SPACECRUISER
INQUIRY

SPACECRUISER INQUIRY

True Guidance for the Inner Journey

DIAMOND BODY SERIES: I

A. H. Almaas

SHAMBHALA
Boston & London
2002

Shambhala Publications, Inc.
Horticultural Hall
300 Massachusetts Avenue
Boston, Massachusetts 02115
www.shambhala.com

9   8   7   6   5   4

Printed in the United States of America

⊗ This edition is printed on acid-free paper that meets the American
National Standards Institute z39.48 Standard.
Distributed in the United States by Random House, Inc.,
and in Canada by Random House of Canada Ltd

LIBRARY OF CONGRESS CATALOGING-IN-PUBLICATION DATA

Almaas, A. H.
Spacecruiser inquiry: true guidance for the inner journey/
A. H. Almaas.—1st ed.
p.   cm.—(Diamond body series; 1)
Includes index.
ISBN 978-1-57062-859-7 (alk. paper)
1. Spiritual life.   2. Ridhwan Foundation—Doctrines.   I. Title.

BP605.R53 A56 2002
291.4'4—DC21
2001049804

To our teachers and guides,
who guide us at each stage of life.
And also to all explorers and researchers,
who love the adventure of discovery.

CONTENTS

INTRODUCTION TO THE
DIAMOND BODY SERIES

THIS SERIES OF BOOKS is an attempt to outline the methodology of the Diamond Approach, a contemporary spiritual teaching with its own direct understanding and view of reality. The Diamond Body series refers to the practice and embodiment of the Diamond Approach, as a complement to the Diamond Heart series, which pertains to the direct experience of true nature on this path, and the Diamond Mind series, which relates to the objective knowledge and conceptual understanding of this teaching.

The series will range from direct discussion of methodology, to the illustration of various applications within different contexts, to the integration of some of the classical methods of spiritual work into this teaching. Some of the volumes in this series illustrate the methodology through actual work on elements of the body of knowledge that is unique to the Diamond Approach teaching, such as the aspects of spiritual essence, the dimensions of reality, and the facets of mind.

To appreciate the place and function of the methodology in any approach to spiritual work, we need to understand how the methodology relates to the view of reality on which it is based and to the teaching that arises from that view. This understanding will help clarify the role of this series of books in the revelation of the Diamond Approach.

Throughout history, human beings have felt the need for intentional, focused work and guidance, to be able to advance beyond the average human development known in most societies. Much of our human potential lies in realms not accessible or even visible to normal consciousness. This is specifically the case for humanity's spiritual potential, which is the ground of human consciousness and the source of true and lasting fulfillment, peace, and liberation.

This situation has led to the arising and development of many teaching schools throughout the ages, inner work schools that specialize in the development of the total human being—particularly the actualization of the depth of human potential. Such a spiritual school is usually built on a teaching that emerges from a specific logos—a direct understanding of reality and the situation of human beings within that reality. Through the teaching, the logos reveals a path toward the actualization of our human potential. The methodology of the path also reflects the wisdom arising from this direct understanding. It is not just a haphazard collection of techniques aimed at helping students to arrive at certain inner states. The methodology will be successful in unfolding the path when it is a faithful expression of the particular logos of that teaching. You could say that practicing the methodology of a teaching is the specific key needed to open the door of this teaching's logos of experience and wisdom.

This understanding of the relationship between logos, teaching, method, and reality has another important implication. As a methodology is practiced within the logos of a particular teaching, objective reality will reveal itself in forms relevant for the journey of self-realization undertaken through that teaching. In other words, a profound and fundamental manifestation of reality characteristic of one teaching may never arise for followers of a different teaching, because each teaching orients to reality through a different logos.

One way of understanding this is that because each teaching traverses different terrain in its unfolding journey, the same underlying reality will be revealed in different forms along the way. Consider, for example, that the Inuit people of the Arctic Circle recognize more than twenty forms of snow and ice. These are true forms of physical reality never recognized by someone living in temperate latitudes, because the climate and the demands of the environment are different. In a similar way, followers of a spiritual teaching will encounter distinct experiences of objective reality that are appropriate to the journey of the soul addressed by that teaching.

This awareness is especially important in understanding descriptions of essential reality in the books that come out of the Diamond Approach. The methodology of the Diamond Approach prepares the soul to experience, perceive, and appreciate that Being appears not only as needed at any given point in her journey, but also in specific forms—which we call essential aspects—that arise in response to the constantly changing needs of the individual soul. However, though these states and qualities are referred to as universal and fundamental to all human souls and to reality itself, this does not mean that people engaged in deep spiritual work based on another logos will encounter reality in the form of essential aspects. Other teachings align the soul for traversing other paths of realization, so essential reality may appear differently.

The central thread of wisdom informing the methodology of the Diamond Approach is that our normal human consciousness does not possess the knowledge or skill necessary for traversing the inner path of realization. However, the intelligence of our underlying spiritual ground tends to spontaneously guide our consciousness and experience toward liberation. This spiritual ground, which is the ultimate nature of reality, is unconditionally loving and compassionate in revealing its treasures of wisdom to whoever is willing to open to it. We simply need to recognize the truth about our present experience and learn the attitudes and skills that will invite the true nature of reality to reveal itself. Toward that end, this methodology brings together classical spiritual techniques and new practices that can help us be open and vulnerable to our true nature.

The task of communicating the teaching and logos for this method is the central function of the Ridhwan School, its teachers, and all the literature of the Diamond Approach. Like any genuine spiritual teaching, the degree to which this logos reveals itself depends on how faithfully the method is applied. And the skill in applying the methodology develops over time as the experience and understanding of the teaching matures.

However, since this method arises from a true logos of reality, and therefore is inherent to objective reality, it is available for anyone to learn regardless of whether they are in contact with the Ridhwan

School—if they are able to recognize the truth of this view for themselves. This means that it is possible to connect to this logos and practice its particular method by seriously studying the teaching on one's own. To do so, however, requires an unusual degree of sincerity, devotion, and intelligence. Such is the limitation of the printed word, in contrast to the direct transmission that can occur when one is in contact with an exemplar of the teaching. Hence, we can only hope for limited benefits when the method is practiced apart from the active guidance of the teaching and the teacher.

Still, we believe there is value in providing some understanding of the methodology of the Diamond Approach. This is not only for the benefit of the students directly engaged in this work, but also for readers who would like to learn and practice some of the elements of the method on their own. In addition, we hope this series will be useful in appreciating the contribution of this approach to an overall understanding of reality, human nature, and what it means to actualize humanity's full potential.

Because the heart of this methodology is a disciplined invitation to reality to reveal its secrets, the Diamond Body series offers the unique benefit of supporting both the pursuit of the inner path of realization and the exploration of the deeper principles of investigation and study that are relevant in any research discipline. Using elements of the Diamond Approach methodology can lead not only to a quickening and an openness to aspects of our inner potential, but also to the development of skills that can be useful for study in other fields within the sciences and humanities.

This is the universal message of the Diamond Approach: When we learn how to invite our true nature to reveal itself, it will guide us toward realizing our spiritual ground and, at the same time, actualize our potential in all walks of life.

A. H. Almaas
Captain Cook, Hawaii
2000

ACKNOWLEDGMENTS

THIS BOOK, AND ALL the perceptions and insights that have gone into it, would not have been possible without the contribution of many people, from many epochs and many persuasions. I have learned a great deal from the work and the example of these individuals, who showed me various ways that the inner guidance of Being—what I call in this book Diamond Guidance—may manifest and function. I mention only a few of these individuals: Socrates; Shakyamuni Buddha; Albert Einstein; Idries Shah; Tarthang Tulku Rinpoche; the Fourteenth Dalai Lama, Tenzin Gyatso.

Spacecruiser Inquiry started as a transcript of teachings I did ten years ago, which I then prepared and organized into the material for this book. However, it was the indefatigable work and dedication of my editors, Byron Brown and Elianne Obadia, and their love of the subject matter, that turned it into a beautiful and readable account. I would also like to thank Charles Miedzinski, Loie Rosenkrantz, and Sherry Anderson for their feedback during the editing process. Lastly, I am grateful for the care and support of Shambhala Publications in doing the work necessary to produce the finished book that you hold in your hands.

EDITOR'S PREFACE

SPACECRUISER INQUIRY holds a unique place in the literature of the Diamond Approach because it articulates in some detail the central practice of this approach. The focus here is not on the spiritual knowledge resulting *from* the practice but rather on what it means to fully engage inquiry *as* a practice of self-realization.

Inquiry as it is practiced in the Diamond Approach is a dynamic, exciting, open-ended exploration into the immediacy of our experience. Through exploring the principles, challenges, and rewards of inquiry, this book reveals what it means to engage in this practice as a spiritual path that opens the door to the mystery of who and what we truly are.

The practice of inquiry is based on a simple but profound principle: that Being freely reveals itself to anyone who loves to know the truth of reality and is willing to wholeheartedly surrender to not-knowing and remain open and curious about what that truth is. Practice based on this principle can take one from the simplest discovery about one's motivation in a particular action all the way to the most profound awareness of the nature of the Absolute reality.

More than any other of Almaas's books except *Facets of Unity: The Enneagram of Holy Ideas,* this one embodies the core metaphor of the Diamond Approach: As a diamond has many facets—each one bright, clear, and revealing a different perspective on the whole of the crystal—so each of the chapters of this book offers a slightly different view of the same core principle in order to reveal a deeper experiential understanding of what the practice of inquiry is.

In Part One, Almaas provides both an orientation and a larger context for inquiry as a path of spiritual unfolding. In Part Two, he looks at the fundamental elements of the inquiry process, which include, among other things, the nature of knowledge, the experience of not-knowing, the love of truth, the questioning process, and the personal thread. Part Three focuses on the guidance of Being that is invited into play by the inquiry practice. This luminous richness of our true nature that guides the soul's inner journey is what Almaas calls the Diamond Guidance. Part Four is devoted to investigating this richness and how it can be realized and applied.

In this final section of the book, Almaas looks at many of the essential forms that comprise the Diamond Guidance, including curiosity, boldness, compassion, truth, clarity, personalness, and intelligence. Each of these essential aspect chapters acts as a doorway to eternal yet immediate truths about Being and its dynamic manifestation in the practice of inquiry.

For those who have some experience with personal inquiry into their direct experience, the wisdom presented in these pages will validate, encourage, and clarify the continued pursuit of that exploration. And it may awaken in those new to the practice a desire for the intimate and revealing journey of self-discovery that awaits them. But this book is not a step-by-step manual for learning how to inquire. What it offers is a window into the way that this practice operates as a profound path to spiritual realization.

We can think of inquiry as a spiritual technique, but it is really the development of a natural capacity that human consciousness inherently possesses. So *Spacecruiser Inquiry* reminds us again and again that the journey of the soul's unfoldment occurs not just when we are sitting down to practice—our entire life can be lived as an unfolding inquiry. This material, therefore, is also a guide to a way of life that is continuously self-revealing as it uncovers our deepest truths in day-to-day life.

This book is based on talks that Almaas gave to the students of the Ridhwan School (home of the Diamond Approach) in a teaching segment devoted to the practice of inquiry. Those talks have been edited in order to speak more directly to the reader.

Almaas's presentation of the material emphasizes understanding and practicing inquiry rather than just comprehending the process intellectually. His presence, his words, and his delivery invite the direct manifestation of both the particular essential quality or dimension of Being under discussion and its attendant capacities. The talks often take the form of an inquiry into areas of familiar experience through questioning the often unconscious positions and beliefs underlying that experience. As the students interact with the words and concepts, their inner psychological barriers are challenged and new understandings of their experience arise. This makes it possible for them to be more receptive to the actual energy and consciousness being manifested.

Included in the sessions were exercises designed to deepen the students' experiences further by inviting them to directly and personally explore whatever was being discussed. These exercises were mostly in the form of a structured inquiry that challenged the various inner barriers and explored the capacities and skills needed for inquiry. The exercises frequently penetrated the various subtle dimensions and then continued to explore and investigate the students' newly arising perceptions.

Personal explorations of the subject matter that are similar to those exercises are included in most chapters of this book so that you may also taste the practice of inquiry more directly. At these points, you are invited to explore some element of your own experience in relation to the material being presented. These inquiries may be done as a silent contemplation, as a spoken monologue (with or without fellow explorers present), or as a journaling process.

In several chapters, questions and answers from the original transcript have been included to give yet another flavor of the process of working with the subject matter of the book. These sections of dialog with the teacher illustrate the issues, reactions, and insights that arise as students explore this material for themselves.

The talks were presented to the School at a time when everyone involved had been engaged in the Work for at least five years and had embarked on what Almaas, in chapter 3, calls the second journey. Much of the experience with inquiry in the first years of the Work is spent in the first journey. This is a period when inquiry is a vehicle for learning in detail about one's own psychic stance in life, when one comes to recognize and appreciate the deeper, historical motivations for behaviors, reactions, and patterns. One also learns how these positions and attitudes block awareness of the more fundamental experience of essential presence.

When one's focus is primarily on this kind of psychological and emotional self-discovery, the process feels rich, challenging, and revealing but circumscribed by the familiar reality of being an individual with a personal history, attempting to live a satisfying and successful life. It is easy to miss the ever present spiritual reality that transcends these familiar boundaries and to lose sight of how inquiry is truly a vehicle of that spiritual realm, not of conventional reality. This is the situation that Almaas is addressing directly in this book.

The teaching sessions are both an inspiration intended to draw students to a deeper level of practice and a corrective for the many deadening traps that one encounters along the way. In this process, Almaas is building on the familiarity that each student has with inquiry, and at the same time reawakening beginner's mind in order to clear out the habitual orientations that result from repeated self-study.

There is a paradox in what is presented here. Almaas is speaking about a process that can be applied to any experience regardless of its content. He presents specific examples to help clarify the material, yet the understanding he is pointing to is more about how we orient to our experience than about any particular content of experience. This makes it difficult for the mind to grasp the material in a familiar way. The book is addressing a part of us that does not inhabit the words in our mind but lives disguised in the varied content of our life. We tend to ignore this part or forget that it exists because we are immersed in the content and believe that that is what's real. This book directly challenges that assumption by inviting the part of our soul that gets lost in the content to come forth. This forgotten part in most of us is our spiritual core—what could be called the true nature of our soul.

You are encouraged to read each chapter and allow it to settle before going on to the next. This will allow each facet of the diamond to have its own impact. In a similar way, the students experienced each facet of the teaching during separate weekends, with several weeks in between to digest the experience of interacting with that material.

But it is not necessary to integrate everything you've read before you continue. Ideas or principles that may seem elusive or foreign to your own experience when you first encounter them are usually explained more fully later on. As the book progresses, the material in each chapter will work on you in its own way and in its own time. The repetition of certain principles from slightly different perspectives serves to evoke a felt sense of the experience beyond the simple content of the words. The familiar echo of truth, recognized from an angle that one hasn't considered before, helps to ground and deepen the understanding of the ideas and concepts that were presented earlier. If you remain open and curious, the practice of inquiry itself will reveal, moment to moment, the truth you need to know.

A final note: Almaas has chosen the metaphor of a spaceship traveling in the great expanse of the cosmos to illuminate some of the elements of the inquiry process. This is because the nature of outer space exploration has striking parallels to the journey into our own Being. Outer space conveys the sense of mystery, vastness, and multidirectionality of the experiential field of consciousness better than any other physical metaphor. And the absolute spaciousness of the cosmos, where there are no roads and no confining terrain, vividly captures the openness that is both the potential and the challenge in the practice of inquiry.

Those who have an affinity for space travel will find themselves delighted by what this metaphor reveals. However, it is not central to the presentation of the subject matter and only enters into the flow of the teaching at occasional intervals. So if your personal inclination does not go in the direction of futuristic journeying, you are invited to travel your inner path via the vehicle that best expresses your own dynamic unfolding.

Byron Brown

NOTE TO THE READER

THIS BOOK IS AN exploration of the practice of inquiry. It is more an orientation to the principles and potential of the practice than a manual on how to do it. However, you may find that engaging in the practice yourself will enhance your appreciation and understanding of what is being discussed. This note will help orient you should you desire to explore inquiry on your own as you read.

The way Almaas presents the material is itself an invitation to do inquiry. So feel free to stop at any time and explore within your own experience whatever he is describing. To help you focus your explorations, specific suggestions for inquiry are included in the text. Beginning in Part Two, each chapter will specify an area of inquiry related to the subject matter to guide your exploration and the development of your capacities for this practice. You are encouraged to do these inquiry exercises either verbally or through journaling, alone or with fellow explorers.

If you find that you are drawn to inquiry as a form of spiritual unfolding, initially it is helpful to formalize the practice by choosing certain times to inquire in a focused way in an undisturbed environment. We will discuss here two ways mentioned above, but you can find additional ones as well.

The first approach is through writing in a journal. When there is something in your experience to be inquired into, you can sit down and write your inquiry. Many people use journals just to report the events of the day and leave it at that; this taps only the smallest potential of a journal. A much richer use of a journal is for personal inquiry.

The reporting of experience can be part of what you write; in fact it often may start the process. But in a journal inquiry, you not only track what happened in your experience—you analyze it, explore it, and ask questions, all in writing. In some sense, your journal becomes a silent witness. If you want to, you can go over what you've written, reflect on it, and continue the writing by giving yourself feedback on your process, but it is enough to do the inquiry itself.

You can inquire through writing as much and as often as you want, but it is good to do it several times a week. Just as you might set aside a time to meditate, you can set aside a time to sit down with your journal and write. Since inquiry is based on self-observation, beginning to practice inquiry will mean that you start to pay more attention to your experience: your thoughts, sensations, feelings, and behaviors. Mindfulness of your experience can become a continuous process, providing you with a rich field of observation. As observation begins to reveal patterns in your experience, questions will naturally come up in response to these patterns. Thus, when you come to your inquiry period, the process often will have already begun, so you just sit down and follow the thread of the inquiry.

Another way to do inquiry is with someone else. You could invite one or two friends to join you. If three of you sit down together to do an inquiry practice, you can use the simple format of taking fifteen to twenty minutes each to inquire into some part of your experience. While one person is inquiring, the other two are silent witnesses who are practicing being present to their own experience as they listen in an open, curious way to the inquiry. This is a particular benefit of inquiring with others: Your own inquiry process will be deepened by witnessing others inquiring. You can practice this way as often as you like. You might find two other people who are as curious as you are, and do it together every day.

Initially, an inquiry will often begin with reflecting on a past experience. You have reactions, concerns, residual feelings, or just a curiosity about what you have experienced. A feeling in the moment may be what triggers the inquiry, but exploring that feeling will often take you back to the situation that provoked the feeling. The inquiry then becomes a process of looking to see what the truth is about what happened. Much can be understood if you stay open and curious about discovering the truth for yourself.

If you continue to be aware of yourself as you inquire into the past, at some point your focus will naturally tend to shift to an interest in the truth of your present experience. Then the inquiry becomes more immediate and alive because you are now opening to what is happening in the moment. This movement back and forth between past and present is an ongoing dynamic that is natural in inquiry. However, the more you are attuned to your immediate experience, whether you are inquiring about the past or the present, the more you will be open to the possibility of realizing your own deeper truth.

Inquiry is a spiritual practice, and like any other, it develops over time. Reading and rereading this book as you follow the gradual unfolding of your inner life can support and enrich the depth and subtlety of your inner journey. Finding your own rhythm and pace of opening will thus allow inquiry to reveal the hidden richness of your Being.

Byron Brown

PART ONE

———

Mystery and Inquiry

CHAPTER 1

Why Inquire?

WHEN WE THINK ABOUT ourselves, what do we experience? What do we see? What are our lives like? Most of us live in a continual struggle of seeking pleasure and pushing away pain. For long stretches of time, we persistently feel that our lives aren't "enough"—full enough, rich enough, complete enough.

Once in a while, we find ourselves experiencing contentment; everything seems just right. But usually we feel this contentment only briefly. We then try to "improve" something, or worry about the future, or in some other way fail to simply be with the contentment.

Suppose it is a beautiful day at the beach. Perhaps you are sitting on your blanket, sipping iced tea and basking in the sun. Everything is fine, but after a while you start getting a little bored. You take a book out of your beach bag and begin to read, but you find yourself feeling irritable. Then you realize that the main character in the story reminds you of your father, who never let you have any privacy. Even though you are by yourself, you suddenly get the feeling that someone is standing over you, judging you for relaxing on the beach and getting a tan rather than cleaning out the garage. You decide that it's probably not a very good book and put it away. What you really want, you feel now, is something to eat. Halfway through eating your sandwich and chips, though, you realize you weren't really hungry. Maybe a nap would make you feel better. You close your eyes, but now you are completely restless. The contentment of an hour ago is gone, and you don't know how you lost it.

This is how we live—trying to manipulate the outer world so that our inner world can be at peace. But this struggle is a hopeless task; it is not what will bring us to a state of contentment. This example of our internal process points to a basic fact of our ongoing experience: We don't know how to leave ourselves alone. Every internal action involves some kind of rejection of our present state, our actual reality. And there is a deeper consequence to this attitude of rejection: By rejecting what is so for us in the present moment, we are rejecting ourselves. We are out of touch with our Being. Aiming toward the future, we sacrifice the present. By looking outside ourselves for what is missing, we subject ourselves, our souls, to the pain of abandonment.

But the fact is: Nothing is missing! Our true nature is actually always there. Our true nature is *Being*. And everything is made of this true nature: rocks, people, clouds, peach trees—all the things in our life. However, these things do not exist independently, the way we think they do. What we are really seeing are the various forms of Being. To understand Being itself, the nature of what we truly are, we must penetrate the inner, fundamental nature of existence. To be open to this fundamental nature, we must question what we think we are: Am I really a white male, of a certain height and weight and age and address, who is defined by my personal history? And if that's not me, what is?

We are like the river that doesn't know it is fundamentally composed of water. It is afraid of expanding because it believes that it might not be a river anymore. But once you know you are water, what difference does it make whether you are a river or a lake?

Your Being is what is constantly manifesting as you. It thinks by using your brain. It walks by using your legs. But in your daily experience, you think you are a bundle of arms and legs and thoughts, and do not experience the unity that underlies all of your experience.

When we are not in touch with Being, we experience a kind of hollowness. We lack a sense of wholeness, or value, or capacity, or meaning. We might search endlessly for pleasure or contentment, but without an appreciation of our true nature, we are missing most of the pleasure that is possible in our lives.

Our nature, our Being, is the most precious thing there is, yet most of us lose touch with it as we dream, wish, hope, scheme, and struggle to have what we think is a good life. We want the right diploma, the best job, the ideal mate. But without some appreciation of our true nature, we end up on the outer fringes of life, always tasting a bland imitation of the nectar of existence.

THE SOUL

Being manifests itself to itself through us, as human beings. In us, Being beholds its beauty and celebrates its majesty. Our experience of ourselves in our totality and our tangibility is what in the Diamond Approach we mean by the term *soul*. The soul is what experiences, and it is the lived experience itself. It is the inner, psychic organism, the individual consciousness that is the site of all experience. The human soul is pure potentiality, the potentiality of Being. It is also the way that Being, in all its magnificence, opens up and manifests its richness.

To experience the richness of our Being, the potential of our soul, we must allow our experience to become more and more open, and increasingly question what we assume we are. Usually we identify with a very limited part of our potential, what we call the ego or personality. Some call it the small self. But this identity is actually a distortion of what we really are, which is a completely open flow out of the mystery of Being.

A human being is a universe of experience, multifaceted and multi-dimensional. Each of us is a soul, a dynamic consciousness, a magical organ of experience and action. And each of us is in a constant state of transformation—of one experience opening up to another, one action leading to another, one perception multiplying into many others; of perception growing into knowledge, knowledge leading to action, and action creating more experience. This unfolding is constant, dynamic, and full of energy. This is the very nature of what we call life.

THE DUAL DYNAMICS OF EXPERIENCE

The beauty of life is that it can be a continuous opening to the full range of experience and richness possible for the human being—the dynamic unfolding of the human potential. This life can be a celebration of the mystery of our Being. We can live a life of love, taking joy in ourselves, in other human beings, and in the richness of our home planet. Our life can be full of appreciation, sensitivity, and wonder in all that surrounds us. Such a life can be a thrilling and exciting adventure of learning, maturing, and expanding.

But it can also be a life of strife, struggle, misery, and depression, which frequently becomes filled with suffering, frustration, envy, and aggression. We can easily find ourselves leading a life of selfishness, antagonism, and exploitation. When this happens, life soon becomes dull, boring, superficial—while the undertone can feel sadistic and brutal.

At these times, life never loses its dynamic and transformative character, but the unfoldment of Being reveals mostly the dark and destructive possibilities of our potential, the negative and depressive side of human experience. The freshness and creativity of the human spirit is eclipsed, the joyous spark dulled and muted, and the sharpness of our clarity blunted and mutilated. We tend to live in ignorance, driven by primitive needs and desires. The sense of humanness leaves us: Even when we know we are human beings, we forget the value and exquisiteness of our gentleness, kindness, and vulnerability.

Our lives are rarely the pure manifestation of only one side of our potential—whether it is the freedom or the darkness. Most of us live a mixture of both in constantly varying proportions. Naturally we all work very hard to maximize the freedom and joy, but we know from bitter experience how hard that is to do. We try this and that, listen to this teacher or that authority, lose heart and renew our resolve, but rarely do we feel certain about what will bring us to the states we desire. Rarely do we experience the positive human possibilities we yearn to embody. Yet even when they do manifest in our experience, we frequently fight them or become afraid of them. We yearn to expand and complete our humanity, and make great efforts to do so, but so often end up thwarted and frustrated. Our successes are meager, and never seem to last.

When the dynamism of our Being unfolds our experience in its dark and negative possibilities, we find ourselves trapped in repeating patterns and closed loops. Although these closed loops of perception and action are dynamic, they are also compulsive and repetitive, robbing our experience of its freshness, our dynamism of its creativity, and our life of its expansion and adventure. The vast universe of human possibilities becomes restricted to a very limited region of habitual experience. Freshness, newness, development, and the thrill of discovery are all stifled.

The situation is not hopeless, however, and we all know this someplace in our hearts. We know—perhaps vaguely, perhaps incompletely—that the human spirit possesses the possibility of enlarging its experience, of opening up its richness. We have many strengths to draw on: sensitivity, intelligence, discrimination, the potential for investigation and insight. We have, most of all, the capacity to learn.

A PATH TO FREEDOM

Each of us has the ability to optimize our experience and attune ourselves to the unlimited dimensions of our humanity. We can all learn to open ourselves more fully to the creative dynamism of our Being and the vastness of the human universe of possibilities. But how does this happen? How can we transform our lives into a thrilling journey of adventure, discovery, and wonder? What will help us to recognize and deal with the dark, destructive, and constrictive manifestations of Being in ourselves and the people around us? Where is the path that will show us the way to discover and live what will truly fulfill and complete us, and what will assist all humanity to mature, and all life to flourish? How can we release our spirit so that it can manifest the richness of its humanity and the divinity of its Being?

Many ways and paths exist to lead people to completeness and freedom. In this book we will look at one of those ways. We will explore how inquiry can open our experience to true understanding and how this understanding can become so deep that it unfolds the fullness of our potential.

As we have seen, our soul reveals its possibilities through its creative dynamism in two basic ways. The first is in an open and free manner, the second through a distorted and constricted process. In the former case, the soul manifests itself in a real and authentic way, while in the latter case, the soul becomes diminished, distorted, and disconnected from its true nature. Both of these experiences (authenticity and distortion) are inherent in the potential of our human soul.

It is important to understand specifically and clearly the difference between these two major ways that our experience reveals itself. The most salient feature of this difference is central to our exploration in this book: When our experience is free, and hence authentic, we discover that our soul is in touch with—in fact, inseparable from—true nature. The distorted experience, on the other hand, is characterized primarily by a lack of awareness of this true nature.

THE TRUE NATURE OF THE SOUL

The awareness of the existence of the soul's true nature constitutes the core understanding in all major spiritual teachings. The primary understanding in any authentic experience of spiritual realization is that our soul (our self, our consciousness) possesses a true nature—its essence. Being is the essence or true nature of the soul, as it is of all manifestation. In the Diamond Approach, we use the word *Essence* to refer to the specific experience of Being in its various aspects when it arises as the nature of the human soul.

We experience ourselves as Essence if our experience is free, unfabricated, and spontaneously arising. If our experience of ourselves is not dictated or determined by any external influence—that is, by any influence extraneous to the simplicity of just being—we are the essence of who we are. True or essential nature, therefore, refers to how the soul experiences herself* when she is not conditioned by the past or by any mental images or self-concepts. We experience our essence when we are simply being, instead of reacting or conceptualizing our experience or ourselves.

Essence is not an object we find within ourselves; it is the true nature of who we are when we are relaxed and authentic, when we are not pretending to be one way or another, consciously or unconsciously.

---

*Traditionally the soul is often referred to as feminine. This is partly because soul is a manifestation of the creative and generative dimension of true nature, the logos. Also, soul's relation to Essence is that of receptivity, which is considered a feminine quality.—Editor.

Essence is the truth of our very presence, the purity of our consciousness and awareness. It is what we are in our original and undefiled beingness, the ultimate core reality of our soul. Essence is the authentic presence of our Being; it is, in fact, Being in its thatness.

Different spiritual traditions have given it different names: Christianity, Judaism, and Islam call it Spirit; Buddhism calls it Buddha nature; Taoism calls it the Tao; Hinduism calls it Atman or Brahman. The various traditions differ in how they conceptualize Essence and how much they emphasize it in their teaching, but Essence is always considered to be the most authentic, innate, and fundamental nature of who we are. And the experience and realization of Essence is the central task of spiritual work and development in all traditions.*

The Diamond Approach is characterized by a distinctive realization about our essential nature: Essence manifests in various forms as an intelligent response to the changing conditions of the human soul. These forms, which we call the aspects or qualities of Essence, include the perennial flavors of human experience such as Love, Peace, Joy, Truth, Clarity, Compassion, and Value. Each essential aspect has a distinct experiential reality and function, while all share the basic ground of Essence: presence, self-aware luminosity, and openness.

THE JOURNEY OF INQUIRY

The discoveries that form the basis of our path, the Diamond Approach, offer an original understanding of why the presence of Being, with its essential manifestations, is not active and functioning in most individuals. The fundamental insight can be stated as follows: Being, as manifested in essential presence and its qualities, is a natural and central part of the potential of the human being. This potential inherently and spontaneously opens up and develops as part of an individual's maturation. When this unfoldment does not occur, psychological and epistemological barriers are the cause. These barriers consist primarily of fixed beliefs about oneself and reality in general, deeply held atti-

---

*For a further discussion of Essence and its experiential properties, see Almaas, *Essence* (1986), in *Essence* with *The Elixir of Enlightenment: The Diamond Approach to Inner Realization* (York Beach, Maine: Samuel Weiser, 1998).

tudes and inner positions, and compulsive patterns of reactivity and behavior.

These elements, in turn, are based on and are expressions of psychic attachment (identification) to unconscious and unquestioned images and concepts about oneself and experience in general. These inner attitudes, positions, and assumptions reduce awareness of oneself, limit understanding of what's possible, and impede the natural unfoldment of one's potential.

The Diamond Approach is an open and open-ended inquiry into the various elements of our experience and its patterns. When that inquiry is sincere and intelligent, it is bound to encounter the psychological and epistemological barriers against the free unfoldment of the soul. Challenging such barriers by questioning them leads to the insightful and directly felt comprehension of these barriers. In this way, inquiry and understanding penetrate the barriers and open up our soul to the still-unknown possibilities sleeping in its depths.

Inquiry not only leads to greater awareness and understanding of ourselves, but also invites Being to disclose its hidden possibilities through the process of unfoldment of experience and insight. This activates our essential presence in its various manifestations in a natural and orderly fashion. In turn, these essential aspects enhance the process of inquiry and understanding, taking both to subtler and deeper dimensions of experience and perception.

This means that the activation of the subtle dimensions depends on our understanding, and this understanding reflects our capacity to inquire into our everyday experience. In the Diamond Approach, we don't mechanically do exercises and practices that activate deep energies that we may not be able to understand or handle. Rather, the activation occurs on its own, in response to one's capacity for openness, inquiry, and understanding. And the fact that this capacity increases in direct relation to our level of maturity is the best safeguard against going too deep too fast.

We must emphasize here that the understanding we are referring to is not mental or intellectual comprehension but a direct awareness and experience of oneself that is insightful and clear. It is the clear discrimination of the truth of experience, as an inseparable aspect of that experience. This understanding is the direct response of Being to sincere inquiry.

Embarking on the journey that begins on the following pages opens the door to a profound and intimate relationship with what it means to be a human being. The essential world of being human, being a conscious soul, is opening up, and in each moment you discover it. Not only that—it is arising right here where you are now; it does not exist somewhere else, waiting for you to find it. The journey of inquiry is both the longest and shortest trip you will ever take—you travel simply as far as you need to go to be where you already are.

This book is designed to open you up to the nature of this most mysterious and personal journey. It is not a travelogue of magical and exotic places but an awakening to the capacities and possibilities in your soul for participating in the inner unfolding of your Being. What follows will orient your self-exploration so that you can recognize and encourage the implicit guidance that arises as you travel your own inner space. And as the journey continues and your awareness deepens, you will learn to appreciate the subtleties, the richness, and the intimacy that is yours as you follow the path of inquiry.

CHAPTER 2

Openness in Inquiry

REVELATION OF THE MYSTERY

The human being is a multifaceted, multidimensional reality. To take one part of this reality, or a certain way of experiencing it, and believe that this is the ultimate, that this is what we should accomplish, is limited, partial, and ultimately static. The human being is a dynamic consciousness with intelligence and potentiality that we cannot encompass with our mind. And as far as it is possible to see, there is no teaching, no particular system, that encompasses everything. Each teaching takes a certain segment, a certain way, and says, "This is it." This is a valid way to approach some kinds of realization, but it cannot contain the totality of the human being or the human potentiality.

There is no end to the adventure of Being—Being is infinite and its possibilities are endless. One reason why I prefer the path of inquiry to predetermined and goal-oriented spiritual practices is that it reflects a certain understanding of the nature of being human, which has to do with the essence of Being. The more I know the essence of my Being, the more I recognize that it is indeterminable, it is not knowable in an ultimate and complete way. You cannot say in any definite way that it is a such and such and such. It is the very nature of the essence of our Being that it is a mystery. It is a mysterious essence. Its mystery is not due to a limitation in our capacity to understand it; its mystery is intrinsic to its reality.

This mystery, this sense of indeterminacy, has been explored by many people, and many teachings and formulations exist to describe it. One way of looking at it is that the ultimate nature of things cannot be described, cannot be determined. You cannot make any definite statement about it, you cannot take any position about it. Some equate ultimate nature with emptiness but are quick to say that there is no "something" there called emptiness. Emptiness is simply a way of referring to the indeterminacy of ultimate nature. This means that you cannot say it exists, you cannot say it does not exist, and you cannot say it neither exists nor doesn't exist. This way is called the way of negation, in the sense that you negate everything you can say or determine about ultimate nature.

I think this is a very clever and subtle way of understanding the indeterminacy of the essence of our Being. However, the adventure of inquiry is based on a slightly different perspective on the mystery. Some would say that you cannot say anything about the mystery because whatever you say is going to be inaccurate, and therefore it is better not to say anything. The perspective I prefer is that the essence of Being is amenable to descriptions. You can actually say a great deal about it, just as the mystical poets have been doing for thousands of years. You can say it is emptiness, you can say it is mystery, you can say it is stillness, you can say it is peace, you can say it is neither existence nor nonexistence, you can say it is the ultimate beloved, you can say it is the annihilation of all ego, you can say it is the source of all awareness, you can say it is the ground of everything, you can say it is our true identity, you can say it is dimensionless nonlocality, and so on. Each one of these descriptions is saying something about it.

Thus the mystery of Being can be seen as having two different implications. I believe the more fruitful one is not that there is nothing you can say about it, but that you can never exhaust what you can say about it. We can describe it and talk about it forever. So instead of calling it indeterminacy, I think a better word is *inexhaustibility*: The mystery is characterized by the fact that it is inexhaustible. You can never know it totally.

So, for instance, when you say that the mystery is emptiness, this does not capture it completely. It does not give you the whole picture. You might say it is stillness. Well, you've then discovered something else about it, which helps you understand what it does to desires and agitations. When you realize this stillness, you experience that the whole universe is still. Yet, since you have an innately inquiring mind and you are inquiring into the stillness, the next day you realize that the mystery is not only stillness, it is also knowledge. What does that mean? Well, you *knew* it was stillness, and you *knew* it was emptiness, so knowledge must be intrinsic to it. But the next day, you realize that somehow defining the mystery as knowledge does not do it justice either. You can say that the mystery is stillness, you can say it is knowledge, you can say it is emptiness, but any one of these—and even all of them together—do not do it justice. So every day, you have a new discovery about the mystery, as if you were flying through the blackness of outer space and suddenly found you had alighted on a whole new star system that you can explore with joy and excitement.

But even then, you realize that you have not reached the end, for the glimmer of another star system is beyond this one. Furthermore, you begin to understand that holding on to any of these discoveries will disconnect you from the inexhaustibility of Being—its very essence. You also might realize that you are attached to there being an end to your understanding.

So this is a slightly different approach to understanding the mystery than the concept of indeterminacy. The mystery *is* indeterminate, but not in the sense that it is impossible to make determinations about it. It is possible to make an infinite number of determinations, but these determinations fall short of capturing the essence of the mystery. Furthermore, these infinite determinations are actually the content of our consciousness. What else is there to experience? We can say that the mystery is unknowable and forget about it, but if we do that, we remain limited to the fact of its unknowability. But it is also knowable, much more knowable than anything else—in fact, infinitely knowable. But it cannot be known totally and finally, so we can never say we have finished our exploration.

My understanding of the mystery is that it is an inexhaustible richness, and this richness is inseparable from the mystery. The richness is nothing but the revelation of the mystery, and that revelation is completely inexhaustible. This perspective gives us some basis for appreciating the way of inquiry.

WHAT IS INQUIRY?

When we use the term "inquiry," what do we mean? Inquiry means investigation, exploration, but mostly it means wanting to find out. It is a questioning. "What is this? Why is that? What is happening? Where is it going?"

What is a question? If you really get into a question, what do you find at its heart? The heart of a question is obviously an unknowing. When you ask a question, you are acknowledging that there is something you do not know. However, a question is not just an unknowing, because unknowing by itself does not necessarily mean there is a question. It is possible to not know and not question. A question has an unknowing in it, but the unknowing is a *knowing* unknowing. You cannot ask a question unless you know that you do not know. But it is not only that you know that you do not know; you also know something about *what* you do not know. Otherwise you cannot ask a question about it. The moment you ask a question about anything, you acknowledge that you do not know and that you also have a sense of what you do not know.

So the question is arising from a place where there is a knowing of an unknowing plus a knowing of a possible knowing, and this possible knowing is somehow penetrating your consciousness in a way that emerges as a question.

It is as if something is tickling you from inside, saying, "Look here, there is something here." That flavor of unknowing, of a knowing unknowing, is how the unfoldment is arising. Something is coming up. Being is heaving up, presenting one of its possibilities, and that possibility is approaching your knowing consciousness. However, it is approaching it with something you have not known before. This new presentation is touching you from someplace within your heart. And this touching makes you ask a question. If it did not touch you, you would not ask the question; you would just not know and not know that you do not know. So inquiry means a knowing unknowing, which is the expression of the unfoldment, of the creative dynamism of Being. And this dynamism of Being is a continuous, spontaneous unfoldment.

We see here how inquiry and dynamism are quite interrelated. In some deep sense, inquiry is the expression of the dynamism, the expression of unfoldment. The moment your experience is static, the dynamism is not creative and there is no questioning. Often you live in a rut without ever questioning it. You are not interested, you are not curious, you have no reason to inquire. What does that mean? It means that your experience is so static that nothing is moving.

The moment there is inquiry, we know that the unfoldment is happening again. Something new is emerging, and you find yourself wondering what it is. Or you start to see the old and familiar in a new way: "How come I'm living in such a rut?" However the newness appears, the dynamism has to be presenting something for the inquiry to begin. So as we see, questioning, which is the essence of inquiry, is actually an expression or a reflection of the dynamism.

Inquiry is basically a challenge to what we think we know. We ordinarily believe that we know who we are, what we are, what we are going to do, what life is about, what should happen. Inquiry means challenging all these things. Do we really know?

Through inquiry, you learn how to navigate through your not-knowing. You will find out where you are going through the unfoldment of your own dynamism: "Where is it taking me? Am I going to become a monk? Am I going to become a householder? Am I going to be a computer analyst, a soldier, a teacher, a lover, a husband or a wife?"

The more any inquiry is open ended, the more its power is released. That power is the power of the dynamism of Being itself. This is quite different from the restricted and limited way of using inquiry, which is directed toward a particular result and is determined by an idea in your mind or by something you or somebody else already knows. When I say that inquiry needs to be open ended, I don't mean that you should never take a perspective. But whatever perspective you take, inquiry can move to open it up and reveal what you are inquiring into. And if you inquire into a particular way of looking at things, you might realize, "Oh, this perspective is good for this, but not good for that."

We are discussing inquiry in a very general way, laying the groundwork for looking more extensively into this fascinating part of our work. But the moment you start understanding inquiry, you forget that it is work. Inquiry brings in a love and a joyfulness; it brings in the very dynamism of Being that is needed for transformation.

The way of inquiry is the way of true freedom. If our inquiry is alive and unfolding, we are free—our mind is free, our hearts are free; our souls are free to unfold, and our Being is free to spontaneously manifest what is natural for it to manifest.

OPEN INQUIRY

Inquiry begins by looking at our present experience, but it is a looking that must embody openness. Instead of taking our perceived discrimination as final, inquiry says, "I know what I see, but I acknowledge that I do not know whether what I see is all." You cannot begin to inquire into a perception if you think you know all there is to know about it. The moment you think that you know, the door to inquiry closes. So inquiry begins from a not-knowing, from recognizing and observing something in yourself that you do not understand. This lack of comprehension is not a resignation to ignorance but an acknowledgment of ignorance that has implicit in it an openness to know, an openness to comprehend, an openness to find out what is going on in your direct experience.

This openness in inquiry reflects the openness of true nature. Without this openness, which is a fundamental characteristic of true nature, inquiry will not work. The core of inquiry has to be an openness to what is present in experience, to what you know of that experience and what you do not know. It is openness to seeing things as they are, openness for them to change and for the change to reveal more of what is present. Openness means that you are not stuck in "I know this, and that's it." Openness means that no knowledge is final knowledge. Inquiry is open to the knowledge of now, but also open for the next moment to bring about a totally new and different knowledge. Openness means no fixation, no rigidity, no closing down. It is the expression of a spaciousness in the mind, a spaciousness and awareness in the knowing capacity.

This open attitude of inquiry is the means of engaging not only the dynamism of Being but the spaciousness that is the infinite potentiality of our true nature. Most fundamentally, it is a direct expression of the truth that true nature is ultimately a mystery. The absolute openness of true nature means that you can never know it completely, can never close the book on inquiry into it. You can never conclude the inquiry, because to conclude the inquiry is to stop the unfoldment, to stop the dynamism—and the dynamism cannot be stopped. Why? Because true nature is infinite in its possibilities, and it is infinite in its possibilities because it is the absolute mystery.

The Sufis often quote the *hadith*, or extra-Qur'anic revelation, in which God says, "I was a hidden treasure; I loved to be known, so I created all." God wants to know his nature, his possibilities, his manifestations. This love to know himself, the desire to know himself, appears in us as the love to inquire; it appears in the soul as the love to know herself. Love motivates inquiry, for inquiry is not only openness to what perception presents, but a love of finding out what's really there. If you say, "I'm open to what's there," you're not dynamic yet. It is the love that brings in the dynamism: "Yes, I'm not only open to seeing, I'm going to get engaged in this. I'm going to jump into the middle of the experience with my hands and feet and dig, because I love to find out."

Therefore, one way of understanding the situation is that God's love of revealing the divine manifestation appears in us as love for the truth. These two loves are the same thing, for ultimately there is only one, undivided reality. We do not need to take the Sufis literally; that is, we do not need to believe in a God that loves and wants. When we clearly seeing true nature, we see its dynamic force as a love that manifests; everything arises out of love and celebration. When we experience this love in a limited way, as the soul's love, we experience it as the love of going deeper in order to see the manifestation more completely.

This clarifies what the ultimate service is. You do not work on yourself to become enlightened; you work on yourself so that God can do what God wants to do, which is to reveal himself. So our delight in investigating reality is an adventure of consciousness, which is the human participation in God's enjoyment of self-revelation. People often misunderstand the Diamond Approach to inquiry, thinking that it is a way to solve their problems. But we do the Work because it is a labor of love, a passion, a celebration. We work on personal issues because we need to work on them to be able to continue this exploration, not because we want to get rid of our personal difficulties.

OPENNESS OF MIND

The method of inquiry is an investigation and exploration of reality in one's personal experience in the moment. This exploration uses the mind—which is not only our intellectual capacity but also all the knowledge we have accumulated from the past—yet we are free from the mind at the same time. The advantage of inquiry, compared to many other methods—which also possess their advantages and disadvantages—is that inquiry can use the knowledge you already have. We do not have to invent the wheel every time we inquire. Yet there needs to be a freedom from this ordinary knowledge, because if we are not free from it, we will not ask questions. We will think we already know.

So the questioning in inquiry needs to be intelligent, needs to embody the openness of true nature that can use whatever we know. You know, for instance, that you have an unconscious. You do not have to discover it every time you inquire. So if you have an experience and you are seeing something about it, the fact that you know you have an unconscious makes you suspect that there may be more to what you see. If you say, "Let's not use the knowledge of the mind at all," and then begin to look at what is present in experience, you might have to go through a long process before recognizing that there is a psychodynamic cause for what is arising in your experience. But the fact that you know there is an unconscious, and that psychodynamics exist, opens the inquiry in a whole new way.

At the same time, we need to be free from the mind, because the moment we see something, we think we know it. This is the tendency of the normal mind. Inquiry also uses the mind in formulating questions, in analysis and synthesis, and in using its various capacities, such as memory and correlation. The aim of inquiry, however, is not to arrive at conclusions but to enjoy the exploration and the thrill of discovery. This discovery is the unfoldment of the soul, and expresses the soul's love of truth and reality, which itself is the expression of Being's love of revealing itself.

Openness includes openness to the mind and its accumulated knowledge, but it is also open to the mind's being wrong or incomplete. Furthermore, there is openness to going beyond the mind and its ordinary knowledge. Openness of inquiry also means that whatever knowledge or insight we get to, we do not wrap it up in a package and put it on a shelf. The moment you do that, you close the path of inquiry. No insight is an ultimate insight. As soon as you believe that you have arrived at the ultimate insight, you know you are stuck. Gurdjieff called that position *Hasnamous,* which means a crystallized ego. You can crystallize your ego around very divine ideas. The moment you know reality and then believe your knowledge is final, inquiry stops, the dynamism comes to a standstill, and the old repeats itself. But if our mind is always open, the revelation is endless. Then we are just there for the ride. We merely enjoy the journey itself as an adventure of discovery.

As I said, openness is one of the main ways we experience the inherent mystery of our nature, the essence of true nature. The free, spacious, infinite, unencumbered lightness of our nature appears in the experience of the soul as an openness. The experience is literally a lightness, a spaciousness, a freedom, but psychologically it is an openness. Literally, phenomenologically, it is like space; psychologically, it is openness to possibilities. So openness means a receptivity to experience—whatever presents itself, whatever arises in our consciousness. We do not say that we want to experience this but not that; whatever arises is welcome, is allowed.

Openness also implies that this welcoming is so complete that we are willing to experience exactly and precisely whatever arises. For if we are only interested in experiencing it vaguely, then we are not interested in seeing it just as it is. So openness implies an interest in precision, as an aspect of a complete welcoming, because the completeness implies precision, exactness, and specificity. Thus, the openness is really an invitation to experience what arises in its completeness, precision, and totality.

Openness also characterizes the field that is receptive to what arises. This implies that the experiential field itself, our consciousness, does not have a fixed or predetermined position. There is no position of preference, no position of comparison, no position of judgment. It does not say that one thing is good or bad, does not say that it should be this way or that way. Openness implies that we come from a place that is disinterested, in the sense that it does not have a self-centered interest, it does not want anything for itself. It simply loves to behold what arises. It is very interested in recognizing and committed to experiencing intimately whatever arises in our consciousness, but is disinterested in the sense that it has no goal in being interested. In other words, the openness of our consciousness has no preference for what arises but is simply interested in the truth of whatever arises.

This disinterest, this lack of a fixed position, is necessary for inquiry; otherwise we will have a prejudiced attitude, and this attitude will limit our openness. This limitation of our openness will dampen and limit our capacity to see what arises in its fullness and its exactness. The more openness there is, the more powerful and effective the inquiry.

OPEN-ENDED INQUIRY

So openness obviously means that we do not have a purpose for the inquiry; the purpose is the inquiry itself. We do not inquire in order to get someplace, to resolve an issue, or to eliminate some difficulty. It is true that when we see a difficulty, an obscuration, it perks up our curiosity, but that is not because we want to eliminate it; we simply become interested in finding out what is going on. It is a different attitude than "Oh, here's a blockage; let's do something about it." It is more like you see the blockage and feel that somebody is placing a veil in front of your eyes and you want to look beyond that veil. It is not that you do not like the blockage because it feels terrible; no, it is just that your inner nature is openness, a complete transparent awareness, and it does not feel right to hamper it. It is your nature that you want to see the whole thing.

People inquire in various kinds of ways, but these methods aren't necessarily the inquiry of the Diamond Approach. They mostly are inquiry with an agenda, with an aim in mind. People do this kind of inquiry in various fields, and it has its uses, but when it comes to recognizing reality, our true nature, and the nature of the universe, it does not work. Inquiry needs a vehicle that is a manifestation of true nature, not an expression of our ego-self. Any interest, any position, is an expression of our ego-self; when you start from there, you end up there.

This is very tricky, for you can think, "I get it now. To really get to my true nature, I should not try to get there. Okay, from now on I am not going to try to get to my true nature." This would not work either, because trying not to get there then becomes another goal. But if your love for the truth is present, then you open up this interest in trying to get somewhere and simply recognize it. It becomes a dance, a play. You don't say, "Oh, it is terrible that I have a goal." The moment you say that, you are again taking a position. Then you'd say, "Uh-oh, I'm getting stuck here again." This means you don't want to be stuck, you want to get someplace—you've taken a position again.

Openness can go further and further till it becomes absolute. Once it is absolute, it has no position. The greater this openness, and the deeper it is, the more our inquiry becomes powerful, effective, vital, and dynamic, and the more it explodes the manifestations of the ego-self. But we do not want to explode them to get someplace; we want to explode them to find out what is in them. We want to open up the wrapping of the gift because we want to see what is inside.

When we are open, inquiry is merely the enjoyment of the exploration: having a good time experiencing the path and the terrain of unfoldment. It is an investigation, and an involvement in the investigation. Then there is a lightness to it instead of the dreary heaviness of trying to get someplace. Dreary heaviness means no openness. When inquiry embodies this openness, it becomes an exciting adventure. It is fun. This fun implies not-knowing, but this not-knowing is not a heavy kind of not-knowing, where there is anxiety and self-blame. It is the not-knowing that is the opening to knowing, the not-knowing that eliminates the barrier—which is the accumulation of what you know. It is true not-knowing. It is innocence.

You know that you do not know and you are happy to be on the journey of finding out. In inquiry, you do not know, and you know that you do not know. However, you have some sense of *what* you do not know, and that means you have a general direction—that is what formulates a question. You are happy that you know you do not know, because that means you are getting closer to knowing the truth, which is the beloved of your heart. The truth is ultimately true nature, and inquiry is nothing but the attempt of the love of truth to reveal the fullness of true nature.

If you have an agenda, then you believe that at least you know what is supposed to happen. In this case, there is no longer true openness. But when there is acceptance of not-knowing, an openness about the situation, and a detached curiosity about it, then inquiry becomes quite powerful. It is not only powerful, it cuts through obscurations effectively and in a way that is light, exquisite, and fun.

Openness is the basis, the ground, of inquiry because openness is the manifestation and expression of the depth of our true nature, the fact of its total emptiness, lightness, and mystery. This inherent freedom, this complete mystery at the very depth of our soul, engages its loving dynamism to reveal itself. But we normally experience that as a questioning, as an inquiring attitude. This openness and mystery is the essence of inquiry, but we normally do not see that because we are looking from the outside.

From that perspective, we see the essence of inquiry as being the activity of questioning. But the more we go into the experience, and inquiry deepens and deepens and deepens, its questioning core meets the original openness and lightness, and we recognize that they are one and always have been one. Inquiry finally unifies the soul with its essential home—with its absolute nature—through the bridge of openness.

As I have said, if we are interested in true inquiry, if we really want to find out about reality, then we have to begin with not-knowing. We cannot start from a fixed position, a fixed predisposition, or an assumption about what we are going to find, what is going to happen, what we are going to do, and where we are going to end up.

This is an important and obvious characteristic of true inquiry. The moment we want to accomplish something in particular, such as: "What I need to do is finally unify with God," or "I want to achieve enlightenment, which is the emptiness of all things," or "I am going to work to be free from suffering," we already have a preset destination, a goal. This goal—by the very nature of having goals—is going to limit our inquiry. It is going to constrain us to go this way and not that way because we have already decided where we are going to go, we are already directing the course of our inquiry.

So openness means that in the Diamond Approach, we do not go along with many of the traditional spiritual teachings that posit a particular end state. Since it is intrinsic to the perspective of inquiry and investigation that we do not start with the assumption of a goal, we want to find out whether there is such a thing as an ultimate spiritual goal. We want to find out whether it is possible to even think from the perspective of a final state or realization. There might not be such an end, and yet if there is going to be an end, we definitely want to find out. But we do not start by saying there is an end, and the end is such and such, that we are going to go there and we must do such and such to get there. Positing an end state is definitely a valid way of doing the inner work, but it is not the way of inquiry.

In this approach, we do not have a map that says we should go from here to there; so we don't decide on a particular route that we think will lead us someplace we want to go. Instead, we consider the experiential field we are in at this moment and discern the direction that is emerging from our experience, and then follow that. Then our inquiry is directed by what is happening at this moment, not by some goal in the future we believe we are going to arrive at.

That is what makes the journey really exciting. You never know what the next step is going to be. You never know where you are going to end up—you might fall splashing in the river or find yourself trapped in the middle of the Earth. You do not know. It can be scary, but it can be quite thrilling. Not everybody has the heart or the stomach for this kind of adventure.

INQUIRY AND PROBLEM-SOLVING

As we have seen, to be open ended, inquiry must not be oriented toward an ultimate aim. But it must not be oriented toward any intermediate aim either. Inquiry needs to be free from any aim, at any time, at any stage of the journey. As we mentioned before, it must not be oriented toward solving a problem. The Diamond Approach by its very nature is not oriented that way. If you say, "I have this problem—I am depressed (or deficient, or dumb)—and I want to do something about it; I hear the Diamond Approach is a wonderful method; why don't I try it?" then you're likely to be disappointed.

This does not mean that your need is not valid or not real. We all have problems that we definitely need to deal with. We all had difficulties in our childhood and we have difficulties in our life now that need to be attended to and solved. However, the inquiry of the Diamond

Approach is not the right approach for these things. We can definitely use it to address our problems and difficulties, but that is not the most efficient way, nor is it the best application of inquiry. This is because by its very nature, inquiry is most powerful when it is open and open ended. To give it a limited aim restricts its power; it constrains the possibilities of the inquiry.

Ultimately, and in the long run, inquiry can reveal all truth, so the source of whatever problems you have will be revealed. But that might take a long time, which means that inquiry is seldom an efficient way to solve problems. If you have an aim—"I want to solve this problem"—you are looking at a particular goal and wanting to point the inquiry in that direction. However, for inquiry to work, it must focus right here, at this moment. It investigates what is going on now. If the problem happens to be what is arising at the moment in your experience, then the problem becomes part of what the inquiry explores—otherwise the inquiry ignores it.

So the Diamond Approach is not oriented toward fixing your problems, managing pain, or accomplishing preset aims. Everybody needs to do these things, and you could use inquiry for these purposes. But they are not the most appropriate contexts for inquiry, nor are they the best use of it. You might forget this because inquiry will bring out whatever difficulties you have, and when you are suffering a great deal, you might think that inquiry will ease that suffering and solve your problems. But if you go off on that tangent, it is endless, and eventually your inquiry will come to dead end.

However, if we are on a journey, problems arise and we have to solve them to continue. So if you're traveling in your car and something in the engine breaks, you don't repair it because you like repairing cars or because you cannot stand things to be broken; you repair it because you want to continue the journey. The difference in attitude expresses the nature of open inquiry. So I am not taking a position against solving problems, but it is a general principle that inquiry has to be open ended.

Ultimately, it is the love of the truth and enjoyment of discovering it that powers the journey. Inquiry is at its maximum power when there is no desire to go anywhere in particular or accomplish anything. Then inquiry can truly reveal the fullness of whatever is happening, moment by moment, as our experience unfolds.

LIMITLESS INQUIRY

One of the wonderful things about inquiry is that you can inquire into anything, even into inquiry itself. You cannot bind yourself when you are inquiring, you cannot get cornered, for any corner can be inquired into. It is the very nature of inquiry that nothing can escape it. You cannot say that inquiry will push you against the wall and trap you, because the moment you get trapped, you can ask, "What's making me feel trapped? What is this trap?" You can always ask a question. There are an infinite number of questions because the mystery is inexhaustible.

We have seen that inquiry is a dynamic engagement that needs to be open and open ended, minute to minute, instant to instant. This means that in each moment of the inquiry, you cannot approach your experience by trying to alter it. If you do that, it is not inquiry, it is something else. If you want the inquiry into your experience to be effective, you are going to have to leave it as it is—exactly as it is. Otherwise, what you will be inquiring into is not your experience but something that has been manipulated.

So inquiry requires this lack of limitation, this openness, not only in terms of an end but in terms of the very process itself. Suppose you are experiencing a certain feeling. If you want to really inquire into it, you cannot do that by trying to change it. For example, if you are angry, you cannot inquire into your anger by wanting or trying to make yourself not angry or less angry or more angry. If you really want to inquire into your anger, you want it to be there just as it is, and then you can investigate it.

Furthermore, the limitlessness of inquiry means that you can use anything to inquire—your mind, your heart, whatever capacities or tools you have, whatever techniques are at your disposal. There is no limitation. If you say, "I can only inquire by using my mind," you are placing a limitation on the process. The moment you do this, that limitation is not open to inquiry. And if that limitation is not open to inquiry, your inquiry itself is limited. The moment you set a boundary anywhere, that boundary will limit your inquiry.

You might think, "I can inquire only into my immediate experience." That also sets a boundary, which you cannot inquire into or beyond. But it's artificial because we can inquire into anything. We can inquire into our mental experience. We can inquire into our emotional experience, our physical experience, our spiritual experience. We can inquire into our thinking and thought processes. We can inquire into our body and physiology. We can inquire into our actions and interactions, our lifestyle and beliefs, our fears and interests. We can inquire into energy and matter, into creativity, into stability. There is no limit to what we can inquire into.

If you adhere to a certain religion, for instance, you may be discouraged from questioning certain things—or even forbidden to ask certain questions. Perhaps you cannot inquire into what God is, or you cannot inquire into Christ, or you cannot ask if Buddha's enlightenment had any limitations. This means that there is a boundary around your questioning; certain areas of inquiry are blocked. And that boundedness will limit the creativity and the unfoldment that is possible. So true inquiry has to be absolutely iconoclastic. It must be able to inquire into, challenge, and question any belief, any position, any experience, any supposition, any knowledge, anything and anybody.

As we see, whichever way we look into the nature of inquiry, we find that it has to be open. When you inquire into something, you are opening it up, you are revealing it. Ordinary experience comes in a wrapping. To inquire, you open the wrapping, you remove the veils that obscure it to see what is there. So the very nature of inquiry is a process of opening up; and what you open up are boundaries, limits, positions, beliefs—any stand you may be taking about what you are experiencing.

In other words, we can say that inquiry is a process of always opening and opening and opening, endlessly and freely. And it opens from any place, from any direction, from any level, from any position. If you really want to go into your adventure with no limitations on how far and how fast you can go, openness has to be total and absolute. The moment you limit the openness, you have limited the amount of energy available for the journey. So the process has to be open ended in every way: in terms of how you go about it, what you inquire into, and where the journey takes you. Every limitation has to be challenged, or at least you have to be willing to challenge it.

It is obvious how thrilling inquiry can be if you have the attitude that anything can be challenged. You can take the most mundane experience and open it up. It does not have to be anything special for you to inquire into it. Everything becomes new, disclosing itself in a new light. This opening has a sense of newness, of freshness, of revelation, like a baby just coming into the world. Everything you encounter is seen as if for the first time.

I have been asked, "What happens when I get to complete stillness and my mind is all gone and I do not want to inquire?" When somebody asks me a question like that, I say, "Isn't it interesting that you are asking me a question? What are you doing when you are asking me a question? You are already pointing to the possibility of inquiring while in that state: 'What should I do, leave it or not leave it?' If you find yourself considering your situation in any way, that consideration begins the inquiry."

There can be inquiry even with stillness, when the mind is completely gone. We assume that there is no possibility of inquiry in this state, but that is not true, because inquiry does not have to be verbal. You may think that you have to ask questions with words, but if you say that, you have already put a boundary on how inquiry can proceed. Maybe inquiry can proceed in other ways. Maybe there is curiosity without words, without mind. So even the state of stillness, where there is no mind, can have an inquiring quality to it. There are no limitations.

The fact that experience continues shows that there is an infinite possibility for inquiring. Regardless of how deep and enlightened one's experience is, it is possible to go further, to have experience open up more. When we appreciate this fact, inquiry can bring us an intrinsic energy that has a sense of deep and thrilling freshness, as if your blood were nuclear energy that is moving and bursting with aliveness, bursting with drive. The drive here is not effort but movement—an inexorable, powerful movement, an unfolding. Being is then always opening up with power, with energy, with strength, with intelligence, with gentleness. Sometimes the opening is delicate, sometimes slow, sometimes fast, sometimes bursting, sometimes quiet.

THE JOY AND ADVENTURE OF INQUIRY

As we have seen, dealing with pain is part of our work and cannot be avoided. We deal with pain because we cannot help it, because we are compassionate people. We are happy to be compassionate. When we see somebody in pain, we will do what we can to help. However, this is not the focus of the Diamond Approach nor of the practice of inquiry. The deepest motivation in my own inquiry is a kind of love that is full of lightness and joy. This kind of inquiry makes life a happy engagement. And my interest in teaching, in sharing the journey with you, is not to solve your problems as much as to share with you that joy and happiness. I find that much more important in the long run. Even out of compassion, I think that learning to enjoy yourself is much better than merely learning to solve your problems, although you may need to solve some of your problems to be able to enjoy yourself. We must not forget that the love and the joy are the deeper determinants of how much we can enjoy life. And compassion truly serves that love and that happiness.

Where does that love come from? That love comes from the fact that it is in the very nature of our to love to know itself, to discover itself. Inquiry is actually what invites Being to disclose its richness. But it is really Being that is activating itself to disclose its mysteries to its own perception.

In the beginning, you are bound to experience the journey from the perspective of Being when it is caught and bogged down. When Being is bogged down, when you are merely repeating old patterns, old views, old positions, old knowledge, your experience becomes stale. But when you can disengage yourself from these things and your soul can move freely, your Being can begin to unfold creatively. Then you move from one unexpected thing to another, and life becomes a flow of freshness. Your experience is a flow of revelation of many kinds, many colors, many qualities, and many capacities. Inquiry then becomes an expression and a reflection of the creative dynamism of Being, a dynamism that is inexhaustible as it reveals the infinite richness of possibility.

This is the adventure of inquiry—a thrilling, exciting, unexpected adventure that can become your life.

CHAPTER 3

The Adventure of Being

THE EXPLORATION OF OUR BEING is an adventure, the adventure of Being. The space we travel through is inner space—our consciousness, our experience. And the vehicle for this journey is inquiry. So far we have looked at the basic motivation and orientation for embarking on the journey; now we will look at the context that determines the nature of this particular journey.

REALITY AND TRUE NATURE

All techniques and methods of inner work originate from experiences or perceptions of true nature. True nature is the reality that we are approaching and learning to embody in doing our work. Many techniques have been created based on particular experiences of true nature that arise during the course of the spiritual journey. However, most of the major teachings employ methods that directly reflect the understanding of the actual state of realization, in which one experiences the characteristics and properties of objective reality itself. Only a method based on such a realization can bring about this realization in others, for a method is determined—even constrained—by its view of reality. What better spaceship to take you to a faraway star system than one that originated *from* that star system.

We begin by considering what I mean by "objective reality" because we need a general understanding of some of the main characteristics of truth when it is experienced fully, without veils. Then we can understand better how inquiry works. And since inquiry is also connected to the function of inner guidance, we will see how guidance relates to inquiry.

First we make a distinction between true nature and reality. True nature is the inner nature of ourselves and everything. It is formless, and it is the basis of all forms. As an analogy, consider water: The basic elementary compound of H_2O can manifest as ice, snow, rain, steam, or fog. To recognize that the essence of all of these is water is to see beyond the different manifestations or forms in order to recognize their common nature.

Similarly, true nature is our innate essence, but we can perceive it only when we see through the particular forms, which is possible only when we experience without any veils or distortions. In our conventional everyday reality, our unconscious prejudices and conditioning distort and limit our perceptions such that we cannot see what is most fundamental. Usually we see the appearance of things and take it to be the whole of reality, meanwhile missing the essence of all we see. This is why conventional reality lacks a spiritual ground. We are seeing the appearance as if it were separate from or without its true nature. It is like believing the true nature of ice to be the little cubical shape it takes on in the freezer tray. We believe that the many forms that life takes are inherently different and separate and their nature is defined by their physical properties.

However, when we see without veils, we experience that the whole of existence possesses a single true nature—its common essential ground—and we find no distinction between appearance and true nature, for nothing can be separate from its nature. This is objective reality—all of existence perceived in its true, unobscured condition, in which everything is inseparable from its true nature. Experiencing this is enlightened or realized experience. We understand then that everything is really true nature, that the whole world is nothing but true nature displaying its inherent potentialities. We still see the many forms that reality takes, but those forms are transparent to their true nature, the essential ground of all of reality.

On the journey of self-realization, it is important to learn to differentiate true nature from the familiar forms of everyday experience.

Our very inability to do this accounts for much of the control that conventional reality has over our awareness. Unless we discriminate this formless ground, we will never be able to perceive the forms of reality in their true fullness. Therefore, true nature must first be discriminated in order to serve as our orientation for the inner journey. In the realized state, this discrimination is transcended and true nature is finally recognized in its truth—as inseparable from reality.

THE FIVE CHARACTERISTICS OF REALITY

Our true nature is a sense of presence, the quality of immediacy, of beingness. That is why I frequently call true nature "Being"—it only exists in the direct present-time experience of being here now. I use the term "Being" in a general way, to refer to the whole range of subtlety in how presence manifests. The purest experience of that presence is true nature. True nature is the absolute purity of Being.

When we recognize that true nature is presence, we also see that this presence has many properties that let us approach our beingness in various ways. Each spiritual method can be seen as reflecting certain of those properties. The practice of being present is a method that comes from the recognition of presence as the fundamental nature of reality. The practice of inquiry, which incorporates the practice of presence, reflects other properties of true nature as well.

As a context for beginning this in-depth exploration of the method of inquiry, I will discuss five facets or characteristics of true nature, the formless ground of everything. I will first present these characteristics from the perspective of the realized state, where reality is inseparable from true nature. Then I will discuss how they manifest in normal perception—that is, how their reflections appear in conventional experience when they are seen through veils. As a starting point, I will be correlating my discussion of reality with the Buddhist notion of the five wisdoms or awarenesses of the Buddha, the five *Dhyani Buddhas*.

1. Awareness
The first quality of true nature is that it is inseparable from awareness. Our true nature is inherently aware. This is the fact of luminosity, the fact of light, the fact of consciousness. We know this because when we

experience any of the essential manifestations, we recognize that Being is inseparable from some kind of awareness, sensitivity, in-touchness, or consciousness. Awareness is not something in addition to true nature; it is an inherent and inseparable characteristic of true nature, the way heat is inherent in and inseparable from fire. This fact is reflected in our normal experience in the recognition that we possess awareness; we are innately able to be conscious and aware. This understanding of awareness is similar to the Buddhist notion of the "mirror-like wisdom."

Awareness is coextensive with, coemergent with, completely pervades true nature. Awareness in this sense is not *aware* of presence, it *is* the presence. Presence is a self-aware medium. In contrast, awareness in normal experience is patterned by the dichotomy of subject and object. There is always an awareness that is aware of something, where the awareness is the subject and the something is the object. Furthermore, awareness is commonly held to be a by-product of our brain and the physical senses. We tend to consider it to be a capacity inherent in certain sentient life-forms, directed and controlled by them, and limited in various ways by physical reality. The fact of awareness is, however, still present. The fact of consciousness is preserved; it is basic to experience.

2. Oneness/Unity

The second characteristic of true reality is that this field of awareness, this field of presence, is pervasive and infinite, and includes everything within it. In fact, it is a oneness, an indivisible unity. This is similar to the Buddhist notion of the "wisdom of equality or evenness." The fact that there are patterns within the field does not mean there are discrete objects. So in our experience, the fact that there is sadness and pressure and temperature and softness and hardness does not mean that different objects are there. The field is all one consciousness with different patterns in difference places. So the entire soul is unitary as well. When we recognize true nature and we lose the sense of boundaries, we recognize that oneness pervades the whole universe. God has one mind.

The primary affect in the unitary consciousness is an appreciation of the interconnectedness of everything. The quality of love is implicit and pervasive in the oneness of true nature; it is the inherent goodness and positivity of reality. When we are no longer conscious of the fact that true nature is a unitary field, the feeling of connectedness—or at least the possibility of connection—is all that remains. In our normal consciousness, we experience this as the feelings we have for other people and objects in our world—including the feelings of disconnection, such as longing, sadness, envy, and hatred. The fact that we can feel, that we are sensitive to what we interact with, is the way the underlying unity appears in our experience. The capacity to feel is ultimately based on the capacity to love; and love unifies—it is an expression of oneness. The basis of the heart is love and love is the expression of the unity of Being.

3. Dynamism/Change/Transformation

The third characteristic is that true nature is dynamic. Reality is moving and changing all the time. This is obvious when you notice that your perception of your inner experience—or of the whole world—is not a snapshot; it is a movie. It is inherently in a constant state of change and transformation. It is not a static presence. This is related to the Buddhist notion of the "all-accomplishing wisdom." Reality is a dynamic presence that is always changing through shifts in the manifest patterns. In fact, the presence of change is implicit in the fact of awareness; without it, there is no awareness. If there is only a snapshot and the observer is part of the snapshot, the observer will have no awareness of anything.

Change is necessary for awareness. If you are aware of the Absolute, only the Absolute, and nothing but the Absolute, then you have no awareness of anything. That is why this experience of the Absolute is called cessation. But usually when you are aware of the Absolute, you are also aware of the manifestation, the dynamism, or the flow that is obvious in your own experience.

The human experience, or the experience of the soul, is in constant flow and change and transformation. When we see this characteristic on the level of true reality, we recognize it to be a creative, dynamic force, always creating the forms that we see. Ibn Arabi, the primary mystic thinker of Sufism, called it "new creation" or "continual creation." That is how God creates—by transforming reality. In our normal life, we see the dynamism as the changes and movements we go through, the flow of thoughts, of emotions and actions. Then the experience of change is not characterized by creativity and transformation, but more determined by cause and effect. We see this dynamism as more linear, and experience it as change in time.

The dynamism of Being is creative; it is what underlies all change and movement in the universe. At the same time, since Being is essentially true nature, free and open, this dynamism possesses an inherent tendency to reveal true nature, with all its purity, beauty, and subtlety. This revelation appears as an inherent direction of the dynamism in the human soul. In other words, when the dynamism functions freely and spontaneously, without the cramping and distorting influence of our conventional minds, it tends to transform our experience and perception toward greater clarity, knowledge, openness, truth, and freedom. We call this evolutionary tendency the *optimizing force* of the dynamism of Being.

We experience the dynamism of Being in the fact that our personal experience is constantly changing. One state follows another, one feeling replaces another, thoughts and images come and go in a never ending stream. But when the optimizing force is operating in us, our experience begins to deepen and expand, revealing new states, dimensions, and capacities. We refer to this changing, evolutionary flow of our experience as *unfoldment*. Our soul is then revealing its inherent potentialities. From this we see that the unfoldment of the soul is a direct expression of the optimizing creative force of Being's dynamism.

4. Openness/Spaciousness

The openness of true nature is its fourth characteristic. Openness means an infinite number of possibilities—open to be anything, open to manifest as anything, unlimited in its potential. This is the indeterminacy and inexhaustibility that we discussed in the last chapter. Reality is always changing because its true nature is completely open. This is the space dimension of our Being: When you recognize true nature, you find it to be spacious. In other words, spaciousness is inherent in the presence that is true nature.

The whole universe is a deep mysterious nothingness, openness, lightness, and complete absence of any heaviness. And this very mysterious, delicate spaciousness has a luminosity inherent in it, a glimmer, a radiance that gives it awareness of itself. This radiance appears in the various colors and forms we see as the many objects of discrimination. But it's a unified radiance—one field of light that is in dynamic flow and constant change. This fourth characteristic is related to the Buddhist notion of the "wisdom of the reality field," also called *dharma-dhatu,* one of the awarenesses of the Buddha.

Before the realization of true nature, when you experience Essence as a presence inside you, you experience the spaciousness as an inner quality separate from Essence. Space feels empty of substance—it is a lightness and openness—whereas Essence is presence that has a substantial quality. You experience Essence arising in space. In the awareness of objective reality, Essence and space are recognized as the same thing; they are coemergent. So Essence is a presence that is spacious, that is aware, and that is continually transforming and creative.

We get the sense of time from the perception of change, so time reflects the dynamism of Being. Similarly, spatial extension reflects its openness. The openness and spaciousness of true nature, which is also the sense of depth, mystery, and infinity inherent in it, appears in our normal experience as the sense of physical space between, around, and within manifestation. Our experience has spatial extension; we cannot have perception without spatial extension, just as we cannot have it without change. Shape and size, distance and extension, all reflect the inherent characteristic of openness. True nature has no boundaries in terms of size, shape, or distance. In fact, true nature is beyond extension. When we fully experience true nature, the concept of space disappears. When that occurs, we recognize that there is no such thing as either distance or no-distance. The concept of extension disappears; we then experience it only as openness, as possibility. And because of this possibility, everything manifests, all the colors and shapes.

5. Knowingness

The fifth major characteristic of true nature is that it is not only awareness, oneness, dynamism, and openness, but also knowingness. This is similar to the Buddhist notion of the "wisdom of discrimination," or the discriminating awareness of the Buddha. It is inherent to essential presence that it is not only awareness of presence but simultaneously the discrimination of the particular quality of presence, such as Compassion or Peace. This knowingness is inherent to presence, inherent to the awareness of presence. It is not that presence arises and a separate awareness knows it as Compassion. In fact, sometimes a quality arises that you are not familiar with, but the presence itself tells you what it is. Many people, for instance, do not know there is such a thing as the presence of Value. But if they pay attention when it arises, they recognize, "Oh yeah, this feels like value. I feel worthy, I have worth." So presence has in it—intrinsic to it—knowingness.

At the beginning of the inner journey, we usually experience Essence in one of three ways: as a presence that arises inside us, or that appears outside us, or that comes into us from the outside. These forms of experience, though real, are due to limitations in our perception, and can become veils if taken to be final. These experiences can be seen as an intermediate stage between normal experience and the objective experience of reality. When we experience true nature objectively, without veils, we recognize that it is neither inside nor outside. It's everywhere—outside, inside, and in between. The field of awareness has no boundaries. This presence is an infinite field of awareness, which means that true nature is not the true nature of the human soul only, but the true nature of everything. True nature is nothing but presence, which is at the same time awareness, oneness, and knowingness.

The moment you recognize that true nature is not bounded by your skin, that it is pervasive not only in the body but in everything else, you recognize that intrinsic knowingness is not the experience of one part of reality recognizing another part. The intrinsic knowingness is the fact that the inherent mirror-like awareness, which is everywhere and everything, has a discriminating quality. It can discriminate the variations that exist within itself.

Objective reality is like an energy field with patterns and colors and forms, and this field has its own inherent capacity to know what these elements are. It can distinguish the red from the blue, the blue from the green, the rough from the soft, the soft from the hard. It can distinguish the fluid from the solid and the solid from the gaseous. This capacity is what we are calling discriminating awareness.

Discrimination means not only the differentiation of patterns, shapes, and forms, but also the inherent knowingness of what these forms are. Seen from this perspective, the whole universe is nothing but the discrimination inherent in true nature.

The ability to discriminate is inherent in our consciousness; that is why you can distinguish the pressure in your knee from the tension in your back. That is why you can differentiate the warmth in your heart from the heat in your pelvis, the emptiness in your belly from the thoughts in your mind. You can also differentiate the sounds you make from the ones you hear. But what are these things? They are knowledge, knowingness. The thoughts you are experiencing are nothing but the knowingness of the thoughts. The pressure that you experience in your knee is a recognition of what that awareness is. It is an awareness of an impression and the recognition that it is a tension or a pressure. That is knowledge, basic knowingness.

You can say, "But there is actually a knee with pressure in it." Isn't that just a story you learned? If you forget all your knowledge from the past about human physiology and just pay attention to that area, what you find is a knowingness. This knowingness, what we call *basic knowledge*, is there all the time, and exists prior to commentary. You can say, "Well, there is me and I'm feeling this warmth in my heart." But in fact, saying, "There's me, who is knowing the warmth in my heart," is nothing but the knowingness that there is something there that is aware of warmth and something there we call the heart. Even the commentary is part of the knowingness; its existence is knowingness of the commentary itself.

So the whole field of experience is pervaded by knowingness, constituted of knowingness. If you look at a mountain, you say, "I'm seeing the mountain." Are you seeing the mountain or is there an awareness of a knowingness of seeing the mountain? All you can be aware of is your knowingness that there is a mountain. The knowingness is the object and subject of awareness, for the experience itself is nondual. You are in touch with knowingness in a nondual way. To say that there is a mountain is entirely another step. I am not saying that there is no mountain, but to assert that there is a mountain is a whole other step in addition to the fact of knowingness, which is immediate and direct.

You are aware of me talking to you; this is your knowingness. Apart from that knowingness, I cannot exist, as far as you are concerned. That does not mean that I do not exist; that is not what I am saying.

What I am saying is that as far as your experience is concerned, I do not exist apart from your knowingness. Reality inherently possesses not only awareness, but a discrimination, a faculty that discerns what is encompassed in this awareness.

LIVING IN GOD'S MIND

So the field that is reality is not only a presence that is awareness, but an awareness that is knowingness. Now, this discriminating awareness recognizes the whole as a field that has within it patterns that can be of color, form, shape, texture, smell, sound, or all these. These are the universal patterns. The inherent knowing of this whole field, with all its patterns, is sometimes referred to as the Divine Mind, or the mind of God. In other words, the knowing of all that exists is nothing but God's mind. So if you take Being as the presence of God, then what we are saying is that the inherent knowingness is God's mind. In that sense, because we discriminate ourselves from the whole field, we are all living in God's mind; we are creations of God's mind, contents of God's mind. In fact, we are nothing but God's ideas, because from the perspective of the presence of Being, all these forms are discriminations or concepts, and in some sense, words. Each form is a distinct vibration, with its own sound, but because each sound is known—inherently knowledge—it is also a word.

"In the beginning was the Word, and the Word was with God, and the Word was God" (John 1:1). What is the Word? Everything. My understanding of this statement from the Bible is that God is the presence, so the Word is with God, which is the knowingness. The Word is God because this knowingness is completely inseparable from the presence of God. You cannot separate them, except for purposes of discussion. The existence of the world and the differentiations within it are not separate. The world doesn't exist apart from the mountains and the oceans and the stars; they are the same thing.

True reality is presence that has self-pervasive awareness that possesses at the same time a discriminating knowingness. This fact, which is important for inquiry, can be recognized in your own personal experience. Your normal experience is of being a person with awareness and a capacity to discriminate. But this discrimination is not a result of the mind's labels; the labeling comes later. The inherent discrimination happens as a part of the awareness. You might discriminate the pattern of a tree outside your window and call it a tree, but your ability to discern the pattern of the tree is already there before you call it a tree. It is the same with the capacity to discriminate your inner impressions, such as various emotions, sensations, and thoughts. For example, your inherent recognition of sadness—the soft, warm dissolution of holding in the chest—exists prior to your mind's labeling the experience "sadness."

When the sense of inherent discrimination is obscured to us, it manifests in our normal experience as thinking and labeling, what we ordinarily call knowledge. However, this is a reflection, one step removed from the true knowingness. In other words, the normal knowingness that has to do with thinking, memory, reasoning, and labeling is how true knowingness appears in our ordinary egoic experience. It is *ordinary knowledge*, in contrast to basic knowledge.

KNOWINGNESS IN THE HUMAN SOUL

Whereas the awareness, the oneness, and the openness are constant and unchanging facets of reality, and the dynamism is the experience of change, it is through the knowingness that we experience what is and what changes. Knowingness is the dimension that recognizes all the various manifestations of our life. And the details of knowingness are always different from moment to moment. That is why it is said God never repeats himself. The status of the universe is always different, always new. This is not an esoteric idea. If you think of yourself, you will recognize that no second in your experience is truly like any other. It's always changing, always different.

The knowingness inherent in presence, referred to earlier as the Divine Mind, was called by the Greeks *nous*, or higher intellect. When the Greeks, as in the case of Plotinus, used the word "intellect," they did not mean discursive thinking. In fact, in Western languages, the word "intellect" originally meant "the inherent knowingness." However, this changed mostly in the sixteenth or seventeenth century, when "intellect" began to refer to the representational knowing that goes on in our mind. Now "intellect" is applied only to mental knowingness, the egoic reflection of true knowingness.

The inherent knowingness, or nous, was called the *logos* by some Christians, total intellect by the Sufis, and discriminating awareness by the Buddhists. Now, this discriminating awareness or knowingness is the source of all experience—the various impressions, forms, and colors. Whether they are ordinary physical experiences or unusual spiritual experiences, they are all the same to the inherent knowingness—they are all knowingness, at different levels and intensities of brilliance. The ego experience is just dull knowingness, while the essential experience is a bright knowingness, a luminous presence.

DIAMOND GUIDANCE

This inherent discriminating knowingness of true nature encompasses the content of all that exists, all that can possibly exist, and all that has ever existed. While it transcends the experience of the human soul, it nevertheless appears within our individual consciousness in a specific essential form. More precisely, this knowingness, which is itself the knowledge of everything, manifests in the soul as the specific capacity of discrimination. In other words, the Divine Mind can manifest in the soul in miniature form—a microcosm of that macrocosm. We call this microcosm the *Diamond Guidance*.

The label "Diamond Guidance" reflects the way this essential manifestation of true nature functions, as it reveals the inherent discrimination in experience. When this essential presence manifests in the soul, she can discriminate with the clarity, precision, and penetration of a diamond what is actually present in her field of awareness. The Diamond Guidance can guide the soul all the way from recognizing an emotional truth in the moment to the discernment of the inherent discrimination in reality. That is why I said before that a spaceship that originates from the star system we are traveling to is the most reliable vehicle we can use to go there.

So the Diamond Guidance is the specific manifestation of the Divine Mind arising in our soul as a personal capacity. It is what gives our soul the ability to know exactly what is going on and to understand our experience. Understanding our experience is knowing what it is, directly feeling it, and having insight into that feeling, all as part of the immediate experience. Because it is a reflection, an emanation, or a particularization of the Divine Mind, the Diamond Guidance has the capacity to *reveal* our experience, to penetrate its obscurations all the way to clarity and truth. I call the Diamond Guidance a vehicle of real knowledge because its specific capacity is to make it possible for the soul to know herself. And if you know yourself, then you know your source, because this source is your ultimate identity.

The totality of the soul is a microcosm of all of reality, the unity of Being. The Diamond Guidance is a microcosm of the characteristic of the knowingness of God, the macrocosm of reality. But remember, on the level of true reality, the five characteristics are inseparable. The five facets are all intertwined and happening at the same time. We have described them separately in order to reflect on them, but they are all one reality. Consequently, the Diamond Guidance reflects all the five facets: awareness, oneness, dynamism, openness, and knowingness. However, the most important one, the most central one it reflects, is knowingness.

I sometimes call the Diamond Guidance the essential nous, the individual soul's version of the universal nous of the Greeks, as described by Plotinus. In Sanskrit, the essential nous is referred to as *prajna,* while the discriminating awareness—the universal nous—is called *jnana.* It is known in both Buddhist and Hindu teachings that you use prajna to arrive at jnana. Prajna is referred to as discriminating insight and jnana as inherent knowingness, or discriminating awareness. So prajna is the recognition of patterns, understanding, insight, realization, while jnana is the inherent self-knowing of pure awareness. Jnana is not the experience of a specific insight or understanding; it is the recognition that all experience is knowledge, and that you exist as knowingness, as knowledge.

Now, as I said, true nature is also dynamic, and its dynamism is creative. It is always creating new forms, and this creation of new forms is a development, a change. So the Diamond Guidance implies a dynamism, a creativity. With this creativity, what is known is an evolving, changing knowingness. You do not just know something and that's it: "Oh, I'm sad," and nothing more. You can relate to a feeling in that way, but not much will happen out of that. Acknowledging the feeling is only the beginning of the real process.

DIAMOND GUIDANCE AND INQUIRY

So what do we do so that the knowingness can unfold? We do inquiry. We ask, "What is it about? Why am I sad?" To initiate movement that can bring us to deeper and more precise discrimination, we need a dynamic engagement that will invite the Diamond Guidance so that new revelations can arise. This dynamic engagement is what we call inquiry. So inquiry is really a manifestation of the creative dynamism of our Being. Inquiry invites new knowledge, and knowledge will develop and reveal the possibilities inherent in our Being.

We begin to see here that in our method of inquiry, we use properties inherent to true nature: dynamism and discriminating awareness. The discriminating awareness is the presence of the Diamond Guidance itself, with its insight, intelligence, and precision, and its capacity for synthesis, analysis, and discrimination. We see here the connection between the method and the reality we are moving toward. We also see that inquiry and the Diamond Guidance are quite intertwined, for inquiry not only invites the Diamond Guidance, it is also an expression of the Diamond Guidance. In other words, the Diamond Guidance unfolds or guides the inquiry.

How does it guide the inquiry? By revealing new and meaningful understanding. This only happens, however, if the inquiry is relevant, as this brief story shows: A Sufi master was talking to the public, and he wanted to give them the opportunity to inquire. He said, "I know a lot more of what's in Heaven than what's on this Earth, so you can ask me anything you want." One person raised his hand and asked, "How many hairs are on my head?"

Since the answer to such a question would be irrelevant to self-understanding, the question is useless; it's unintelligent inquiry. So we can inquire—and many people do—but if the inquiry is not intelligent, if it is not an expression of the true creative dynamism of our Being, it will not engage the Diamond Guidance. The Diamond Guidance will not guide the inquiry, and no new revelation will occur. We will just go around in circles. We will keep seeing the same knowledge over and over again—maybe in different forms and shapes, but basically the same. Inquiry needs to involve elements of true nature itself to take us beyond conventional experience. If we use only elements from ordinary experience to guide us, inquiry—or any method we use to consider our life—will merely repeat and confirm this ordinary experience.

The Diamond Guidance can be accessed and used not just in our work but in many ways—for example, in a philosophic or scientific inquiry. In the Diamond Approach, we inquire specifically into our own personal experience. Inquiry is an application of the Socratic method to the immediate reality of our life.

It is worth noting that many people, when reading books about the Diamond Approach or when first coming to the Ridhwan School, believe they know how to practice inquiry. This is especially so if they were trained in philosophy or psychotherapy. I am sure that many people know how to inquire, but that does not mean it is the inquiry we are discussing here. We do not practice inquiry as it is conventionally understood; we do it from the perspective of our true nature.

Inquiry that is open ended, that is an expression of the openness, true knowingness, and creative dynamism of Being, is not just any inquiry. It is a matter of actively using the various qualities of our deepest nature. This is a very unusual and rare capacity. It takes some people a long time—in fact many years in this work—before they recognize, "Oh, this is not how I usually inquire. It is not inquiry the way I have always thought of it."

When one first practices the inquiry of the Diamond Approach, it appears very similar to what is commonly done in other forms of inner work: You ask questions, analyze, look at things, experiment, examine defenses and reactions and psychodynamics, and all that. Anybody who has read any book on depth psychology might feel, "Of course, I know how to do that." However, if these people know how to practice inquiry in the way we do, why don't they arrive at experiences of Essence and true nature? The differences in methods of inquiry may appear quite subtle; nevertheless, they are profound. We need to recognize these differences in order for inquiry to have any true capacity to bring about the unfoldment of the soul.

It is worth looking a little deeper into the confusion that can arise between the type of inquiry I am describing and the analytic exploration you may have been doing. I am not saying that you can never use your mind to do analysis in inquiry—but this is not the method we are using here. We want the inquiry to be a pure act of Being. Analysis might arise as part of the dynamism of Being, but we don't do it intentionally. As soon as we have a desired end in mind, the inquiry is not coming out of the openness, it's coming out of a fixed place. When we analyze from a purely open, investigative space instead of trying to get someplace, the source is openness itself.

THE PATH OF INQUIRY

By understanding inquiry, we learn the posture of the soul that will invite the Diamond Guidance. When we inquire from a posture or an attitude that approximates the qualities of the Diamond Guidance, we will invite its presence, which will then guide the inquiry more directly and more precisely. Practicing this inquiry is a matter of finding a certain kind of openness, a particular attunement, using ourselves and our capacities in such a way that the soul becomes the right kind of vessel for the Diamond Guidance to enter and guide the inquiry. Part Two of this book focuses on the basic elements of the inquiry process that align the soul for guidance to appear.

We will explore how to be open to and recognize the guidance of Being, and how to allow the guidance to function through us. As the guidance functions through us, it not only guides the inquiry and gives it objectivity, openness, precision, clarity, and all of the other qualities, but it also guides the unfoldment of the soul itself. This is because the guided inquiry inherently evokes unfoldment. So the soul herself becomes guided, and that is why we use the term "guidance" for this essential vehicle. Part Three explores in greater depth the nature of the Diamond Guidance, how it arises, and what blocks its functioning in our inquiry.

By manifesting the various essential aspects that compose this vehicle of knowingness, the Diamond Guidance keeps on correcting our perspective in the inquiry—balancing, expanding, or focusing it. Each one of the essential aspects both expresses and serves the true nature of our Being in our experience, life, and actions. They are necessary in all areas of our life, but we will study them here specifically in terms of serving, supporting, and expressing our way of practicing inquiry. Studying them with this perspective will increase our clarity and understanding, and generate the needed perception and experience. Part Four investigates in some depth eleven essential aspects as they arise in the Diamond Guidance to support inquiry.

When inquiry flows freely, it is a true manifestation of openness and love of the truth, and it expresses the spaciousness and dynamism of Being. This dynamic openness will precipitate the presence of this vehicle, the Diamond Guidance. Then the Diamond Guidance will guide the inquiry; it will help us see very precisely what is present in our experience. It will also guide our questioning so that our inquiry will be relevant, precise, and specific.

The Diamond Guidance uses the mind, instead of the mind being in control, or in the foreground. It guides the mind, but it is actually the guide for the soul toward individuation and maturity, toward self-realization and the journey home. This is similar to the Sufi view that what is needed for the awakening and transformation of the soul is the "higher intellect" more than anything else. The Diamond Guidance provides the soul with the objective discriminating capacity that she needs to understand more and more deeply what reality is. This discrimination and understanding is not only the process of the work of inquiry, it is the nature of a true life. Inquiry can become the center of our entire life as our life becomes the unfoldment of our soul. If our life is not a continuing inquiry that is always engaging the unfoldment of the soul—if it is not an ongoing transformation—then we are stuck; in a deep sense, we are dead. We will be mired in inertia, repeating the same patterns forever.

Inquiry breaks this cycle, the self-perpetuating cycle of beliefs: "Yes, I know who I am—I'm this kind of person. . . . Of course people always reject me. . . . My father and mother did this to me, and I'm going to be like this forever and ever; the best I can do is give somebody else a hard time. . . ." This goes on year after year. Inquiry opens it up: "Wait a minute; is that true? Is that why I'm feeling this way?"

If you open up and start inquiring, you will have a chance to find out what is going on. If you stop taking your beliefs at face value, you will stop identifying with them. Not questioning the old knowledge means that you accept your identification with it and accept that it is ultimately true. To inquire means to begin to recognize what it is from the past we identify with. The past survives in our memory knowledge, but we can penetrate it by staying in the present and opening up our experience to our immediate knowingness. In this way, our life becomes a continual living openness, an openness that is a revelation of Being's mysteries.

Then our experience becomes more than just a series of haphazard, disconnected occurrences, as is usually the case in normal egoic life. It becomes a flow of awareness and insight that has a pattern of opening, unfolding, and optimizing. That is why, when we take the attitude of inquiry, understanding keeps happening on its own and new insights emerge. Our experience keeps moving deeper and deeper, becomes more and more expanded, freer and more transparent, until at some point it coincides with the qualities of our true nature.

CHAPTER 4

Spacecruiser *Inquiry*

Throughout this book, I use some concepts from science fiction to help illustrate inquiry because I find them specifically illuminating for understanding inquiry as journeying. Spacecruiser *Inquiry* is the name I sometimes use for the vehicle of this spiritual path—the practice of inquiry. When you begin doing inquiry, you are learning how to use this vehicle for traveling in your own inner space. Spacecruiser *Inquiry* is a gift to you from your own true nature, a method of self-understanding that is designed to reveal deeper and deeper truths about who you are and what reality is. In the last chapter, I gave an overall perspective to orient us for our journey aboard Spacecruiser *Inquiry*. Now it is time to go aboard. First we looked at the ship from the outside, saw the door, and familiarized ourselves with it. Now we can go inside and look around, get familiar with the control console, and then become skilled at actually flying through space.

When I say that inquiry is our spaceship, I don't mean that you actually experience inquiry as a spaceship. I'm using the word metaphorically here. So don't look for some kind of an experience of a spaceship in the process of doing inquiry. Inquiry is a process, an actual dynamic engagement. It invites Being to exhibit its richness and reveal its mysteries, and it does this by activating and engaging the Diamond Guidance, which is a subtle, essential intelligence. Inquiry cannot operate fully without engaging the Guidance—just as a spaceship cannot operate without a guidance mechanism—because inquiry requires real intelligence in its operation.

After taking a tour around the ship, we are ready to consider what it means to take a journey and what different kinds of travel Spacecruiser *Inquiry* can engage in. The nature of our journey is determined by three distinct but interconnected aspects of traveling. First is the mode of journeying, which is expressed in terms of three successive drive mechanisms—the power drive, the hyperdrive, and the superluminal drive. The second relates to the fuel for the journey—what powers the drives at the different stages of the journey of inquiry. The third comprises the intelligent control mechanisms that make our spaceship function most effectively.

In this chapter, we'll explore these aspects and see how they move the individual through what I call the three journeys.

THE FIRST JOURNEY

The first journey takes us to the beginning of experiencing our Being, as we have our initial glimpses of our true essential presence. To begin this journey, the spaceship needs to be able to travel within the same star system, or planetary system, in which it finds itself.

However, at the beginning of the inner journey, we find ourselves earthbound, gravity-bound, caught in an inertial orbit. We are stuck within unchanging patterns, going around and around the same experiences, perceptions, and knowledge. Inertial orbits do not need any power; these habitual behaviors just keep on going, fueled by energy generated from the momentum of our conditioning, which is the gravity that is always pulling us to return to the same terrain.

So first our spaceship needs to be able to disengage from the gravity that keeps us in the static orbit of habitual experience. It needs to be able to reach other orbits—thereby expanding our range of normal experience—and then travel to other areas within the same star system. For our vehicle to be able to travel freely within the same star system, we need an appropriate driving mechanism.

We need to have a drive that can power our spaceship and give it the necessary escape velocity—the *power drive*. In science fiction, the power drive (also called impulse power) is used for traveling between planets or around Earth, in what is considered regular space travel. When we are journeying using the power drive, we continue in the same dimension of reality we are already familiar with, but are able to experience different domains within it. For example, experiencing the unconscious dynamics underlying our normal feelings and actions is part of the first journey.

Inquiry propelled by the power drive is space travel in which the normal concepts of time and space still operate. We are still in normal reality, and within that reality we are exploring our personality and mind, our patterns and feelings—the various conventional conditions of existence, whether neurotic or normal. This process begins to break the grip of our conventional experience, exposing its limitations, and opens us to the possibility of other dimensions.

The supports for this personal exploration are the awareness practices of concentration and mindfulness. In concentration, we learn to focus and sustain our attention on our present experience without allowing habitual distraction from our mind. If we cannot do this, we will never be able to concentrate our energies to break out of familiar orbits of consciousness. At the same time, we must learn mindfulness, which means expanding our awareness to include as much of what is present in our experiential field as possible. In perceiving more, we learn to challenge our conditioned beliefs about what is important in our experience and what is not. This will introduce new elements into our perception and juxtapose things that would never have appeared connected in our normal frame of mind. These two capacities of concentration and mindfulness are central to the power drive and implicit in the more advanced drives.

The first journey I call the *journey to presence*. Our inquiry is primarily in our familiar conventional reality, exploring the beliefs and barriers that keep us from resting in the immediacy of our present experience. In this journey, the functioning of the essential aspects, the various qualities of our beingness, serves to motivate our inquiry. For example, the presence of compassion is what allows us to tolerate our hurt enough to open to it and explore its origins. Strength gives us the capacity to defend our vulnerability against self-criticism, and personal will is called upon when we commit to aligning with the truth in our inquiry. These are three of the five essential aspects known as the *lataif*, which we will look at in detail in Part Four. These five qualities are basic supports in the first journey for keeping us on track in the inquiry process.

We may not know these manifestations of Being in a direct way as essential presence, but they are operative in our soul and instrumental in our travel. Though they arise from a different dimension, the essential qualities are still recognizable within our conventional reality, for we can appreciate their importance through their impact on our soul. Thus the power drive gets its energy from these aspects of Being, as Being calls us toward the knowing of our own presence.

THE SECOND JOURNEY

The second journey begins as we learn to recognize Essence, the dimension of essential manifestations of Being. Now we are approaching the farthest reaches of the power drive; we are at the edge of our star system and are beginning to have glimpses of other dimensions of experience. Most of us will need the help of a teacher, the captain of the spaceship, who can take us into the second journey. A teacher helps us to pay attention to and discriminate the subtle and previously unrecognized aspects of our experience that open the door into the realms of essential perception.

However, the power drive will not be sufficient to take us on the second journey to other star systems or other galaxies. With the power drive, our spaceship cannot exceed the speed of light, and other star systems are tens, hundreds, and thousands of light-years away. Because the power drive operates within regular space-time, we won't have sufficient time to travel to other galactic systems, or even other star systems, which in our work means to other dimensions of experience.

To reach the next level of space travel, we need what science fiction calls the *hyperdrive*. The hyperdrive is powered not only by the qualities of Essence that are the manifestation of the actuality of Being, but also by the openness characteristic of Being itself. This openness transforms the concepts of time and space, allowing hyperspatial travel, which is space travel outside of ordinary space and ordinary time. *Star Trek* introduced the term "warp drive" for this mechanism. Warp drive operates according to principles that transcend our usual laws of physics, allowing us to travel at speeds that exceed the speed of light many times over.

So the hyperdrive is necessary in order to traverse the vast distances of the second journey, to go to other star systems, even other galaxies. But when you go to another star system, you do not know what kind of reality you will find there, so you cannot go with any preconceived ideas. Having preconceived ideas about what you are going to find will prevent you from reaching another dimension. That is why we need the hyperdrive—which requires us to eliminate all our concepts about what space is, what time is, what reality is, what can happen, what cannot happen—to be able to move to a dimension that is totally new, one we never perceived or even conceived of.

In inquiry, hyperspatial travel means effortless and spontaneous unfoldment, for inquiry now is increasingly powered by the openness of Being. This second journey is a *journey with presence*, meaning that the dimension of the essential manifestations of Being is available to our experience as a matter of course, whereas in the first journey those manifestations are tasted only occasionally and serve mostly as incentives to continue the journey of discovering Being.

So, on the second journey, as new dimensions begin to arise, one after another, we need a nonconceptual openness to drive our inquiry. The more freedom we have from concepts, the more profound the openness that powers our inquiry, and so the more we can engage the hyperdrive, allowing a spontaneous and natural flow of revelation. In hyperdrive, the support for this openness with its unfolding flow is the constant practice of presence. Developing this capacity for immediate and direct contact with one's experience and the understanding of how this contact is available at any time becomes an ever present ground for the open not-knowing that characterizes the second journey.

THE THIRD JOURNEY

The hyperdrive can take us through the second journey all the way to the third journey. The third journey is a way of referring to *journeying in presence*, in nondual reality. With hyperdrive, inquiry is driven or motivated by the openness itself, but traveling the third journey requires the hyperdrive to attain maximum, one hundred percent efficiency and power. This means that inquiry is powered by total openness, absolute openness. In science fiction, this drive is sometimes called the superluminal drive.

With the superluminal drive, travel is no longer spatial or even hyperspatial. Hyperspatial travel means that you are traveling in spaces—such as hyperspace, or subspace, to use another term from *Star Trek*—that are not regular space. But these still have limitations because they are still defined by the concepts of space and time, even if they are not ordinary space and time. But since absolute openness has no limitations of any kind, our inquiry is not limited even by the concepts of time or space.

Superluminal travel is more like time travel, but not conventional time travel, because here the concept of time is transcended. Traveling superluminally means experiencing the very creation of time, as the unfoldment of all that exists. In superluminal flight, we cannot even talk about the drive as coming from the openness of Being's essence. It is more that the openness is the vehicle itself. So the essence of Being, the mysterious emptiness, creates time. As it creates time, it creates experience, and this creation of experience is instant and immediate realization. In other words, in the third journey, the traveling is an immediate and continually spontaneous manifestation of realization.

We call it superluminal flight because it is the recognition that perception at that level is nothing but the illumination of the Absolute essence of Being. There is the perception of this mysterious depth, and its glimmerings are the manifestations of the various dimensions, the various star systems. Whereas in the second journey, the manifestations of Being continually shift from one to the next in a dynamic movement of the soul's unfolding experience, in the third journey the unfolding is no longer a movement through time but a constant arising of all experience from the absolute source in the now. There is no spatial travel, no sense of process taking us to another dimension. The dimensions manifest spontaneously and instantly, as the continual emanations from the mysterious essence of reality. It is as if you remain in the same place, and experience merely manifests differently, through and around you, revealing new dimensions and realizations. This is in contrast with the first two journeys, which involve traveling in both space and time.

THE FUEL FOR TRAVEL

So we have three drives that we need to engage as we learn to pilot Spacecruiser *Inquiry*: the power drive, the hyperdrive, and the superluminal drive. In the beginning, we need to learn how to engage the power drive and the hyperdrive. These two drives are related, and we can see this by addressing the question of what motivates inquiry. Motivation fuels the driving force of inquiry. This motivation, which is Essence and openness, develops and transforms as we go through the three journeys.

The specific way that Essence functions in the power drive is through the love of truth for its own sake. What does this mean? Inquiry proceeds by being guided by the truth. In fact, inquiry can *only* proceed on the basis of finding the truth; there is no other way of inquiring. When we inquire, we investigate to find out what the truth of a situation is. We do not try to change anything, we simply work on opening the situation by inquiring into it until it reveals its meaning. So inquiry is basically an investigation to apprehend the truth, the meaning, of what is going on. Frequently, the truth is hidden or not seen, or is distorted by our positions, beliefs, and identifications. We want to see through all that fog to find out what is actually happening.

There is a place in us that loves to know the truth, that wants, values, and appreciates the truth. Only inquiry inspired by this love can serve the functions of activation and transformation. If we inquire out of love to know the truth, our inquiry will naturally disclose the truth that we love to know. We all need to inquire into our own hearts to see if there is a place in us that really loves to know the truth, where we love it enough to do whatever we can to inquire, to investigate. This loving to know the truth is nothing but the response of our Being to its own dynamism. The dynamism is revealing something new, and it manifests initially as the soul's interest in discovering the truth for its own sake.

Our Being loves to rend the veils obscuring it because it loves to find out as much as possible about its truth. Our soul loves to travel into inner space, from one dimension to another. The journey is filled with thrill and excitement, with a celebrative and appreciative quality. When we are motivated by this selfless love, we want to call upon all our possibilities, all our capacities; we want to establish all the support we can for the journey, without caring about how difficult it is or about what is going to happen. We need to find that love because otherwise the only reason and motivation for inquiry is a particular goal or aim, or to confirm an established position. Then we would ultimately be trying to assert a particular identity we've defined ourselves by, and that motivation will not take us anywhere new. Inquiry will not be possible because it is not open ended, and it will become locked into known territory.

When loving to know the truth becomes the specific motivating power for inquiry, the qualities of Essence are able to contribute their specific capacities. These capacities are what fuel the power drive. During the second journey, the openness becomes the inner core of the love, and the hyperdrive engages. It is then that the love becomes coemergent with the mystery. The love of the mystery reveals its mysterious power of revelation and transformation. Loving the truth then becomes a direct manifestation of the openness of Being: It is recognized as the other side of the openness, as its dynamic side.

Loving the truth for its own sake continues to be the motivation for inquiry throughout the second journey, but it is now a more primary motivation than during the first journey because it is a love that has as its base the freedom of the openness of Being, and is a direct expression of that openness. The openness eliminates all the boundaries and positions that can limit our love, and it makes that love completely selfless, totally focused on truth. Love of truth here reveals its inner secret, as the love of Being to reveal its mysteries, as the force of the dynamism of Being that reveals the inexhaustibility of its essence.

INTELLIGENTLY RESPONSIVE INQUIRY

Inquiry is a science in the sense that it can be very objective, very precise. It goes beyond merely inquiring into facts in order to find the truth; it is also an art that needs an organic, wholehearted, comprehensive kind of responsiveness that is not rigid or bound by rules, concepts, or positions.

Inquiry is a dynamic functioning of our consciousness, of our soul, that has to be flexible, responsive, and playful for it to be truly intelligent. It has to be inspired by intelligence and informed by understanding. As you inquire, you need to use your intelligence, and you need to apply whatever understanding you have to the experience of the moment. Inquiry is not a matter of asking a question haphazardly; all questions have to be asked in an organic way. That is what intelligence is: an organic and appropriate responsiveness to each situation.

Intelligence gives our inquiry the capacity to modulate itself according to the particulars of the situation. Sometimes you recognize the need for a great deal of determination, a lot of power and will, to penetrate through a certain manifestation, for there might be a stubborn inertia or fear. Or perhaps the situation can become so subtle that you do not see it, and you need to become quiet, peaceful, and delicate so that your inquiry is a very gentle probing into the situation. In this case, even the will becomes a gentle receptiveness, an effortless presence, as you probe very delicately into the situation. Sometimes the situation requires the tenderness and warmth of compassion because pain and hurt arise. Sometimes you need the humor and playfulness of joy for the inquiry to continue to unfold in the face of hopelessness and despair.

So inquiry doesn't operate on only one wavelength. Because of its intelligence and responsiveness to the unfolding situation, inquiry always modulates itself so that it is appropriate to what you are inquiring into, adjusting as the subject of inquiry changes. For instance, if you inquire into a certain state and a defense arises, you would not ram the defense, since you already have some understanding that you cannot penetrate a defense by ramming into it. This understanding makes your inquiry more intelligent, and you can apply the inquiry to the defense itself. Inquiry is then guided by your intelligence and your already acquired understanding. The skill required here is knowing how to use your previous knowledge and experience as understanding that will inform your inquiry. Thus you can inquire in such a way that this intelligent understanding will not block the inquiry or create boundaries that limit it.

In any inquiry, you have to consider that everything is constantly changing, that experience never remains fixed. For example, you might be experiencing a certain anxiety. As you inquire into your experience, you might encounter some kind of tension or a particular judgment.

You have to take this into consideration in your inquiry; you cannot keep investigating the anxiety regardless of new factors, for the experience is no longer just anxiety. Defenses will arise, and different states and feelings will emerge, so inquiry will have to intelligently modulate itself to respond to this constantly changing scenario.

Inquiry can be so responsive that at times it recognizes that it needs to cease for a while. You can reach a place where you feel it is the time to not ask a question but just to be in complete stillness. Inquiry can then reemerge spontaneously on its own, with fresh possibilities.

Inquiry is also intelligent in its application of mindfulness and concentration. Inquiry requires the global awareness of mindfulness without identification so that you can see the entire situation you are working with. As you take on the whole situation, you start recognizing patterns. As you see the patterns, the inquiry starts focusing and concentrating on where all the patterns lead. For a while, the direction in which the patterns are leading becomes an object of inquiry, which you address with intense concentration. But the inquiry is intelligent enough that even when it is concentrating, it is still mindful so that there will be feedback. As you focus on feeling love, for instance, and are investigating it, you might have all kinds of reactions and responses to that feeling arising. Without mindfulness, you will miss those things and won't take them into consideration as you investigate the state of love.

Mindfulness and concentration occur in varying proportions as the situation being inquired into changes. Sometimes you engage mindfulness as the main capacity used in inquiry, and sometimes concentration becomes dominant. Sometimes mindfulness has an element of concentration in it. At other times, concentration takes over to the point that you forget mindfulness. But generally, mindfulness is needed and is almost always present because it is very rare that only one thing is manifesting in your experience. One thing always brings other things, and that will require the general and global awareness of mindfulness.

THE POWER OF NO POSITION

The intelligence we use in inquiry is the intelligence of the mystery of Being. This essence of Being is the zero that is the source of all infinities, the indeterminacy that is the source of all determinations and discriminations. More specifically, for intelligence to engage the hyperdrive, it has to have as its core the complete openness of indeterminacy, the absolute emptiness of the essence of Being. Otherwise, intelligence will be limited by the various ideas, positions, and concepts in the mind, by our ideas of what can happen and what can be.

So intelligence needs to have as its source that indeterminacy, that complete mystery which gives it its maximum power, where intelligence can use all the understanding, all the knowledge we have without limiting the functioning of that intelligence. It can use its power, it can use its compassion, it can use its gentleness or determination, without the limitations of preconceived ideas or already established positions or beliefs about what is supposed to happen. It is completely fluid.

So for inquiry to engage the hyperdrive, it has to be powered by the freedom of this nonconceptual openness. This amounts to inquiring without having an identity, since identity is based on the positioning we take. We take a position in order to establish a sense of identity. So not having a position means we cannot have identity. That is why the essence of Being, the Absolute, is the experience of no position.

When the inner core of intelligence is this absolute indeterminacy, then your inquiry flows without operating from any established position. You do not even adhere to the position that you are a human being—or beyond that, that you even exist. The next dimension might be complete nonexistence, so if you adhere to the position that you exist, how are you going to arrive at that dimension? Believing that you exist, or that anything exists, could become a barrier. But indeterminacy does not say there is either existence or no existence. It does not say anything. Indeterminacy means that you do not take a position, no assertion whatsoever. Complete freedom.

During some stages of the journey, your travel is both spatial and hyperspatial. You alternate: Your power drive serves as the main propulsion system, and once in a while, when your identity is less fixed, you engage the hyperdrive. But as soon as your sense of identity reasserts itself, you have to go back to using the power drive. Then you are once again moving at sublight speeds and your travel is limited within one dimension. In order to reach another dimension, you have to lose your identity, for the fact that you are shifting dimensions means that you have to let go of your position.

So the more open we are in our inquiry, and the more open ended the inquiry is, the more we can engage the hyperdrive. The unfoldment of our soul then becomes natural and effortless. We can easily move from one dimension to another, for our mind is not limited by what we believe reality is. Then Being is not coaxed, it just manifests naturally, freely, and we are traveling in complete freedom. In the first journey, when we are still using the power drive, we need to use effort, we need to struggle, we need to discipline ourselves. At that point, inquiry cannot happen except with disciplined determination, commitment, and strength, with the intentional application of our intelligence. We have to use our own power. But when the hyperdrive is engaged, there is a spontaneity and a flow. We do not know where we are going; all movement becomes spontaneous, and our spaceship has become a spacecruiser, enjoying cruising from one star system to another.

However, inquiry can be so open ended, so open and free, that sometimes it even allows certain fixations or positions for a while. Positions are different states you can experience: "I am this, I am that. I am peace, I am stillness, I am love, I am space. . . ." In its intelligence, inquiry can recognize that one of these positions might be useful for a period of time. So when you recognize the value of taking a particular position temporarily, your Being will allow you that. Within the perspective of inexhaustibility, you can take a position, but you do not adhere to it; you are able to get off that position. The shifting from one position to another has to remain free. In this sense, the infinite number of positions is itself the inexhaustibility.

No matter what form inquiry takes, it is always responsive to the unfoldment of Being because it is an invocation of that unfoldment. Inquiry is inseparable in some basic way from the unfoldment. At some point, the inquiry and the unfoldment become one thing: the process of manifestation, of Being manifesting what it loves to manifest. That is the point when you enter into the third journey. When the hyperdrive becomes completely established, your experience becomes an uninterrupted unfoldment in the eternal now. This is what we have called the superluminal drive.

We will not discuss the superluminal drive further here. We have mentioned it mostly to give a complete picture of the movement through the three journeys and because it is useful to understand that a form of inquiry is possible that cannot even be called inquiry in the usual sense. When you finally embark on the third journey, that which invites the unfoldment is completely inseparable from the unfoldment itself. This is nondual realization, where experience is pure illumination and unfoldment, where every moment is a spontaneous inquiry, a revelation of the inexhaustibility of Being.

PART TWO

The Fundamental Elements
of Inquiry

CHAPTER 5

Ordinary Knowledge

W HEN OUR BEING IS FREE, it unfolds spontaneously, revealing its mysteries and its inexhaustible richness. We can live within a flow of revelation of many kinds, many colors, many qualities, many capacities, many kinds of experiences. In order for us to engage in the kind of inquiry that will support and participate in this dynamic mystery, it will be helpful to appreciate the relationship between truth, understanding, and knowledge. The relationship can be expressed as follows: Inquiry invites understanding through the revelation of truth, thus transforming knowledge. To begin to know what this means, we will consider the question: What is knowledge?

KNOWLEDGE, UNDERSTANDING, AND TRUTH

This invitation/revelation/transformation—this unfolding of the soul —is what we call the adventure of Being: the open-ended journey in our Spacecruiser *Inquiry* to the farthest reaches of space. However, to take part in this adventure, we must comprehend more fully and exactly what knowledge is, and how it is relevant to our inquiry.

If you look at your experience at any moment, you will see that it is a kind of knowledge. Experience is inseparable from knowledge, and in fact is completely knowledge. Experience is so intertwined with knowledge that you cannot say, for example, "My knee hurts," without the knowledge that you have a knee, what a knee is, what hurt is, and

63

the various other pieces of information that constitute your experience of the knee hurting. All of this is knowledge. You cannot say, feel, or think, "I feel loved by you," without knowing there is a you, there is a me, there is love, and what love feels like or means. All this is knowledge. Even not-knowing your experience is knowing, is knowledge. Even "I don't know what is going on with me" is knowledge.

What is understanding, then? How is it different from knowledge? Understanding means that you not only have knowledge of what is going on, you not only have the experience, but you also are in touch with the *meaning* of the experience. There is not just the knowledge of the fact of the experience itself, but also a cognitive appreciation of its significance. For instance, you are sitting with somebody and you are feeling uncomfortable. This is experience, and it is always connected with knowledge. At some point you investigate, "Why am I uncomfortable?" You hold this question until you see some truth that you haven't seen before—perhaps you want to go to bed with that person but are afraid to say so. You are afraid of even knowing it. This is the truth you didn't see before that gives meaning to your discomfort.

The moment you recognize that truth—which is a certain element of experience that was unknown to you that gives the experience a fuller meaning or significance—the experience transforms. You become aware of how turned on you are, and how scared you are that you are turned on. But being turned on is also knowledge, and so is fear.

So by now your experience has changed from one thing to another. We can also say that what transformed is knowledge. This transformation of knowledge, through which more of the meaning of your experience is revealed, we call understanding. Understanding is thus the dynamic, creative flow of knowledge and knowing. Knowledge creatively transforms through the seeing of truth, and the truth is what transforms the knowledge from one form to another, taking it to a deeper, fuller, and more meaningful level. On the other hand, when you don't recognize that you are uncomfortable because you want to go to bed with the other person, the experience doesn't change. It keeps repeating itself every time you are with that person; then we say you don't understand your experience. So, at least in this particular instance, there is a direct relationship between truth, knowledge, and understanding.

Another example: You notice by being mindful of your experience that it is important for you to be successful, that throughout the years you have been after success in many ways. As you inquire into this tendency and are open to this question of success, you might become aware of an agitation that drives you. You can't sit still; when you sit for a short time you get restless, so you get up and do something. This agitation is a new piece of knowledge that transforms your experience. You now have more than just the knowledge of merely getting up and doing something. If you are curious about this agitation, you might ask, "How come?" and then you might begin to recognize an underlying emptiness. This is a new truth that you have found: It is this underlying emptiness that is driving you toward success.

So the truth changes: The first truth you discovered was the agitation, the next truth was the emptiness. Both truths are relative: Each is true as it is happening, but later on it is no longer relevant. And if you explore the emptiness with the same openness and interest you had during the initial experience of restlessness, you might recognize that the emptiness makes you feel that you are not a competent person because you interpret it as a lack of capacity. Again, inquiry invites the truth, and truth transforms knowledge, resulting in understanding.

DYNAMISM AND ORDINARY KNOWLEDGE

Our openness to the presentations of our soul gives Being the space and freedom to creatively unfold, revealing its hidden possibilities. If left to its own resources, Being will spontaneously unfold in a creative way, revealing whatever is inherent in it. This creative unfoldment is a natural property of our Being. This means that if you don't put limitations on your Being or try to channel or restrict it, it will of its own accord be creative in presenting to your openness whatever possibilities reside in it as potential. What is revealed might be suppressed painful memories from the past, or newer capacities and skills, or even new dimensions of experience.

Since it is inherent to our Being that it is dynamic and tends to optimize our experience, it makes sense that what is needed is the openness to the unfoldment that occurs as the result of our inquiry. Openness implies a trust in the inherent intelligence and lovingness of this dynamism: "I trust that my Being will move the way that is best for it to move, so why should I interfere? This allows me to be really open to it." The openness becomes an invitation.

The optimizing thrust of Being can become bogged down, however, and then we get stuck in a cyclic repetition, a repetition compulsion of old patterns and stale impressions. This is the fixed and rigid inertia of conventional experience. What is responsible for this fixation?

To answer this, we need to appreciate that knowledge comes in various forms, the most common of which is ordinary knowledge. Ordinary knowledge is what is generally meant by the word "knowledge"—all the knowledge you have in your mind. Whenever knowledge becomes a memory, it is ordinary knowledge. It is the totality of your accumulated information: things you learned in school and things you were told or have read about, as well as things you have learned from your own direct experience.

For instance, you have learned from experience that you have a body. That is ordinary knowledge. You were told you *are* that body, and that too becomes remembered knowledge. Now, if you take the concept that you are the body and adhere to this ordinary knowledge as truth, it will limit your openness to the creative dynamism. You will not be open to that dynamism to reveal that you are not a body but something else—consciousness, for instance. This example makes it easy to appreciate that our optimizing dynamism becomes bogged down due to our identification with images, structures, points of view, positions, concepts, beliefs, preferences, prejudices, and so on—all forms of ordinary knowledge. This thwarts and distorts the creative unfoldment of our Being.

In other words, our openness to the dynamism is limited when we adhere to what we call ordinary knowledge, especially when we take that ordinary knowledge to be ultimate truth, truth that should continue forever. When we take our ordinary knowledge as a faithful description of reality, we erect walls around our inherent openness.

Our past experience as a whole, which includes both pleasurable and painful impressions, becomes the content of ordinary knowledge that ends up patterning our experience. It is true that Being always unfolds—dynamism cannot be stopped or completely thwarted. However, it unfolds either freely or in a distorted way. When rigidity patterns our experience in a fixed way, this distorts the manifestation of the dynamism, and the creativity of our Being comes out in a darkened, dull, and disordered way. Understanding these distortions reveals the qualities of Being that are being blocked by the distortions, and thus helps us to see how the creativity of Being itself is distorted and constrained.

Whatever arises is the manifestation of Being and always has a meaning, whether it is distorted and constrained or free and open. The distortions, including emotional pain and difficulties, are nothing but the presentations of the dynamism of Being happening through the filter of our ordinary knowledge. Fixed beliefs, attitudes, and positions, mostly based on ego structures and defenses, impede and distort the flow. What you end up with is a painful, constricted, and dark repetition of old knowledge.

What inquiry does is activate and invoke the optimizing thrust of the dynamism, inviting Being to exhibit its hidden richness. Inquiring opens up our knowledge by challenging it, questioning it, understanding it, and this happens by seeing the truth that transforms, rejuvenates, and deepens our experience. By understanding the distortions, we can see and get to what Being is trying to unfold. At some point, that unfoldment will appear in pure manifestations—the direct, unobscured experience of true nature.

Such an experience of true nature transforms our direct knowledge, taking it to new and fresh dimensions. So the transformation of our experience is the transformation of our knowledge.

REALITY AND ORDINARY KNOWLEDGE

Our experience is mostly determined and patterned by self-images and internalized relationships from the past. These images and memories form most of the content of our ordinary knowledge.

Ordinary knowledge is not inherently constricting to our unfoldment; however, the degree of freedom or restriction depends on how we relate to it. We need ordinary knowledge for practical living, such as finding our car when we go to the parking garage. Without ordinary knowledge, we won't know which car is ours, how to start it, or how to drive. All of that is ordinary knowledge. This kind of knowledge provides necessary assistance and guidance in our daily life; the problem is that we tend to use it for more than that. For example, it is useful to think of your car as a separate object you can drive. However, if you adhere to that position as ultimate, you'll never arrive at cosmic consciousness, because cosmic consciousness reveals the underlying unity of everything.

So ordinary knowledge is useful, but we need to see our true relationship to it, and its relationship to reality. We need to take it as a tentative categorization of reality but not as ultimate, final, and universally applicable. The fact that I am a body is useful when I am crossing the street, but is not useful when I am sleeping. I don't need to think I am a body when I am sleeping. It doesn't matter what I think I am when I am sleeping. But most of us will continue believing we are the body through our sleep and our dreams too.

All of our prejudices, beliefs, positions, and preferences, all of our ego structures and identifications, are either ordinary knowledge or based on ordinary knowledge. And it is the adherence to this ordinary knowledge—taking the position that a particular piece of ordinary knowledge will apply to every moment forever as absolute truth—that limits our openness and thwarts the dynamism from engaging its optimizing evolutionary thrust.

For example, to believe that I'm not a body but I have a body is very useful at some point when I begin to recognize and deal with my body image. As I begin to realize that I am identified with a body image, it is possible for me to recognize that I am a consciousness or spaciousness that has a body. This insight may manifest as truth at some point, which then transforms my experience. But this truth is not final. A year or two later, I might start having certain issues that I recognize are there because I make a separation between my body and my soul. I think I am a soul that has a body or a body that has a soul. At the time, it was useful for me to recognize that I am a soul that has a body, but a year later that truth becomes a falsehood because I recognize then that the body is nothing but a manifestation of the soul. There is no body separate from the soul. The soul doesn't have a body, like a possession; the body is as much a part of the soul as my feelings are a part of the soul.

If I hold on to the insight that "I am a soul that has a body"—which was a truth, a new manifestation of knowledge that at one time transformed my experience—it becomes ordinary knowledge. And if I adhere to that insight as an ultimate truth, there will come a time when it will limit my openness, and the dynamism of my unfoldment will not flow into new dimensions of experience. So truth is something we recognize at the moment, but it is not something we need to adhere to forever. We need to take ordinary knowledge tentatively, and that includes whatever we think and experience as truth, for in the next moment it might not apply.

The truth, then, is a moving point. The moment truth becomes knowledge, it quickly becomes what I call ordinary knowledge. The moment the elements of ordinary knowledge become positions, fixed views of self and reality, they become barriers to the inquiry. Knowledge then becomes a barrier to the openness that is the very heart of inquiry. We can say, then, that understanding and transformation are a matter of freeing our experience from old knowledge, from ordinary knowledge.

INQUIRY AND ORDINARY KNOWLEDGE

In order to understand inquiry, what to inquire into, and what the point of inquiry is, we must understand how ordinary knowledge can thwart the unfoldment and distort the dynamism.

Ordinary knowledge includes what we think about ourselves and reality, what we take ourselves and reality to be, what we think we want and don't want. Anything we put in a conceptual framework is ordinary knowledge. So ordinary knowledge is old categories, information, beliefs, philosophies, ideologies, positions—whatever we believe we know and take to be truth. We ordinarily experience ourselves through the veil of this knowledge, such that our experience of ourselves and everything else is not an immediate, direct, free, spontaneous contact with what is. It is indirect and filtered through knowledge, and this filtering is largely what patterns the experience. The filter patterns experience to a degree we would be appalled to realize.

For instance, our knowledge patterns our experience to the extent that we actually experience a physical reality. We end up believing that there is such a thing as physical reality and physical matter. In fact, we are completely convinced that physical reality is a fundamental truth. In objective reality, there is no such thing as the physical world that we know. If we experience our body without the filter of ordinary knowledge, we will not experience a physical body, we will experience a fluid patterning of luminosity. Our experience is so conditioned and determined, that not only do we believe we have and are a body, we believe in something more basic that underlies this belief: that the body is the body as we take it to be. For most people, this is absolutely true: The body is physical matter that is born and hurts and dies. From that point of view, how can we possibly think of it as a fluid patterning of luminosity? This is just an example, maybe a little extreme, to tell us how far the patterning of ordinary knowledge goes.

In the initial stages, the process of inquiry is mostly an investigation of ordinary knowledge. Why? Because it is an investigation of our present experience, and if we have an experience and don't know its meaning, that tells us there is a piece of ordinary knowledge implicit in it that we don't see yet. So by exploring your present experience, you are actually exploring how ordinary knowledge is patterning it.

A good example of this was mentioned earlier: the unconscious belief that you are an incompetent person, which underlies your drive for success. This unconscious belief is part of ordinary knowledge implicit in your present experience, determining that experience without your knowing it is there. From this insight, you recognize how events that happened in your childhood—perhaps you were put down by your teachers, or your parents didn't believe you could do anything well—caused you to start believing you are incapable. That became a self-image impressed in your mind, which is a piece of ordinary knowledge that now patterns your experience in such a way that you are always driven toward success. So investigating your present experience at first often means investigating how ordinary knowledge is patterning your experience.

Inquiring into how our ordinary knowledge determines, patterns, and limits our experience enables us to learn a different way of approaching the content of that knowledge. Usually we take our knowledge as the determination, as the boundary, of what is possible and what can be known. However, if we understand indeterminacy, the openness of inquiry, in time we learn to take the knowledge not as a boundary but as a pointer. We can use our words, concepts, and thoughts as pointers toward truth, toward what is possible, rather than as boundaries for what can be known: "This is a possibility" instead of "That is what you will find."

If we can inquire into our experience by using knowledge as a pointer, it becomes a helper, a kind of guidance. For instance, we know that anger frequently hides hurt. That becomes knowledge from repeated experience. The next time we see anger, how do we use that knowledge? Do we say, "There must be hurt there; let's find the hurt"? Or, rather than making this automatic assumption, are we open to the possibility that there is hurt, which then can guide our investigation? If you assume that you are hurt, you might be wrong, for once in a while hurt does not underlie anger. There are always exceptions. Knowledge can be used in a way that will aid our inquiry, but we usually use it in a way that limits and binds our inquiry.

TRUTH AND ORDINARY KNOWLEDGE

Usually we equate knowledge with truth; otherwise we say it is falsehood. However, knowledge is not really truth, for truth is always in the moment. Truth is dynamic and in some sense mysterious. We can never fix it and make it static.

Many problems arise when you take knowledge to be truth. The first is that beliefs and information can be incorrect. This is not unusual, as the history of science illustrates. Science is a set of approximations that are always being corrected. We usually characterize our knowledge in physics or mathematics, for example, as absolute knowledge or absolute truth, when it really is just an approximation. At one point in history, people believed the Earth was carried on the back of a turtle; this was a widespread theory. When somebody asked the theologians—who were the scientists at that time—"What is the turtle on?" the answer was, "On the back of another turtle." Later on, people believed the Earth is flat. It was "scientifically proven": Scientists looked as far as they could and concluded it is flat. At that time, that was science, and it worked fine for a while; it was useful knowledge.

The second problem is that indirect knowledge—knowledge you get from other people—is not true knowledge even if it is correct. It is not yet what we call personal truth, not experiential or perceptual truth. People tell you things, you learn things in school, you hear or read things. All this is not true knowledge, it is only secondhand belief and conviction, beliefs taken on faith. There is no certainty here, and yet your belief may prevent you from perceiving reality in any other way. For instance, each one of us believes that our body is composed of atoms. Do we really know that? We have heard it, read it in chemistry books, but it is not direct knowledge. We don't really know. It is knowledge based on faith. It has been useful in the development of our technology to think that our body is composed of atoms, but if scientists took this as absolute truth, our science would not advance.

The third problem is that reliance on information and assumptions communicated by others establishes in us the habit of not exercising our own intelligence. Then our capacity to know, and our love of knowing, weaken in ways that we do not even notice, especially in terms of experiencing and knowing ourselves. That is why it is important to find out what is true through your own direct experience and knowledge. If you only listen to others, you don't exercise your own muscles of inquiry or your own intelligence. If you adhere to—and are satisfied with—indirect knowledge, you will disconnect from the immediacy of your experience.

So our work has to do with inquiry into the very consciousness and perceptivity of our experience. We need to rely more and more on our own immediate, direct knowledge. However, even true knowledge based on our own experience is composed of concepts, labels, ideas, images, and so on. So it exists only as a memory. For instance, you work on yourself and you have the experience of being an ocean of consciousness. This is a true, direct knowledge of your consciousness. But the next moment, it is just memory, an image, concept, idea, impression from the past. It is true knowledge in that you got it directly, but it immediately becomes ordinary knowledge, old knowledge.

If you keep thinking that who you are is an ocean of consciousness, this will disconnect you from your immediate experience, even though the statement is both true and experientially derived. These concepts, labels, and ideas that come from our direct and true knowledge have to be taken as symbols or pointers to the realities that they refer to. They are not the truth. If you talk about your experience of being an ocean of consciousness, the recounting of that experience is not the truth. It is truth only if it is the immediate experience of essential reality now. Your immediate experience might not be of Essence at all, or of Essence manifesting in the same way. If you are holding on to the thought, "I am Essence," that thought becomes another self-representation, another self-image. Maybe your experience this moment is of being space, or love, or just a clunky body. Even though you have had an authentic experience of Essence, to identify with it through ordinary knowledge disconnects you from the immediate experience of its actuality and presence. This is because the experience of Essence is the immediacy of experiencing your Being and you cannot connect to that immediacy through a remembered concept.

Certain concepts such as that of an essential self are useful for certain times and purposes but not for all times. If you take any concept to be applicable all the time, it becomes a rigidity that freezes the dynamism and blocks the openness of inquiry, closing it down.

However, the transformation of knowledge is a much more encompassing process than merely the transformation of the old knowledge that patterns our experience now. Understanding reveals how present experience is patterned by the past, by old knowledge. This understanding, which arises through the revelation of truth, liberates our experience to unfold freshly and spontaneously. Our experience then becomes more immediate and more intimate.

Practice Session: Your Past Experience with Inquiry

With this chapter, we begin an ongoing structure in the book called a *practice session*. This is a support for you to experience the inquiry process for yourself. We will suggest specific questions related to the material of the chapter for you to investigate. You are encouraged to do these inquiry exercises either verbally or through journaling, alone or with fellow explorers.

A good place to begin now is with an exploration into your past experience with inquiry. Give yourself fifteen minutes to sit with and reflect on these questions and any associated insights that arise. What kind of self-inquiry have you done? Did you like doing it? Was it revealing, satisfying, challenging, disturbing, or something else? How do you see your concerns, your capacities, and your limitations in relation to inquiry? How fixed is this knowledge about yourself? How does that knowledge affect your experience of inquiry now and your openness to pursuing it further?

INQUIRY AND THE MYSTERY

When inquiry is open and open ended, it discloses the knowledge that is always available within experience. An open-ended inquiry means that the rigid patterns in our experience can be transformed into fluid patternings of a self-organizing flow. Before we enter into the process of questioning and inquiry, our experience is rigidly patterned; it arises in repetitive, compulsive, obsessive patterns. When we look into and challenge what is determining and fixing these patterns, their rigidity dissolves and our experience starts unfolding in new ways.

Even with that dissolution, our experience doesn't lose its sense of pattern, and this is because pattern is the sense and meaning of experience. We still recognize patterns in our experience, but there is a more fluid and fresh patterning to the flow of experience. It has a fluidity and smoothness, a lightness and spontaneity to it. We feel free. When your experience is in rigid patterns, you are in prison. When your experience flows in fluid patterns, you feel the freedom of experience.

This freedom of experience is the adventure of Being. For an adventure to be really thrilling, we have to go to places that are completely different. That kind of adventure, with its exhilaration and wonderment, is implicit in our Being. In time, your response to experience is not only delight but pure wonder. You come upon an experience and your mind hasn't got the vaguest idea what it is, but it is so beautiful, you are full of wonderment. You can't experience this wonder, though, if you hold on to a particular identity and frame of reference, if experience continues in its rigid habitual grooves. Wonderment arises when you are open to something that is mysterious, new, and fresh, when your old knowledge is completely suspended for the moment.

In other words, Being reveals its mystery through revealing its truth. By revealing to us more of what it is and how it functions, Being shows us how little we know. It also shows us that the more we know, the more we know how little we know. The journey of inquiry takes us from knowledge to mystery. Our inner guidance reveals to us the truth and richness of our Being, but the more it reveals the truth and richness of our Being, the more we are in touch with the mystery. It is a strange, paradoxical situation: Inquiry reveals to us more and more about our true nature and about reality. However, the more knowledge and understanding we gain through this revelation, the more we approach the depth of our Being, and its essence, which is mystery.

To go from knowledge to mystery means to jump into the unknown.

CHAPTER 6

Basic Knowledge

W E HAVE BEEN MOSTLY using our power drive to discuss inquiry; in other words, we have been considering our familiar
experience by looking at certain patterns that are revealed through the
concept of ordinary knowledge. Now we will shift to hyperdrive to
take us beyond the reality we are used to and into a much subtler
awareness that challenges our usual assumptions. We need the hyperdrive to jump to this different dimension and understand a different
kind of knowledge that we call basic knowledge.

The focus of the previous chapter was on how our old knowledge—
our ordinary knowledge—patterns, influences, and determines our
present experience and how inquiry opens up our present experience
by questioning that patterning. We have also discussed briefly how
experience in general, even in the moment, is inseparable from knowledge because of the way it is patterned by past experience.

DIRECT KNOWLEDGE

Experience is inseparable from knowledge in a much more fundamental way, however, than being patterned by old knowledge. In fact, our
experience *is* knowledge. How so? Take the simple case of experiencing
your knee. Included in that experience is the knowledge of what a
knee is, what seeing is, what sensing is, what the body is, and what

pressure is. So you cannot experience the knee except as a collection of various pieces of knowledge.

But the experience is also knowledge in a more fundamental way than that. If you reflect for a minute, it is not very difficult to see that your experience of the knee is knowledge. But it is not merely that you know what a knee is. You do know what it is—and that knowing is knowledge—but knowing what a knee is is ordinary knowledge.

Your experience of the knee is one of shape, sensation, and pressure. What is that? An impression. This impression has information: the contours, the shape, and the various sensations. If you consider this further, you will see that your experience of your knee in this moment is nothing but an impression, an inner perception.

We can say that this impression or perception consists of sensation, or shape, or pressure. But what are these? Knowledge. More specifically, they are a knowingness of some kind of information. An impression is knowledge, but it is not ordinary knowledge. It is information that exists right in this moment, regardless of what you think about the experience or what you know about knees.

Can you experience your knee apart from the sensations and impressions? Is there a knee in your experience apart from the impressions? You might separate sensation and shape into different categories, but they are both knowledge that is not ordinary. They are not knowledge that is in your mind, they are knowledge that is in the moment, here in your present experience. The experience of the knee is nothing but a knowingness of a particular impression or perception. And the perception is inseparable from the knowingness of the perception.

This is what we call direct knowledge, or knowledge acquired through directly perceiving something in the moment. It is not second-hand. You might not even call your knee a knee. You might forget everything about what knees are, but the sensation will still be there, the shape will still be there, the temperature will still be there, and you have a general impression of something, which is a piece of direct knowledge. You can call it something other than a knee, or you might not call it anything, but there is definitely a specific piece of information that is very different from the experience of your stomach, for example. This gets us closer to what I mean by basic knowledge.

Take another example. You are feeling some kind of emotion, let's say fear. It is true that the feeling of fear is your experience in this moment patterned by old knowledge about what in the situation makes you afraid. But what is fear itself? Direct knowledge. When you experience fear, you know fear, even though you might not call it fear. There is a knowingness present of some quality of feeling that is very different from sadness, for instance. The direct knowingness of fear is the same as the experience of fear. Is there any fear apart from the experience of the knowingness of fear? No. This knowingness of fear is what I call basic knowledge of fear; it is fundamental to our experience. Our actual experience is nothing but this basic knowledge.

EXPERIENCE AS BASIC KNOWLEDGE

So our experience is not knowledge in the usual sense of knowledge. It is not what we call ordinary knowledge—the information we have in our minds that we remember about things in the past. It is knowledge now. Basic knowledge is always direct knowledge in the moment—the stuff of our immediate experience. We usually don't call it knowledge; we call it experience, and if we are a little more sophisticated, we call it perception. Perception carries more of the sense of being aware of your immediate experience, which is the palpable sense of knowingness that is basic knowledge.

Our usual perspective is that there is experience and then there is knowledge about it—the knowing is separate from the experience itself. And sometimes the experience happens without any knowing at all; it seems to come and go, and we are clueless as to what happened. However, the fact is that there is no experience if there is no knowingness; otherwise how could you say there is an experience? You may not know what the experience means or even recognize it based on past experience, but you know it as experience and can discriminate elements of it. This is basic knowledge, which means that the knowingness exists in the very moment of experiencing—there is a recognition of something in the present. Experience is always a discrimination, an apprehending of something.

Now, this knowingness of our experience in the moment of perceiving it has a profound and unsettling implication if we pay attention. This is the hyperdrive jump that shifts us out of our familiar mind.

Usually we think of our experience in terms of the duality we have developed as the experiencer and the experienced, the perceiver and the perceived. In terms of the example of fear, we would say, "There is fear and there is me perceiving the fear." We think fear exists someplace on its own, and the perceiver is someplace else, looking and thinking, "Oh look, there is fear." This is the familiar and assumed position that we are in some separate place of observation viewing the world and our experience. But when you experience fear, are you the perceiver separate from the fear? Remember, we are speaking now about the immediate level of direct perception. Can you ever separate in your experience the perception of the fear from the fear itself? It is not possible. The perception of the fear is the same as the experience of the fear, which is the same as the presence of the fear. It's as simple as that. The perceiver and the perceived actually exist together as the experience. If we set aside the duality of the perceiver and the perceived, then what is actually there is consciousness aware of itself as fear.

More accurately, there is a consciousness aware of a manifestation within itself as fear. This becomes clear and distinct when we have direct knowledge of what the soul is, for the soul is the experiencing consciousness. The soul is a field of consciousness that has experience because the experience is an arising within the field of that consciousness. Its experience does not happen outside of that field. Thus the soul is both the experiencer and the medium of experience. So the experiencer and what is experienced are not separate. The soul manifests part of itself as fear. It is not a soul over there experiencing its fear as separate from itself, as if through a telescope. The awareness, which is the nature of the soul, is in the fear itself.

But the dualistic knowledge that we learn in school and in society at large makes us think that an observer exists someplace and fear is someplace else. This kind of knowing is based on many dualities: the observer and the observed, the individual and the experience, the consciousness and the body, and so on. So we have to go through many pathways to investigate these dualities before we finally come to the recognition that they don't exist.

What exists is consciousness that is experiencing fear as part of its manifestation. Consciousness knows part of itself as fear, and this knowing of part of itself as fear is the same thing as having knowledge. In other words, the knowingness of fear is the fear, hence the fear is knowledge. In the same way, feeling sadness is the awareness of the sadness, which is the same as the knowledge of the sadness, and so the sadness is inseparable from knowledge.

Again coming back to the example of the knee: If you don't think with your ordinary mind—which overlays ideas and frameworks onto your experience of the knee—there will only be basic knowledge. In other words, if you don't rely on your ordinary knowledge—in this case, what you know of anatomy—what presents itself is simply immediate experience, an awareness that is a piece of knowledge right here. Furthermore, everywhere you look, hear, or sense, there is only knowledge. All of your experience of yourself is simply knowledge in the moment.

ESSENCE AND BASIC KNOWLEDGE

The exact nature of basic knowledge can be understood more precisely when we consider essential experience. At the beginning of inquiry, what you are exploring is relative truth, the truth of conventional experience. In the territory of relative truth, the fact that whatever you are experiencing is basic knowledge is not strikingly obvious yet. You do experience sadness and sensations, but you are still not recognizing those perceptions as knowledge, or knowingness, because of the dichotomy of observer and observed. Knowledge is still seen as the meaning or insight that you discern from your immediate perceptions. You believe that it is something added to the simple perception. Thus in conventional experience, when you see some relative truth, you end up with insights, and the content of those insights is considered to be knowledge.

At some point, however, you come to the recognition of what we call "essential truth." Essential truth is not an insight about something but the apprehending of the immediate reality of the moment. This immediate reality is presence—the quality of beingness—as when one is experiencing an essential aspect, such as Compassion or Strength.

We find out here that one of the most important characteristics of essential presence is that it is self-aware consciousness. So if I am experiencing the presence of stillness, which is one flavor of essential Peace, nobody needs to be outside the stillness to be aware of the stillness. I and the stillness become one thing. My familiar sense of being a separate observer dissolves. There is no observer and no observed. The stillness itself, Essence itself, is awareness, but awareness with a quality of stillness and peace. And the awareness is pervasive throughout the presence of the stillness. The presence is completely aware—a medium of consciousness characterized by the quality of stillness.

When we appreciate how knowing occurs in essential experience, we know clearly what basic knowledge is, because Essence knows itself only through basic knowledge—through being present to itself. That is why we call it presence. When we begin to think *about* our essential awareness, the presence and the consciousness are no longer one, and the knowing shifts to ordinary knowledge. Furthermore, Essence, which is consciousness and presence as one, is an awareness that not only is aware of its own presence and the fact that it is presence, but is also aware of the distinctive quality of that presence—in this case, stillness and peace.

Our mind can associate all kinds of things with peace—what it is not, what agitation is, what it would mean to be peaceful. All of these things are ordinary knowledge, but the direct apprehension and recognition of the stillness is what happens right at this moment and is independent of what our mind says. In fact, we might not even call it stillness. If we don't speak English, we won't call it stillness, but it is still the same experience.

In this case, what is stillness? Knowledge, basic knowledge. If you call it presence, then it is knowledge of presence, but the knowledge of presence is not separate from the presence. There is no presence separate from the awareness of the presence. They are the same thing. It is the same as the experience of the sun and its light. You cannot experience the sun except through its light. It cannot be perceived otherwise. So how can you separate the two? They are the same thing, which means that the presence of stillness and the direct knowledge of stillness are the same thing.

We see here that by encountering essential experience, we begin to have a new kind of knowledge that we didn't anticipate when we were within the restricted boundaries of ordinary knowledge. If we were to go along in our inquiry thinking that ordinary knowledge is the only knowledge there is, we wouldn't find out about this new kind of knowledge, which I call basic knowledge. And even now our mind may simply want to create a category called basic knowledge in which to deposit certain kinds of experiences such as essential ones. This is once again treating basic knowledge as if it were a new kind of ordinary knowledge. The fact that this is a different kind of knowledge, one that cannot be stored and manipulated by the mind, has very profound implications for inquiry, as we shall see.

Not only is basic knowledge "live" in the sense of existing only in the present, and thus unstorable like random access memory (RAM) on a computer, but it is also "live" unlike any computer knowledge, in the sense of being self-aware and self-knowing. One of the most important things we learn when we start to experience Essence is that the presence knows itself, but the presence and the knowingness of the presence are completely indistinguishable; they are not two things. This is similar to the way water is wet, yet the wetness is not separable from the water.

Our essence has the capacity to know itself completely and directly, independent of what we have known in the past. The knowingness is inherent in the essence itself, in such a way that it not only is aware of itself as existing, but is also aware of the quality and characteristics of this existence. This is an expression of the discriminating awareness, one of the five major characteristics of true nature.

EXPERIENCE AS BASIC KNOWLEDGE

By going from relative to essential truth, we travel to another dimension and recognize a new way of knowing. If we continue in this dimension (the second journey), we find out that the new way of knowing is not that new. Basic knowledge always underlies our ongoing experience, but we could not see it before, because of the usual dualities in our mind between the observer and the observed. We usually think, "The knowingness is in me as I observe my body," instead of recognizing that there is knowingness that is itself the body. The moment you recognize Essence, it is possible to transcend that duality. In knowing Essence, we begin to recognize basic knowledge, and we embark on a journey into a new way of knowing, a direct and immediate knowing.

When we are aware of our presence by being present, there is a new knowledge, and we call this knowledge Essence. At that point, we have the opportunity to begin expanding our inquiry into the nature of all of our experience. We recognize that not only is self-knowing intrinsic to essential presence, but this way of knowing is fundamental to our soul, the consciousness that is the ground of all our experience. We recognize that the soul herself has presence. And how does the soul know herself? How does she experience herself? She experiences herself the same way that Essence experiences itself—through the direct awareness and direct contact with her very presence. In this presence, various things manifest. Sometimes an essential quality manifests, sometimes a feeling or a sensation, an image or a thought.

We usually think, "There is me, aware of a thought." If we inquire a little deeper, we recognize that this statement is based on ordinary knowledge, the belief that there is an observer separate from the thought. If we continue this self-reflection, especially when we go beyond our belief in the observer, we recognize that the thought itself has awareness. We are aware of the thought because the thought itself is luminosity with a certain flavor and information. The thought itself is not separate from awareness, and awareness is knowledge; thus the thought itself is knowledge. It is not that the thought carries knowledge, as in ordinary knowledge; the thought *is* knowledge. It is consciousness with a certain form, and we call that form information. The knowingness pervades the thought itself as if the thought were some kind of fluid moving around and taking a shape. The shape it is taking is a concept or word that we recognize from ordinary knowledge. But the whole thing—the consciousness arising as thought fluid, which is formed into concept shapes—is knowledge, for it is consciousness with content.

At any moment a tremendous amount of information is presenting itself in our experience—things that we see, hear, sense, feel. We are aware of these perceived things as the ground of our experience, as basic knowledge, and we give labels to those parts that we want to think about or communicate. However, if we have the global awareness that comes through the development of mindfulness, it is possible to recognize that the true ground of our experience is actually a medium of awareness, rather than a collection of perceived objects. This medium of awareness that we call the soul has things bubbling in it. The bubbles are not separate from the medium, and the medium itself is self-aware. The bubbles are different colors and shapes: This bubble feels like sadness and that bubble feels like pain, this bubble feels like the idea of a bird and that bubble feels like the thought of a person, and this bubble is an image of our home. All these bubbles are arising in the same medium.

When our experience is freer from ordinary knowledge—from the patterning influence of all the positions, beliefs, and ideas implicit in it—then we can discern basic knowledge more purely. We become aware of what our experience actually is because we know it directly, without the filter of ordinary knowledge. In fact, we can now see that there is nothing but knowledge. We can say there is nothing but experience, but that implies that meaning or interpretation must be added in order to have knowledge or to understand experience more deeply. To say that there is nothing but knowledge means that nothing needs to be added to experience to get knowledge, that each part of our experience is the arising of knowing and is an opening into deeper knowledge. With experience we ask, "What is next?" but with knowledge we ask, "What is this?" and all kinds of possibilities open up. When the nature of experience is nothing but knowledge, we recognize that knowingness is an inherent dimension of being an experiencing consciousness or soul. You can't be a human being without every moment being an experience of knowing.

Some people feel that they don't know anything. Others may experience that their head is literally empty. But what is that emptiness except knowledge? What is the experience of being stupid? Knowledge. What is the experience of not-knowing? Knowledge. What is the experience of intelligence and brilliance? Knowledge. Knowledge is the ground that underlies and allows all possibilities, qualities, discriminations, and actions.

This sense of all experience being knowledge also holds true in the realm of action. What is action? You can say, "I moved my hand." Is moving your hand separate from the immediate knowingness of the experience of moving your hand? What is the actual experience of moving your hand? It is information unfolding. Taking an action is nothing but a flow of knowledge. That is what we call "unfoldment," and we call it unfoldment because there is change. An action is some kind of change. And change or action is nothing but a flow of knowledge.

BASIC KNOWLEDGE AND INQUIRY

We are discussing basic knowledge to begin appreciating that knowledge is not just information someplace in our brain, it is not just computer memory. A computer cannot have basic knowledge; it can only store ordinary knowledge. A human being is capable of basic knowledge, which is the source of all ordinary knowledge. Without it, there is no knowledge of any kind, even ordinary knowledge.

Where does ordinary knowledge come from? It comes from direct experiences that have already happened—either direct experiences in your consciousness or direct experiences of something you have heard or seen or read. What is reading but the knowledge of the experience of reading? Reading the book itself is knowledge. I don't mean the knowledge of the content of the book; the very process of reading the book is knowledge. The whole experience is knowledge. This basic knowledge is the source of ordinary knowledge that you store in your mind. Even ordinary knowledge is basic knowledge because it cannot arise in our immediate experience except as basic knowledge—where each thought and memory in the moment of being experienced is basic knowledge.

Ordinary knowledge is in some sense a subset of basic knowledge. However, because we can think of ordinary knowledge as knowledge that is stored someplace and becomes accessible at certain times, we can conceptualize it as not an experience, and hence as separate from basic knowledge. But in reality, whenever there is ordinary knowledge in operation, it is arising as experience in the moment and thus is basic knowledge. If you think of your experience yesterday, that act of thinking is basic knowledge. So ordinary knowledge always originates from and operates within basic knowledge.

So how are inquiry and understanding related to basic knowledge?

When we inquire, what we are actually inquiring into is basic knowledge. Basic knowledge is never static; it is always moving. Now you are sad, now you are angry, now your knee hurts, now there is a thought, now there is an image. It is always moving and changing. This is the nature of basic knowledge.

And because basic knowledge is a presence of self-awareness and self-knowingness, inquiry, then, is actually basic knowledge inquiring into basic knowledge. What happens in inquiry is that basic knowledge is inquiring into itself, and through this inquiry is liberating itself from the influences of a subset of itself, which is ordinary knowledge.

Ordinary knowledge is knowledge that comes through memory. In conventional experience, basic knowledge does not experience itself directly but through the veil of these memories. Inquiry penetrates these veils so that basic knowledge can begin to experience itself without their influence. So experience is always basic knowledge, but that knowledge can be more or less direct, more or less immediate. The more immediate basic knowledge is, the more luminous it is and the more it embodies the sense of truth, presence, and awareness. When this purity is complete, we have arrived at the discriminating awareness of true nature, the wisdom of discrimination. The less direct it is, the more it lacks implicit meaning and understanding, the more distorted it is, the heavier and more stale it becomes. But it is always basic knowledge.

Basic knowledge means experience right now, the direct knowingness of your experience this moment. It is discriminated information that is happening in the moment inclusive of the observer and the observed. But then you have thoughts about this arising information, reflection on it, and a framework through which you look at it, and that is what we call ordinary knowledge. Inquiry helps you see how ordinary knowledge is affecting your direct experience now. To be liberated from ordinary knowledge means that you feel what you are experiencing right now freshly, without this overlay of old information.

The moment you are consciously in touch with basic knowledge, you realize that nothing can escape it. No concept exists outside of it because any concept is ultimately basic knowledge—even God. What is God? Basic knowledge. What is the Absolute? Basic knowledge. Basic knowledge has many qualities, many levels, many refinements, and many ways of manifesting itself. The point is that in any experience, there is knowingness, and if you eliminate the dichotomy of observer and observed, you see that this knowingness is the same thing as the known, which is the same thing as the knowledge. This is a different way of defining knowledge than the ordinary way of defining it. This knowledge is a more direct, immediate, and experienced knowledge, and yet it is still knowledge that includes the discrimination and recognition of the meaning of the experience.

Practice Session: Your Experience in the Moment

In this inquiry, you will not be exploring a particular issue or subject but observing and investigating what is arising in your experience moment to moment. Take fifteen minutes to stay with this present-time exploration. Begin with simply being aware of the various elements in your experience: bodily sensations, emotional feelings, mental activity, what you see and hear. Report or write what you are aware of and notice how that process affects your experience. Notice what draws your attention in your experience and then look more closely at that, describing what you see. Be aware of when you relate to your subject of inquiry through old ideas or positions and when you experience it with more immediacy and freshness. See if you can tune in to the sense of immediacy and openness of direct contact with your experience in contrast to the familiar feel of what you already know. What is it like to be in touch with and perceiving your experience so directly? What do you feel you have to give up in order to be so immediate? What draws you back into the familiar territory of ordinary knowledge?

DIFFERENTIATION AND DISCRIMINATION IN BASIC KNOWLEDGE

At some point in our second journey, our spacecruiser takes us to a realm of experience where we recognize ourselves as awareness. This awareness is not only aware of its own presence, but it also has the capacity to discriminate. The fact that my experience arises indicates that there is differentiation in this awareness. In other words, there is experience because there is an awareness of different elements that make up my experience and those elements change. Otherwise, there would be no experience.

Pressure feels different from heat, heat feels different from sadness, sadness feels different from anger, anger feels different from pain, pain feels different from relaxation, and so on. Even if I remove all the names and labels from the elements of my experience, even if I suspend all of my knowledge from the past, my experience will still remain differentiated. Not only differentiated, but discriminated as well. In other words, this awareness, which is my presence, is capable of recognizing the differentiated qualities.

So our awareness recognizes that one quality is different from another—this is differentiation—and it can also recognize the innate givens of each quality, independent from comparing one quality to another—this is discrimination. When you experience Strength or Compassion, you don't need to compare them to each other to know them. You can know the Strength Essence just by experiencing it; you recognize how strong and hot it is on its own. When you experience the Compassion Essence, you directly experience the gentleness of it, the warmth of it. When you feel Strength, your intelligence makes you act in a way that you wouldn't act when you are feeling Compassion. Even if the functioning of your mind were suspended, making all ordinary knowledge inoperative, you would still tend to move your body in a strong, expansive way, speak loudly, and assert yourself—all characteristics of the Strength Essence. This means that our intelligence has the capacity to inherently discriminate and recognize a particular quality, not just differentiate it. All these functions occur before the mind begins labeling.

Experience ordinarily includes various kinds of psychic operations, all simultaneously present and functioning at different levels in experience. There is consciousness, then there is differentiation, then there is discrimination, and then comes labeling. They all go on at the same time but are interrelated in a nearly instantaneous chain of arising.

As soon as labeling begins, ordinary knowledge comes into operation. The act of labeling creates the link that associates information from the past—ordinary knowledge—with what is occurring now in your experience, that is, with basic knowledge. When you recognize that your consciousness has inherent in it a discrimination that is inseparable from the capacity to discriminate and is prior to labeling, you are recognizing basic knowledge, which is the ground and the basis of all experience. From basic knowledge arises every kind of knowledge, experience, insight, and action.

INQUIRY AS KNOWLEDGE IN ACTION

We have seen that inquiry will remain limited as long as it is understood as a means for attaining the personal goals that we adopt on the basis of our ordinary knowledge, for our personal goals are based on what we believe we already know, on our already possessed knowledge. Since our goals are based on this knowledge, if we believe that the purpose of inquiry is to fulfill these goals, our inquiry is bound to be narrow and limited.

A more encompassing and open inquiry will disclose to us a discriminating knowingness not bound by ordinary knowledge and its positions, but simply aware whenever positions are in operation. The more open your inquiry becomes, the more you are able to see how ordinary knowledge creates a film through which you are always peering into what you are experiencing right now. Through inquiry, you open up this recognition, this basic knowledge; it begins to become available. By dissolving or parting the veil of ordinary knowledge, you start looking directly, immediately, and intimately, and the experience is now more purely basic knowledge. Observer and observed dissolve. This movement, which is a transformation of awareness, happens through understanding.

However, this understanding/transformation is not just a movement from ordinary knowledge to basic knowledge. The change can be the unfoldment in the purity of basic knowledge itself. This is especially true in the third journey, where there is no filter of ordinary knowledge. Experience is direct, immediate, and pure presence that manifests with differentiated qualities. The presence appears as differentiated qualities and forms that are recognized and discriminated as they arise. As the quality or form arises, the consciousness knows it. When the Strength Essence arises, for example, the consciousness feels the heat and the strength without having to have a thought about it. Even if a thought arises, the thought is not separate from the presence; it is just a blip, a pulse, in the presence.

Basic knowledge has the capacity to separate itself into parts and begin experiencing itself as one part (such as the head) viewing another (like the knee)—as if the experiencing consciousness were located in one part and not in others. Basic knowledge does this by unfolding a part of itself through a piece of ordinary knowledge, such as an image of a self in a separate body, and that knowledge or image becomes a veil it looks through. This veil makes it see a duality where there isn't one. Similarly, basic knowledge has the capacity to free itself by becoming intelligent about seeing through these limitations, by recognizing more of its possibilities.

The optimizing thrust of Being is an inherent, dynamic intelligence in basic knowledge that, when left to its own without our interference, will tend to create more luminosity in its knowingness. So the optimizing thrust is a movement toward more lumination in basic knowledge, and inquiry is an expression of this movement, this intelligent dynamism. When basic knowledge frees itself from the influence of ordinary knowledge, it becomes more luminous and begins to experience itself more immediately and more intimately. In that process, it will also come to know itself as presence, as beingness.

When inquiry is open and open ended, it discloses the knowledge that is always available within experience. Knowledge is available all around us all of the time, in total abundance. If we allow ourselves to be open to it, this knowledge will manifest more and more knowledge, more qualities that we can call new knowledge. Whole new dimensions are part of this new knowledge. We are a total richness of knowledge.

Inquiry itself is knowledge in action; it uses ordinary knowledge in conjunction with our innate intelligence to open up basic knowledge. It is informed by knowledge, is open to knowledge, and invites further knowledge. Knowledge in action is both inquiry and understanding, which is also the unfoldment of Being. We can say that understanding liberates basic knowledge from the rigid patterning of ordinary knowledge, freeing it to unfold according to its own intrinsic patterning, which we experience as inherent discriminating wisdom.

To put it succinctly, ordinary knowledge is carried by thoughts whereas basic knowledge is carried by perception. Ordinary knowledge cannot be separated from thoughts, and basic knowledge cannot be separated from perception. Inquiry is the action of the optimizing thrust of Being's intelligent dynamism that opens up basic knowledge, liberating it from the cramping influence of ordinary knowledge. When basic knowledge is liberated from the filter of ordinary knowledge, it reveals itself as the discriminating awareness of Being, the wisdom of discrimination. In other words, we recognize that this inherent discrimination is the source of discrimination in basic knowledge, and hence in ordinary knowledge.

Basic knowledge spans the distance between the wisdom of discrimination—one of the fundamental characteristics of true nature—and conventional experience, which is basic knowledge filtered through ordinary knowledge. From this perspective, it is possible to see inquiry as a vehicle that takes us from conventional experience to enlightened perception, through the understanding that transforms basic knowledge back to its source, the wisdom of discrimination.

Remembering that another characteristic of true nature or reality is its unity, we see another important fact about basic knowledge. Not only is our inner experience knowledge, and not only is our experience of external phenomena knowledge, but all phenomena—inner and outer—are knowledge. The wisdom of pervasiveness, of unity, eliminates the boundaries that separate percepts in basic knowledge, revealing them only as the lines of demarcation that allow discrimination. We then see that all of reality, the whole universe, is knowledge.

CHAPTER 7

Not-Knowing

FREEING UP BASIC KNOWLEDGE

We have seen that in a fundamental way, experience is basic knowledge, which is the expression of the innate discriminating wisdom of Being. We have also learned that we can be aware of this innate discriminating wisdom of Being in a distorted way or a pure way. When our awareness is distorted, we live inside ordinary experience. When it is pure—liberated from ordinary knowledge—we experience the discriminating wisdom of basic knowledge as a display of luminosity and presence. But for most of us, most of the time, basic knowledge is determined and distorted by our ordinary knowledge.

As human beings, we naturally want to free basic knowledge, for this means freeing our experience. That is our liberation. Freeing basic knowledge means freeing Being to manifest itself in whatever form its intelligence guides it to. Our Being is then spontaneous, free, and truly responsive to the particular situation instead of being held captive by the demands of our past, especially the constraints imposed by our conditioning. Our liberation is a matter of releasing basic knowledge from the distorting and limiting influence of ordinary knowledge, so that experience becomes the pure, direct display of the discriminating wisdom.

Our basic knowledge can be freed by liberating the optimizing force of our Being from the limitations of our ordinary mind and identifications, allowing it to unfold our experience toward greater truth and freedom. But how does this happen? How do we liberate the optimizing force so that it will resume its natural function of revelation and unfoldment of the incredible potentials within our Being?

Our experience is a manifestation of basic knowledge, which is a display of qualities and possibilities from the depths of our Being. However, our experience is usually limited and repetitive. It tends to become stale because of the heavy inertia and fixed boundaries imposed by our ordinary knowledge. Because of these boundaries, we experience ourselves and the world as objects, as entities interacting and doing this and that. We tend to always experience ourselves as this object that we call a self, which goes to sleep and wakes up and has a job to do, and likes certain things and doesn't like other things.

For instance, you might wake up one day and feel, "God, what a terrible day; I have to do all these things I don't feel like doing." This is connected to a self-image of being a person whose life is always an imposition, who always feels put upon. You live as if your life were always limiting you, putting pressure on you to behave one way or another. And you can live your life like that forever.

But this limitation of the display of our Being is due to the content of our ordinary knowledge, which accumulates from all our past experiences. This old, accumulated knowledge limits and constrains our everyday experience by patterning it according to the beliefs, positions, and images that form the content of this knowledge. Because we take this old knowledge to be true and final, we end up living in what appears to us to be a familiar world inhabited by our familiar selves. In other words, we wake up every morning and find ourselves to be this familiar self inhabiting this familiar world because of the positions we have taken based on the dictates of that old knowledge.

But this is a delimitation; we have determined what reality is: "I am such and such, this is reality, this is how I live, this is what I do." And we take the position that these definitions are final and non-negotiable. However, we have seen that the essence of reality is indeterminacy. So how can we take the position "Well, I am this kind of a person and I live my life in such and such a way, and that's non-negotiable"? The moment we do that, we destroy the indeterminacy, we destroy the essence of reality. We lose touch with true reality.

In other words, because of our total reliance on our old knowledge, we take the position that we know the present manifestations of reality. Don't we? Don't you believe that you know what is going on? Don't you feel and think you know who you are, what you are; who and what the people in your life are, what they want from you, what you want from them? Most of us walk around full of this non-negotiable knowledge of what things are all about. You do this even in your spiritual practices: You have all kinds of deep experiences, yet you look at them from the perspective that you know what is supposed to happen to you. You believe you know what is good for you. You take the content of that old knowledge as if it were absolute truth.

And, of course, the more we do the Work, the more the structure of ordinary knowledge becomes shaky. Under ordinary circumstances, it takes a great deal of work to shake it even a little bit, for we have all kinds of maneuvers to try to substantiate and ground our old knowledge. We believe that spiritual development is supposed to happen according to what our old knowledge says is good for us, instead of recognizing that spiritual work means looking at the old knowledge and recognizing it as just ideas, concepts, and beliefs from the past.

In some fundamental way, you don't know at all what is happening right now. You don't know what is going to happen. And the purpose of spiritual work is to pop those old beliefs and concepts, one after the other, until you realize that you do not know what is really happening. Every time you pop one, this is called having an insight. Normally you try right away to fit your insights into the framework of the old knowledge. But these insights are actually puncturing your familiar experience of the world. And in time, you start realizing, "Wait a minute! I am having all these insights, and they are punching holes in my world." You are feeling a loss of support, and at a certain point things might open up in you and you feel, "I am going to fall forever!" But where you are falling is within your own mind. And if the insights are fundamental enough, you might fall *out* of your old mind!

Taking the position that we know the present manifestations constrains these manifestations to appear within the conceptual confines determined by this old knowledge. This limits the dynamism of our Being to fixed, rigid, and repetitive patterns. It destroys the freshness of the moment and separates us from the wonder of the mystery that is always confronting us. We lose touch with the mystery if we go about our lives believing that we know all these manifestations that appear to us. You look at a person and say, "Yes, I see; she is made out of skin, nose, eyes, colors. . . ." Everything is known. Door closed. No investigation, no inquiry, no mystery, no wonder. After a while, you get bored.

If you look at reality this way, you are shutting away the mystery and destroying the freshness that is possible in experience. It might feel secure for a while, but it really isn't. Many kinds of situations and experiences—the most important of which is death—show us that this view of reality does not keep us safe or secure. One day you might be confronted by this event we call death, and it will make you wonder, "Uh-oh, what is all this? Do I really know what life is about?" When the time comes, you may only have ten minutes to find out. This is one reason why I sometimes say that the Work is partly a preparation for death.

We not only believe that we know ourselves and the world around us; we also end up adhering to these beliefs and creating in our external reality what we believe we know. This is because what we believe we know actually patterns the manifestations of our Being, our direct experience of ourselves and the world. We end up seeing what we expect to see. If I believe I am a deficient person, I keep seeing myself as deficient over and over again, and somehow life and the universe always seems to manifest me as a deficient person. In reality, there is no such thing in the universe as a deficient person. That concept is nothing but a certain boundary set on the manifestation of Being by a particular piece of information that I accept as true knowledge. I take this constraint on my experience to be what I know about myself—I say it is reality—because years ago I experienced myself this way and this impression became stuck in me as a certain boundary, an outline for the manifestation of my being.

Most of us do this constantly. You conceptualize a past experience as a piece of knowingness that becomes some impression in your mind, integrated later on with other impressions, thus creating an image that determines your present experience. Your old knowingness and your present experience become inextricably linked. You become trapped in a vicious cycle of inertia, repetition, and stagnation.

This cycle must be interrupted if we are going to regain the freshness of nowness and the wonder of the mystery. We can do this by realizing that we do not truly know what we believe we know and by not adhering rigidly to the positions dictated by our ordinary knowledge.

INQUIRY AND NOT-KNOWING

Not-knowing is the door to the true, direct, fresh knowing. In the preceding chapter, I related inquiry to knowledge, but in this chapter we are exploring it in relation to not-knowing. To inquire into basic knowledge, we must respect and appreciate not-knowing. We need to become comfortable with not-knowing, we have to embrace not-knowing—not as a deficiency or lack, but as the manifestation of basic knowingness. Not-knowing is itself knowing, for it is the way basic knowingness first appears when allowing the possibility for new and direct perception—basic knowledge. Otherwise what we experience will be the repetition of the same things we have known in the past and believe we know. In some sense, not-knowing is the transition from ordinary knowledge to basic knowledge.

So inquiry begins with the recognition of not-knowing. The moment you recognize that there is something you don't know, inquiry may proceed. If you take the position that you know, then no inquiry is possible, for we must first perceive and acknowledge that there is something we don't know. Not-knowing, regardless of how uncomfortable it is, is the starting point of inquiry. And to recognize that you don't know is a very deep thing, as we will see.

When we say we don't know, we are usually looking at the situation from the perspective of ordinary knowledge. It is like saying, "I've studied chemistry; I studied the acids, the bases. But I haven't studied organic chemistry, so I don't know about organic molecules. I need to explore those so that my knowledge will be more complete."

This is how we ordinarily think about not-knowing; it is not-knowing from the perspective of ordinary knowledge. But there is a much more profound not-knowing, a much more basic not-knowing that underlies all of our knowingness, all of our knowledge. As you listen to me, you believe that you know me in a certain way. But most of what you know about me comes from experiences in the past. At this moment, if you really investigate, you will discover that you don't really know me. Maybe I have changed since last night. How do you know? Maybe I went through a deep metamorphosis. Maybe I am not what I was yesterday or a few years ago.

There is a basic not-knowing that is present all the time, in a fundamental and simple way. You look around you and say, "I'm sitting here with these people, inside these walls," and you think you know who the people are and what the walls are. This is ordinary knowledge. And this ordinary knowledge from the past is actually determining your perceptions right now. In reality, you don't truly know in this moment what a wall is. You call it a wall because you know things about walls, and you put the wall in a certain category that fixes and rigidifies it. Of course, it appears to be a normal wall. But what you are knowing is basically your mind. More precisely, you are knowing this presentation, which we call a wall, through the filter of your mind. But do you really know the wall at this moment? Do you truly know what this thing is in itself, without your ideas about it?

You don't know what's here directly and fundamentally. You will not know unless you divest yourself of all your ideas about walls and people completely and look totally openly to see what you find. Then what you can experience is a basic, direct knowingness. But that can start only from a not-knowing. And you cannot take even this fresh, basic knowing into the next moment. In the next moment, you might need to penetrate even deeper to experience directly what is in front of you.

Let us suppose that now you look at the wall and it looks as though it were painted in a shade of white. If you eliminate your ordinary knowledge and look at the wall, you might recognize that it is really more black than white. That is what I see right now. More black than white, even though it is white in ordinary experience. As you see, we think we know even simple things like color. What is the color of this wall? On a certain level of perception, it is white. But we are not seeing the wall in the most complete way possible. We are looking at the wall through certain beliefs and ideas we already have, which we imperceptibly impose on our perceptive apparatus. We look through those ideas and see things in certain forms, certain colors, certain appearances. Our perception is not pure and naked.

In saying that inquiry begins by not-knowing, I am not referring to something circumscribed; not-knowing is not a certain quantity or area of information that you don't know. Not-knowing is omnipresent. However, it *begins* with certain circumscribed areas, for they are part of the not-knowing. For instance, you experience a certain manifestation and feel a particular reaction: Suddenly you're frustrated and scared and you don't know why. This is a not-knowing that can begin inquiry. The more you are aware of what happened—"I just went through this door and saw all these people, and I am scared and frustrated"—and realize you don't know why, the more likely it is that inquiry will begin. Of course, right away you may find a reason to explain your feeling: "Well, I am just scared of crowds. Too many people here." This is a piece of knowledge derived from previous insights, but you can use it to close down the not-knowing. Maybe there is more to it. If you investigate, you might realize that you are not scared of crowds; you might discover that the reason why you are afraid is a deeper one. For example, you might be concerned about losing yourself in such a situation.

It is important that we explore more thoroughly this not-knowing. We usually think that not-knowing is a gap, a deficiency, in our ordinary knowledge. That is why we judge ourselves, that is why we feel bad or get threatened and scared when we realize that we don't know something. We think it's something we could have known, and that if we know it now, the not-knowing will disappear. This position implies that we do not understand that not-knowing is how basic knowledge first reveals itself, that not-knowing is really a knowingness. Not-knowing already implies knowing, doesn't it? You know that you don't know. In the very not-knowing, basic knowledge is functioning. In other words, one of the main ways basic knowingness functions is in the feeling that you don't know.

This possibility of not-knowing thoroughly permeates our experience all the time, in all possibilities and all situations. It is fundamental to our knowing capacity. In fact, our basic knowing capacity begins by not-knowing. How can you know if you don't first not know? We tend to be scared of not-knowing; we are unable to see that it is the pervasive ground of our knowledge. Not-knowing, in some sense, is where we live all the time. Every piece of knowledge is situated in not-knowing. It is the space where all knowledge is. So we can say that basic knowingness is the field of not-knowing, which can manifest forms within itself that this knowingness recognizes.

It is clear that not-knowing is basically of two kinds: Just as there is ordinary knowledge and basic knowledge, there is *ordinary not-knowing* and *basic not-knowing*, Ordinary not-knowing is the absence of certain information. Basic not-knowing is a quality of experience, an omnipresent quality necessary for our knowingness. It implies knowingness and it is the entry into knowingness. Basic not-knowing is actually the openness of Being that allows the dynamism of Being to disclose new possibilities of experience and perception.

RECOGNIZING OPENNESS IN INQUIRY

We have previously discussed how openness is necessary for inquiry. What is this openness for inquiry, and how do we recognize it? We see now that a fundamental characteristic of this openness is not-knowing. You are not open to find something out if you do not acknowledge and respect your not-knowing of what you are investigating. The not-knowing and the openness to find out that is at the heart of inquiry are really expressions of the same thing. The more we think we know what is going on, the less open we are to find out; the more we acknowledge that we don't know, the more open we are to discover what's there. This means a greater possibility for inquiry, and a more effective inquiry.

So not-knowing is an important manifestation of the openness of our Being. In recognizing that we do not know, we realize that not only do we know it is time to inquire, but we also know where to direct our inquiry so that knowledge can emerge. In fact, inquiry is guided by the thread of not-knowing. The pattern of unknowing is, in some sense, the guidance of our inquiry. When you recognize that there is something you don't understand while investigating your experience, what you are actually following is the thread of not-knowing. That is what guides you. What is it that makes you ask a question when you recognize that there's something you don't know? The moment you feel, "Oh, this I know," inquiry in that direction stops. It's a dead end. However, when you feel, "Oh, I don't know this," inquiry moves in that direction. So we can say that not-knowing is a knowingness necessary for inquiry.

Inquiry invites basic knowledge to speak—for instance, in disclosing the limitations in our knowledge and experience. It investigates the possibility that knowingness can appear within what we do not know. Inquiry involves a not-knowing, but it also involves investigating what you do not know, which allows knowledge to emerge. In inquiry, there is an interplay between knowing and not-knowing, but the ground is not-knowing. This ground of not-knowing is what expresses the necessary openness. And as you investigate, this openness allows Being to disclose the truth of the situation. Finally you arrive at new knowledge, but this knowledge emerges within not-knowing and continues to be surrounded by it.

Practice Session: Your Experience of Not-Knowing

A good place to start exploring your own experience in inquiry is by looking at your relationship to the experience of not-knowing. Under what circumstances do you avoid not-knowing? When do you tend to welcome it? Do you have associations with or judgments about your own not-knowing?

Think of something specific in your experience that you would like to explore. Make a list of everything you think you know about it. Then list everything you don't know about it. What is your relationship to knowing and not-knowing in connection with the issue you have raised? Notice what happens when a sense of knowing or not-knowing arises as you are inquiring. When does the inquiry seem to open up? When does it become narrower or start to close down?

NOT-KNOWING AS MYSTERY

Every insight you arrive at is a burst of luminosity, but surrounding that insight is a sea of mystery. This sea of mystery is fundamental for the arising of the insight; without it there will be no space for this burst of luminosity. At the same time, this luminosity is an expression of the mystery and helps us to approach this mystery. In contrast, when we live in the realm of ordinary knowledge, our mind is thick with knowledge. Knowing is all around us, in the form of things we know—rocks, people, likes and dislikes, colors, feelings, memories. Everywhere we turn, there is only old knowledge, no mystery—except in mystery stories.

Our conscious minds would have us believe that we are living in an environment of ordinary knowledge, while what really surrounds us is an environment of mystery, of not-knowing. That which truly exists at any moment is not-knowing, with few little bursts of luminosity, of direct, basic knowledge. Yet we do not find ourselves in this reality; our identity is located within our mind, this universe of thoughts and concepts and memories that would have us believe that we know what is going on. Once in a while, when there is a little gap in that knowledge, we freak out: "Oh, there's something here I don't know. What am I going to do next?" In reality, however, not-knowing is so fundamental, so important for us, that without it we can never know anything new.

One corollary of the fact that not-knowing underlies all knowing is the recognition that knowing is not something we must have. Knowing is a transitory phenomenon. Something arises and you know it; the experience of knowing it at that moment is what matters. What is important for your liberation is not that you've just gotten a piece of knowledge, which you then store in your brain in order to increase the amount of knowledge you have. What matters is the direct experience of the luminosity. And this direct experience of the luminosity needs and requires the ground of not-knowing.

Ordinary knowledge can be used to either support inquiry or block it. For instance, if you know about resistance, you may recognize that your response to a certain experience is resistance, which then will help you to inquire. If you don't know about resistance, you will not know how to inquire into your response effectively. However, if you always interpret your response to be resistance, that can block your inquiry. Even though the manifestation you are taking to be resistance is most often resistance, to always assume that it is resistance will prevent you from seeing that it could be something new.

For example, let's say you feel something hard in your head. You know well that you feel tension, so you conclude that this means that some sort of defense is operating. You investigate and try to open that up. Once in a while, though, that hardness might turn out to be an essential presence that is as hard as a diamond. So thinking that hardness in your head is always resistance—which is a piece of knowledge—might distort your inquiry. Even if the hardness is an essential diamond that is pushing through, you would probably want to push against it, and then it would feel even harder.

That is why I sometimes ask a student, "What happens if you don't fight the hardness?" Sometimes the response is, "Oh, it starts shining!" If you always take the hardness as resistance, you close yourself off from the possibility of experiencing the shining; yet knowing that resistance appears as hardness is definitely a very useful knowledge. So this is one way that knowledge can be used to direct your inquiry and to discriminate. We need to use knowledge in a way that doesn't become a barrier, that doesn't become rigid. We need to see knowledge as pointing somewhere, instead of saying what that somewhere is. In other words, ordinary knowledge can be useful as a pointer to what is possible, instead of being a final conclusion about how things are.

What I am saying is that for inquiry to happen, we first need to see and acknowledge what we do not know. This requires investigating what we believe we do know. And that means we need to be courageous enough to be open to the possibility of questioning everything we believe we know. The more we are willing to accept not-knowing, and the more this not-knowing pervades our experience, the more our inquiry embodies courage and openness, which will make it more effective. In other words, we need the courage and openness to embody, to embrace, the not-knowing all the time. The moment we rest, having concluded that what we know about something is final, we close the door to knowledge and we inhibit Being from disclosing its further and infinite possibilities. We lose the sense of adventure in our experience. To be an adventurer of Being requires that we stay always on the edge of knowledge, where knowledge appears and disappears, where it is created and destroyed. This is the nature of revelation: It is a process of the creation and destruction of knowledge because not-knowing is the ground from which knowledge arises.

This demonstrates another reason to have a healthy respect and appreciation for not-knowing: Not-knowing is the entry to the adventure of discovery. In time, you may recognize that not-knowing is the way Being opens up to its own mysteriousness. In fact, this not-knowing is the direct expression of the Mystery itself.

What does "mystery" mean? When you say, "There is mystery" or "I experience mystery," you are experiencing not-knowing in a palpable form. Mystery is the essence of Being itself, which manifests in inquiry as an openness that appears as a not-knowing. Entering into that openness of not-knowing is the work we do in the Diamond Approach. We question one thing after another—everything we know about ourselves and about reality. And every time we recognize that we don't know, a new kind of knowledge is revealed.

We need to remember that basic knowingness is the field of Being as it manifests in our soul. Inquiry is a dynamic stream that meanders according to its knowingness of what it does and doesn't know as it flows through the field of the soul. This field, however, exists within a larger field of not-knowing—a boundless field of mystery and the ground of all of our experience, perception, and knowledge. The not-knowing of inquiry is like a spring bubbling up in the stream of knowing from the underlying ground of Being's mystery, indicating the undiscovered treasure that lies beneath.

CHAPTER 8

Dynamic Questioning

W̶E DISCUSSED IN THE last chapter how inquiry requires acknowledgment of and respect for not-knowing. We have seen
that for there to be any inquiry at all, we need to see that there is
something we do not know. Not-knowing on its own, however, does
not initiate inquiry, even though it is necessary. Not-knowing is a passive condition, whereas inquiry is a dynamic engagement. For inquiry
to start, not-knowing must become dynamic, active, and engaged.
Many people can recognize they do not know something about themselves, but they do not go further; they leave it at that.

DYNAMIC UNKNOWINGNESS

Not-knowing is a state of knowledge; it indicates an innate, basic
knowingness. It happens within a field capable of knowing. As we have
seen, recognizing that you don't know is a function of knowing, is an
expression of basic knowledge. A dynamic not-knowing implies an
unknowingness that is moving toward knowing, an unknowingness that
is interested to know. It is an unknowingness that wants to know, that
loves to know. In a very direct way, dynamic unknowingness is the
expression of dynamic knowingness.

In other words, dynamic unknowing is the operation of a knowingness that knows that it does not know. And the fact that it is knowingness gives it the dynamism to actively move toward knowledge. Not

only do you need to recognize that you don't know, but the not-knowing must also have a dynamism that moves it toward knowing what you don't know. Otherwise, your not-knowing will not be inquiry.

What I am saying is that a dynamic not-knowing is one that is open to knowledge. It is not just a passive attitude that leaves things as unknown. It is a not-knowing that is full of interest, passionate about knowing, in love with discovery—a not-knowing that points to the possibility of further knowing. In terms of basic knowledge, this possibility leads to further discovery, further experience, further expansion.

Let's take the example we used in the last chapter: You walk into a room full of people and recognize that you are scared, but you don't know why. You can leave it at that, or you can become curious about finding out why you don't know. What is this fear about? This attitude toward your experience is dynamic unknowingness, which is an expression of basic knowledge. It is basic knowledge moving toward optimizing its condition, for further knowledge is a greater illumination. More accurately, it is basic knowledge embodying the optimizing force of Being.

An important thing to see concerning this dynamic unknowing is that it is the essence of a question. The core of any question is a dynamic unknowing, an unknowingness that is moving toward knowing. This is, in reality, the most important element of any question; it is the power and force of any question. Whenever you ask a question, a dynamic unknowingness is involved. The core and heart of your question is an unknowingness that loves to find out. So a question expresses not only an unknowing but an unknowing that wants to know.

We can say, then, that inquiry is a questioning whose dynamic essence is a knowingness that knows it does not know but is interested to know. And since it knows what it does not know, this knowingness knows where to direct its openness. It can direct its openness by knowing where the gap in knowledge exists. In other words, a question is really an elegant and beautiful embodiment of the dynamic unknowing of Being as it optimizes itself. It expresses basic knowingness by embodying at its heart this dynamic unknowing.

THE OPTIMIZING FORCE OF BEING

The optimizing force of Being's dynamism is a will and movement within the manifestation of Being that guides the dynamism to move toward more openness, greater illumination, greater maximization of reality, awareness, light, and truth. This is exactly identical to the core of a question, which means that the dynamism of Being can and does operate as the dynamic essence of a question. That is why we have often said that inquiry activates and engages the optimizing force of Being's dynamism. Inquiry engages the optimizing force because the essence of a question is this unknowingness that is full of love for knowing.

Inquiry dynamically expresses the openness we can have toward the manifestations of Being, in order that Being may unfold and express itself and disclose its further possibilities. Your Being will unfold if you approach it with a genuine question. If you sincerely question your experience, your Being will automatically and naturally disclose its possibilities, which will arise as the discernment of the truth, which in turn will lead to greater understanding.

What happens when you inquire into your experience? You notice that after a while, certain things begin changing, moving, and manifesting the various feeling states, beliefs, and associations involved in your experience. These arise as you question your experience. Do you ever wonder why? What is it about questions that does that? A question is really the functioning of both the dynamism and the optimizing force of the dynamism. When we inquire, Being's dynamism moves toward expansion, toward light, toward understanding, toward truth. We experience this in the process of questioning. Or we can say that the openness toward the expansion and understanding is manifested through a question, for a question allows the possibility or the space for Being to manifest, to display whatever it is that we call an answer. But the answer is not just another piece of ordinary knowledge; it is a new experience, a new perception, a fresh insight. And this new experience, this fresh insight, is the output of the activation of Being's dynamism.

It is true that a question includes concepts, words, and previous knowledge, but what is its living force? If it is a genuine question, the living force in it is this unknowingness that wants to know, this dynamic unknowingness. The openness manifests at the beginning as not-knowing. And as questioning continues, this not-knowing proceeds toward the revelation of whatever manifestation will occur in that space of not-knowing. So the not-knowing, in some very real sense, invites the answer. That is why I call it dynamic.

A question is an interesting manifestation of the soul. It is not just a string of words in your mind. If it were only that, there would be no movement in your inquiry. A question has to have a heart to it, a living force. This living force is the unknowingness that is dynamically moving toward knowing.

If you directly sense this self-directed movement of aliveness, you can actually experience the flow of the soul, the dynamic nature of who you are, separate from any particular content. In this way, the soul directly links the unfoldment of Being with the asking of a question.

So the openness, the unknowingness, the investigating, can be expressed with words, but the questioning itself doesn't have to have words; the dynamic unknowingness is the questioning itself. And you will find that sometimes your question doesn't have words, it has only this dynamic unknowingness. But since you are investigating something in particular, you build on that wordless unknowingness by formulating words and concepts and bringing in what you know from the past. But the force itself, the current that moves, is a dynamic unknowingness, which is an expression of our Being.

Now it is becoming clear how inquiry is the expression of the dynamism of Being. The center of inquiry is questioning, and a question is a direct experience of this dynamism. Dynamism generally manifests as an actual unfoldment, a presentation of Being, but it can also manifest as the part of the unfoldment that activates the dynamism.

Our soul can inquire because it can question, and by questioning it opens up its basic knowledge for Being to disclose its mysteries. This disclosure of the mysteries of Being is the optimization of this basic knowledge. We are then embodying a dynamic openness that expresses a dynamic knowingness.

Inquiry includes other elements such as knowledge, observation, awareness, concentration, reflection, intelligence, and so on. Yet questioning stands as the central initiating process that acts on all these others, integrating and directing them toward a specific object of investigation. Therefore, to learn to inquire, we first need to learn about questions and questioning. We need to liberate our questioning mind and to expand the dynamic openness at the center of our questions. Inquiry then becomes the manifestation of unknowingness in our experience and the moving toward illuminating this unknowingness. This illumination of unknowingness becomes the emergence, the arising, of new dimensions of experience, the unfoldment of our soul. To learn to inquire means to learn to question your experience in a way that will cause it to unfold.

Practice Session: What Limits and Stops Your Questioning

A good place to start this exploration is to find out what stops you from asking questions and what limits the questions you do ask. Many kinds of limitations exist in questioning. You may limit where you let your questions take you, for example, or perhaps how intensely you can ask a question. Why do your questions stay in one area instead of expanding into others? Why do you ask little questions instead of big questions, or complex questions and not simple ones? Some people don't ask questions when they are stuck, others don't ask questions when they are feeling good. So there are obviously many individual differences in how and when questioning occurs.

Choose an issue that you would like to inquire into further than you may have in the past. Notice your mood right at this moment, and your initial attitude toward questioning in this area. Do you feel excited? Wary? Curious? Impatient? Confident? Tense? How do your feelings affect your approach to questioning?

After you have asked the questions that seem relevant and allowed them to trigger other questions, step back and notice: What was the movement and nature of your questioning? Did you begin in one area and move into another, or several others? Was your questioning passionate? Distant? Persistent? Did you get stopped by a thought, a belief, or a position that blocked you from freely continuing? Did your mood shift during the process, and how did that affect your questioning? Observe as much as you can about the pathways your questioning took, and what that might mean about your attitude toward asking questions.

LIBERATING QUESTIONS

For some people, one of the major obstacles to questions results from secrecy in childhood. If you had to keep your own feelings secret or protect the secrecy of others, it would have been very difficult to ask questions. So you may have developed a great deal of anxiety about asking questions or an expectation of severe punishment for wanting explanations. Parental attitudes toward sexual curiosity in childhood also affect questioning. Children have a lot of sexual curiosity, and an unsupportive environment could put a damper on the questioning mind.

Questioning needs to become multidirectional and open ended, with no limitations, no boundaries, no constraints. You need to develop the capacity and the willingness to ask any question, about anything, anything that is germane to your experience. For we're talking here about questioning the important, fundamental things about life, about your life. Working on questions and liberating them is very difficult, but it is important if we want to inquire effectively and powerfully.

A question expresses both the fertile openness of true nature and the love that characterizes the dynamic creative force of that nature. The question invites revelation because its love for knowledge engages Being's love of revealing itself, and the openness of the question expresses Being's infinite and unlimited potentiality—both the source of all manifestation and the space that allows those potentialities to arise. From our limited individual perspective, we are aware of the herald of Being's new revelations as a question. For a question is how the creativity of Being's dynamism appears in our limited mind.

A question is a holy thing, a holy manifestation. A question is an amazing phenomenon—because its heart is the openness of true nature and its activity is a creative love to know the truth, but it also implies a knowingness. It is true that its core is an unknowingness, a mystery, but you cannot ask a question if there is no knowingness at all. You first have to know that you don't know, and then, to ask any particular question, you have to know something. For instance, the question "What's this sweetness in my heart about?" implies that you already know there is sweetness in your heart. So both knowing and unknowing are needed for there to be a question. Without any knowing, there won't be any question, and without any unknowing there won't be questioning.

So a question is a dynamic manifestation that integrates in itself the openness of true nature, the dynamism of true nature, and the knowingness of true nature, all at the same time. By extension, the entire process of inquiry also embodies the openness of true nature, the knowingness of true nature, and the dynamism of true nature. That's why inquiry is not just a passive witnessing, it is an active engagement. When I ask a question, I'm interested to know; I'm not just sitting here watching what passes in front of me. When something passes in front of me, I'm going to inquire into it—dissect and analyze it, contemplate and question it.

I call this the Socratic method because Socrates was the first major figure we know who engaged this process directly, who sat down with people and asked them pointed questions such as, What is courage? Everybody thought they knew what courage was, but he led them in inquiry, first showing them that they did not know, and then guiding them through questions so that they could find out for themselves. He knew the answer for himself, but when he asked the question, he asked it from the place of not-knowing. He knew, but he knew that he didn't know everything, and because of that his inquiry was always alive. That's why so many people flocked around him; they were excited by that energy of inquiry. He could have just told them the answer, but they wouldn't have learned anything, for the important thing is to learn how to inquire, how to ask questions.

That's why a good teacher is somebody who knows, but knows that she or he does not know everything. A teacher who knows everything is dull, can't be spontaneous, can't be creative. If you already know, you will just be saying what you know from memory; you might just as well write one book that contains everything you know and leave teaching to somebody else.

BEING A BURNING QUESTION

The soul can always be ready to inquire, to know and discriminate what arises. You can be a question mark, an excited, exciting question mark that is constantly throbbing. You want to know and you are interested to know completely and fully. You don't stop at "Oh, I'm feeling good today." It's fine that you know something about what you're feeling, but that is not the end. So I ask, "What do you mean? What kind of feeling good?"

"I feel full in my stomach."

"Oh, good, now we're getting someplace. What kind of full in your stomach?"

"It feels something like milk in my stomach."

"Oh, did you have milk this morning?"

"No."

"Well, then, what do you mean, milk in your stomach?"

"That's interesting! It seems like milk, it even looks white like milk. It tastes like milk."

So you begin with feeling good, but end up discovering that Essence can arise in the aspect of Nourishment, which is like physical milk. Through inquiry, knowledge deepens and expands, increasing your understanding. That's what we mean by discrimination: More precision means more revelation. If you say, "Oh, I'm feeling good today" and you leave it at that, then when you feel depressed the next day, you won't know what happened. There will be no revelation, no dynamism. The inquiry brings in greater discrimination, which helps you see exactly what is. Awareness expands, becomes brilliant, and the dynamism is engaged.

Questions are always a response to what is happening in the moment. We ask questions to clarify the dullness of obscuration in our experience, using the drive toward more precision and specificity. In this way, we arrive at greater and more brilliant truth. A question arises because at any moment our experience is not completely illuminated. If it were, we would be in total, objective reality. For us, there is always some dullness here and there, which means we don't understand something, we haven't penetrated it; the discrimination is not complete. So a question arises in response to the recognition that there is something we don't understand.

And our question is not just theoretical. The inquiry has to be fired with a burning question if it is going to ignite the dynamism of our Being, if it is going to turn on the engine of our spacecruiser. It has to be about something we don't understand in our immediate experience, in our daily life—something important and relevant. So inquiry begins with the recognition of an obscuration, a dullness, a lack of understanding, or a lack of complete knowingness and awareness of our experience. This knowingness, combined with the openness inherent in our beingness and its love of revealing the truth, initiates the questioning. The questioning is the beginning of illuminating and clarifying this dullness, this darkness.

DYNAMIC OPENNESS AND WONDER

A question has enfolded in it many elements. In fact, it would be difficult to isolate all of them, for they overlap and interact with each other. Let's go more deeply into four that are vital to the effectiveness of the question. We are trying to study inquiry in as much detail as possible so that we can discover more about its components and how we can maximize them.

We have seen that, more than anything else, inquiry requires an openness to transformation, to new presentations—an openness to seeing the truth. It is a dynamic openness, an openness that has the potential to unfold, to open up to new possibilities. It is not just space, it is a fertile space, and the fact that it is a space allows manifestations to emerge within it. It is a space that has the potential for creation, for creating content within it.

Not-knowing is the way we enter into this dynamic openness, and this unknowingness is the essence of a question. The dynamic openness manifests in inquiry as a question, as a questioning movement. So the central element of a question is the unknowingness that expresses this dynamic openness.

Furthermore, the dynamic openness needs to be multidirectional, directed not merely toward what you think you are inquiring into, but toward the totality of the experiential field. This means that when we are inquiring into a certain experience or manifestation, there is a constant questioning of the inquirer throughout the process, regardless of the object of inquiry. The openness is only maintained when the questioning moves in both directions. If you are focused only on the object of inquiry without looking at yourself, your questions will be dictated by your biases, positions, and unexamined assumptions. This ordinary knowledge will then guide the questioning. However, if the questioning also includes an awareness of and an inquiry into where you are coming from, then you will have a greater openness to seeing more of the truth of the situation.

Let's go back to the example we discussed earlier. You arrive here and you are scared about walking into this room. You can look into this feeling of being scared, but your inquiry needs to also involve your attitude toward the fear. If, for example, you have the judgment that it is better not to feel fear, this is a bias that mitigates against openly inquiring into the fear. The inquiry needs to always be aware, in a questioning way, of where you are coming from.

Inquiry is something that arises in the midst of your experience—as part of your experience, not separate from it. In other words, there is not a person here inquiring into something over there. The inquirer has to be within the field of inquiry itself. This is different from inquiry in natural science, where the object of inquiry is outside you and all that is needed is to not interfere with it. In fact, as it has been stated in the Heisenberg uncertainty principle, even in physical science we cannot separate ourselves totally from the object of our inquiry. In our work, however, since you are inquiring into your consciousness, to make that separation will effectively stop the inquiry. When you are inquiring into yourself, the soul is a field of inquiry that is alive and active, where the inquirer, the inquiry, and the object of inquiry are the same field.

The point is that when we inquire into something, we also always inquire—though not necessarily in an explicit manner—into our positions and biases, judgments and assumptions, identifications and reactions, into all that might limit our openness. This will expand the openness at the heart of our questions. If you don't understand this, you can't truly engage in an effective inquiry.

The dynamic openness implies a lovingness that expresses our love of discovery, our love to know the truth, our love of the mystery. This makes it possible to behold all of our experience—in any moment—with wonderment. When we are aware of this lovingness implicit in the openness, then we are coming not only from a place of being open but a place of wonder. You do not ask questions only to find an answer;

you ask because you are full of wonder. This becomes more obvious the more comfortable we are with not-knowing.

What kills the wonder is asking questions only in a utilitarian way, to get something out of the answer. Such an approach makes it necessary to find the right answer. But in inquiry, it is not important to be right. We do not ask questions to find the right answer; what is important is that there be an unfoldment, an illumination, an openness that is fertile, that keeps opening up, that keeps expanding.

Being right is ultimately meaningless, for there is no final, absolute knowledge about our experience. Most of the time, we are probably right to some degree, wrong to some degree. Whatever knowledge you have is limited, approximate; regardless of how precise it is, it is never the end.

It is important, of course, to value your perceptions and insights, but the point is not to find an answer, which is a destination. It is to keep things rolling, so that the flow continues and the natural dynamism is liberated. Never forget that what matters is the movement, the expansion, the freedom—not which bit of information you have arrived at.

Our inquiry is then filled with wonderment, which is the integration of the love of truth with the openness that arises as unknowingness. We find that the inquiry, and all of our experience, embodies an appreciative quality, a heart quality. Sweetness and appreciation pervade the openness.

Wonder can become the source from which questions arise. It becomes the heartfelt dynamic essence of inquiry. If we let our questions arise from this true wonder, they will open to further questions, which in time become free from bias and positions. Our questions will call forth a knowledge that reflects the power to go beyond the known, transforming our basic knowledge into forms and dimensions our ordinary knowledge can never imagine.

DIRECT OBSERVATION

What we are interested in is the inquiry into our basic knowledge, which is our immediate experience. To inquire into your experience, you need data that comes only from direct observation. So your questions, if they are going to be effective, need to be grounded in and based on this direct observation of yourself, your experience, your life, your environment—moment to moment, day to day.

If we are interested in understanding our experience, we cannot depend on abstract ideas and thoughts to guide our inquiry and our questions. Sometimes people sit around a table and ask all kinds of questions based on an argument or abstract thinking. That becomes sophistry. You can do that, but that is not the Diamond Approach.

It is important that you inquire specifically into what is significant in your experience. What is significant in your experience is what presents itself and impacts you, and you can see this only if you are aware of your experience. If you are only thinking about your experience, or somebody has given you some ideas about it and you inquire into these ideas, your inquiry is not going to be effective. It is not sufficiently grounded, not guided, and will not engage the dynamism of Being. It will engage your thinking process, which is a kind of dynamism, but a very limited kind.

Questioning based on observation addresses the quality of knowledge in our experience, so that our participation in basic knowledge becomes open and direct. Direct observations—the fruits of our mindfulness—give our questions the necessary direct data for us to use our intelligence. Observation also functions to guide our inquiry by directing our questions to relevant areas. Even to recognize an unknowingness, we have to be observing our experience.

This brings in the elements of mindfulness and concentration as described in chapter 4. Let's look at an example of direct observation: I am sitting here and I recognize that there is a tickle in my belly that seems to be out of the ordinary, for my belly doesn't usually tickle like that. I can inquire directly into this. I do not need to check any book; I can just apply my mindfulness and concentration with a questioning mind.

The tickle can be the tip of an iceberg. Many other things might be happening in my belly: The tickle might turn out to be the tip of something that extends all the way through my pelvis and down through my legs. If I use my concentration and am not dissuaded by all my ideas, reactions, and superego, if I stick with my experience and my attention is not deviated, my mindfulness might inform me that the phenomenon doesn't stop at my feet. In my seeing that, another layer of unknowingness has arrived. What is this tickle that begins in the belly but doesn't stop at my feet?

This is an example of an inquiry based on direct observation, which also includes a dynamic openness. It demonstrates the usefulness of developing mindfulness and concentration as supports for the direct observation necessary for inquiry. In using these capacities, I recognize that there is something there I don't know, and I am interested to find out what it is.

USING ORDINARY KNOWLEDGE TO INQUIRE

The capacity of mindfulness, however, which provides the global awareness necessary for observation, is only one of the necessary elements of questioning.

Asking questions also involves knowledge, both ordinary knowledge and basic knowledge. We ask a question about our experience, and the question itself is basic knowledge, which is patterned by our ordinary knowledge. Ordinary knowledge comprises all experience from the past. Without any experience from the past, it will be impossible to ask a question. We might have the dynamic openness, we might have the unknowingness and the interest in knowing, but without ordinary knowledge, we wouldn't know in what direction to inquire, what kind of thing we want to know. So ordinary knowledge gives us an orientation for inquiry.

As we discussed in the chapters on basic knowledge and ordinary knowledge, first we need to understand that ordinary knowledge is the natural result of basic knowledge; basic knowledge becomes ordinary knowledge as time passes. You have an experience or observation, which is basic knowledge, but after a few minutes it becomes ordinary knowledge, stored information.

This alone is not a problem. But one difficulty we all get into when doing spiritual work is that the mind starts functioning like a computer; it takes a piece of information as unchangeable, as final. A piece of information is one bit stored in the mental computer. When a piece of knowledge is needed, it is reproduced exactly as it was stored, without the possibility of modification. So we tend to take the content of our knowledge as final and absolute, and our memory becomes a boundary for what is possible in experience.

One element that characterizes the Diamond Approach is the way we use ordinary knowledge. Many spiritual approaches say to drop your mind, throw away your knowledge, just be in a mindless space. You can do this, but that is not inquiry; it is something else. In the Diamond Approach, we use our ordinary knowledge in a specific way, an intelligent way. We use ordinary knowledge—all our concepts, ideas, realizations, and memories—as pointers to something in reality without taking the position that that knowledge is final and unquestionable. If we don't do that, it will be the end of our inquiry. After a while, we won't find anything vital inside the wrappings; nothing alive will remain within the concepts. Then we only live within wrappings, within shells of reality. We have all these packages all around us and we call it experience, and our living knowledge self-destructs.

So inquiry and asking questions use ordinary knowledge, but with an appreciation of the nature of this kind of knowledge. We need to use all this knowledge—all this experience we had before—with intelligence, in a way that allows this knowledge to help us open the door instead of closing it. Then our ordinary knowledge can inform our inquiry, can guide our questions, by our intelligence using all of our experience in the present moment to open up this door further.

Suppose that you had an experience that propelled you for the first time to work on the issue of doubt. Inquiring into the doubt led you to experience a wonderful black peacefulness. Having had that experience, you now know that the Black aspect of Essence is peace. (See chapter 16 for further discussion of the essential aspects and their colors.) This is stored in your memory as ordinary knowledge. The next time Black Essence arises in your experience, your mind remembers peace, so Black always becomes experienced as peace. If you remain fixed on the knowledge derived from this experience, you will never discover qualities about Black Essence other than peace.

It is true that in your first encounters with it, the Black Essence arises mostly as peace, but when you further investigate this peace, you might recognize that the peacefulness is related to an exquisite, calm stillness. When you experience this stillness, you may think of it as peacefulness, but the concept of peacefulness doesn't exactly capture the flavor of the experience. Stillness as the direct inner experience of the Black Essence is slightly, subtly different from peacefulness.

And when you contemplate the stillness and explore it, you might find out that stillness is not static. This is difficult for the mind to grasp. Usually you think that stillness means stillness—nothing moving—which your mind understands as static, so that is generally how it is remembered when the experience of stillness is stored in your mind. Now when Black returns and you bring back the remembered experience, which has become a concept of stillness, you don't recognize that stillness has a dynamic effect; you think of it as static and unchanging. In actuality, there is nothing static about the Black Essence. The dynamic effect—which is felt at the moment stillness comes in contact with the mind—is to erase the mind. It destroys its content, annihilates it, and makes the mind still like itself.

When you recognize this annihilating action of the Black Essence, you can begin to understand the relationship between peace, stillness, and annihilation. And if you stay open, without allowing the concepts of annihilation, stillness, or peacefulness to limit your contact with what you are experiencing, you might recognize that the Black Essence is also powerful, for it can quiet down the agitation of the mind easily and effortlessly. This might allow the Black Essence to arise as power, and you can then recognize that Black is the essence of power.

Now we have gone from peace to power, though we wouldn't initially have seen any connection between them. If we had remained bound to the memory of our original experience of Black as peace—filed it away in our computer as a bit of final knowledge and closed our mind to further possibilities—we might never have arrived at real power.

But even power is not necessarily the end, because if you stay with your experience in an attitude of dynamic openness, the Black Essence can also manifest as the essence of magic and the essence of beauty. And if you continue to be open and curious, you might see, "Oh, it is some kind of unfathomable mystery." And so it goes, as the unfoldment of the richness of Being continues endlessly.

This doesn't mean that the Black Essence is not truly peace, it doesn't mean it's not true stillness or true power. It is all of these, but we need to remember that the essence of Being cannot be finally determined—this is what I call the inexhaustible mystery of Being. You can know it and know it and know it and know it, but you can never exhaust it. This is true about any manifestation of Being—in fact, about anything in life, anything you experience. You can know the experience precisely, but this precise knowledge is never final. It is this ultimate mystery that allows the unknowingness to continue being there, for regardless of how much we know, we still don't know. There is always unknowingness.

ORGANIC, FREE INTELLIGENCE

In inquiry, many elements interact, including dynamic openness, observation in the moment—which uses the skills of mindfulness and concentration—and the content of ordinary knowledge, all integrated in an intelligent way. So the fourth element is an intelligence, an organic, free intelligence that can operate while taking the nature of ordinary knowledge into consideration. This is not an operation that a computer can do; computers relate one thing to another in a linear fashion. The intelligence that inquiry needs is a nonlinear and responsive kind, which can respond even when there is insufficient information. This intelligence is part of the dynamism that gives our questioning a penetrating quality, a sharp quality, a synthetic quality, a brilliant, luminous quality. With this kind of intelligence, our questions become powerful and relevant.

The intelligence I am referring to is inherent in our Being, a specific aspect of Essence that characterizes the optimizing force of Being's dynamism. This optimizing force is movement toward greater and greater illumination. Illumination, when it becomes intense, is brilliance. Brilliancy is intelligence. So intelligence is the organic recognition and responsiveness within the process of inquiry that skillfully moves it toward more optimization—which means more awareness, more light, more love, more expansion, more depth, more significance.

However, our organic intelligence can illuminate our inquiry only when two things happen. First, we must have the direct data of our observation, arising from our global awareness of what is going on here and now. And second, we need to use our ordinary knowledge appropriately to inform us of what we have observed in the past.

As we have seen, there is a place for ordinary knowledge, as long as we know how to use it intelligently. But ordinary knowledge by itself won't work without the raw data of direct observation. And these two together will do nothing for our inquiry if we don't have the dynamic openness. All of these elements need to operate as one in a field of openness that emerges as a dynamic questioning that invites experience to open up, unfold, and flower. Then our inquiry is full of wonder, a thrilling and satisfying adventure, taking us to places maybe no one has gone before.

Practice Session: Your Experience of Questioning

Now would be a good time to explore your own experience of questioning. What are the strengths and weaknesses of your questioning capacity? Explore this through an inquiry into a specific matter that you are seeking to understand more fully. Begin by asking questions about what you don't know, what you would like to know, what puzzles you, or what interests you. Write the questions down as they come to you. Pursue your inquiry as it unfolds from the questions. See where the questions lead you. What answers arise? How are new questions stimulated? Where do you hit a dead end? Stay with this process for twenty minutes to half an hour.

Then look at your list of questions and examine them in terms of the four factors described above: dynamic openness, intelligence, ordinary knowledge, and direct observation. How did these factors come into play in your immediate investigation? As you consider these different factors, did you notice any feelings or beliefs that restrict your ability to deeply inquire into your experience?

Questions and Answers

STUDENT: I was struck by my experience that when all four of these elements are present, it means the loss of identity, of the sense of who I am.

ALMAAS: It's good that you brought that out, because this has been happening since yesterday. People's identities are screaming. The not-knowing challenges the identity because the most important thing for everybody to know is who they are. If you don't know, you wonder, "What is happening to me?" That is definitely challenging.

STUDENT: There was a moment when the pain stopped and the painlessness was the loss of the identity, which actually felt like a loss of dynamism. It was as though the whole aliveness of me just dropped out.

ALMAAS: The ego identity is a fake dynamism; it is always running around, always burning rubber. In contrast to this agitation and busyness, the true dynamism of Being may initially feel quite subtle and undramatic.*

STUDENT: Isn't basic trust necessary to allow that unknowing and the loss of identity?

ALMAAS: By basic trust, you mean the experience of implicit faith in the optimizing force of the dynamism of Being—that if the unfoldment of experience is allowed, what happens will turn out for the best. This sense of trust is inherent in our natural connection to Being and the universe, but for most of us that connection is lost in childhood. And you are right that basic trust, and the sense of holding that comes with it, is fundamental, as well as other elements that we haven't discussed. All the aspects will ultimately be needed.

Basic trust is related to the holy ideas, which form the view of reality that underlies this method.† Thus the entire process of inquiry is supported by that view, and basic trust returns naturally as we come to know the holy ideas and understand the view of objective reality. This means, of course, that our inquiry will have limitations as we go on, because we have yet to recognize, know, and understand reality in this way. Thus most of us don't have complete basic trust.

STUDENT: So the more you develop basic trust, the more your inquiry develops.

---

*See *The Point of Existence* (Berkeley: Diamond Books, 1996; Boston: Shambhala Publications, 2000), chap. 8.
†See *Facets of Unity: The Enneagram of Holy Ideas* (Berkeley: Diamond Books, 1998; Boston: Shambhala Publications, 2000), chap. 4.

ALMAAS: Yes. In time, you develop basic trust and you learn to trust the dynamism of the inquiry. This will happen as a result of several things: First, clearly recognizing the optimizing force in the dynamism of your own unfolding; second, truly seeing that optimization is the nature of the dynamism; and third, having faith that the optimizing is occurring even when you can't feel it in the moment. Then you are trusting the guidance and the unfoldment. Basic trust—the knowing that you just need to relax and things will work out fine—is an automatic result of this developing knowledge of reality.

STUDENT: When you were talking about wonder, I realized that I feel the openness as a place where my mother can get in. So my inquiry is fueled by running around trying to stop up all the holes.

ALMAAS: So your motivation is fear; you are scared of your mother getting in. This is an example of what I was referring to as bias. This is a bias that can distort the inquiry. We have all kinds of biases. It's completely normal—each of us has millions of them. And you just recognized a big one of yours.

STUDENT: I got into an interesting place of feeling wronged and wanting to be held and feeling as if my mind were gone. And I realized I had lost complete touch with my body. When I was able to connect again with my body, it brought back continuity to the inquiry and also the feeling that I could nurture my own little self, be a holding presence for myself. Since then, I've realized that losing touch with the body means losing the whole field of inquiry.

ALMAAS: I have said that direct observation is the grounding for inquiry, what keeps it anchored here in the present, and that includes everything, especially your body. The more total the observation—the more it includes everything—the more your inquiry is effective.

STUDENT: I am trying to understand the particular way I experience the process happening in our inquiry in relation to asking questions. Sometimes there is a sense in my process that I can touch into the unfolding and then it moves by itself. When I can just be, when I feel open and allowing, things come up and the unfolding simply happens without questions. I am trying to understand whether there is an implicit questioning going on in this experience, or whether there is possibly something missing in just allowing it that way.

ALMAAS: Unfolding can happen without questioning, for unfolding is more fundamental than questioning. The questioning is to energize the unfolding.

STUDENT: So when there is a particular stuckness or deadness that comes in, or some kind of resistance . . . ?

ALMAAS: Usually it comes because you're identified with a certain position, something you believe you know. That blocks the unfoldment, and by questioning it you remove the barrier.

STUDENT: Does this mean that questioning sometimes isn't needed or appropriate?

ALMAAS: I am not implying that we should be engaged in inquiry all the time. There are other things to do while living. Inquiry is only one important thing.

STUDENT: So are you saying that we need to inquire only when the unfoldment gets stuck?

ALMAAS: Not necessarily. Inquiry is motivated by not-knowing. Sometimes the unfoldment gets stuck, and you know there is something you don't know, so you inquire. Sometimes the unfoldment is moving right along, but in a way you don't understand. Most of the time, people have experiences they don't understand. When inquiry occurs at such times, the unfoldment appears in a different way, with more insight and more understanding.

STUDENT: It almost seems that if the unfoldment contains all four elements you discussed, then it is fully happening and questioning is not needed.

ALMAAS: Right.

STUDENT: If one of the four elements is not there, then at some point inquiry becomes useful because the unfoldment is missing something.

ALMAAS: Inquiry is a practice. And like any other practice, it can take itself to silence, where there is unfoldment with understanding and insight, without a need for questioning, because the openness itself allows things to emerge. The dynamic openness functions then as the free unfoldment of our experience. Inquiry basically opens up experience to this unfoldment. When the dynamic openness is present in our experience, a question will arise when there is something we don't understand. It is a spontaneous movement—a flowering—within the open and flowing unfoldment.

As we have seen, inquiry uses many faculties, capacities, and skills. It uses mindfulness and concentration. It uses reasoning and intuition. It uses analysis and synthesis. It uses observation and knowledge. It uses energy and intelligence. All of these we will explore in more depth as we go along. But inquiry's central tool is a question. Here we have been exploring four factors in asking a question: first, the unknowingness, which expresses the dynamic openness; second, direct observation of our immediate experience; third, ordinary knowledge bringing relevant information from the past; and fourth, the organic, self-responsive intelligence.

We can say that inquiry is mindfulness with a dynamism that is open to seeing what it does not know, plus concentration with an energy that loves to find out the truth that it does not know. Concentration is necessary for staying on track and not getting distracted by stimuli that aren't relevant to the particular inquiry. Mindfulness provides the capacity to be aware of anything that emerges in experience, regardless of how minute or subtle. The global awareness of mindfulness reveals the patterns of unknowing in experience. And questioning directs consciousness to investigate the not-knowing.

Inquiry, based on love and dynamic openness, is a journey of wonderment whose center is a question that embodies knowing and unknowing. That dynamic openness makes all our questions penetrating and encompassing, which activates the optimizing force of Being—in the form of the Diamond Guidance—so that it may reveal the hidden truth, the truth beyond the known. What is needed now is love of the truth for its own sake to give that questioning power and urgency, enough to carry our spacecruiser out of our earthbound orbit and into the depths of the mystery.

CHAPTER 9

Loving the Truth

THE DEVOTIONAL ATTITUDE

Our inner guidance will naturally begin to function when we learn the precise attitude needed for discovering the truth. This is the most important part of the teaching on how to open oneself up to the optimizing force of Being. Because without the correct motivation, inquiry just won't work. Even if you become relaxed about not-knowing and are willing to ask questions, this in itself is not sufficient to open up your inquiry.

The motivation we need is the sincerity of wanting the truth for its own sake, loving the truth for its own sake. This happens when truth becomes what we want, what we value, what we appreciate, what makes our heart happy. This is not a matter of ethical sincerity—of telling the truth—which is how sincerity is usually understood. The attitude here is more of a state of the heart, a devotional attitude.

We want something for its own sake when we truly love it. There's no other way to want something for its own sake. Conversely, when we appreciate something for its own sake, we call that love. So loving truth for its own sake brings the heart to a devotional attitude, an attitude of selfless affection and dedication. It is the heart's openness, the heartfelt appreciation and longing, the gravitational pull that makes us want to see the truth, to be closer to the truth, to be intimate with it.

The heart's love of the truth is not a thought or an idea. It is not a matter of trying to live according to an ideal. It's not a motive that comes from the mind. It is an impulse from the depth of the soul, a deeply felt motive from the heart. It is not that we think and deliberate and decide that truth is good for us, so we end up wanting it. Love of the truth is not utilitarian. The truth often ends up being utilitarian, but that is not what inspires the right attitude for the journey. The correct attitude is that of a lover who wants to be close to the beloved.

When utilitarian considerations predominate in a love relationship, we will experience many difficulties. For example, one may begin wanting to live with one's lover because it will reduce one's expenses. Looking at your intimate relationship from this point of view will usually affect the love itself. But when there is real love, you can't help feeling happy in your beloved's presence. You can't help but feel, "I want to be there, regardless of whether I save money or not."

So we see that we can't approach the work on ourselves—the work of going toward truth—from a mental perspective. We can't approach it from a strictly practical perspective. We can't approach it from a needy perspective. It will have to come from an appreciative place, from a giving place, from a selfless place.

When we inquire and explore from that place, we act from one central motive. It is difficult to even call it a motive, because we usually think of motives as being oriented toward particular ends. The motive of loving truth for its own sake doesn't have an end in mind. The point is just to know the truth, whatever it is. What will result from that is not a concern.

This orientation toward truth is different from how our society appreciates truth as a virtue. It is generally agreed that it is a good thing to be truthful, to acknowledge the truth, to confront the truth, and so on. However, we usually tend not to focus on the truth until things get tough. When things are going fine in your life, people don't tell you, "Well, you'd better see the truth about your situation." They tend to believe that the truth is needed just to help resolve problems or when things aren't going well. So the general cultural or societal attitude about appreciating the truth is not the attitude we're looking for.

When you inquire and are exploring your experience, you need to be inspired by a sincere interest in finding the truth. You're seeking the truth not because an experience is difficult or painful, but because there is something in the experience you don't get, something you don't understand. It's not that you have a problem and you want to solve it. It's not because you're confused and you don't like feeling confused. It's not that you're trying to get to a certain state of clarity. It's more like you really want to recognize what's going on.

Of course, most of us have myriad motivations most of the time. This is normal when we're not mature enough for our heart to be integrated. Having many motivations means our heart is divided. It loves many things. Yet if love of the truth for its own sake is not present, Diamond Guidance simply won't show up. However, if you really love the truth for its own sake—even if you want to know it for only an instant—Guidance says, "I'll show up. You'll find me there at the launching pad."

Now, this can be a very tricky situation. You might say, "Oh, good! Tomorrow when I work on myself, I will want truth for its own sake." Well, what's motivating you when you're feeling that way? If what's motivating you is another goal—to use loving the truth as a new method for working on yourself—it won't work; you won't get the truth. The heart itself has to quicken. You have to feel that inner desire for the truth itself. When that almost magical turn in the heart occurs—when for an instant you forget all your concerns in the world and want to know the truth only out of love—the Guidance reveals itself and guides you to the truth.

Love of the truth for its own sake differentiates our work—traveling on the Spacecruiser *Inquiry*—from many other kinds of things we do in our lives. Inquiry in the Diamond Approach is a concern of the heart, a particular orientation that goes counter to how we generally think and feel and organize our life. Our heart needs to be involved in a pure, selfless way. Selfless means that we don't want anything for ourselves. We investigate because we are turned on to the truth. We inquire because we can't help it, because we can't help liking the truth. We inquire because we really want to find out. What we find out might be wonderful or beautiful, and it might be painful, scary, or difficult. We might even get burned in the process. But none of that matters to the lover.

To desire truth for its own sake means that the inquiry is not for your benefit, it's for the sake of the truth. Yet this is the way that your heart can find its most complete contentment. This is paradoxical because if you are really dedicated to the truth for its own sake without thinking of yourself, if you give yourself over to it, in time the truth will give you back a lot more than you give.

The truth is not merely a matter of not lying; it is seeing what the truth is—the essential truth, the absolute truth, which finally reveals the real world. This has been called the Kingdom of Heaven. However, you cannot take the perspective of trying to get to the Kingdom of Heaven. You can't say, "Well, I'm going to love truth because I know if I get to the truth, then I will feel wonderful."

Practice Session: Your Motive for Self-Exploration

You might at this point want to explore your motives for doing inner work. To do this, you need to have some sincere desire to discover the truth. Take some time to sit and explore the following questions: Why do you work on yourself? You have all kinds of motives. What are you hoping to achieve in the process? How much are you motivated by love—for yourself, the process, the insights? What are your other motives? Which motive tends to predominate? Have you experienced the selfless motive of loving truth for its own sake? If so, how does its presence affect your inner work? You may find it useful to write down what you discover as you inquire.

GIVING UP THE SELF

As I've said, it is a law of Being that its Guidance manifests when we want to know the truth. This is not a moral injunction. It's not ethics. It's about how reality works. It means that ultimately truth is the nature of Being. So Being says, "I'll open myself to you only if you're interested in me. But if you want something else, that's what you'll get—you're not going to get the truth."

In other words, the revelation of the Kingdom of Heaven is the action of the optimizing force of Being, and only the love of truth can invite and activate that force. The optimizing force guides experience toward greater optimization, which means contact with deeper levels of truth. So loving truth for its own sake unites the heart of the soul with Being's love of revealing its own riches.

This revelation is not an intellectual exercise. You can't do it through a reasoning process. You can't do it through logical deduction. The mind at some point is incapable of telling you what is needed to reveal the truth. It is the heart that knows, because the heart loves the truth.

To love truth for its own sake means that at some point you give yourself over to the truth. This, however, is not a consequence, not a matter of cause and effect. It's not that you give yourself over to the truth and then the truth reveals itself. It's not even that you give yourself up to the truth *because* you love the truth. Loving the truth *is* giving oneself up to the truth. To love the truth for its own sake means that in the very instant of loving the truth, your self-centeredness has vanished. This is very profound, yet it can be very, very subtle.

It means that in the moment I'm exploring, in the moment I'm investigating, I am in an attitude of giving. I am in a non-self-centered attitude. All of my consciousness, all of my attention, is sacrificed for the truth. Even "sacrificed" isn't correct—it's more like, "Whatever needs to happen, I am willing to do it." Frequently, that doesn't mean sacrificing anything. It's more that loving the truth for its own sake means an implicit readiness to let go, to give up the self.

To give up the self means, "I am willing to not protect myself against the truth. I am willing to not defend or resist." Most of the time, giving ourselves up to the truth means giving up our defenses, manipulations, positions, and strategies—all the things we use to shore ourselves up or to continue to preserve ourselves. And because loving the truth arises from a place where we are willing to be selfless, we cannot try to figure out how to be selfless. The self cannot figure out how to give itself up, because in the very act of thinking, the self keeps on preserving itself.

FOOD FOR THE SOUL

Initially the truth might be a specific insight, some connection we make between various elements in our experience. But as the soul gives herself more to the truth, the truth becomes essential truth, and ultimately the absolute truth—the ultimate nature of everything in all its beauty, magnificence, and splendor. When we finally behold the absolute truth and see its beauty and magnificence, we understand. We recognize it as the source of love. We love it because it's lovable. We love it because we are loving our true self. We love it because it's natural to love the truth. Not because it's correct, ethical conduct, but because in some very deep place in us, the truth is the Beloved.

But even in this place, the question of loving the truth for its own sake can get subtle and problematic. When we see the beauty and magnificence of our own Being, we love it—but how do we love it? When you truly love somebody, you want to do things for them. You're willing to go through discomfort in your life, you're willing to give your time, your attention, your energy, but not because you're going to get something from it. You want to give because the heart is overflowing out of love. That's what love means.

It is the same thing with loving the truth. Loving truth for its own sake means that you want the truth to be as deep as possible, as complete as possible. That's implicit in loving truth. If you love truth for its own sake and you start seeing the truth, and that truth is not complete—there's still more that you don't see—the love you have will impel you to go further, to see deeper, to experience more fully. So you're not oriented toward an end result. You're oriented to the truth itself. That by itself will guide you toward deeper truth, bigger truth, fuller and more complete truth.

Recognizing our love for the truth is a very joyous feeling. The heart now has found itself. It knows what it feels. It knows why it feels it. It knows what it truly wants. There's a melting excitement, and a wonderfulness.

It has been said that people can't live by bread alone. True. Bread is important, but the food for the soul is truth. The body needs food, security, and safety; we're not saying these things aren't important. But at some point, we need to attend to the nourishment of the soul. We need to go to the next stage of evolution, we must travel to another star system. And it's the heart that leads the way.

No matter how you feel about it, at some point you must face the fact that the process of inquiry, of investigation, of understanding your experience, is a heart involvement. It is an affair of the heart that represents the spiritual dimension of your life. It is the lifeline of the soul. This means that regardless of what is happening in your life, there can be a thread of luminosity, sweetness, and intimacy running through it. You can love what is true and life can be a love affair that goes on regardless of what is happening.

THE DIVIDED HEART

Truth is such that when you love it, it will tend to own your love. In other words, when you love truth for its own sake and allow that love to deepen and develop, you begin to see that loving anything else takes away from love for the truth. When you love something else besides the truth, there will come a time in the journey of inquiry when you are going to be faced with a choice. More precisely, the more you experience the love for truth, the more you will recognize that this love must become the dominant and overwhelming love in your life. It can't be just one of the loves.

If you love truth but you also love comfort, loving comfort may at some point become a barrier to recognizing the truth. For example, you might want to lie to yourself so that you can have the comfort you love. The only way you can continue to see the truth about comfort is by loving the truth more than you love comfort. Comfort is one example, but it could be pleasure, riches, fame, love, recognition, creativity, company, and so on.

We recognize at some point that our love for truth is natural; it is inherent in our heart. The heart loves what is true. We also recognize that loving truth is the intelligent thing to do because the truth is ultimately what will free us. It is of ultimate value, and it is the source of all value. Life is incomplete—it lacks depth and genuineness—when there is no truth. But even though we might recognize all of that at some point, we still experience the conflict with other things we love.

Most spiritual literature takes the position that there is a conflict between loving the truth and loving the world in the form of possessions, pleasure, comfort, fame, and so on. This is an important truth, but in fact, there is no inherent conflict between loving truth and loving other things. The literature refers to the fact that most spiritual aspirants experience a big struggle when they recognize that not only do they live in the world and interact with the various things within it, but they also love all these things of the world.

At some point, that love of worldly things can become a barrier to loving the truth. This happens when you want to preserve your possession of or connection to the things of the world at the expense of recognizing the truth. That's when you experience the truth and the objects of the world as competing for your love. You don't have to go very far to see this conflict. When you're a parent, for example, it is very difficult to see the truth about your relationship with your children because you are afraid the truth is going to disrupt that relationship. You're afraid of losing what you have.

So to love truth requires that you recognize that truth is your primary love—Love #1. In fact, the situation can go as far as truth becoming your *only* love. This is when love is most effective, most powerful for the journey. This is when the heart is fully cognizant of its Beloved. But that's not easy, for the heart is normally divided. The heart has many love objects, many beloveds.

It might be easy to see that some loves are not good for us, such as cigarettes, too much sugar, or violence. But we love many things that seem to be good for us, and this brings the subtlety of the situation to the foreground. The love for these things can become a barrier, for it will compete for your heart, and your heart will not be completely united in its love for the truth. Part of it loves the truth, but another part loves this person, and some part loves that other person, and another part loves tennis. One part loves food, and another part loves to watch TV, and yet another part wants to spend hours and hours conversing with friends, and so on.

As I said, there isn't an inherent contradiction between these things and the truth. However, the experience of most people is that this situation does become problematic. It is the natural tendency that when you love something, you don't want to lose it. You want to have it. You want to be close to it. You want to protect it. And quite frequently, this means protecting it from what the truth might reveal.

Furthermore, loving other things in such a way that they become a competition for your love of the truth indicates that your love is not completely selfless. It is still self-centered love. You still want something from whatever it is you love in the world—the object, the person, or the situation. You don't love food selflessly, do you? No one loves food selflessly. When you love food, you want to have it, fill your stomach with it.

It is especially difficult to love other people selflessly. Even if you have some degree of selfless love for another person, ordinarily a large part of your love will be selfish. In fact, nowadays people think that selfish love is fine, that it is the right thing. The whole growth movement seems sometimes to be about that: "Don't love somebody else selflessly. You have to be selfish, you have to take care of yourself. You have to assert yourself, claim your rights. If this person isn't giving you this or that, you should ask for it, even demand it." This indicates that our culture is becoming disoriented because we are forgetting what selfless love is.

Most people think that selfless love means that you have to be self-sacrificing in a masochistic way, that you allow other people to walk all over you. But selfless love can be pure giving without a masochistic kind of sacrifice. Of course, this subtle point gets missed. It is missed because it is not easy to get to that place. It is very difficult to really love somebody or something selflessly. Most of the time, loving somebody or something becomes competition for our love of the truth.

So we often end up in situations where our hearts are divided. And when the heart is divided, the process of inquiry is less effective. However, the more the heart is one in loving the truth, the more our unfoldment will be optimized. The understanding that we need to love the truth and make it our dominant love—even our only love—lies behind the need for discipline, behind the view of renunciation, behind the view of detachment. When it is said, "Renounce the world, leave the world," what does that mean? The idea is not that the world is bad. The point is that if you love it to the extent that you don't want to see the truth, then the world becomes a barrier to the truth. You feel that the truth will threaten that love for the world, so some of the time you will choose the things of the world over the truth.

Most of the time, choosing the truth over everything else does not mean that you have to renounce the world. It only means that the world is your second choice. But this is very difficult because of our divided heart. The heart is not powerful enough, courageous enough, strong enough to go charging after the truth regardless of what happens. You feel that you're going to be rejecting and ruthless if you do that. You're always concerned about this, about that, about what's going to happen tomorrow. What is this person going to think of me? What is going to happen to my mother? What is going to happen to my child, my wife, my husband? You continue in the condition of having a divided heart.

As I said, though it is difficult, it is possible to arrive at a place where you love only the truth. This is not, however, required to activate the Guidance or to allow the unfoldment to happen. What is needed is only the pure, selfless love of the truth even if you have competing loves. But the Guidance can work most effectively when the love of truth outweighs our love for everything else.

When does our love for the truth become the only love? When we recognize that there is nothing else but the truth. When our perception has opened up to the extent that we see an expression of the truth wherever we look, then we love only the truth. Then truth is not at all in contradiction to the other loves. We love everything. This is a beautiful condition to get to. We arrive there, however, only through first preferring the truth over everything else. Unless we truly perceive that everything *is* the truth, we cannot say, "Well, since everything is the truth, let me love it as much as the truth." That won't work.

For us to say that everything is the truth, we must be actually perceiving for ourselves that this is the case. Before that, everything is not the truth, at least not as far as we are concerned. To say, "I love that," about someone or something in your life without loving the truth in that moment indicates that what you are seeing is not true. You're actually looking at falseness and that's what you're loving. In reality, there is no such thing as a person separate from the truth. So, if you love your husband, for instance, yet you are not loving him as a reflection of the truth, then what are you loving? Either your husband reflects the truth or you're loving something that is false—some idea in your mind that is bound to take you away from the truth and be in competition with it.

So loving the truth for its own sake confronts us at some point with a choice between truth and our other loves. There is no way around the step of preferring the truth over other things. If our heart is going to move toward what it really loves—the truth for its own sake—the heart will need to see that all these other loves are not as important as the truth. That has to happen if the truth is going to continue emerging.

Of course, you can't force yourself. You can't punish yourself for loving the movies better than the truth. If you see that this is the case, you need to acknowledge it, for that's the truth of your situation. You can't say, "No, that shouldn't be true. Let me change it." That again is fighting the truth. We need to look at the truth and understand it. Your understanding might reveal to you what your preference is really about. That will orient your heart in the right direction. It's a process through which love of the truth will eventually reveal itself as the first priority.

LOVE AND THE ANIMAL SOUL

The next issue we're going to deal with is how objects of desire compete with the truth for our heart's love. The objects we crave compete for our attention, our interest, our time, and our commitment. This is because of what we call the libidinal soul, the primitive and animal level of our soul, the part that is run by instinctual drives. At some point, we recognize the libidinal soul as one of the main barriers to the love of truth.

Love of truth is a subtle thing; it is the illumination, the radiance, and the melting sweetness of the heart. The animal soul, however, doesn't love the truth. Not only that, it doesn't even recognize love. This soul is dominated by cravings, by animal desires: "I want it because I gotta have it. What has love got to do with it?" This is just like when an animal feels, "I gotta have this meat." It's not out of appreciation or love. It's more like, "If I don't have it, I'm going to die."

This level of need and desire becomes the main barrier—and the most difficult one—to deal with when it comes to recognizing our love for the truth. This is the level of animal instincts, where motivation comes from instinctual needs for survival, pleasure, and social connections. These are very powerful drives that live at the bottom of the unconscious. More than any other influence, they make us forget about or ignore the truth. You may see the truth, but when an instinctual need comes up, you not only stop seeing the truth, you actually feel,

"Who cares about the truth? If following my instinct means that I'll survive, and I don't know if I'll survive if I follow the truth, then the choice is obvious." Survival is what you go for. You forget truth because it feels like a luxury.

In fact, the animal soul doesn't just forget truth; its attitude is, "What's that? What's truth? You can either eat it or you can't. If I can't put truth in my mouth, what good is it? If I can't play with it, what is it for? If it's not fun, if it's not filling, if it doesn't make me feel safe and secure, I'm not interested." The animal soul manifests as many kinds of desires, cravings, and needs. Pleasure is paramount. Even when truth comes, it's good only if it is pleasurable. If it feels sweet, nice, yummy, that's good. If it's bland or bitter, it's not the truth that's wanted.

This level of soul exists in us all. At this level, it is not a question of having difficulty with the truth due to a divided heart. The animal soul does not have a heart yet! It's operating on the lower chakras; only the stomach and pelvis matter here.

What's important to see is that ultimately, all animal instincts amount to the basic drive for physical survival. And all our powerful needs and instinctual drives can become a force that completely eclipses the love of truth. This is true whether the survival instinct manifests as the need for security, support, safety, affection, social contact, comfort, or money. In reality, all social and sexual instincts are linked to survival. For example, you may just want somebody around or someone to talk to on the phone, and it doesn't matter whether truth is involved. Just talking is what's needed. What's really happening is that you can't be alone; you are operating unconsciously from the assumption that social contact is a survival need, and that takes precedence over the love of the truth.

We need to deal with this level of our soul if we are to liberate our heart, for our heart can truly love only when it is free. The heart exists at the level of the human soul rather than at the level of the animal soul. And unless the instinctual drives in the animal soul are confronted, they will confine—and ultimately control—the human soul and heart.

One way that the instincts manifest themselves is in aggression. When getting what we want is blocked or frustrated, we often feel anger, hatred, and revenge. These feelings and our desire to express them can become powerful forces against our love of truth. We're more interested in getting angry than in recognizing the truth, more interested in making somebody suffer than in inquiring into what's going on. These tendencies are driven by an instinctual force. Of course, fears are also involved because we are anxious about survival and anticipated losses.

So the level of the instincts, the animal level, looks at the world in terms of objects of gratification—going after things that will make us feel good, gratify us, and help us survive. These are real needs for human beings; they are not made up. We need food to survive. We need some kind of security. We need to have some pleasure; human beings can't survive if all they are experiencing is pain and suffering. We need some kind of company, some kind of social contact, some kind of family. The question is not whether these things are needed, but whether the expression of these needs is more powerful than the love for the truth. When it is, we stay on the animal level. This doesn't mean that anything bad is going to happen. It just means that we're going to continue living as animal souls; we won't take the next evolutionary step toward becoming truly human souls.

Many people go into spiritual practice without dealing with their animal soul, without recognizing that there is such a thing. Some even become enlightened but never find out that they still have an animal soul. This means that the animal soul is living in the dungeon, waiting for a chance to come out. The moment the observer inside relaxes and a wonderful object of gratification appears on the horizon—perhaps an object more wonderful and available than ever before—that's when the animal soul will come out.

The love of the truth is in some sense our beacon, our way to become more human, more developed, more refined. And this does not happen by abandoning our animal needs—you can't abandon these needs—it happens by not putting them ahead of the truth.

Practice Session: Your Instinctual Needs and Your Love of the Truth

You might want to explore in yourself the relationship between your heart's love for the truth and your animal instincts and needs, your libidinal soul. Make your inquiry specific: You want to see what your situation is right now. You want to arrive at the objective recognition of how much your love for the truth has developed in relation to the power of your instinctual needs.

Bring to mind an issue that has pitted your love of truth against your instinctual needs. The areas of sexuality and power are usually fertile ground for this kind of exploration. As you inquire into this situation, notice what happens. Are you loving the truth for its own sake? What power do your instinctual needs have over you? You want to see where that dance happens, where the conflicts occur in this particular instance.

Then you can return to a consideration of these conflicts in a more general context. Be willing to see the details and recognize which one wins most of the time. In what situations does the love of truth win out over your instinctual needs? When does the reverse happen?

Inquiring into and understanding the animal soul is a more effective way to work with our instincts than attempting to control them through renunciation. If you just renounce your cravings, your desires, your passions, then you're not dealing with the animal soul. When you say, "I don't want to engage with the animal soul. I'm not going to do anything to it, and I won't allow it to do anything to me," that pushes it to the side, and its tendencies are suppressed. But just as renunciation will not bring us to the place where our love of the truth is primary, neither will acceptance. Even after you recognize the unsatisfied needs and wants of the animal soul and how they were rejected—and then work with them and accept them—that does not necessarily translate into allowing the love of truth to dominate.

The animal soul has its own fixations and objects of satisfaction. We definitely need to allow the animal soul to feel all its wants and desires and we need to accept them. However, that is not enough for the animal soul to be able to let go of them. It can still be dominated by them even after accepting them. There are people whose animal needs have not been rejected. This does not mean that these people are not dominated by the animal soul. In fact, their needs might have been overgratified, which is just as difficult a problem. It's easy to get stuck in that. These individuals are used to being gratified and they feel that's their right. Because they're used to getting what they want, it's very difficult for them to let go of the focus on gratification and love the truth. So both the rejection of and catering to animal desires are barriers to the love of truth.

In reality, the animal soul is the primary barrier to spiritual development. It's difficult for us to see this because we're usually not dealing with a healthy animal soul; we're dealing with a damaged, distorted, or arrested one. So we're always dealing with the distortions. We don't know how big a barrier the animal soul itself is because we're busy trying to turn it into a more "normal" animal soul by freeing the instincts that were repressed in childhood. That in itself is not easy. But even if you can accomplish that, you recognize, "Oh, what did I do? I thought this animal was going to turn out nice and cute." You didn't know it was going to become a huge hungry monster that declares: "Good! Now I am strong, I have my energy. Now I can get what I want!"

It's not as if the animal soul never feels peace and happiness. It does—when it has gotten what it wants. The animal soul becomes beautiful and graceful—but only after gratification of its desires. There's no freedom in this. You're at the whim of your desires. In this way, the animal soul is like a small child. When things are going fine, the child is happy. He is an angel. When something goes wrong and he is not getting what he wants, or you want him to do something he doesn't want to do, the child can become angry and even vicious. Give the animal soul what it wants and it becomes relaxed, happy, and generous. But the next day, when it is hungry again or somebody crosses its path, it behaves very differently.

So there are two stages of working on the animal soul. First, allowing it, accepting it, and letting it be there—recognizing that there is such a thing and that it's normal and human to have all these desires. The next stage is its transformation. The transformation of the animal soul happens as you live your life according to the truth that you have discovered. If you don't live your life according to the truth that you know, then you continue being an animal soul that has spiritual experiences once in a while.

THE HEART AND THE HIGHER INTELLECT

There is a specific reason why loving the truth for its own sake is important for the revelation of truth. This has to do with the relationship of love to the optimizing force of our Being, and the relationship of the latter to the Diamond Guidance. Being is alive, dynamic, and creative. The creativity of our Being is what we experience as revelation in our journey of inquiry and understanding.

The dynamism of Being can move in an optimizing way or can just be repetitive, depending upon whether we are open or closed to the dynamism. If we're closed—meaning that we are clinging to our positions, identifications, and structures—that situation will trap the energy of the dynamism, which will then move in circles. That is what happens in the experience of ego. We have fixed, rigid structures, and they need the dynamism in order to keep re-creating themselves.

However, when we are open to the creativity of Being, the dynamism engages its optimizing, enhancing, evolutionary force. Then there is not just a movement that is dynamic, but the dynamism moves in an evolutionary, expanding, deepening, life-enhancing, optimizing way. It's a movement from the inside out.

If we inquire into the energy of the optimizing force, we find that it is love. Love is the creative energy that disposes the dynamism to move in an optimizing way. This makes love the fuel of inquiry—and points to a very clear relationship between love and the revelation of truth: When we love truth for its own sake, we truly love. When our love is selfless and genuine, it is the love of what is real. This shows more specifically why it is the energy for the optimizing, energizing, evolutionary force. Love, by its very nature, is a matter of revelation, of unfoldment. It is a manifestation of Being whose very nature is a matter of opening up and unfolding, like the unfolding of a rose.

Rumi once said in a poem, "This is love: to fly heavenward. To rend, every instant, a hundred veils." To love is to rend the veils. What does it mean to rend the veils? To reveal. So love is Being in the process of revealing its truth. It is the dynamic, revealing energy of Being.

This unveils two things about the engagement with the Diamond Guidance. First of all, the Diamond Guidance is the discriminating intelligence of the optimizing thrust, the guiding intelligence that specifically reveals through the recognition of what is being revealed. There is a dynamic interaction between this Guidance and love, an interaction related to the optimizing force of Being. Love is the energy of the dynamism that displays the truth, while Guidance is the magnifying lens of Being that helps us recognize what is being displayed. Furthermore, the Guidance is the discriminating intelligence that opens the way for love to display the truth. The two things need to happen together for there to be a revelation: Our spacecruiser needs a navigational system with its sensor array, and it also needs an energy source powerful enough to take us beyond the gravitational pull of our conventional experience.

So the love and the operation of the Diamond Guidance work in consort, reflecting the heart and the higher intellect. That's why it is not enough to have a good teacher. There also has to be a good student for the learning to happen. Some students say, "I want to work with the most enlightened teacher." But the most enlightened teacher is not necessarily going to be able to do anything for someone who is not a good student. You need both: the active force—the love itself—and the Guidance. The two working together is the alchemical combustion, the revelation.

THE QUICKENING OF THE SOUL

Diamond Guidance always reveals something new. It discriminates the creative display of Being. That is why it is the nous, the higher intellect. The lower intellect is our usual discerning capacity, similar to that of a computer. It merely discriminates a different form of what it already knows. This activity is the repetition of the knowledge of the past, or of different combinations of things we've known from the past. It puts one thing and another thing together and, using reason, it comes up with an idea. But that idea can never be original.

We have seen that love of the truth for its own sake is an invitation to the Diamond Guidance, and engaging the Diamond Guidance manifests the discriminating intelligence of the optimizing force. At the same time, when we love truth for its own sake, we engage the very energy of optimization, the very energy of the evolution of the soul. We are fueling the unfoldment. We are powering our spacecruiser's drive. When we have only an intellectual curiosity that comes from an ego position, experience will not unfold, because the unfoldment needs its own particular energy, which is the love of truth. So loving truth for its own sake activates the unfoldment itself, the journey; it engages the drive and steers the spacecruiser.

We can also say that loving truth for its own sake in the process of inquiry and understanding is the way that the heart and mind are united, becoming one—which *is* the revelation. This is the way to quicken the soul. In inquiry there is interest, excitement, and initiative. It's as though a light in the heart had been turned on. Thus, the opening of the heart has to do with the quickening of the soul.

So it is important to see that loving the truth for its own sake is not just an invitation to the Guidance, it is also the quickening of the unfoldment itself. We're not usually in touch with our heart in this way, but the heart is the source of the energy of unfoldment. Even if we have a great capacity for clarity and discernment, it may be that nothing new will arise. Many people are very good at logical analysis and discernment, but they don't know anything important about reality. Their experience is limited because the heart is not open. The love of the truth is not active.

This also teaches us that techniques and practices on their own are not that effective. Merely having a method or technique for accessing Being is not going to be very effective because the unfoldment has to do with love. At some point, which practice we use is not that important if we don't have the devotional energy. Some practices might help open the heart and put us more in touch with that love of truth, such as prayers and invocations. But whatever practices we do, what's needed is to develop our love for the truth. This is something innate, inherent in us, not something we impose on ourselves. It is something we discover, nurture, and allow to grow. The heart is love, and love means appreciating what is real.

When I say that techniques or practices are not effective on their own to activate the unfolding, this applies equally to inquiry. Inquiry will not work if we don't love the truth for its own sake. It just becomes an intellectual exercise. If we are disengaged from our heart, we might understand something but it won't bring about the revelation or unfolding. Our experience won't evolve.

Of course, other attitudes are useful as fuel for doing the work. Some of them are effective to some extent—for instance, the attitude of helpfulness. Some people do the work because they want to serve and liberate other people. This is a kind of devotion that is based primarily on compassion. However, even here, if this compassion is not based on love, it is not going to be very effective. Why do we want to help other people? The attitude that will make us more effective in helping others is the understanding that helping other people means that we want to help them see the truth. If we really want to help the other person recognize the truth, live the truth, appreciate the truth, then we already have the loving attitude. But if we just want to help them so that they don't feel bad, so that they don't suffer, that is not yet spiritual work. It is something else. A spiritual attitude is not an attitude that is just focused on eliminating suffering. It's true that it has to do with eliminating suffering, but a spiritual attitude understands that suffering is only a side effect of not realizing our Being.

There is another reason why we need the heart for the process of inquiry, a reason we do not appreciate until we go very far in our journey. The heart is the specific abode of the truth. It is the particular place where the absolute truth will emerge and declare, "This is my place. I made this heart my throne, for me to dwell in." This can happen when we recognize that the Absolute is one hundred percent what the heart wants. The heart recognizes its ultimate function as the place, the particular abode, where the truth resides. It has been said that to look for the Absolute, you cannot look in any temple or place, but must look for it in your own heart.

There is an inherent reason why the heart loves the truth. More than any other expression or manifestation of the truth, the heart is designed so the truth can reveal itself there most fully. It's just like when we make a ring for a particular stone. The ring is made for that stone to fit perfectly. That's what the heart is—a particular setting for the precious stone that is the truth. This is a very subtle, deep perception that we can recognize at some point. We see its reflection when we feel that we love and want the truth.

The heart loves to have its master present, longs for its true occupant to dwell within. Before that, the heart is occupied by many kinds of things that are mistaken images of what the truth is. All these things that we love and want do not fit the heart exactly. As a result, the heart is constantly discontented, for its setting is designed for one thing in particular. Only that one thing will fit one hundred percent perfectly. The heart will know when the truth appears. It will then be fulfilled. And the Diamond Guidance is the specific guidance that leads the heart to fulfill its purpose.

HISTORICAL BARRIERS TO LOVING THE TRUTH

The heart is the feeling capacity of the soul, the soul's capacity to know intimately. In the process of developing love of truth for its own sake, we encounter various kinds of difficulties besides the ones we have discussed. Things happen in the heart that tend to close it down, things that make it difficult to open up to the truth, to feel the desire to see the truth. Because of our experiences in the past, we may have developed fear of the truth itself. For various reasons, we might become afraid of recognizing the truth. For instance, as the heart begins to love the truth, and the soul reveals its truth, the soul will naturally reveal whatever places in it have been closed down or stuck. These have to open up for the deeper truth to come out.

These are places that were shut down, isolated, or suppressed at times when the truth was painful or difficult. There were times when we felt rejected as little kids, or not loved, or punished, or abused. That was part of the truth of the situation. At those times, it was too much for the young soul to take, so the heart closed down in order not to feel the pain, the hurt, and the fear. This will manifest at some point as a limitation in our love for the truth. So we don't want our love for the truth to open fully because it will reveal the particular truth that we know unconsciously we're unprepared for or are afraid of experiencing. That's why the process of opening to truth is challenging—because it requires us to feel our various resistances.

It is not only that we fear the truth due to pain and difficulties. Some of us might end up hating the truth. Because of the harm we have experienced—which we saw as the truth of the situation—we might feel, "What do you mean, love the truth? That painful family situation I grew up in was the truth, and look what it did to me! I hate the truth!"

Others might end up distrusting the truth. As children, we were innocent and frequently spoke the truth, yet sometimes we got punished for it. The result was that we felt we lost something important to us, such as our parents' love, so we don't trust the truth to support us.

Other early experiences may result in the belief that the truth is going to be our enemy. This might be true for children who tend to lie to get what they want or to get away with things. For them, the truth may feel like an entity they are at war with, like it is siding with their parents or with bad luck or deprivation. Sometimes they end up lying so much that they actually forget what the truth is.

Children are naturally truthful, vulnerable, and curious. So if they are exploited or misunderstood, disappointment in the truth can easily arise. Loving truth for its own sake is bound to not only confront this barrier of the painful truths of the past, but also confront us with the threatening truths of the present. We might not want to be aware of the truth in a certain situation. We may prefer to deny it.

The cause of this particular barrier is that we as children were unable to discern the whole truth of our situation. The feeling of being disappointed by the truth is not actually caused by an experience of the truth but comes from an experience of partial truth. When as a child you feel that you are being unfairly punished, you may feel that if the truth is supposed to be fair, then the truth has let you down. However, it is not that your parents know the truth and are ignoring or rejecting it, which is what you think they're doing. The real problem when your parents punish you, hurt you, or violate you is that they are ignorant.

If your parents had really seen the truth of the situation, they wouldn't have done what they did. But you as the child didn't know that. So you might have blamed the truth, or blamed reality, for causing you pain or not protecting you. This early belief will then remain attached to the experience of truth in painful situations, so that you are convinced that truth will only lead you to more pain.

If our entire environment in childhood tended to deny and not want to look at the truth, we might have identified with this attitude. To love truth in such an environment makes us feel isolated. So we may have pushed away and rejected the truth and our love of it because everybody else was busy living their life of lies. We ended up not feeling our love for the truth because we adopted the attitudes of the significant people around us. How many children have shut off the experience of grief after a death in the family because no one else would acknowledge it? Most of the time, it is an unbearable situation for a child to feel alone and isolated because it is in touch with some truth that everyone else denies.

This brings up a basic assumption in any spiritual work, investigation, or inquiry: the notion that confronting and accepting truth is helpful. We take that as implicit, but not everybody believes that. To accept, or even know, that knowing the truth is helpful, our heart must not have been so hurt or closed down that we lost all contact with our love. If we were hurt so badly that we can't open up, it might be difficult for us to feel that discovering the truth is a good thing. We might want to dissociate and not be aware of the truth.

The question of whether the truth is going to feel overwhelming to us is sometimes a realistic concern. For some people, recognizing certain truths might be too much due to their lack of inner strength and development. And left to itself, the soul tends not to open up to such an overwhelming truth. Usually the soul has built-in defenses to prevent what is overwhelming from arising, unless life presents it with a situation where it can't use these defenses. Sometimes the truth might arise as overwhelming, but that's not generally the natural process of the unfoldment.

Usually, if we are attuned to the truth in our own experience, our inquiry will tend to reveal things in a way that is exactly what we need and what we can handle in the moment. Guidance never reveals things to us that we don't need. The revelation of truth is what Being presents in our experience, and Being is intelligent, compassionate, and loving. It will present exactly what is needed in the moment. That is why inquiry is generally a much safer approach than many other methods we can use. It *follows* what arises, it does not push, because it is not trying to get somewhere or achieve some goal.

Practice Session: The History of Your Love of the Truth

Now is a good time to explore your love of the truth in terms of how it developed. You want to see specifically how your history affected your love of the truth. What kinds of experiences around truth did you have as a child? Did they open your heart to the love of the truth and allow that part of you to grow and develop? Or was your history such that you ended up distrusting the truth, being afraid of it, and resisting your love for it? Be specific. What happened that made you not want to love the truth for its own sake? What childhood experiences might have helped you in your development?

LOVE VERSUS INERTIA

As we have discussed, the love of truth is the energy, the fuel, of the optimizing evolutionary force of our Being. This means that loving truth for its own sake will naturally and automatically open us up to unfoldment, to the revelation of our own nature. We will be inviting the optimizing dynamism, which means undergoing continual change and transformation. We will experience ourselves in new ways, and experience and know things about ourselves and the world that are fresh and different.

So to love truth for its own sake also implies a transformation of our experience and perception. This fact will present us with a specific obstacle that we have not discussed so far. The barrier I am referring to is a particularly tough one: the fact that our sense of self in the ordinary world has a component or characteristic that resists such transformation.

Our sense of self is based on fixed structures. In fact, that sense of self is *itself* a fixed structure. So our feeling of identity is ordinarily unchanging. Our sense of who we are has a conditioned quality to it, which means that we have a habitual tendency to experience things in a certain way, to think of things a certain way, to know and do things in a certain way over and over again. And it is not only our perception that tends to be confined to a certain groove; even our experience of ourselves is limited and constricted within certain boundaries.

This rigidity of the ego-self, its inflexibility, can be experienced as inertia: the habit of going on and on in the same way, in the same direction, without change. Our perception, experience, and identity contain this inertia. Inertia can also be expressed as an automatic tendency to continue with and live out the status quo. The personality becomes part of the status quo; consequently, its way of perceiving, being, and operating can't help but perpetuate the way things have been.

This means staying at the same level of experience, the same level of discourse, having the same patterns and the same identity, and being the same kind of person year in and year out. This can manifest in specific and clear ways, such as the inflexible tendencies that are hard for us to break even when we want to. We might be always busy, always afraid, always angry. We might habitually watch TV. We might habitually spend time in social conversation or gossiping. Even though we want to change those behaviors, it might be difficult due to the inertia of the personality.

To love the truth for its own sake means that we're going to be happy to see something new in our experience. Our inertia, our inflexibility, on the other hand, operates in just the opposite way. It resists change and thus becomes a limitation on our love for the truth. It is obvious how this works, but we need to see it in our personal everyday experience. We need to recognize how our inertia—our habits, our lazy comfort in the status quo—inhibits, limits, and even blocks our love for the truth. The truth, in contrast, is a quickening, a movement, a change.

One specific form that inertia takes is identification. The more we are identified with a particular position, the more unwilling we are to move from it. If I am angry, that's it—I want to be angry. I am identified with that emotion and feel justified in it. This means that I am not interested in finding out about the anger and its underlying dynamics. Another example is being identified with a certain self-image. If I am a certain way and I am identified with it, I believe it is me and I am not open to exploring it. So the identification blocks the heart movement, the love of the truth that would allow me to find out what is really there.

One particular identification is especially challenged by the love of the truth: our identification with being small, deficient, inadequate, incapable, and not up to the task. This belief in our deficiency can prevent us from opening to the love of truth because this love will expand us in a way that we're afraid we won't know how to handle. It seems much easier to stay with the status quo and its cozy familiarity.

If we allow the love of truth to become powerful, we will be confronted with this identification with inadequacy.

There are offshoots of all these obstacles, but it is enough to mention these as beginning points for your own continuing inquiry. The more you work on these obstacles, the more the space opens up and allows the love of the truth to manifest or to expand and deepen.

The love of the truth is a subtle and refined quality in our consciousness. It tends to be hidden behind many veils of emotion, instinct, and identification. It may not be easy for you to contact this deep movement of the heart. Yet without the experience of loving truth for its own sake, regardless of the consequences—without the willingness to completely open your heart to the fullness of your own truth—you will not have the energy or the motivation to go beyond your familiar reality. Spacecruiser *Inquiry* will not be able to engage the hyperdrive to enter the depths of the mystery of Being.

CHAPTER 10

The Personal Thread

A T THIS POINT HAVING activated our questioning engine and engaged our love of truth fuel on board Spacecruiser *Inquiry*, we shift
from our power drive and again engage our hyperdrive to travel
through hyperspace, the space of the second journey. To support our
inquiry in the second journey, we will now explore what we call the
Point Diamond dimension of Essence. This dimension is fundamental to
the continuity of essential realization. It provides inquiry with a very
important orientation, one that expands inquiry's openness and gives
it an effectiveness not envisioned before entering into the second
journey.

Understanding the dimension of the Point Diamond, as I call it
in the Diamond Approach, becomes experientially accessible through
personal work on the Point, the aspect of Essential Identity.*

THE POINT DIAMOND TEACHING

Exploring this new dimension will bring up many issues, and we will
discuss some of the major ones here. The understanding that results
will also challenge many ideas, positions, and beliefs that we may have
adopted by listening to spiritual jargon. It will also set the work of
inquiry apart from other kinds of inner work.

---

*See *The Point of Existence* for a detailed discussion of the Point and its relationship to the
issues of narcissism and self-realization.

We can call this segment of work by different names, each of which gives us an initial impression of what the Point Diamond teaching is about. We can call it the work on the lifeline. The term "lifeline" originated as part of Einstein's relativity theory; it refers to an event curve in Minkowski space. Minkowski space, named after the Russian mathematician, is the four-dimensional time-space continuum in which our life happens, in the sense that at any moment, you find yourself at a certain location in space and time. In other words, you are always physically locatable in Minkowski space. So your life is physically composed of a series of these locator points in space-time. When you connect the points, you get a line called your lifeline. Every physical object has its lifeline.

The teaching we are discussing concerns more than your physical body, so it is related to a different kind of Minkowski space—a spiritual or inner Minkowski space. Thus, the lifeline we are exploring is not only your location in time and space, but your location in terms of where you are in your experience; it is the lifeline of your soul's unfoldment. You can always find yourself in a certain state, or experiential configuration, at any point of your unfoldment. Your soul's phenomenological configuration in any moment corresponds to the location in the space dimension of Minkowski space, and the point where you are in your unfoldment corresponds to the location in the time dimension. Understanding the significance of these correspondences becomes the teaching of the personal lifeline.

Another name for the teaching of the Point Diamond could be the teaching of the freedom of movement of the assemblage point. The notion of the assemblage point is a central part of the teachings of Don Juan as related by Carlos Castaneda in his books. According to Don Juan, reality is composed of many bands, dimensions, or rays of manifestation. You experience yourself at any given moment in one or a cluster of these bands.

The band where the ego normally crystallizes is where the assemblage point is fixed. The teaching is to discover how to free yourself from this fixation—how to move your assemblage point without constraint—so that your perception becomes liberated, thus allowing you to roam through the experiential bands and be open to experiencing the totality of your potential.

We can also call the Point Diamond realization the teaching of the personal thread, in the sense that your lifeline can be seen as the thread of your evolution, of your unfoldment. If you really investigate, inquire into, and understand your situation fully, you can find out at any moment where your thread is, which is where you are experientially.

A central issue that arises in finding and aligning with your personal thread is the nature of external influence. How is your relationship to your own unfolding experience affected (or controlled) by the books you read, the people you listen to, even the teaching you are following? How can you be true to exactly where you are at the present moment without being influenced by beliefs, suggestions, and ideas absorbed in the past?

This issue helps us see that the personal thread's being free from influence is ultimately the same thing as the freedom of movement of the assemblage point. The ability of your assemblage point to move freely is what allows your personal thread to be free from influence. Thus, this can also be seen as the teaching of freedom from influence. This teaching provides us with an understanding of influence and what it means to be free from its limitations. When you have this understanding, you are able to fully realize the uniqueness of your personal thread.

DYNAMISM AND THE CURRENT OF EXPERIENCE

Inquiry implies that experience doesn't stay the same, that there's change—or at least possible change. You explore and you find out something you haven't seen before about yourself or reality. This indicates a change in perception, a change in experience, or a change in consciousness. This change points to the dynamism of our Being.

The word "being" connotes simple beingness, or thereness. You investigate and you find that your nature is Being: you're just there, pure presence. This, however, doesn't mean that beingness stays the same; otherwise, how can we account for the various manifestations, the various ways we experience our Being and ourselves? So Being is inherently dynamic, and its dynamism is creative and transformative, in the sense that Being is always creating new forms, constantly manifesting different appearances.

In the second journey, we are engaging our hyperdrive, which is similar to *Star Trek*'s warp drive, the type of propulsion system that allows space vehicles to travel faster than the speed of light. What I have called the power drive is the equivalent of impulse power on a starship, used to travel at sublight speeds. Full impulse power is only one-fourth the speed of light. So when you are operating the warp drive, the laws of sublight physics don't apply, and you find yourself traversing huge distances in extremely short periods of time. For example, even at warp factor 1, which is the slowest faster-than-light speed, you can reach the moon—400,000 miles from Earth—in 1.34 seconds. This can give you a sense of the speed of unfoldment that is possible on the second journey. You can find yourself accelerating so quickly that it seems as though you have instantaneously transported yourself to another place.

Being's dynamism implies more than the fact that experience and perception change; it also implies that the change is due to a transformative and creative inherent power. It's not solely a matter of cause and effect, although cause and effect is part of it. When I say "dynamism," I mean a living force similar to the biological evolutionary force: It doesn't always respond in the same way or in predictable ways. It is intelligent, and therefore its manifestations keep shifting around, moving toward more optimization of life. This is why I say that Being inherently possesses the optimizing force, or the optimizing thrust.

When we think only in terms of cause and effect, the dynamism, the intelligence, the power, the force, and the aliveness within our Being are all left out. We're thinking only within a mechanical framework, holding a mechanistic view of how change happens. But human experience cannot be completely explained as a function of cause and effect or any other predictable construct about change. We can never systematize life changes completely, for we will always find exceptions. There will always come a time when things happen differently.

This intelligent dynamism expresses the freedom and the inexhaustibility of the mystery. Because this mystery—which is fundamental to Being—is inexhaustible in its possibilities, Being's response can change, can be totally new and fresh. And there's no end to this variability. Dynamism, intelligence, and the inexhaustibility of the mystery go together; they are reflections of the same truth.

The simplest and easiest way to see the dynamism is to look at your constantly changing experience. Even when it is repetitive and feels familiar, the repetitions are only of certain things, certain landmarks. Regardless of how patterned your experience is or how stuck you are, there is always some change. In fact, in an absolute sense, your experience is never the same; it never repeats itself one hundred percent. If it weren't for this constant change, this dynamism, there would be no perception, no awareness, and no experience. If you took the whole world and froze it, there would be no perception, and it would be the same as if there were no world. So the dynamism and the awareness of our Being are two sides of the same phenomenon.

This is an interesting point because we naively believe that if we experience something that does not change, in a situation where we have no other experience—either internal or external—we will continue to experience that something. If you think about it clearly, you'll realize that this is not possible. Imagine that you are in the center of a completely spherical room and that this sphere is all one color—white, for instance. And suppose you do not experience any memories, associations, reactions, or ideas, either about your perception or in general. In other words, you have no inner experience whatsoever, not even perceiving your body—there's nothing but the whiteness all around you. Will you see white? No, you will not see anything.

This is just a thought experiment to simplify the question, but it shows that without some kind of change either inside you or outside you, there will be no perception. Change is necessary for perception. Either the external or the internal has to change; otherwise it's similar to being in this spherical white room. When you come out of that experience, you won't remember anything. This is called the experience of cessation.

From this example, we see that experience, awareness, and dynamism are very much interconnected. There is a movement in your experience—a current, a flow—from one impression to another, from one perception to another. In fact, that's your life: a current of experience, of impressions and perceptions that we can call a lifeline. Perhaps you usually don't think of it this way. You probably see your life from a physical perspective: There's physical space, and you have a physical body, and that body goes around in this physical space and does things or doesn't do things, makes noises, and so on. Maybe you also include your inner experience and external perception, but these you probably situate within this physical perspective.

However, you can also look at your life and reality in general as a series of changes in perception, and this perception includes the body and its movements. We ordinarily think that perception and experience are secondary to the physical space and the physical body that's in it, but can you ever experience the physical body in physical space without perception? Can there be any life at all without perception, and specifically, without changing perception? No.

Therefore, we can say that one's life is a current of experience, a current of perception, a current of impressions. Experience includes all the modalities: vision, hearing, feeling, sensing, thinking, imaging, all together as one unified current. If you close your eyes, the current continues; only the patterns and colors change. Certain things are not there, other things are there. Certain things appear, others have disappeared. You may say that you closed your eyes, which is the familiar way of expressing this experience, but what happens is that the current is presenting different perceptions. At least, this way of viewing it is just as valid as the notion that your eyes open and close. In fact, if you investigate it philosophically, or completely scientifically, you will find no proof that you have closed your eyes. All you can assert without further assumptions about reality is that impressions changed and perception changed, because the explanation that you closed your eyes is itself an impression that is part of the current.

This is an interesting shift in our way of looking at things. Things continue to be the same, but we can look at them slightly differently, which can bring in a different perspective. Usually we think that reality is out there and that we're here interacting with it, and that this interaction creates our experience. In this view, experience comes and goes, sometimes occurring inside, sometimes outside, but always in fragments and pieces: "I had this experience . . . I had that experience." It is external reality that appears to be continuous, not our experience. What we don't see is that everything that's happening is simply a change in the stream of our perception. The continuity, the current, of experience is constant and includes everything—there's really no inside or outside.

In any case, there's a current of experience, regardless of how we think of it or explain it, whether it needs to be proven or not. There is a flow, a progression, from one impression to another. And it is this flow, this progression—one event following another, one event fading into another—that makes it possible for us to speak of a journey. It also makes it possible for us to speak of inquiry.

OPTIMIZING THE UNFOLDMENT

Inquiry is basically a matter of participating in the stream, cooperating with the current, going with the flow, in such a way that you are aligning yourself with the optimizing force. In other words, inquiry is more than just a continuous movement with the current. In all experience, the current expresses the dynamism, but this dynamism may or may not be optimized. In inquiry, we are aligning ourselves with the optimizing force in the dynamism, which means that the current of experience moves toward becoming brighter and clearer, more beautiful.

This beauty and clarity can be conceptualized in many ways—as fulfillment, as heightened awareness, as depth, as expansion, or as more reality, more fullness, more objectivity. However you experience it, the optimizing current is further revealing the mystery of Being. As long as there is consciousness, the current is always there. Without optimization, it flows only on the surface of reality—moving in one or several directions, or circling back on itself. Even though there might be changes, the current stays on the same plane, repeating the same fundamental outlines of experience—as the surface itself is infinite. This is life when it is lived solely on the ego level.

But the current can also flow deeper, which means that it begins to manifest the underlying potential of Being, revealing new and unexpected planes of experience. The current then becomes creative—not only in the sense of being generative, always producing, but in the artistic sense: Something new arises, something original manifests; an enhancement happens, an optimization.

So when we discuss unfoldment, we add another element to the idea of the current of experience. We now have a current that is creative, unfolding, that is revealing new aspects, new possibilities, that is manifesting more elements of the inherent potential of Being. The potential that has always been possible is now becoming actual. When unfoldment is occurring, the current is more luminous, more radiant, more alive, revealing newer possibilities. The more the current that is our life reveals new possibilities, and the more it becomes creative and unfolds in an optimizing way, the closer we get to our true nature, the pure essence of our Being.

In fact, you might even say that we are then approaching the source of the current. Which also means that we are approaching the fullness of what we can be. By manifesting our possibilities, by actualizing our potential, by creatively bringing out our further possibilities, we approach our completeness, our wholeness. More of us—more of the potentialities of our soul—is experienced, is conscious. We sometimes call that maturity, but really what we are approaching is completeness, totality, wholeness.

In other words, if we participate in the current and cooperate with its optimizing force, the current tends to complete itself, tends to move in such a way that experience becomes more of a wholeness, and more dimensions emerge and are integrated. This is the essence of the spiritual journey: As you move toward wholeness, you see more and more of reality, and more of your nature is accessible and expressed.

MOVING TOWARD WHOLENESS

Although the current will move toward wholeness when we align ourselves with Being's optimizing intelligence, the wholeness does not immediately arise every time we align ourselves. Wholeness is simply the natural direction, and it will naturally arise whenever it is the appropriate response. Being's intelligence is responsive to where the current finds itself at the time of change. Therefore, the nature of your situation, which is the totality of your experience, changes and transforms depending on how it is manifesting at the moment. The intelligent movement directly responds to your experience; it doesn't just leave whatever is present in your experience and abruptly move to the wholeness or to the Absolute.

I'm saying this because many teachings assert, "Leave what you are experiencing now and go to a higher state. The practice is to actualize wholeness in the present moment, to actualize the mystery right now." This may be one way of doing it, but the natural intelligence of our Being doesn't function this way. It does not skip the present and its content, no matter what it is, and jump to the ultimate. This is because Being's optimizing intelligence is responsive to the specific details of this moment. Sometimes the wholeness of Being will be the appropriate response to the situation of the moment; most of the time, that is not the optimal response.

You might very well ask, "Well, if the movement is not going toward wholeness now, but it ultimately will, why not push it that way?" But are we as intelligent as Being itself, in its natural responsiveness? Do we know what the next step will be? Are we as omniscient as Being itself that we can determine how the current should go? How do we know that the way the current naturally is flowing when we are aligned with Being's intelligence is not the most efficient route toward wholeness?

So understanding the dynamics of Being reveals a trap that many people fall into: attempting to twist God's arm or second-guessing Being, trying to help it along by pushing its current in a particular direction. This tendency to orient our experience toward a particular state reveals more than anything else the identifications and positions we have learned from various teachings. Most teachings actually say, "This is where you're headed, so let's go straight there." This is especially a danger when we become attracted to teachings referred to as sudden, direct, or fast methods. Such approaches might seduce you into believing that you can jump into the final realization without going along with the dynamism itself. The possibility definitely exists that this jump will be successful, but it is a minuscule possibility, and whether it can happen depends on where you are in your journey.

Approaches based on the belief that you can bypass Being's dynamism—or more specifically, that you should go toward a particular state—tend to create a big problem and a painful conflict for most individuals. You will always be comparing where you are to this place you're supposed to get to. You will always be pushing yourself to get there. Then you will develop a superego, or inner critic, that is always looking over your shoulder and telling you: "The goal is over there; how come you're still here? When are you ever going to get there? You know you're not doing very well."

These teachings apparently have their logic and their own context, and their methods obviously work in some situations. Nevertheless, the work we're doing here has to do with cooperating with the natural intelligence of the dynamism of our Being. Our approach is to piggyback on the natural wave of Being's optimizing force by harmonizing ourselves with its flow.

So the Diamond Approach says that wholeness is available, is possible, and it will arrive in its own time. The ultimate nature of the wholeness doesn't mean that it is available to you at each moment. Being just does not operate this way, which should be clear from most of our observations. The dynamism doesn't thrust wholeness on you. It responds appropriately and intelligently to your unique situation in each moment. It is intelligent, perceptive, sensitive, and empathic in its responsiveness. When you are aligned with Being's intelligence, the current of your experience in any given moment is either in the condition of wholeness or approaching more wholeness and more integration. The wholeness is the source of the intelligence; in fact, this intelligence is nothing but the expression of the wholeness, through the response of Being's dynamics. Therefore, it is natural that when you completely and deeply relax, your experience will spontaneously settle in the condition of wholeness.

But many things can get in the way of this settling—glitches, misunderstandings, conflicts, wrong views, conditioned responses, feelings and thoughts that need to be dismantled or clarified. The intelligent dynamism will respond to these interferences as it moves toward the wholeness. The intelligence might operate at one moment by manifesting in you a feeling of strength, for example, to deal with your condition. Or it might arise in you as a condition of boundless love or another of the infinite possibilities of Being. Being's intelligence responds differently not only to different individuals, its response varies in each individual at different times and under different conditions.

If this were not so, there would be no such thing as a unique personal thread. Each person's field of experience is individual; it has different components, different manifestations and influences, a different history. The optimizing intelligence will transform each person's experiential situation in a different way. Another way of saying this is that each person's current will be unique. All currents move toward the same reality—toward the wholeness—but this movement will meander through different terrain for different individuals. One person will be going through a valley while another is going over a mountain.

Speaking in terms of the lifeline, we each begin from a different place, with different initial conditions, and this is another reason why each of us will have a unique lifeline. Within these differences, however, are similarities between lifelines, for the laws that govern our currents are the same. Nevertheless, the curve that is your particular lifeline will be different from the curve of someone else's lifeline, even though we are all moving in the same direction—toward wholeness.

Practice Session: Your Personal Thread

You might find it useful now to stop and explore for yourself what we have been discussing. Have you been in touch with a current in your inner experience? If so, what is your experience of this personal thread? To help you answer these questions, choose an issue that you have been aware of or working with for some time and begin to tune in to your feelings and attitudes about it in this moment. What is your experience of yourself in relation to this issue now?

Then look back at the time when the issue first arose for you. Can you identify a thread of experiences that has brought you to your present position in regard to this issue? Did you lose touch with that thread from time to time? Under what circumstances? How did you reconnect with it again?

Looking in this way at your history around an issue can reveal how your process is more like a thread unraveling than a problem being solved. How do you know when you are in touch with the thread and when you aren't? Looking at the overall process of working with your issue, can you see how the thread might be tracing an unfoldment in your soul? If so, how would you characterize that movement?

THE MANDALA OF THE SOUL

A useful image to help us conceptualize the thread of personal unfoldment is the *mandala*. By a mandala I mean a field with a midpoint, such as a sphere with a center. The field is the totality of your experience—your thoughts, feelings, sensations, perceptions, actions; it is the totality of your life at each moment. The center is where Being's dynamism touches your field, touches your mandala. This is where the transformation of experience begins, which then ripples through the whole field. The center is where you are—the essential aspect or state in which your soul is manifesting, which is where you find your identity, your true nature. Being interacts with your mandala by touching you right at the center—in fact, the touch is what makes it your center—which has a rippling effect throughout the whole mandala.

For instance, there might arise at the center an intensification of awareness, or boundless love, or power, which then has a rippling effect throughout the whole mandala, which is the totality of your experience. How Being touches your center, or what it touches it with, depends on the whole mandala at each moment, the totality of what's going on with you. It doesn't just touch you with any element haphazardly. So your experience at each moment reflects the totality of the mandala and the force touching it that is generating a change.

The way I have described the mandala does not exactly apply in the first journey; it is a picture more appropriate to the second journey. This is because in the first journey, the optimizing force is not yet a directly felt experience, not a direct recognition. It is experienced more in the effect it has on the mandala, for even though the movement is toward presence, presence isn't manifesting in consciousness yet. In the second journey, presence manifests directly in experience, and this presence is the center of the mandala. That presence, that center, is you, and the mandala is the totality of your experience. In the third journey, the center and the mandala become coemergent, for everything at this point is presence.

We are discussing the mandala in relation to the second journey because that's where we can understand the question of personal thread most clearly and specifically. This is because the personal thread, the lifeline, is most obvious, most delineated, most specifically clear in this journey with presence. We can then use this specificity to understand the first journey more precisely. The personal thread is not so clear in the first journey because you are not directly in touch with the dynamism. Therefore there is no clear and specific center—it is as though you're swimming in a sea that is your field of experience.

But I am not saying that you cannot follow your personal thread in the first journey. It is simply more difficult because the thread is not characterized by an awareness of the mandala's center. The question of personal thread, or of uniqueness of unfoldment, is relevant in all three journeys, but there are differences depending on which journey you are on. These differences have to do with your identity in each journey.

THE PERSONAL THREAD IN THE THREE JOURNEYS

In the first journey, your identity is on the ego level, which is the familiar sense of self-recognition. This identity is a reflection of the particular ego structure that defines you in relation to your experiential field. In the second journey, the identity is the Point, the point of light and existence, the Essential Identity. In the third journey, the identity is the mystery of Being itself, the Absolute. These differences create some variations in the nature of the thread in each journey.

However, all three journeys are similar in terms of what following your thread means. Following your thread means that it is possible to see objectively what is going on with you, moment to moment. More specifically, this means that you become aware of your experience through the global awareness that arises from mindfulness and then investigate and inquire to find out what's going on. You may, for instance, observe irritation, sleepiness, and a reluctance to talk to people, but you don't know exactly why. This unknowing can then activate a questioning attitude toward these impressions, and at some point the understanding might arise: "I see, I'm just angry." Now you are beginning to find your thread.

This process is the same in all of the journeys. However, the thread in the first journey has no single element that consistently characterizes it. The thread can be: Now I'm angry . . . now nothing is happening . . . now I'm eating my dinner . . . now I am stuck. As a result, the thread in the first journey meanders over a large territory, without clear connections, though sometimes in hindsight you can see what they are. So even though you can find your thread, there is no inherent feeling of "Yes, here I am." The moment you say, "Oh, here I am," you are already in some sense entering the second journey, as you begin to recognize yourself independent of the content of any particular experience.

Inquiry begins with the desire to find out what's going on. You want to understand your experience in the moment. Inquiry leads you to greater and greater understanding of yourself in general, but it does this by helping you to understand yourself from moment to moment. In the first journey, this moment-to-moment understanding changes, transforms, becomes more, becomes less, moves in this direction, moves in that direction, and so on. We can say that in the first journey, your personal thread is the thread of understanding. The thread of your understanding is what tells you where you are in the first journey. This usually happens toward the end of it, when you can know where you are continuously, in the sense that you have an unbroken understanding of what is going on: what you are feeling, what you are experiencing, whether you are stuck or not, what kind of defense is going on, whether you are reactive or not reactive, what issues you are dealing with, and so on. This can never be done perfectly, but it is possible to do it more and more effectively as you move through the first journey. The whole thrust of the work on the first journey is to become aware of yourself to the point of knowing where you are at any given moment.

THE THREAD OF ESSENTIAL PRESENCE

When we inquire into our consciousness, we find that it has certain manifestations. Inquiry is not only a matter of being aware of these manifestations, which make up our mandala, but also of understanding them in a coherent way that tells us where we are experientially. This is our thread at that moment. But by "thread," we also mean something slightly more than knowing where we are; we mean being aware of the process of the unfoldment within us as well. So the thread means really recognizing and understanding what's going on with us as a continuous process.

The more aware you are of what's going on—that is, the more you are in touch with and understand your personal thread—the more the optimizing force can impact your experience. This optimizing force always occurs when we align with any of the qualities—such as awareness, understanding, or in-touchness—that the optimizing intelligence naturally manifests when Being's dynamism is allowed in our experience.

We see this most easily in the second journey, which is the journey with presence. You are aware of your essential presence, but other things are also going on in your mandala. You may be experiencing a particular quality of presence, such as the Personal Essence or Peace or Compassion. This quality constitutes the center of the mandala, and the rest of the mandala is composed of your feelings, your memories, your internal dynamics, your actions—the whole emotional inner atmosphere and how it manifests in your life, as well as the entire perceptual sphere. So we can say that the way Being is manifesting in you at any moment is the center of your mandala. Being touches your mandala through its essential manifestations, which are its center. This center is a changing point, and this point, as it changes, forms a thread—your essential lifeline. Thus, in this journey, the mandala is quite clear, and it is easy to see the thread.

In the second journey, the distinguishing characteristic of your personal thread is the essential presence, something that is not available in the first journey. Because of this, we can't clearly talk about unfoldment—the direct impact of the dynamism of Being in the soul—in the first journey, even though there is a current of experience. We can speak about unfoldment quite precisely in the second journey because the center, which is the essential presence, is arising as one quality after another.

Inquiry in the second journey means inquiring in order to know where you are—finding out where you happen to be on your journey. I don't mean just your location in the field of the mandala—the manifestations of your life such as your emotions, thoughts, or actions. I mean where you are at the center, the place that is touched by Being. This means finding your place, recognizing your location in the essential space. Two elements are involved in this inquiry: first, seeing the center of the mandala, which means being aware of your presence and knowing exactly the quality of this presence; and second, being aware of and understanding the totality of the mandala, that is, the reverberations of the presence through the rest of your consciousness, and vice versa.

Interactions are always happening between the center and the field of the mandala, for the quality of presence arising is responsive to and impacting what's going on in the totality of the mandala. If, for instance, you are feeling powerless and helpless, the center of the mandala becomes the Black Essence (the quality of essential power) after a while because it is responsive to what's happening in the mandala. The response is also related to the history of your mandala and its location in the universal mandala. In other words, your personal mandala, which is your experiential world—the totality of your consciousness with its essential presence—is the result of both your personal history and your interaction with the larger mandala of the whole world, within which it is situated. However, beginning in the second journey, your experience within the mandala is determined not only by these two factors, but also by Being's optimizing dynamism arising through the center of your mandala as essential presence.

FOLLOWING THE THREAD

We can also discuss the mandala in terms of the soul. The soul is the totality of the mandala. Essence arises in the soul, but for a long time throughout the second journey, the soul is not completely essentialized; only part of it is. The rest of the field of the mandala—the rest of the consciousness of the soul—is composed of all your mental, emotional, and physical experiences. The thread is defined by the center of the soul, and we can know that center most specifically and in a delineated way by recognizing the essential presence and what quality it is manifesting. This is the journey with presence, where the soul is moving toward wholeness, toward the integration of the mystery, through the dynamism manifesting the essential presence in its various qualities and dimensions. This is what really transforms the mandala, what actually changes the soul. The mandala can't be truly transformed without the essential presence.

Inquiry in the second journey is a matter of following the thread, which means that you are aware of the presence and understand its qualities, and you understand how the presence is affecting the rest of your experience. You see your issues in relationship to whatever essential quality is manifesting, and you also see and understand how your life experience is limiting or affecting the essential presence. The essential presence becomes the guidance. It is a thread of Essence continually becoming brighter, more luminous, and that thread of brightness can move through our experience. In contrast, there is no thread of brightness in the first journey. It just blips once in a while.

So in effect, the optimizing thrust and the thread and the guidance are all one; they are different manifestations of the same thing. And being in alignment with the optimizing thrust means that you are in contact with the guidance and are moving in the direction that allows the presence to manifest more and more. However, for that to happen, you will need to have realized the Point to some degree, the Essential Identity. To recognize Essence as your center, you have to have some identification with essential presence; you have to have recognized, "Oh, that's me." This is the experience of the Point: Experiencing that you yourself are the purity of Being. However, you won't know that this is *you* if you have not worked on the Point and the narcissistic issues surrounding it.

But when we are discussing the possibilities of the second journey, we are not just talking about a discrete experience of recognizing that your essence is you. We are talking about a continuity of recognition, a current of realization that stays at the center of your experience. That's what you want to actualize in the second journey. When you really have actualized the second journey, you are always aware of presence, regardless of what happens. Other things might be going on that are not presence, but there is always presence. Before this stage, you go back and forth between the second and the first journey.

TRYING TO CONTROL THE THREAD

During the second journey, you need to trust that there is nothing to do but stay with the thread. The question of trust activates the specific issue that makes it difficult to stay with the thread. The specific issue of any essential aspect is the issue that arises in everyone regardless of personal history, as a barrier against realizing that aspect. The specific issue for the Point Diamond is the belief that you need to be someplace in particular. "Maybe I should be experiencing the mystery. I should be in the unchanging silence beyond all of appearance. That's realization." No! Realization is knowing where you truly are, not experiencing some state that you can only sometimes reach.

The point is that the dynamism is manifesting its pure quality within *your* mandala in a specific form, with a specific quality, for an intelligent reason. Dynamism has its own purposes in presenting itself within you the way it does. You can say, "No, that's not what I want," but this comes from a will disconnected from the Divine Will. Because of this self-centered willfulness, it is said in some of the theistic traditions that harmony with the Divine Will is a higher realization than God-realization. Going along with where Being puts you is a much deeper realization than just becoming intimate with the wholeness of Being.

So the dynamism presents itself to your mandala, giving you the opportunity to be moved by the Divine Will in whatever way it wants. Another way of saying this is that your mandala, which is the totality of your experience, is touched in the center by the Divine Will. The particular way in which you are touched is the manifestation of Divinity itself, which is the essential presence. This is also called the elixir, the transforming agent that can transform the totality of the mandala and move it toward greater optimization. Our personal contribution is to investigate our experience to become aware of and understand what's happening, because if we don't understand it, we will tend to push against it. Not understanding it means that we are acting according to some other impulse that originates in a more superficial part of our soul. The movement of the whole mandala is then being directed by this superficial part, which most likely is a remnant of our personal history.

In the first journey, you can't help but push all the time; this is all that is possible for you. In the second journey, presence has been recognized and is becoming integrated. This presence now transforms the mandala by moving it deeper and deeper, by manifesting at the center of the mandala whatever qualities are needed to transform that mandala. And as the optimizing thrust penetrates the various barriers in us, the experience of the whole mandala begins to change. This is because our experience is affected by all these barriers. The quality of awareness, the quality of consciousness, the quality of responsiveness, the quality of contact and action—all these elements of experience are largely defined by our internal barriers.

TRANSFORMING THE MANDALA

But the optimizing thrust does not function only by focusing on the problems or the barriers. It illuminates the entire mandala. Sometimes the illumination is focused on understanding the essential presence itself. Engaging in that understanding can lead to the central part of the second journey, which is the luminous thread itself, the awareness of the presence itself. You are aware of it, and you are feeling it as the center of your experience because it is the deepest and most trans-formative force in your experience. And it will affect the totality of your experience. I don't that mean that it will transform your experi-ence totally every time this awareness arises. But it is a force, so it will begin impacting, transforming, and clarifying your experience.

So the work, then, which is the work of inquiry, is a matter of being present, being aware of the presence, and of understanding it and its interaction with the rest of your experience. The presence will change from one quality to another, from one dimension to another, and these transubstantiations will bring about changes in the totality of your mandala. They will activate different object relations,* different identifications, different feelings, different memories. All the situations and relationships in your life will be impacted.

What is required of us is not just to know the thread, but also to know its relationship to the totality of the mandala. Because if we focus on one or the other, we tend to split our experience. If we focus only on the thread, only on the essential presence, without paying attention to the totality of the mandala, then we can become spiritual material-

---

*An object relation is a psychic structure consisting of a self-image, an image of the other, and the feeling that connects them. These units, established early in life, are the building blocks of the ego and the psychic determinants of most personality patterns.

ists. Some essential development will occur, but it will be split off from the rest of your soul, so a large part of your soul is not touched, not transformed. On the other hand, when people always focus on their problems and difficulties, or only on their external circumstances, they lose track of their essential presence. Either way, there's an imbalance. So we need to be aware of understanding both the essential presence—the center of the experience of the mandala—and the totality of the mandala.

Let's look at an example of how the interaction between the center and the field of your mandala might occur. Suppose you're experiencing the presence of Clear Essence. It is clarity and transparency, which teaches you that your nature is lucid and clear. You may begin then to see a thickness around your head. You can investigate this thickness much more effectively while the clarity is present because the clarity reveals the thickness, the obscurations, in contrast with its own clear nature. You start seeing the history of this thickness and what it is connected with—the object relations and their history—and at some point you realize that one object relation becomes more dominant. You realize that your clarity wasn't seen, wasn't recognized or appreciated by your parents when you were a small child. As you are dealing with the issue of your clarity not being recognized, you notice that your essential presence has changed from Clear Essence to Amber Essence. This is because the issues that you are encountering have changed to those of value. The dominant quality of your essential presence might be value for a few hours, a few minutes, a few weeks, maybe a few months. During this time, the transformation will activate all the questions relating to value at different levels.

Here we see how the essential presence determines the thread of your understanding by unfolding it, which makes it the center of the mandala. The presence transforms from one quality to another, from one dimension to another, which determines the issues pervading your mandala, with their feelings and memories and their effect on your life.

LOSING THE THREAD

Of course, your essential presence will not determine your mandala completely because your mandala is also impacted by the universal mandala. But the more involved you are in the inner work—the more the work becomes your first priority—the more the essential presence becomes a greater determining force than external reality. If your involvement is more in the world and less with essential realization, your experience of what happens in the world will determine your mandala more. Of course, in the second journey, the movement frequently goes back and forth. You might move all the way to the external and lose the essential thread; then you are back in the first journey. At that point, all you can do is explore what is going on. If you find out how you got disconnected from your essential presence, you reconnect with it and pick up the thread again.

Whenever you look at where you are during the second journey, you will find some quality of essential presence, which is very important for understanding the totality. You can never really understand the wholeness of your mandala without being aware of the essential presence and knowing what it feels like and how it affects you. Losing the thread in the second journey means losing the awareness of this essential presence. Maintaining the thread means that you're always aware of your presence, whatever is going on. When issues come up, for example, dealing with them doesn't mean that you leave essential presence and jump into the first journey; you can continue being aware of the essential presence as the issues and the feelings around them arise. This awareness gives you a much greater power and effectiveness in dealing with your issues than is possible in the first journey. This is because being centered in the essential center of the mandala makes all the issues look much smaller, and accompanying emotions and reactions are not so overwhelming.

In contrast, during the first journey, you usually identify with one image or another—most of the time with an image of yourself as a child. When intense feelings arise, such as pain, it can be too much to stay with, and self-awareness is easily lost. Essential presence, on the other hand, doesn't feel pain. There can be a great deal of pain, but essential presence makes the experience of pain secondary for the soul. So the totality of the mandala is always secondary to its center, which is essential presence. The contact with our true nature is essential presence, which in time becomes more powerful, more grounded, more solid, and pervades the mandala more and more as it moves toward the third journey.

The essential presence, moved by the force of its optimizing intelligence, reveals more of its qualities and the understanding of those qualities, moving you to deeper and deeper dimensions of presence. This is a very organic, interconnected, synergetic process. The mystery that is our ultimate nature—inexhaustible in its possibilities—guides us by means of this dynamic force of intelligence, affecting our experience in a way that eventually reveals the original mystery.

Questions and Answers

STUDENT: Earlier you said something about focusing on the world versus focusing on the inner work. I guess I'm not sure what you mean by focusing on the world, because I feel I am just finding my world, my relationships, my job, and everything else. I'm finally in the world and experiencing presence with it. That's how I'm doing the work.

ALMAAS: What I mean is: Which is the priority—being in touch with your thread or focusing on all these other involvements? In the second journey, the priority needs to be the thread of the essential presence; otherwise, you lose the thread on which to base the other priorities. This doesn't mean that you are not in the world, or that your experience in the world is not important.

STUDENT: I'm just struck by the support that was created from the environment here during the exercise and how vital it is to me in my work. I'm aware of how it helps me feel safe and accepting so that somehow Essence easily emerges and finding or contacting it is not even an issue.

ALMAAS: As you inquire, you realize why you are sometimes present and sometimes not. The question of support is usually primary: How can I support myself, how can I support my realization, both inside and outside? Supporting your realization means living in such a way or finding or arranging a situation so that you can continue to be aware of your presence. If you continue being aware of your presence, it will unfold. If you lose that awareness and don't find where you are, you will tend to feel meaningless, and your experience will seem to lack significance. When you find where you are again, however, the meaninglessness is gone.

STUDENT: Would you talk about the difference between just being aware of the presence and being aware of the presence in some precise way? You seem to be emphasizing the quality of presence that we're aware of.

ALMAAS: Awareness of presence is fundamental, and that will determine whether you are on the second or the first journey. I don't mean here simply being present in a general sense, as it is commonly understood; I mean being aware of your essential presence, which is the kernel and source of feeling generally present. It doesn't matter what quality of presence is manifesting when you're just trying to distinguish which journey you're on. However, part of the work in the second journey is to inquire into the presence itself, in order to know it more precisely. As you go through your day, being present is basic. An added refinement is to find out what the presence is, what quality it has. That moves you further along on the second journey. The point is that you never understand exactly what's going on if you don't know which quality of presence is manifesting. The presence might be the Strength Essence or the Will Essence, or any of the other qualities, but if you don't know which one it is, it will be difficult to understand why you're behaving a certain way. It's important that you have this precision in order to move in the second journey effectively.

STUDENT: The inquiry felt very, very personal, and filled with love and compassion. It was all on a very subtle level and very intimate.

ALMAAS: That's one reason why I call it the personal thread—because you need to be personal with yourself to engage the inquiry fully. You have to be personal with your process instead of looking at it from some abstract or external perspective. It has to be intimate to you. When you know where you are, it is personally *you*. You begin to feel this personalness, and with it can arrive the love, the sweetness, and the compassion.

STUDENT: It seems to be such a contrast to the way I am used to looking at myself. There is more awareness of the things you just mentioned: love, compassion . . .

ALMAAS: Sounds good; you must be feeling better about yourself. When that happens, it's easier to follow the thread.

STUDENT: . . . not only a willingness, but an excitement and enthusiasm.

ALMAAS: It's exciting, you know, to be yourself. That's what it means to find where you are: to be yourself continuously instead of just having blips of yourself. You're being there, you're being personally *you* and going through your life. That sense of being there becomes the center of your life. Your life is the whole mandala and the flow of that mandala—and you become the center of it, its identity. Then there is an intimacy and a personal quality to your life. You are finding your truth—not in contrast to somebody else's truth, but yours in the sense that it is personal to you.

CHAPTER 11

Journey without a Goal

THIS EXPLORATION WE ARE involved in will highlight a component of the Diamond Approach that is, generally speaking, not
addressed by the Eastern spiritual traditions. These traditions, which
have become increasingly accessible to Westerners of the past few decades, are generally oriented in a different way from what most people
are comfortable with in this culture: away from life. For them, realization is not the fulfillment of human life on Earth, it is the freedom
from that life. The Eastern approach usually defines liberation as freedom from cyclic existence, that is, from being born again on Earth.
Therefore, the focus is more on the realization of ultimate true nature
that transcends all life.

This realization is also an important part of our work in the Diamond Approach. If we are going to be truly free, we do need to
understand and realize our true nature in as transcendent and fundamental a way as possible. However, just as important is how to apply
this realization of ultimate true nature in everyday life. "Fine, I know
what my true nature is, I can *be* my true nature, but what does that
have to do with cooking dinner? How is it relevant to interacting with
my family? How does it relate to living my everyday life?"

The Eastern spiritual paths traditionally oriented themselves toward
monastic life—being a monk or a nun. In fact, that is the form that
most Eastern religions began with. This is because monastic life makes
spiritual work easier, simpler. The subtleties that arise in meditation

and in other spiritual practices and exercises are not as difficult to deal with as the situations of everyday life; the latter are much more complex and difficult.

So concerns such as these come up all the time when you want to live a normal human life: Can I earn my living? How much money do I need to support myself, and can I stay in touch with my true nature while I do that? What kind of a living situation should I choose? What kind of people should I associate with? How much time should I spend with them, and what should I do when I am with them? What do I really need? These questions need to be addressed just as comprehensively as the realization of the subtlest inner nature. It is also necessary to be compassionate and loving not just in one's inner practice, but also when dealing with people in ordinary life. This requires intelligence, efficiency, action, strength, and will—all the capacities needed for ordinary life.

INTEGRATING DAILY LIFE INTO TRUE NATURE

In our work, we address both sides of human evolution: the realization of true nature and the integration of everyday life into that true nature. For the Far Eastern religions, the integration of the world of appearance into true nature results in nondual experience. This is still an impersonal and universal perspective, where all that appears to perception is experienced as inseparable from true nature. This is not what we mean by integration of life into true nature. The Diamond Approach supports living a personal life in relationship to other human beings and engaging in other human activities besides spiritual practice. Integration of appearance into true nature functions as the ground of this personal integration; it does not stand on its own as the only value. Being manifests not only in the transcendental, but also in down-to-earth, practical, and personal forms that are relevant to everyday life. And daily life itself can become spiritual realization.

It is worth noting, however, that as Eastern traditions have become more established in this country over the past few decades, they have begun to pay more attention to the blending of true nature into daily life. Some, for example, have begun to seriously undertake service to the greater community. But several thousand years of nonconcern about external life have had a defining influence on Eastern spirituality, and the integration of the spiritual and material is still the exception rather than the rule.

The Diamond Approach is also in contrast to the Eastern guru-disciple model, that is, surrendering to an individual who is detached from the world and who lives in transcendence of personal life. I am not saying that this isn't a valid model for some people, even in our Western culture, but you will not find those people in our school. The traditional image of the guru has also undergone change in recent times, as some spiritual teachers in the West become more modern in their approach and recommend that their followers involve themselves in worldly concerns. But again, these are exceptions to the norm.

The understanding of inquiry we are discussing highlights the integration of true nature and everyday life through finding your thread—being where you are, moment to moment, and following your immediate experience. As this luminous thread, which is the center of your life, manifests and unfolds, your daily life becomes an appreciation and celebration of the continuing manifestation of true nature in its various qualities, colors, and forms. This flow of experience, of manifestations, is what we call living the essential personal life, in which the various situations of personal life become the context for Being to manifest its many possibilities.

For example, if you go off to court because you have been sued, Being manifests in a specific form for you to be able to deal with this situation. It will be a different form from the one that will manifest when you go to bed or sit down to talk to a friend. And even in the latter case, Being will manifest differently when your friend is suffering from a relationship breakup than when your friend is putting you down and arousing your anger.

Thus the events and activities of your personal life become as much an expression of true nature as the inner process of self-realization. It is natural, then, that certain questions and conflicts will arise in our attempts to understand what it means to follow our thread. These are important and relevant questions for inquiry in general, and thus worth looking into more deeply.

GOALLESS INQUIRY

As we have seen, inquiry is, by nature, open ended if it is true inquiry. You cannot truly inquire if you choose to go in a predetermined direction, as when you say, "I want to accomplish such and such in my inquiry." By definition, this is not inquiry, although some traditions call it that. What is frequently called inquiry in the East, for instance, is what we consider in the West to be proof of a theorem, such as a Euclidean proof: "This is the theory; investigate and find out that it is true." As a specific example, in the Buddhist tradition, inquiry is the investigation of phenomena in order to discover that they are all ultimately empty. So emptiness as the ultimate nature of things is posited from the beginning.

That is not what we do in the Diamond Approach. We merely inquire into phenomena so that the truth can reveal itself. This is a very important attitude for finding your thread, for your thread can be anywhere, anyplace. Further, your thread is a process, so any state that arises is not permanent, but keeps changing. Therefore, following your thread requires an open-ended inquiry, which is in direct conflict with any attitude or method that says, "Let's develop such and such a condition, let's move toward such and such a state." This latter attitude asserts, "We know where we need to be, so let's work to get to this realization." This is not an open inquiry, and your personal thread will not be able to unfold your experience when you take that attitude.

Your personal thread is unique to you and can be in any place at any particular moment. Therefore, finding your thread—being where you are—cannot happen when you are working toward a particular aim or toward a particular state. You can't take the position that you know what the enlightened state is, for example, and work toward making it happen, because the moment you do that, you close down inquiry. Then it is no longer inquiry, it's something else, and you will have lost your thread. Similarly, if you do a particular practice and actualize some kind of expanded state, it may be unrelated to where you truly are. And if it is not where you are, you'll feel a sense of meaninglessness. The meaninglessness will stick with you because this state is most likely not you; it is something accomplished, not a place where Being's dynamism has freely situated you.

Questions and Answers

STUDENT: This approach seems to preclude the idea of intervention by a teacher or even intervening in one's own process.

ALMAAS: That's correct, unless the intervention is a matter of guiding you to explore. If the intervention is for the purpose of guiding and supporting your inquiry, then it falls within this open-ended attitude. But intervening to make certain things happen would be contrary to the way of inquiry.

STUDENT: Are you saying that there is no place for goal-oriented work within the Diamond Approach? You once said that getting help outside the School for a specific issue might bring some resolution more quickly than only doing the continual inquiry toward the truth that we're doing. Isn't that moving toward a particular goal?

ALMAAS: I did not say that it is bad to go toward a particular goal or that you shouldn't do that. I am merely saying that this is not what we do here. This is why I suggest going somewhere else if you have a particular goal. If you are sick, for example, and you have a goal of getting healthy, it's good to go to a doctor.

STUDENT: Isn't it something of a goal to allow whatever is a barrier, whatever obscures the truth of our experience, to emerge and be released?

ALMAAS: You can take something that happens in the process of inquiry as a goal, but no particular occurrence within the process is the goal of inquiry. The goal of inquiry is the adventure itself, if you can even call that a goal.

STUDENT: Isn't your goal for us to reach our true self?

ALMAAS: The orientation of inquiry is to inquire into your experience as it happens. As we do that, we notice an optimizing force that leads us to our true self. However, we also notice that the true self doesn't say, "I want you to go toward your true self." The true self does not operate with that intention. So we do not work with that intention; instead we want to harmonize ourselves with the true self, which is goalless, endless.

This is very tricky. You can always say, "The true self is pure awareness, so let's develop awareness." Or you can say, "The true self is lovingness; let's develop love." The true self means no blockages, so you can say, "Let's work on blockages." Many teachings do exactly that, but the true self does not say any of these things. The true self never tries to make anything happen. It does not have a particular position. It embodies an attitude of complete allowing and freedom: Whatever arises is fine. The true self will just guide you toward understanding your experience, appreciating it, and moving on.

Finding your true self is a good thing, but there are many ways of going about it. In the Diamond Approach, we don't look for it; it happens as a natural consequence of our inquiry. If you trust the process of following your thread, the optimizing dynamism will manifest whatever is supposed to happen. You do not even need to have the concept of true self. The true self may arise, but you might not even call it the true self. Because if you say, "Let's look for the true self," you create a concept, which then becomes an ideal and a goal. This is the beginning of developing a spiritual superego, which uses spiritual ideals to evaluate you, but is a superego nonetheless, and then you are back where you started—at the same impasse. We will look later at the problems that come up whenever the superego gets involved and you become trapped in comparative judgment.

STUDENT: I want to understand what you are saying in terms of the bodywork that is done in the Diamond Approach. For example, in the breathwork that we do, isn't the suggestion to begin a particular breathing pattern or to make a sound instead of just lying there a form of goal orientation?

ALMAAS: I am sure that is how many people look at it, but we really use bodywork techniques to help people become aware of what is going on in their experience. These methods are aids to inquiry. So you work with the blocks sometimes because that helps you to see what is happening. You are not trying merely to remove the block; you are working to see what is going on in your experience, which is the first step of inquiry.

STUDENT: So a method that exposes the nature of your experience is not considered intervention per se; it is not an attempt to change what is there.

ALMAAS: Right. We can say that there is less intervention with this kind of approach. There is still some, but your attitude toward that intervention is what matters. Your attitude can be, "Okay, let's get rid of this block," or "Let's actualize the orgasm reflex." Or you can say, "Let's use this method to inquire, because this blockage is preventing the awareness of what's going on in the moment."

STUDENT: How about what happens in weekend groups when you have us work on a specific state, such as joy or compassion?

ALMAAS: That is a good question. It has to do with trust. Let's say— let's hope at least—that I'm guided enough to see what the thread of the group is. So whatever I introduce is for the purpose of helping the group become aware of the central thread unfolding for it. This would be the best scenario. It doesn't always work, though, especially when we use specific structures or exercises, for then we are not following the Diamond Approach exactly. When we work within these organized structures, our method is not pure, which means that it is less powerful.

STUDENT: It sounds like we are using inquiry as a clever way to isolate our process from any ego intervention.

ALMAAS: In some sense, yes. That is one way of looking at it, but only one way. Another way is to see that inquiry is an invocation, an invitation for the optimizing dynamism to reveal the richness, the treasure of our Being. We call this process unfoldment. And when we open ourselves to that unfoldment, we do not go along with the ego activity, with the usual hopes and desires of the ego-self.

STUDENT: So when you give us a topic to look at in exercises, we're actually doing an inquiry process, though there is a background topic that we have to focus on. We keep that theme in the background while we are inquiring into what comes up.

ALMAAS: Right. When we do the work through organized exercises and processes, we are only approximating the Diamond Approach. It is very difficult to find structures that allow us to do it purely. Ulti-mately, you can't have a structure for pure inquiry because the moment you have any structure, you are interfering a little bit. Our orientation in the School is to do the process as purely as possible.

BEING PERSONAL WITH YOURSELF

As we have seen, if you have a particular goal, a particular orientation toward what you want to happen, then your inquiry is not open ended and most likely you will miss the thread. This means that for your inquiry to be open ended—in order for you to find your own thread and follow it—you need to proceed without any particular goal, with-out any end state in mind. You must proceed without believing that any particular state of being or realization or enlightenment should happen. You cannot do inquiry and have the attitude, "I'm going to inquire in order to accomplish this state," even if it happens to be what actually arises when you inquire. The more you inquire from the perspective of a particular end state, the more you make the inquiry into a mental process instead of a real, living one.

The moment you have a goal in your mind in terms of how you are going to experience yourself, you are not being personal with yourself. Personal means that right this moment, where you are is where you personally are—it is *you* now. The moment you say, "I'm going to go someplace" you are no longer personally relating to your immediate reality. You have adopted an abstract, impersonal aim from some source. So looking from the perspective of a certain state or aim is not appropriate to finding your thread. It is forced and unnatural because the particular state or aim that you have in mind is most likely not what is going to happen at this moment.

You are in fact trying to force something on yourself instead of finding out where you are. This is true even if the state you are wanting to go toward is wholeness or the Absolute. You are trying to put your-self in a certain place instead of finding where you actually are. Then you are not following the Holy Will, which is the natural flow of the unfolding of reality as a whole; you are just being willful. You are not cooperating with the intelligence of your own being; you are superim-posing a direction on top of your Being's true movement.

So following your personal thread is not a matter of cornering your-self in some inner state, regardless of how wonderful that state may be. The direction of your Being, if you allow it, will go toward the ultimate state. However, the particular route it is going to take is something you cannot know. The route for most people is not a direct one; you do not just jump. You go through many kinds of experiences in a sequence that is in accordance with the nature of your particular mandala. Each person is different, and that manifests in what I have referred to as the uniqueness of one's personal thread.

If any ideal can be said to exist in terms of the practice of inquiry and in the teaching of the personal thread, it is the freedom from fixation on any state or any goal. However, being oriented toward a goal is not something that is so easy to avoid.

CONDITIONING FROM SPIRITUAL TEACHINGS

Goal orientation in spiritual work can take several forms: The most common is that you read or hear that the true self or ultimate reality is such and such and then adopt the aim to arrive there. You then constantly push yourself from this side and that side, manipulating yourself in hopes of finding the right way to that particular place. But this is not participating or cooperating with the unfoldment that is naturally and spontaneously arising.

Since the sixties, people in this country have been reading books on Zen, Taoism, Vedanta, Yoga, and Buddhism, so their minds are conditioned by the ideas and concepts in these teachings. Therefore, when you start to inquire and want to allow your nature to manifest, many of these concepts from Eastern paths, or the ones from indige-nous religions, will tend to arise in your mind: "Aha! This is what Vedanta says . . . and Buddhism believes that . . . and here is what Christianity teaches," and so on. You become mentally involved and excited: "Oh yeah, that's what the experience I just had means," and you try to fit what is arising into a certain mold. You tend to feel happy when you fit within a certain model for a while. You take that as a corroboration or confirmation of your experience.

Everybody needs the support of confirmation during the early stages of the journey. However, seeking it by trying to fit into a model or ideal is a very powerful trap on the path and a great barrier to open inquiry. The conceptualizations become ideals and goals that we try to emulate, giving our ego another motive to keep on manipulating experience instead of letting Being flow and guide it. This conceptual trap is very deep and subtle, and an amazing amount of suffering arises from it for spiritual seekers. The question is, how can we learn from all these conceptualizations without getting trapped by them?

For example, you hear or read about certain ideas or possibilities, but when the experience you thought you understood arises, you realize that it is not exactly as you conceived it. You might have been close to the truth, but your understanding cannot be exact because you learned about the experience conceptually, and conceptual learning never exactly matches the experience.

In fact, the traditional teachings always state that. They warn that the finger pointing at the moon is not the moon. They say that the concept describing the reality is not the reality, it only points to it. But the mind takes that pointing and begins to look for something that looks like the pointing finger. And the truth isn't going to be something like that at all.

You see, our nature is positionless. Or, more accurately, reality always presents itself in positions—especially when we speak about it—but these positions are never fixed or rigid. Being's dynamism is a process of positioning, but it's a positioning that's always fluid, always changing from one position to another. Being cannot be pinned down in one position. We can take these positions as pointers, but not as a frame into which to fit our experience. Being is not an image to fulfill and not a goal to try to attain by pushing our experience in that direction.

When you are inquiring, you want to be totally open to what is present without any preconceptions, without any preset ideas, without any particular orientation. So you cannot take a position that I may have enunciated at one time or another—or that you got from some teacher or teaching, or even from your own previous experience— adhere to it rigidly, and expect your inquiry to be free and open ended. Your inquiry will be predetermined, set in a particular direction. It will not be free. And it will very likely distort what is going on or obscure the clear perception of what's truly arising in your experience.

This situation points to why a necessary part of our work is the integration of one's own inner support. For as long as you don't have your own inner support, you're going to rely on external supports, and frequently these will be concepts, ideas, and positions taken from the outside. Then, of course, you get yourself in a big knot and begin rebelling against these influences because you don't like the fact that your mind has become dependent on them. You might feel that you want to be free from external influence, so you try to free yourself by pushing it away, which just does not work. You cannot be free from external influence by pushing it away. What you need to be free from is your mind and its impressionability to external influence.

The reality is that there's always external influence as long as you have a consciousness. Somebody sitting beside you is an external influence. Reading the newspaper is external influence—actually, reading the morning paper will influence you a lot more than listening to teachings. We are seeing here the subtle but profound implications of the true freedom in your inquiry. It must be free from the influence of your teacher and the teachings; but even more important, it must be free from all the ongoing, unconscious influences in your life.

As your teacher, when I intervene in your process, I am inquiring into it so that you will see where you are. This will allow your process to flow. I do not know where your process is taking you next, and I am not invested in making it go in a particular direction. All I can do is work with you so that you will be open to whatever Being is presenting in your mandala. We can call that intervention or influence, but it is neither, because I am not taking you to any particular state.

Questions and Answers

STUDENT: But you are focusing my attention on something that you are choosing to focus on.

ALMAAS: No.

STUDENT: Yes. *(laughter)*

ALMAAS: Only if I am off in my guidance. In the Diamond Approach, my job as a teacher is to serve as an active mirror when something is present in your mandala that you do not understand and for some reason are not paying attention to. Then, to help you become aware of it, I inquire into why you are not paying attention to it. But I do not point to something that is not there in your mandala. In fact, even when I inquire into why you are not paying attention to something in your mandala, or why you do not understand it, it's not to get you to pay attention to it. I am not interested even in this outcome. I am simply curious about your attitude and interested in understanding it, in seeing its truth. In this process, you too might end up understanding your own attitude, and when this happens, it frees your awareness to include more of your mandala.

STUDENT: But sometimes you do direct a student. Sometimes you'll ask, "What's happening in your head right now?"

ALMAAS: Right, but this is because I am aware that there is something happening in your head that you might not be aware of, or might not believe is significant. It is not because I think something in particular should happen in your head.

STUDENT: When you talked to us for days about the wonders of the body of love, weren't you orienting us toward the notion that this would be a good thing to experience?

ALMAAS: Yes.

STUDENT: This isn't open-ended inquiry.

ALMAAS: Right. In teaching I sometimes do introduce certain things. At those times, I am not doing pure inquiry, even though inquiry is the central practice in the Diamond Approach. We do many practices besides pure inquiry. Sometimes we do limited or circumscribed inquiry, as when we work on a specific essential aspect. We inquire, but we inquire specifically into that quality of Being, not just into anything that happens to be arising in your mandala. Our central practice, though, is pure open-ended inquiry, which distinguishes the Diamond Approach from most other paths and approaches.

Practices that aim to put you in a particular state have a whole mind-set attached to them, which is the mind-set of that particular state. The problem is that this can become *your* mind-set, providing you with a mental framework, which means a particular orientation toward your experience. And we want to be free from any mental framework. So true meditation, true practice, according to the Diamond Approach, consists of following your thread, which means being where you are and continuing to be where you are without trying to make your experience go in any particular way. This requires practice because most of the time, you do not know where you are, you do not understand where you are, or you are fighting and rejecting where you are.

This is the normal state of the ego-self, for the ego is always trying to get someplace, to make itself be a certain way. The ego-self is constantly judging and rejecting its arising state and trying to fit itself into a certain ideal. It is not just being where it is and allowing itself to unfold freely. As a result, it does not understand where it is, for it is invested in being somewhere in particular, being a certain way, or in satisfying a particular ideal. And even if this ideal is taken from spiritual teachings, the same mechanism of ego activity is in operation. Trapped in the ego-self, you do not trust that Being itself will take you where you need to go.

STUDENT: Then you as a teacher are attempting to sensitize us to the process, and once we're on our own, we're on our own. We become our own teachers, so to speak. And it just looks to some people that you may be interfering or establishing some goal or setting some direction, when in fact you are just sensitizing us to the process of inquiry.

ALMAAS: When I am attuned and the circumstances are right, I am only sensitizing you to where you are. But I am not always able to do that purely. The teaching situation is complex, especially when we have a large group like this. Different students in the group are in different places in their understanding. Usually I am addressing the general current, which means it is not one hundred percent relevant to everybody. Frequently, the majority of the group will feel it addresses their state or condition, depending on my delivery and the accuracy of my perception of where the thread of the group is.

STUDENT: I see how inquiry is a very open attitude. It seems, nevertheless, that it does involve us in efforting to be a certain way, which is that of inquiring, which emphasizes certain aspects of Being rather than others. It emphasizes the dynamic aspect rather than peace or stillness, curiosity more than love. The way we do inquiry seems more open than other methods, but it is not entirely open because as long as I am trying to do anything, including inquiring, it is not entirely open.

ALMAAS: That's not true. You may think of inquiry as a restriction or as a chosen direction, but if you look at it more fully, you will find that this is not so. It is an openness to your experience, but that doesn't mean allowing unconscious, limiting behavior to go unexamined. You are defining openness as whatever happens, even if it is actually a resistance to openness, which happens to be the habitual condition of the ego-self. I am not defining openness as going along with whatever happens without being aware of how open or closed the experience is. If we define openness this way, then most of the time your experience will be that of an unexamined, closed mind. This is the state of the ego-self, which is not openness, and which tends to block Being's optimizing dynamism. There is no spiritual practice then, only ego activity that is compulsively trying to get someplace.

So I do not think that a person who is distracting herself is being open. If a person is going along with a distraction, which is the usual condition of the ego-self, I don't call that openness. Inquiry tends not to go along with distractions; it tends to focus you on what is actually going on. So there is a discipline in inquiry, but discipline does not necessarily contradict openness. In fact, you need discipline for a long time in order to be open because you are accustomed to being closed and distracted.

STUDENT: Inquiry is a direction, however.

ALMAAS: It is definitely a direction—toward openness. That is exactly what it is. It is a direction away from being closed minded and toward being more open minded—which is toward the natural condition of our Being if it is left to its own inherent tendencies.

STUDENT: Is it correct to say that we are doing inquiry in order to get the inner guidance?

ALMAAS: I myself do inquiry because it is fun. (laughter) We can, of course, say that we do inquiry because it opens us up to the Diamond Guidance. You can say that we do it because it moves us toward the optimizing thrust, or because it moves us toward the wholeness. All this is true. However, if you listen to your spirit, your essential being, why is it doing inquiry? Because it is its nature to do so. It is not really for any of those other reasons. Those reasons are hindsights—valid hindsights, but still hindsights. Our true nature is inherently character-ized by an openness and a dynamism toward revealing its potential. And these characteristics express themselves naturally and spontane-ously, sometimes as an open-ended inquiry.

I do inquiry because it is a direct and natural expression of my nature, and not for any reason. I do it in the same way the sun radiates light and the flower opens up. Does the sun have a reason to shine, does the flower need a reason to bloom?

I am saying that the teaching I do here is to guide you into the attitudeless attitude of doing inquiry from the perspective of no reason or aim. We sometimes talk about these spiritual reasons to help us understand the process, but that is because of the limitations of our realization and understanding, not because of the nature of inquiry. Sometimes we use concepts to help us understand the process or to motivate us to engage the process.

STUDENT: At the moment that guidance strikes, does the inquiry have to shut down? When guidance arrives, does that mean you are not open any longer because now you know?

ALMAAS: That is not what guidance means. You think guidance tells you, "Go this way" and then you are off and running in that direction. Guidance doesn't work like that. Guidance works in a micro way: a little bit here, and then, in two minutes, it needs to arise again to show us what is next. The guidance needs to be continuous in the process of inquiry.

I'm trying to clarify what we are doing when we inquire, what we are engaged in. I am not making value judgments about other practices, and I think that many people here are starting to see that. Value judg-ment can be part of the problem in inquiry, as we will see later. There is something, however, that is more immediate in our consideration. We are concerned with what happens when you take a position that a certain state is reality, when you say, "That is the truth, and we are going to go there." The moment you take a position, you lose your thread. You go toward a goal instead of being where you are in the moment. This will tend to disconnect you from where you are, which will disconnect you from the true guidance, which will disconnect you from the optimizing dynamism of Being. I am not saying that one cannot do spiritual practice in other ways, but I am saying that in the kind of practice we are studying, this disconnection will happen whenever you are after some goal.

We said earlier that adopting a position from a certain teaching, teacher, or philosophy is one form of goal orientation to avoid. I will continue to delineate some of the other ways in which you can disconnect from your personal thread. These situations are all problematic for your inquiry because they go counter to the natural unfoldment of Being.

CONDITIONING THROUGH PERSONAL EXPERIENCE

The barrier to inquiry, to finding your own thread, can be a state posited by your own past experience. Disconnection can happen even out of experiences that arise from the true dynamism of Being. For example, you work on yourself, and one day you experience a wonderful state. You inquire into it and understand it, and you also really like it. If you have not already been clobbered by this dilemma many times, your mind will begin to look at your experience from the perspective of the state you just encountered. Your whole soul will try—perhaps subtly and imperceptibly—to balance herself, correct herself, in order to reproduce this state in the next moment. You thus become conditioned by something you have experienced yourself.

So the barrier to inquiry, the barrier to finding your own thread, can be a state posited by your own past experience. Your past experience might even be of the ultimate state, enlightenment—if there is such a thing. You then become prejudiced by your own enlightenment, which of course becomes an ideal to orient yourself toward. So your attitude is no longer completely open. And if this state is not your thread at the next moment, Being is not going to manifest in this way. Your aim of again attaining this state, regardless of how subtle that aim is, will become an obstacle to the free unfoldment of your soul, to the optimizing dynamism of your true being. You might not notice any gross self-manipulation, but the more subtle interventions, such as starting to think from the perspective of the state when the state is not present, can be easily overlooked.

Suppose the state that you have reached is of empty and undifferentiated Being that has no particular quality. You might begin to inquire with the idea already in the back of your mind that this is what you are again going toward. But that is not fundamentally different from the ego attitude of trying to be one way or another. The danger here is that experiencing and liking a particular state might become an orienting factor for your consciousness. But what if the Absolute wants to manifest in you as something different the next moment? Maybe you cannot tolerate the Absolute in its undifferentiated qualityless condition, so the Absolute manifests itself to you in another way—in the quality of compassion, for example. You might start to feel warm and gentle in a very differentiated way. If your orientation is toward something undifferentiated and unspeakable, you are liable to misinterpret the compassion. You might not see it, and you might even push it away. Then you become disconnected from your own thread, which also means that your inquiry is not open ended.

So the end state you posit can be something you have taken from an external source or from your own experience in the past, but neither of these is different from having an ego ideal. Taking a position is identical to developing an idea from your childhood that you are going to be a good girl, a strong boy, or a loving person. In either case, an underlying background goal is orienting your consciousness, though perhaps unconsciously and subtly, in that direction. You end up trapped in the same process, and it does the same thing to you—it disconnects you from your personal thread, from the truth of your experience in the moment.

THE TRAP OF COMPARATIVE JUDGMENT

The moment we posit a particular state as ideal, we also fall into the mode of comparative judgment. We're comparing where we are now with that ideal state. This becomes a fertile ground for the superego. The superego loves this position. This is exactly the gap it needs to enter into your experience. When you make a comparative value judgment, you become engaged in: "Here's where I am, and over there is where I am supposed to be. Where I am is not as good as where I'm supposed to be, so where I am should change to be that other place." When you say this, you are rejecting where you are at the moment. And when you reject where you are at the moment, not only do you disconnect from your personal thread, you also disconnect yourself from your true nature, from your beingness itself. When you reject where you are at the moment, you cannot simply be, because merely being means not acting on yourself in any way.

Comparative judgment disconnects you from Being whether the comparisons you make are accurate or not. This happens when you take a position about what's supposed to happen and then try to practice from within that context. For example, you may realize that the way you are right now is not the fullness of humanity; it is not the most realized, most whole, deepest possible condition. You may be aware that feeling compassionate toward someone would be more effective than the resentment you are feeling. And sometimes you can't help but know that there are conditions that feel better than what you are feeling at that moment.

But if you use that understanding to judge where you are, to reject where you are and try to manipulate yourself to fit better into your ideal of where you think you should be, you are engaging in the normal ego activity of rejection. This will merely inhibit your development. No matter where our particular focus is, the orientation of the Work is always to align ourselves more and more with the nature of Being itself.

So the question is, how do you act when you are tempted to try to change yourself in this way? You act according to the recognition that your ideal or preferred state has no judgment! You don't reject yourself or manipulate your experience. You remember the wisdom of that supposed ideal position, rather than focusing on your memory of how the ideal state feels and trying to reproduce those feelings.

So to continue the example: If you're feeling resentful, you might remember how much better you feel when you are compassionate. You remember that when you're compassionate, you feel open and caring, so you tell yourself, "I should be caring," thereby rejecting your state of resentment. Does that work? No. The compassionate state itself doesn't have the attitude of rejecting you or your present state. Engaging in the rejection of any experience will go counter to this compassionate state and not toward it. This is a difficult lesson to learn, but if we inquire long and sincerely enough, we will probably get it at some point.

But comparative judgment is a trap that all beginners fall into. Whenever a teaching is formulated, you take it to mean that you should change your state in order to accomplish the ideal of that teaching. You can't help but take it from a comparative perspective. And you then run all kinds of trips on yourself. But this trap is not something that needs to continue forever, and the sooner we are free from it, the better it is for us.

How can you know and understand what is possible for you without judging or rejecting where you are right now? This is difficult, but it is exactly what is required of us in order to practice inquiry. It is possible because Essence does present itself before we are one hundred percent realized. The guidance of essential presence itself makes it possible to learn to attune ourselves to our true nature because, as the presence manifests, it informs our consciousness of the right attitude, the right direction, which is beyond judgment.

Essence never judges. Essence never tells you that you shouldn't be this way, that you should be some other way. It just gently and lovingly melts the position you're in, without judgment or rejection. It melts it with acceptance, with compassion, with understanding, with love, with sweetness. It reveals a deeper possibility.

COMPARING YOURSELF WITH OTHERS

Comparative judgment and disconnection arise not only from positing an ideal condition to move toward, but also by comparing your experience with other people's experiences. This might occur especially in group settings where people express themselves freely in reporting their experiences, getting feedback, or informing the teacher what is going on with them. So if you are listening to people talk about experiences of red diamonds, boundless love, or whatever, it's easy to fall into the trap of comparing their experience with yours and judging the situation.

This comparative judgment can go either way. You can say, "Well, I don't experience things the way that person did; that means something is wrong with me and I'd better change my condition right now." If you do that, you end up hating yourself, and as that hate increases, you will probably end up hating the other person too. That's a natural development if we take the position of comparative judgment. You can also make the judgment the other way around: "Oh, my experience is better." What you might do then is reject the other person or feel superior, which is again a position of ego, and that will disconnect you from where you are that you think is so wonderful.

There's another alternative that is more aligned with the truth, which is that everybody is where they are. You are where you are, and what's important for you is to be where you are with full awareness. To be fully where you are *is* your realization. What's important for the other person is to be where they are. That is *their* realization. I am being authentic and doing the best I can if I am in touch with where I am and following that thread. Where I am is not a static thing but a dynamic movement that will go wherever it will go. As I stay with the continuity of being where I am, my experience will deepen and expand and reveal more.

True sincerity and honesty are not reflected by the attitude: "I'll stay where I am because my state will grow and expand, and maybe in a couple of months, it will become as good as the other person's." That attitude shows that you are still caught in a comparative judgment. The absence of comparative judgment means that you are where you are, accepting wherever you are with a delight, a joy, a satisfaction, a peacefulness. It doesn't matter whether where you are goes somewhere or not, nor does it matter where it goes; it doesn't matter whether your state is going to be like the other person's or not. What's important is that you are where you are, and that you are authentic in your experience.

Comparative judgment is a big barrier. It is a very powerful barrier even though it is very subtle. But subtle doesn't mean unimportant. This barrier affects your state, your experience, and even your perception. It pushes you this way and that way. It is a big veil over your perception that makes it impossible for you to realize where you are. So if we understand and embrace the attitude of open and open-ended inquiry, and if we integrate this dimension we're discussing, the dimension of the Point Diamond, we are not concerned whether where we are is better or worse than where someone else is. Someone else's experience can actually become a source of learning rather than generating comparative judgment and rejection of oneself or the other. When someone expresses something that you don't know, that can help you be open to other possibilities. In fact, when you're curious about what you are hearing and learning, the communication will influence you, and your state will shift one way or another as you consider both that influence and your own experience.

On the other hand, let's say that the person is communicating something you're already experiencing. You might also learn something from that. "Oh, this doesn't happen only to me. Maybe it happens to everybody under these conditions." Now you have a further insight and understanding about what you are experiencing. So you might feel supported. You might feel that human beings are similar in a particular way, and this may open up your appreciation for people or for the other person.

Practice Session: Your Relationship to Goals and Comparison

The deepening of your personal inquiry will be supported by exploring your relationship to goals and comparison. You might want to take the time to do your own inquiry into this question. How do goals play a part in your inner process? In what ways are you influenced by the spiritual reading you do, the stories you hear from other people, and even the experiences you have yourself? How do these influences affect your ability to stay in touch with your own inner development?

Once you have answered these questions about your experience in general, you might want to take a closer look at them in a specific context. Here's one possibility: Bring to mind the different ways you see yourself as a seeker. For example, you might experience yourself as the devotional type, as more oriented toward an intellectual approach, as a serious, disciplined meditator, as someone for whom service is an essential part of the journey, or some combination of these. Can you identify any goals that are linked to your sense of self? When you read or hear about others' journeys, do you tend to compare your inclinations and personal style to theirs? Do you experience yourself losing touch with your own process when this happens? If you shift from one mode of seeking to another, do beliefs based on past experiences you have had in one mode tend to interfere with the unfoldment that occurs within another?

A PATH OF FREEDOM

So now we have the understanding that taking any condition or any state of realization as an aim can adversely affect our process; the aim can distort it and might actually block it. As long as we have this attitude of trying to influence our experience toward a particular direction—whatever that direction is, and whether it has its source in our childhood, our adult life, our spiritual experience, or a spiritual teaching—we're going to have difficulty with the dimension of the Point Diamond, because this dimension means hanging loose, simply being without a position.

Many of the traditional paths that use techniques oriented toward accomplishing certain states teach their students in advanced stages of practice to let go of those techniques. This is referred to in different ways: the end of the search, nonmeditation, beyond practice, and so on. This relates to the kind of open-ended inquiry we are talking about here. But the difference is that nonmeditation is inherent in our way of inquiry from the start. It is the approach we use in our work from the beginning of the path of inquiry, not only in advanced stages of realization. We don't have to wait until we reach a certain state to engage this free attitude. We can let ourselves be from the beginning. We may not be able to do it, because it's subtle and tough. But at least we know from the beginning that ultimately there is no point in efforting. We make effort sometimes because we have to, because there is no other way. But we know from the start that effortlessness is the way.

We can engage in comparative judgment and its attendant rejection in any of its forms, or we can merely continue inquiring. Inquiry is always for the purpose of finding out the truth, so it does not need to be motivated by comparative judgment. It is motivated purely by the love of truth. Inquiry can continue whether we are in an enlightened state or caught in an ego reaction. And whenever judgment arises, we can inquire into it like anything else.

When you really like to discover the truth, when you just like to see and feel what's true, this indicates that you like being yourself. It is lovely to be where one is without rejection, without the need to be somewhere else to be okay. In this place, the heart opens up, and there is enough space to feel joy. There's contentment and peacefulness, and a personalness to the contentment and peace that gives the feeling of intimacy. You are intimate with yourself when you're simply being where you are.

PART THREE

———

Diamond Guidance

CHAPTER 12

Guidance of Being

THE GUIDANCE THAT INQUIRY INVOKES, which is the guidance relevant for our Work, is not the simplistic kind of guidance that many people believe in today. Guidance doesn't mean that somebody will tell you, "Don't do this, do that." In your meditation, you won't necessarily hear a voice that says, "Tomorrow you should meditate for only thirty minutes, not forty-five." Guidance doesn't appear as an angel standing in your room and telling you, "Yes, marry her, she is the right person." That can happen, but that is not what we mean by guidance in the Diamond Approach. The kind of guidance needed in inquiry is an intelligence inherent to our Being that will guide us through our development, to unfold our soul to maturity and realization.

Various teachings have different formulations that suggest different ways to listen to or connect with guidance. In the Diamond Approach, guidance is connected to the comprehension of the messages and indications that are arising in all the levels and parts of our experience. Guidance doesn't appear only, or mostly, in the form of an angel or a wise old woman or man. It usually appears in the context of our normal everyday experience: in our relationships with our family and friends, in the state of our physical body, in our job situation, in what we feel and what emotional conflicts we are having. We want to be able to discern the guidance in all of these experiences so that our soul will unfold toward optimization.

And since our mind can never know all the elements and forces involved in our experience and unfoldment, we need to listen to the guidance of Being itself—the guidance that is an expression of the intelligence of Reality. This is inherent to our Being, whose intelligence is in contact with everything.

DYNAMISM AND THE OPTIMIZING FORCE

This chapter will lay the ground for understanding guidance, by presenting a view of what guidance means and how it is relevant to inquiry. We begin by looking more closely at the dynamism of our Being, because we cannot understand what guidance is if we don't understand that dynamism and its optimization. If we don't have an appreciation or an understanding that there is an evolutionary force at work, then guidance becomes something completely different; it becomes the guiding of a being who doesn't have a potential. But we have a potential, and this potential has a force, and that force embodies an intelligence.

These concepts can also be seen in relation to the soul. As we have discussed, our soul is a living organism of consciousness. It has a dynamism inherent to it, and a dynamic force that powers it. The soul is a presence that is continually moving and changing; it cannot be static. The dynamic force underlying this constant change possesses an evolutionary bent, an optimizing property. It inherently tends to move the soul toward more optimal experience and life. It brings in more life, more energy, and more light. It is an organic, nonmechanical force that evolves and optimizes our experience. And it empowers our soul to develop and unfold, not in isolation but in relationship and response to what is going on in our life. In that sense, it is a conscious force, an aware, intelligent force.

This optimizing force manifests in many ways. Normally it manifests in actual states, experiences, perceptions, and various life situations and opportunities. But it also manifests in guidance. The optimizing force appears in the optimization of your experience, and guidance is one specific form of this optimization. One way of stating it is that the optimizing dynamism is the force, and the guidance is the eye of that force. Or—returning to our spacecruiser metaphor—the optimizing force is the drive of our spaceship, and the guidance is the sensor array and data analysis systems needed for its navigation.

We tend not to see the dynamic quality of our soul directly, especially its optimizing tendency. But if we reflect on our experience, we can discern this tendency. For instance, if we are sincere with ourselves, we realize at some point that we want to experience love. The soul inherently wants to give and receive love, to expand and deepen love. Our soul also seems to like it when things are true and genuine; she naturally wants to go toward more genuineness and authenticity. She also naturally prefers to feel more open, relaxed, and happy.

We take all these values for granted, but they are actually indications of the dynamic optimizing force of Being in the soul. That is exactly how the force manifests in our experience: as a tendency toward maximization of love, pleasure, openness, truth, and authenticity. We are not like machines that run according to a certain programming. We have motives and drives that spring from the depths of our Being and impel us to go in certain directions, causing our experience to develop and evolve toward optimization and enhancement.

Our situation is not so simple, however, for sometimes we move in directions that are not healthy or useful. We sometimes move toward destructive aggression, revenge, ignorance, stagnation, or toward contraction instead of expansion. Therefore, to understand the evolutionary or optimizing force and its underlying dynamism means to see that the presence of the optimizing force also indicates the presence of barriers to that force. It is difficult to conceive of an optimizing force without also picturing what resists it: barriers to go through, obstacles to overcome, and issues and conflicts to resolve.

DISTORTIONS IN THE DYNAMISM

One way to conceive of the dynamism of Being is that it's totally free and unprejudiced, and open to all possibilities. It can manifest itself in a positive or a negative way, in evolutionary or devolutionary directions. This means that the optimizing force can appear in its primordial state—that is, free and unhampered—or as distorted and constrained. Either way, the optimizing force is always working, because it is inherent to our humanness. We sometimes just don't see it as optimizing because it is filtered through barriers that distort it.

All of our experiences, all of our perceptions, are basically due to the dynamism of our Being. And all of them reflect the optimizing force functioning in either a straightforward manner or a distorted manner. There are, in other words, no accidental experiences, no chance inner states. Whatever arises is in us, whatever we experience in the world is a response, or manifestation, of our Being. And our Being is functioning as optimally as it can, given the presence or absence and the quality of our filters.

Many kinds and levels of distortions can exist. There can be a slight distortion, as when another car comes across the road you're driving on and won't let you pass. The optimizing force in this case can manifest as your finding another route around that other car. If it is more distorted, it might manifest as your getting irritated and angry, or grumbling under your breath about the inconvenience. You might yell at the other driver to get out of the way. Or, if the optimizing force is very distorted, it might even manifest in some crazy way, such as your pulling out a gun and shooting the driver for being in your way. All of these responses are a function of the optimizing force.

You are going someplace, and you want to get there—that's where it all starts. *How* you get there depends on you. It depends on whether there are distorting filters and what they are. The fewer filters you operate with, the more the optimizing force will function from its own radiant intelligence, with its clarity, strength, power, and sensitivity. The more your experience goes through filters—the ignorance that comprises our ego structures, beliefs, images, and fixed patterns—the more it becomes twisted and distorted. Then your actions can seem counter to optimization.

OPTIMIZING OUR DEVELOPMENT

The direction of the optimizing force is toward developing and unfolding our experience so that we can actualize the complete human being that we are, the wholeness we can be. However, we do not have to think in terms of goals, for this would be anthropomorphizing Being's dynamism. Being's gravity simply moves it toward settling into its original, primordial, and pure condition, just as turbid water tends to settle, returning to its clear and transparent original condition. We recognize this gravitational pull of true nature as its optimizing force, for optimal experience is nothing but the experience of true nature.

Being is always inherently optimizing our experience. The optimizing force is aware and intelligent, trying to go around obstacles or go through them, whichever way will allow the optimization to continue. Realizing that our experience, both inner and outer, always reflects the action of our Being's dynamism means that, in principle, it is always possible to know whether we are aligned or not with the optimizing force of Being, to discern whether we are progressing, backtracking, or on idle. We don't need someone else to tell us. All the information we need is in our experience at each moment if we can perceive it clearly.

How do we come to know our relationship to the optimizing force? It is not enough to simply pay attention to our thoughts, or our thoughts and feelings, or even our thoughts, feelings, and behaviors. We must open to all dimensions of our ongoing experience, which might include sensations, beliefs, attitudes, judgments, preferences, patterns of attention, and so on. Our awareness of all these dimensions will clarify the nature of our soul's unfoldment in the moment and also reveal the degree of our alignment with the optimizing force that is moving us—that is, whether we are evolving, devolving, or stuck, the only three possibilities.

In other words, if by opening to an awareness of the totality of our experience, we see that our soul is actually moving in a direction contrary to openness and luminosity, then we recognize that we have not been aligned, that we have in fact been distorting our unfoldment by being out of touch with the optimizing force.

THE DESIRE FOR GUIDANCE

Guidance is a way of referring to the discriminating intelligence of this optimizing force of our Being. So experiencing guidance does not mean that you are a child who is going to be taken by the hand from one place or experience to another. Guidance is the accurate discerning of the optimizing direction for experience, moment to moment. It is needed when the soul is not living from her true nature—when she is in the familiar situation of obscuration and distraction.

If the soul is operating from her own inherent capacities—from true nature—she will not need guidance for her development. Then unfoldment will happen on its own because that is what an optimizing force means. It is a force within our soul that is intelligent, responsive, and aware. It will respond to things accurately, intelligently, and appropriately to develop the soul in the best way that she can develop. And that is what we want when we seek any kind of guidance—internal or external. Inner guidance means the directing of our unfoldment so that the unfoldment will optimize itself all the way to wholeness. Inner guidance guides the soul in her unfoldment so that she will unfold in the right direction, correctly, toward maximizing and optimizing her life and experience.

The more deeply we become involved in our unfoldment and the more we align with it, the more our external life situations become part of that unfolding. Issues such as which girlfriend or boyfriend to have, which business to be in, where and how to live, and so on, will become subsumed into the unfoldment. This is not necessarily true at the beginning of the journey, and it depends on the relevance of the particular situation to the overall unfoldment of the soul. For example, sometimes deciding which job to take is crucial for your unfoldment, but sometimes it isn't. Guidance will function to help you see which job to take if that choice is relevant for your overall unfoldment. All the practical choices we have to make in life can be within the range of inner guidance if we look at them from the perspective of what will optimize our overall development.

In other words, what determines whether guidance will function or not is not what you want the guidance for, but what your motivation is. If you want guidance about a job because you want to make more money, that is not relevant for the guidance. If you want guidance about jobs because you want to see which one is going to enhance your soul's development, you will probably get guidance. So the more aligned and attuned we are with our optimizing force—with the inherent evolutionary movement in our soul—the more the guidance arises. That's why people who are externally oriented tend not to be guided in the way we are talking about here. They are being guided, but by external considerations.

This principle of the relationship of motivation to guidance is also fundamental in one's work with a teacher. A teacher functions basically as the guidance, or as the representative of the guidance. This means that the teacher is aiding the development and unfoldment of the soul, functioning in alliance with the optimizing force. If you want your teacher to help you solve a problem because you don't like feeling bad, you will likely be frustrated with your teacher's apparent lack of interest in your goal. However, if your desire is to understand what is creating this problem in your life and what it means for your development, your teacher's guidance will likely feel responsive and helpful.

In the Diamond Approach, the reason one needs a teacher is that one is not yet attuned to one's own inner guidance. In time, you learn from your external teacher how to orient toward your own deeper unfoldment, and thus to become a guide to yourself. In that way, you reconnect to your inner guidance, which simply means that you can recognize how the optimizing force is functioning in your life.

Practice Session: Your Relationship to Inner and Outer Guidance

This would be a good time to look at your own relationship to both inner and outer guidance. Do you see your own experience as a potential source of guidance? Do you believe that guidance must come from some source other than you? If you are currently working with a teacher, how is the guidance you receive from him or her different from or the same as your inner guidance? Do the two work together? Do they seem antithetical at times? Do you have different expectations of outer guidance than you have of inner guidance?

If you are not currently in relationship with an outer guide or teacher: Do you seek out guidance or desire it? If so, what would you want guidance for? Have you had an experience of your own guidance? If so, what seems to cut you off from that experience at other times?

HOW GUIDANCE MANIFESTS

Guidance manifests in many ways and means many things. But what is really happening when we say we are getting guidance? We are recognizing the discriminating intelligence of the optimizing force. We are seeing whether a particular direction is going toward more optimization, or, if there is a distortion, what the nature of that distortion is. The messages of guidance that we get are nothing but the comprehension of whatever experience is going on, and the meaning or significance of that experience. You become guided about whether or not you are going in the right direction, how you may be stuck, what the difficulty is, how to go about dealing with the difficulty, and so on.

Thinking of guidance as a voice or a person telling you to do this or that indicates that you are not in touch with your own optimizing force. You are identifying with a child who is in need of a parent's guiding hand for wisdom and direction. But the reality of our Being is that we have an inner force, an inner life that wants to express itself and actualize itself. And it is constantly doing that—in all kinds of ways, some successful, some not. Guidance is then a matter of recognizing which ways are successful and which ways aren't. We need to know where our unfoldment has gotten bogged down, and how. That means that we really need to listen and receive the manifestations of the optimizing force in our experience. Only through understanding these impressions can we begin to recognize the messages of guidance—the signposts along the path of our continuing development.

Guidance works in many ways, not always by giving you flashes of insight and understanding about your situation. If you need to learn about being vulnerable, for instance, it will place you in a situation where you get threatened. The manifestation of relevant situations is one effective method of the guidance. So, as in this example, if a threatening situation shows up, and you believe that you need to learn to *not* become vulnerable, then you are not reading the guidance correctly; you are reading it according to your filters and obscurations.

Guidance, then, can create barriers for us so that we pay attention and learn. But in a deeper sense, it doesn't need to create barriers, because the barriers already exist in the obscurations that distort our perceptions. So what we call barriers, or difficult experiences and situations, are nothing but the optimizing force coming through our filters and manifesting as a certain kind of experience that we find painful and perceive to be a barrier. If we understand the meaning of that experience, however, we have recognized the guidance.

For instance, let's say the optimizing force is taking you toward the quality of peace. Stillness and peacefulness happen to be the next things for you to learn. But you hit a certain barrier, which is a deep longing for your mother. The conjunction of the two—the movement toward the peace of Black Essence and the longing for your mother—may appear as a pattern of falling in love with people who have dark features. You find yourself always attracted to women with black hair and dark eyes. Every time you fall in love, it feels great. You feel, "Now I've got it, now my love is going to be peaceful. Now I'm going to have what I want." But then you keep losing your lovers; the relationships never work out. You are seeing something true about the peacefulness—that it has to do with the blackness and the darkness. But it is mixed up with a need that you haven't finished with: You still want your mother. So this combination manifests as falling in love with someone who is like your mother: a woman who also is like peace—dark.

You could call that a barrier—you might even say that the optimizing force has created this barrier. It is more accurate, though, to see it as a manifestation of the optimizing force as it interacts with your mind. If you are attuned to the guidance and you are really observant, you might realize while you are fantasizing about your dark-haired lover that what you are seeing in your mind is that black, shining hair. That might make you wonder, "Why that black, shining hair, why always black, shining hair? What does that make me feel?" You might discover that it gives you a sense of richness, a sense of mystery. This line of inquiry will access the guidance, which will lead you to what it is you are really after.

Our actual situation is more complex, however, because there is not just you in a static universe. There are other people too, with their own unfoldment and processes, and constant interactions between everybody. Add to that the evolution of Earth, of humanity, and of the whole universe. All of this is being guided. The guidance is not only in the unfoldment of the individual soul; there is an overall, universal unfoldment that has its own optimizing force. And that unfoldment appears in all of us, in all human beings, as it interacts with each person's mind. So the messages that appear in your environment relate to your own unfoldment, the unfoldment of other people, plus the unfoldment of the entire situation around you.

This unfoldment, however, is invisible for a long time because it is so hard to separate our notions of guidance from the early imprint of being led through life by a wise and kindly parent. This deep unconscious association blinds us to the liberating reality of inner guidance. True guidance is nothing but the awareness of the intelligence in the dynamism that permeates all manifestation. As we have seen, the dynamism of Being follows an organic path of unfoldment as it draws all manifestation toward the realization of its true nature. This optimizing force is inherent to the dynamism itself and is therefore operating at all times.

However, at the surface of consciousness where our soul has become identified with external life, the optimizing force is generally obscured by the soul's outward fixations. The unconscious longing for parental guidance continues to dominate the soul's journey through life. From this level, the soul, as it develops, appears undirected, ignorant, and therefore in need of external guidance. As long as our orientation goes outward in order to seek meaning and direction, we will be unable to recognize the optimizing force that is already operating within us. True guidance appears only when we are willing to value our own experience as it is, and in that way attune ourselves to the signs and messages of optimization that are always present in the field of our experience.

CHAPTER 13

True Guidance for Inquiry

THE NEED FOR GUIDANCE

We all need guidance. We need it because we are lost. Without guidance, we will just move from being lost to being lost. Many of us get more lost as our lives progress, even when we believe we know what's going on. This has been understood for thousands and thousands of years by all people who have been guided. Of course, I'm talking about the spiritual journey; I'm not talking about trying to get from your house to somebody else's house, even though frequently we need guidance and directions in that situation as well.

Through trial and error, you can find your friend's house even if you don't have directions—given enough time. But in the spiritual domain, it's not as easy as that. It's not a matter of trying this street and that street until you finally find the right one; you don't even know what is a street and what isn't a street. And even if you can discern what is a street, you can't tell whether it goes up or down. The whole terrain is a new reality. Trial and error doesn't necessarily work, even if we have unlimited time, which we don't. Our time is precious and must be used wisely. So when a person finds guidance, internal or external, that person is fortunate, blessed. And generally speaking, people who are cynical about guidance just keep getting more lost, and don't even know what they're missing.

We are lost because all we have when we begin the journey is what everybody else in society has: a package of experiences, beliefs, and ideas absorbed from the culture and from our parents. All these are expressions of the conventional dimension, the ordinary and prevalent cultural wisdom. This wisdom is not bad, but it usually does not deal with or originate from the deeper dimensions. And we cannot guide ourselves by using the kind of knowledge that comes from the mind that is the product of this conventional dimension. If the guidance comes from the same dimension you are operating in, it is not true guidance yet—at most, it is a limited guidance. True guidance means insight, understanding, discernment, and indications originating from a source beyond where you are, from the dimension you move into as your spiritual experience develops.

Unless guidance comes from that source beyond, we keep moving from one place in the conventional dimension to another place in the same dimension. We haven't got the vaguest idea of what awaits us, of what is possible in our potential. We don't know the extent, the depth, the infinite possibilities that lie underneath the surface. So we tend to judge everything by our knowledge, attitudes, and feelings that come from that surface. We don't know that by taking that knowledge to be final knowledge, we identify with the very barriers that prevent the depth from emerging and guiding us. This is why the conventional dimension is a state of spiritual sleep, of being spiritually lost.

When we recognize that we are lost and that we cannot move out of our lostness with the conventional knowledge we have, we become aware of the terror of our situation. We recognize just how lost we are and how scary that is. We realize that whatever we try to do—read books, practice this or that technique, attend this or that workshop, try to figure out things ourselves—we do not feel any less lost.

Our situation really is much more difficult, much more profound, than we allow ourselves to see for a long time. That's why we speak of the terror of the situation—because it is so frightening to finally realize and admit how lost we are, and how at the mercy we are of so many elements that we have no handle on. The terror of the situation has a lot to do with how much we believe what we think we know, with how much we are caught in the gravity of our planet of conventional reality, believing it to be the center of the universe—and sometimes all that exists. We usually do not realize that our experience of reality has to shift only a little bit and all will disappear, leaving us totally terrified.

Our only hope is a guidance, a discernment, an indication that comes from a realm beyond. There is no other way, there has never been any other way. What you know can only take you further into what you know. Your mind can only take you to another component of itself, it can never take you beyond itself. If we don't open ourselves up to guidance—whether it is coming from the outside or the inside—we are bound to remain stuck. We are doomed to go in circles, orbiting the same planet over and over and over again, gravity-bound.

To get to another planet, we need a spaceship, and the kind of spaceship we need does not exist on this planet. The spaceship we need is a direct manifestation of guidance—the indication, the light that comes through from beyond this reality to show you further possibilities, possibilities you couldn't even conceive of. And when we recognize that guidance, that indication, that insight, that intuition, that discernment, that pointing toward further possibilities, then we open up. At that point, our experience begins to unfold; it deepens and reveals those further possibilities.

THE ROLE OF ESSENTIAL GUIDANCE

As we discussed in the last chapter, guidance is a specific expression of the optimizing force of our Being. The direct expression of the optimizing force is the unfoldment itself, the self-revelation of our Being. It is reflected in the way our experience goes from one depth to a greater depth, from one element to a deeper element, from one dimension to a more expanded dimension. Guidance as a specific expression of this optimizing force makes it possible for inquiry—as an evocation of that force—to engage its power drive, hyperdrive, or even the superluminal drive. It is the intelligence of this evolutionary force. Without guidance, there will be changes in our experience, but no optimization. The guidance guides the dynamism so that the dynamism starts going deeper, which means that our spaceship can leave Earth's orbit and go to other planets. It may even be able to leave the planetary system and travel to another star system.

As the dynamism takes the soul into new realms, our Being reveals many pure qualities, which I have called essential aspects. It displays the quality of Love, the quality of Clarity, the quality of Strength, the quality of Peace, the quality of Truth, the quality of Contentment, the quality of Spaciousness, the quality of Existence, the quality of Passion, and so on. These qualities are elements from the beyond, from the unseen world, and our conventional wisdom cannot fathom them, can't really see or discern their meaning, function, or usefulness.

So how can we discern what these essential qualities are? We need to recognize what they mean; we need to understand how they are related to our conventional experience and how they can optimize our lives. For this, we need a vehicle of understanding—a source of discrimination and knowledge—that originates from the same or a deeper dimension than the one these qualities come from.

The specific guidance that makes this possible is what I call the Diamond Guidance. The Diamond Guidance is itself a pure manifestation of our Being, which is necessary for it to be able to guide us in the essential dimension. Our Being not only displays its richness, it also provides us with the capacity to comprehend, appreciate, and integrate that richness. Without this discrimination, we are only able to approach this richness as candy. We don't understand the significance of the richness, that it is really part of our inner nature, so we just want more and more of the candy—these things that taste sweet and wonderful but are separate from who we are.

DIAMOND PRESENCE

Essence manifests as many elements, many aspects, but it also manifests on many dimensions or levels of those aspects. For example, when you experience the Strength Essence—the Red Essence—you can experience it on many levels of refinement, subtlety, or depth. At the beginning of essential revelation, it's just the Red Essence. You feel the redness, the heat, and the strength, but your understanding and knowledge of the aspect is not precise. Your understanding can still be influenced by your conventional knowledge—by your reactions and beliefs. However, in another dimension of Essence, the experience of the aspect itself and the comprehension of what it is are inseparable. In this dimension, the experience of the Red Essence and the understanding of what it is arise as the same experience, so our comprehension is free of the influence of our mental concepts, free from the conventional dimension of experience. The insight about the Red Essence is now protected by the new level of manifestation of the aspect. This means that as the Red Essence arises, there is inherent in the very experience of it an exact understanding of what it is.

This kind of knowledge is not available in the conventional dimension; it is not conventional wisdom. In some sense it is a magical property, because there is no rational explanation for it. So this knowledge of the Red Essence does not arise from our storehouse of acquired knowledge, it arises independent of our mind. It is real knowledge, authentic knowledge, because you didn't get it from someone or something or arrive at it through logical analysis or deduction. It is a direct knowingness, a new basic knowledge. It's an insight that comes from the very depths of the Red Essence itself. The Red Essence is stating what it is. Not, of course, through one word, one sentence, or one insight, but through an entire gestalt of understanding. And there is no question here about the accuracy of the new knowledge; the only barrier that arises is the veil of our conventional knowledge reacting to this new knowledge and trying to distort it.

However, if the Red Essence arises in this new dimension, which I call the Diamond Dimension, then any conventional knowledge that is trying to impose itself on the true, direct knowledge of the aspect will be exposed. The Diamond Guidance manifests at this point because this capacity of knowing can withstand and transcend the dullness of our conventional knowledge and manifest the truth about the Red Essence. Independent of our subjective mind, it can show us what is objective and what is not. It can let us know what is and what is not completely precise. That's why we say that the aspect is arising on the diamond level: It has clarity, precision, and indestructibility.

On the diamond level, we don't experience the Red Essence in the usual way, as a red fullness, flow, or fire. If it occurred in this way, our knowledge of the Red Essence would be susceptible to our conventional mind, to our beliefs and reactions. Instead we experience a red diamond, a faceted ruby. There is a precision in the experience of a red diamond, an exactness and definiteness. These characteristics simply reflect the fact that we are experiencing the aspect in such a way that its meaning is inseparable from the direct experience of it. We know precisely what the Red Essence is because we are experiencing the Red diamond, which is experience and knowledge as one. So, without the diamond level of experience, there would be no possibility of precise knowing, and hence of Diamond Guidance.

Only people who have experienced the diamond level know its reality. People who have not experienced it cannot know it. This is true about any form of deep spiritual knowledge, for this kind of knowingness does not exist in the conventional dimension. That's why when one *knows,* one seems certain and definite, for one is in touch with the source that is the knowledge itself. It is only then that a person can function well as a guide, not before.

So if we are not in touch with that power, with that manifestation, with that diamond level, we are not in touch with the Diamond Guidance. Guidance means that Essence arises in such a way that it reveals its own truth, its own meaning, its own significance, its own operation, its own function, its own effect. It gives our soul and her intellect the capacity to discern on the essential level. And the capacity to discern on the essential level means the capacity to discern independent of knowledge on the conventional level.

That doesn't mean we can't use the conventional level. When we operate from this Diamond Dimension of Essence, we do use words and the concepts underlying them to transmit and reveal direct knowledge. Words and concepts, which exist on the conventional level, are empty vessels that can carry something that is beyond them, but they are not knowledge itself; they are attempts at elucidating knowledge in order to communicate it. The knowledge itself is experienced, is sensed. When the aspects arise on the diamond level, they impact the soul by touching it in such a way that the soul starts having spontaneous insights about its experience. The diamond quality touches the substance of the soul, which starts to open up, allowing the knowledge that is coming from that aspect to arise. The soul becomes receptive to a knowledge that comes from beyond, from the unseen world. It is revealed knowledge. It is no longer merely the experience of Essence, it is essential wisdom.

Inquiry can open us up to the possibility of revealed knowledge. Although inquiry, exploration, and research by themselves do not lead to wisdom or revealed knowledge, they can help us see our barriers—our beliefs and prejudices—so that we can open up and be receptive to the revelation of direct knowledge. Inquiry invites Being to manifest its secrets, and this manifestation is revealed knowledge, new basic knowledge, timeless wisdom.

We begin to recognize the Diamond Dimension itself as all the essential aspects appear anew, in the diamond form. Now, instead of experiencing a fluid or formless presence, we experience a faceted bright diamond, a ruby, or an emerald, for instance. In the emerald experience, we have the sense of loving-kindness and warmth inherent to Compassion, but with a precision, a definiteness, and an exactness not familiar in conventional experience. The diamond restructures the soul in such a way that its experience is now inseparable from insight, from direct knowledge. Understanding, then, is simply the stream of structuring of our soul by the diamond and what it is communicating.

Revelation, insight, or direct knowledge is nothing but the impact of the essential diamond presence on the soul. The soul's experience is affected and structured by the diamond presence, rather than being patterned by ordinary knowledge. The diamond presence also gives us a sense of precision, definiteness, and objectivity that we call understanding when we describe it. The understanding itself is not the words, rather it is the actual new structuring of the soul. In other words, the arising of Essence impacts our consciousness in such a way that an essential experience arises, a new unfoldment happens. The diamondness of the essential presence gives us the experience of a precise and sharp delineation, a knowingness, a discernment of what is arising. This is real understanding.

Most people take the description of an experience to be the understanding. However, when we use the word "understanding," we mean the actual impression in the soul created by the arising aspect. This is a felt experience, a tasted, touched knowledge, with a direct discrimination of different patterns, flavors, and textures. The discernment of the pattern—not the description or the communicated words—is the understanding. Communication is the use of words taken from the conventional dimension to try to express the already existing understanding. Understanding is experience, but experience with precision and clear discrimination.

What is meaning, in this case, and how does it relate to understanding? Meaning is nothing but the recognition of the structure and pattern of our experience. Meaning is not a word, it is a discernment of what an experience is. When meaning pervades experience, it transforms it into understanding.

In the Diamond Dimension, all the aspects—Compassion, Intelligence, Will, Truth, Joy, Peace, Identity, and so on—arise in the diamond form. This means that each aspect of Essence will arise as understanding or, more precisely, as inseparable from understanding. Will, for example, arises as a new patterning of our experience in which the meaning of Will is already clear in the experience itself. Thus Will arises as essential wisdom.

DIAMOND STRUCTURES

Depending on the situation, the Diamond Dimension manifests as a field in which the various aspects operate as diamonds, or it arises as one presence in which all the essential diamonds are integrated into a single structure, one operating vehicle. Instead of experiencing one diamond at a time, we experience all the diamonds arranged in a particular structure, such as a chandelier, a cathedral, or some other distinctive form. There are many of these vehicles, each of which is an integrated form of the Diamond Dimension in a different shape or configuration. So Being not only manifests itself in aspects, but also in combinations of aspects that we call Diamond Dimensions or Diamond Vehicles. The Diamond Guidance, though experienced at times as an aspect, is actually one of these vehicles.

The Diamond Guidance is an essential presence made out of diamonds, in which all the aspects combine together as one beautiful, colorful, luminous vehicle—not unlike a spaceship—in a precise, delineated form. And since each aspect manifests here as the understanding of the aspect itself, the structure that combines all of these diamonds into one presence operates as the vehicle for understanding in general. This vehicle then functions as guidance on the diamond level. This is a direct description, not a metaphor, of what the Diamond Guidance is.

In inquiry, we learn how to open to the Diamond Guidance so that it will descend into our soul and guide her. This is something magical, really, in the sense that it is not part of our ordinary experience. And because integrated in it are all the colored diamonds, the Diamond Guidance makes it possible for the soul to understand all the aspects, their functions, and their effects on the soul. It is what reveals the meaning and understanding of each aspect, dimension, and manifestation of Being on all levels. It is this manifestation—the Diamond Guidance—that is the true, specific source of the Diamond Approach.

As the source of revealed knowledge, Diamond Guidance arises in a way that doesn't correspond with our rules of logic or the laws of cause and effect in our ordinary experience. Consequently, revealed knowledge cannot be proven in the conventional sense. The same is true of spiritual knowledge in general: It cannot be proven according to the standards of the conventional dimension. However, it can be proven in the spiritual dimension because the standards of proof at that level are different. When we try to logically prove to somebody who doesn't know about the essential dimension that there is such a thing as the Red Essence, for instance, we are bound to fail. You can describe certain experiences associated with the Red Essence and the person may be inclined to feel that there is such a thing, but you cannot really prove that it exists.

THE FUNCTIONS OF DIAMOND GUIDANCE

The Diamond Guidance functions in many ways, all of which are expressions of guidance. How it functions depends on the intensity of your present need, on the depth of experience that is manifesting, and on your receptivity. Receptivity means your capacity, your level of development, your openness, your trust, and your sincerity.

We can recognize the functioning of the Diamond Guidance through its impact on the soul. The soul experiences the structuring brought about by contact with the Guidance* as giving her certain potentials. The Diamond Guidance is thus the source of various capacities that are fundamental to the soul's unfoldment. Depending on one's level of

---

*Whenever the word "guidance" is capitalized, it refers to the Diamond Guidance.

awareness and realization, the Guidance may be felt as the source of these capacities or as the functioning of the capacities themselves.

Here we will look at the most significant of these endowments made available to the soul through the presence of the Diamond Guidance: the capacities for insight, discrimination, direct knowledge, understanding, objective perception, and articulation. All of these capacities operate together in the process of inquiry. In the next chapter, we will explore further the ways in which the Diamond Guidance works directly on the soul to guide its unfoldment.

The Diamond Guidance may appear as a source of intuition and insight—not the intuition or insight itself but its source. As the source, it is the clarity, the light, and the presence that touches our experience and ignites sparks and flashes that we recognize as intuitions and insights. Thus, the Diamond Guidance is the magic source of knowing. When it comes into our experience, it illuminates it. Its illumination comes from itself, not from outside itself; it is inherent, intrinsic illumination.

The Diamond Guidance functions as a source of pure and real knowledge, new basic knowledge, completely fresh discrimination. Because it is made up of elements that are each gnostic, or direct, knowledge about an essential aspect, the Diamond Guidance becomes a source of knowledge about anything it touches in our experience. Real knowledge is not only basic knowledge, but basic knowledge that is free from ordinary knowledge and that originates in reality.

The Diamond Guidance also functions as a capacity for true discrimination. Because each aspect is now discriminated objectively and precisely, the Guidance, which is the vehicle formed of these aspects, has a profound and precise capacity for discrimination. It can discriminate the false from the true, and it can distinguish various shades of truth as well.

We already have a capacity for discrimination in the conventional dimension—we call it intellect. That capacity for discrimination deepens and becomes much sharper when the Diamond Guidance affects our consciousness. In some very real sense, our ordinary capacity for intellectual discrimination arises from the Diamond Guidance. The degree to which our discriminating intelligence has developed, however, depends on how in touch we are with this diamond manifestation of Being. The farther away from it we are, the less sharp our capacity for discrimination is.

Intellectual discernment is an expression of this inherent discrimination, but the capacity for discrimination that the Diamond Guidance provides is not only on the intellectual level. It is on the feeling, experiential, sensing, and perceptual levels as well. The discriminating capacity of the Diamond Guidance can be seen and appreciated as the prototype of the capacity for discrimination at all levels. It is the essential nous, the expression in the soul of the universal nous—the wisdom of discrimination.

To effectively and fully operate using the Diamond Guidance, we need to be able to function on all levels of discrimination. It is important to have intellectual discrimination, for example, not because we are primarily intellectual, but because intellectual discrimination is necessary for describing a feeling, a sensed discrimination, or a perceived one. It is also necessary to have emotional and sensate discrimination to appreciate the subtleties in our lived experience. The Diamond Guidance, in the arising of basic knowledge, gives us the discrimination on the essential level—the spiritual level—but it also sharpens our discrimination on all the other levels, because it is the prototype, the Platonic form, of the capacity for discrimination in general.

We have already discussed how the Diamond Guidance gives us the capacity for objective understanding. Objective understanding is the felt sense of the pattern of meaning in our experience. Since our experience is continually unfolding, understanding is not a static thing but an unfolding pattern of meaningfulness. This meaningfulness can be expressed in concepts and words that we take from our ordinary knowledge; nevertheless, it is independent of ordinary knowledge. Objective understanding is the flow or stream of real knowledge. The flow of new experience is unfoldment, but understanding is the flow of meaning in this unfoldment, which is inseparable from the unfolding experience itself. Objective understanding is a diamond flow.

However, unfoldment can happen without understanding. For example, I may be experiencing a fountain in my chest manifesting different qualities and colors. We would call this perception of the spontaneous arising of immediate experience unfoldment. But I could have this experience without its having any meaning for me and simply relate to it as an unusual, pleasurable occurrence. When the qualities I am perceiving also reveal their meaning and significance, we call it understanding: "I can feel that the fountain arising in my chest reflects the opening of my heart, revealing its true nature as an overflowing fullness. Now I am understanding what is going on."

It is this capacity for effective understanding that makes the Diamond Guidance the revealer of truth in its various dimensions. By giving us the capacity to understand the pattern or structure of our experience, it reveals the truth of our Being.

The Diamond Guidance brings a clarity and precision into our relationship with our ongoing experience, whatever it is. The diamond level of consciousness impacts us by enhancing our perception, our articulation, and our inquiry into what we are in contact with at any moment.

When the Diamond Guidance is present, it gives us the capacity for precise, objective perception in terms of seeing, hearing, touching, tasting, and smelling, as well as emotional feeling and inner sensing. It affects our perceptual capacities in such a way that they become crisp and distinct, transparent, and free from the dullness of accumulated past knowledge. So it makes our perception clear and objective.

The Diamond Guidance also enhances our capacity for articulation. The articulation of experience requires many capacities, one of which is the knowledge of words, syntax, and grammar. But we cannot articulate our experience if it is not first delineated and discriminated clearly in our awareness. If the structure of our experience is not clear to us, how are we going to articulate it, even if we know the right words and how to use them? If our experience is vague, our articulation is also going to be vague. So the Diamond Guidance not only brings a sharpness and precision to our experience, it also helps us to be precise and clear in our articulation, by imbuing our expression with its own properties: precision, sharpness, clarity, objectivity, and discrimination.

The presence of the Diamond Guidance activates, enhances, and sharpens our capacity for inner investigation, exploration, and study. Inquiry comes into its own now, guided by the objective discriminating intelligence of Being, as we will see in future chapters. At this stage, we are engaged in the hyperdrive travel of the second journey. Now, for example, we can discriminate the effects of our past on our present experience and attitudes in greater and greater depth. And through direct knowledge, insight, and understanding, our inquiry can unfold with more efficiency and dynamism at all levels.

Due to all these capacities, the Diamond Guidance functions as teacher, guide, and also as friend. It is the prototype of the friend who truly wants us to return home to what we love most. It is the prototype of the teacher who can reveal to us objective knowledge of reality and our relationship to it. And it is the prototype of the guide who recognizes the meaning and significance of our experience and how it is unfolding toward our true home.

CHAPTER 14

Guidance as Gift to the Soul

THE UNFOLDMENT OF THE SOUL is a truly mysterious process. If we try to analyze it, we find that it is very complex because the elements involved are infinite. But we need to discern only certain factors, outlines, or patterns—we don't actually need to know all the elements—for the unfoldment to happen. Our Being possesses an infinite redundancy, meaning that even if we see only some of the patterns, the Diamond Guidance will still emerge.

So recognizing some of the patterns in our experience begins to liberate and orient our consciousness to receive the Guidance. It is as though our atoms need to be aligned in a certain direction by a set of magnets to create the right space for the Diamond Guidance to descend. This is the function of open and open-ended inquiry—to be the magnet orienting our consciousness with a burning question.

When inquiry opens up the soul and orients her toward receptivity to guidance, one may experience the arising of the Guidance as a descent of presence. The Diamond Guidance descends, and it is as if a spaceship has just landed. The power and magnificence of the descent is not unlike what was portrayed at the end of the movie *Close Encounters of the Third Kind,* when the mother ship lands. The air becomes electrified; all is still and yet pulsing with a brilliance of dancing colors and qualities. One may hear the powerful hum of the spaceship's engines. One can feel a sense of elegance and delicacy. Then consciousness begins to attain a quality of precision, a quality of brilliance, and a quality of exquisite, sharp clarity. It is no longer the normal conscious-ness that is inquiring but the consciousness pervaded and transformed by the pure light of the Diamond Guidance—the variegated, precise, diamond-like brilliance. One may become aware of a sense of divinity and purity, a sense of otherworldliness that has come into this world.

The experience of the presence of the Diamond Guidance is nothing like our ordinary feelings and emotions. It is a feeling of another kind, a freshness and purity that pervades the consciousness of the entire soul. We may feel touched from within by a light that is not only sweet, loving, and kind, but transporting and pure as well. This extraordinary presence changes our experience completely; it is as if the atoms of our consciousness were being cleansed with Arctic ice that has never been touched, with a sense of precision that is crisp and fresh. The sharpness of the diamond consciousness is like the sharpness of an ice diamond: It is always melting at the point where it touches the consciousness of the soul—yet it never loses its precise edge.

The essential qualities appear now as precisely cut diamonds of vari-ous colors and qualities. We experience Strength, for example, as an exhilarating, strong sense of precision, with aliveness and beauty. The joyfulness of the Yellow aspect has an intense kind of sweetness that is almost overwhelming. In comparison to these essential qualities, our usual experience is old and stale. It doesn't have the possibility of true vibrancy or alive consciousness, where each atom feels as if it could open a thousand miles wide and explode at the same time with a delicious, tingling energy.

The experience of Essence on the level of the Diamond Guidance is a kind of consciousness that memory cannot capture. You either expe-rience it now or you don't know it. Even if you've experienced it continuously for ten years, the day you stop experiencing it, you can't remember its quality precisely. It has to be that new and immediate to be known.

INVITING THE BLESSING OF DIAMOND GUIDANCE

In other traditions, the Diamond Guidance is sometimes called the angel of revelation, the holy spirit that brings the word or message from the source. It is the angel that guides us to the Beingness that is our ground, our nature, our source. It is the true friend, the total friend, because the Guidance's only concern is for you as a soul to go back to your source, to be who and what you can be, with total acceptance, total support, total guidance, total kindness.

The soul needs to place herself in the right attitude for this kind of blessing to come. You have to do the work of correctly orienting yourself. Basically this means harmonizing your consciousness with the mode of presence and operation of the Guidance. This is what we are exploring when we discuss inquiry—the right orientation, the right posture, the ways of being and functioning that will invite the Guidance. When we are learning the proper attitudes of inquiry, it is as though we were building the platform, the flight deck, where our spacecruiser can land. Then our inquiry becomes illuminated and guided. It is inseparable from the actual unfolding experience, the actual revelation.

For this to happen, we need to orient ourselves in such a way that our love is for the truth, which is ultimately our true nature. We have to be pure of heart, which means that the whole world with all of its temptations and promises will have to be our second priority. Our love for true nature has to come first. For the Diamond Guidance to come, we have to feel, even if just for a second, that we really want the truth for its own sake regardless of any other considerations. When it does come, we recognize that giving up the world wasn't that much of a sacrifice. What we receive is infinitely more precious, infinitely more fulfilling, more beautiful, more exquisite; we recognize that what we get is the best thing possible. We recognize that the world, and our life in it, is merely a place, a context, a universal vessel for that preciousness to arise. We see that the world is not valuable in and of itself; it exists so that the preciousness of true nature can come into our lives.

Before we can truly say that we are spiritual, we have to recognize that spirit is paramount and the world is only the experiential locus where the experience of spiritual realization can happen. Without this dimension of realization, the world is not only a place of suffering, it is a forsaken world. It is an empty world. It doesn't truly have nourishment, only the illusion of nourishment.

This is one important reason why our inquiry needs to be open and not oriented toward any goal set by the mind, for our mind is oriented toward achieving what the world promises. More than anything else, the seduction of the temptations of the world is what limits our openness. If we knew what is possible for us as human beings, if we just had a little taste of what it is like to behold the Guidance, we wouldn't squander one minute of our life pursuing the promises of the world. The sense we get when we feel the presence of the Guidance is not only wonderful, not only a blessing; it feels right, it feels as if that is what is supposed to happen. We start to recognize our human birthright. We begin to understand what we are here for—why this world exists, why we are alive.

THE EXPERIENCE OF DIAMOND GUIDANCE

When the Diamond Guidance arises, it is like experiencing the descent into stillness of a diamond-like vehicle, so graceful and fine that you can only think of it as an angel or a divine emissary. Not that it looks like an angel with wings, but it has a sense of purity, of divinity, of a transporting quality of consciousness, otherworldly yet infusing this world with light and goodness. It is perhaps these qualities that have caused it to be perceived as an angel in the context of a different logos, such as Christianity.

It actually looks more like a spaceship than what we call an angel. It is a latticed structure of myriad diamonds of pure consciousness. Each diamond is a specific quality and color, and together they create one unified structure that sits on a round platform of pure solid silver, which then sits on a larger round platform of pure solid gold. Gold is the essential truth, and silver is the will of the truth, and together they function as the foundation for all of the qualities that appear in diamond form.

This Diamond Vehicle can be of any size. It can descend and fill a whole room or a whole valley. It can be experienced as arising in the soul. Its mode of operation in inquiry can be experienced at the forehead as an illumination, a pulsation, a tingling, a dancing of presence. But the Diamond Guidance may also descend into the heart or the belly. It can be very tiny or as big as a galaxy. Space doesn't bound it. It is amazing that there is such a presence.

The experience of the Diamond Guidance itself is that of a presence, an awareness inseparable from the sense of hereness. There is a subtlety and a refinement in this presence, a purity and a gentleness. It is both full and delicate, with a gracefulness to the delicacy, a flowing ease that is inseparable from a peaceful quietness.

The discrimination of the Diamond Guidance is different from that of a mind full of thoughts and agitation. Here the understanding is quiet, peaceful, and settled. And this quietness, this peacefulness, this settledness, which is inseparable from precision and clarity, functions as the source of insight and understanding. Insight arises with clarity in the environment of peace.

The presence of the Diamond Guidance is a stillness that is inherently luminous and illuminating, as if the presence had atoms of illumination, of clear light, that illuminate with various brilliant colors. These colors affect our heart with feelings of warmth, sweetness, wonder, and joy, giving a sense of sacredness or holiness to the presence.

Usually the Diamond Guidance operates as a presence in the center of the forehead. When it arises in support of discrimination and understanding, we become aware of an expansion as space opens up in the forehead. With that expansion comes a sense of peacefulness; the Black aspect at the center of the forehead opens and we feel stillness and spaciousness. When the Diamond Guidance arises in this peacefulness, we feel a delicate presence, a pulsating energy that possesses a sense of clarity and transparency, an intelligence, an illumination. This delicate, pulsing, breathing presence appears as understanding, as insight, as intuition. As the forehead opens, we feel the Diamond Guidance as a tingling, an energetic throbbing—but very delicate, very soft, very subtle. If we are not attuned, we might dismiss it as just a physical twitch. Or if there is a lot of blockage, as is often the case in the early stages of our development, the diamond might feel hard. Due to the blockage, it can't get through, so it feels almost like a rock. But if we are relaxed and open, we feel it as a softness, a delicacy.

This delicacy gives our perception a sense of clarity and precision, such that whatever we experience is not only open and clear but also clearly defined. Colors are vivid, sensations are clear, and our thoughts are slow and lucid. Our thoughts become like a gentle flow that expresses the understanding of our experience.

We integrate this presence—that is, we become able to understand

and investigate in this delicate, peaceful, clear, open state—as we understand inquiry and understanding itself. As we inquire into understanding and inquiry, and understand better what they are and what they require, we integrate understanding, which means that we integrate the Diamond Guidance. But first we need to open up to it. We need to allow it to descend into our consciousness before we can integrate it and operate with it.

ATTITUDES TOWARD GUIDANCE

The Diamond Guidance will not descend if we are not open to it. We can block it, or we can refuse it. We can make ourselves thick toward it, resistant to it and its operation. So in order to be open to it, we have to be open to the possibility of this kind of guidance. Inquiry itself opens us up to our experience, but if our openness is limited by the belief that there is no such thing as this presence, then our inquiry will not be sufficiently open. Then we cannot be receptive to the Guidance. If you believe that discrimination can only be mental or that all knowledge is only the normal conventional knowledge and that no other kind exists—that there is no possibility of having direct revealed knowledge—then you won't be open to the functioning of the Diamond Guidance, in yourself or in anybody else.

So we need to look at our positions and attitudes regarding such precise guidance. We need to see and expose our beliefs, our intellectual and emotional biases, and our orientations about such a definite, real guidance. We do not need to adopt a belief in it, for that will not work, but we need to be open to it as a possibility. All of us are full of beliefs, ideas, and reactions about guidance—its possibility, its dependability, its realness, its precision. And if we are influenced by these preconceptions, we won't be open to the Guidance. We will only prove to ourselves again and again that there is no such thing.

Practice Session: Your Experience of Guidance

What are your beliefs, hopes, fears, doubts, and expectations about real guidance? You began this exploration in chapter 12; now you can go deeper and be more specific in your exploration with this expanded awareness of what guidance can offer and how it operates in your soul. Do you have faith that guidance will show up for you? Do you trust that you can follow it and not be led astray?

To answer these questions, look back into your personal history for your experiences with guidance. Can you identify situations in which you called on guidance and were disappointed that it did not appear? Or times when you followed what you felt was clear inner guidance and felt somehow betrayed by the outcome? What feelings or thoughts tend to arise in you when you have the impulse to call on guidance? How do they relate to your past experiences? To what degree is your basic relationship with guidance relaxed and open? cynical? fearful? blocked? How has your personal history shaped your sense of the specific ways that guidance can or can't show up and work in your life?

So in some sense, the first job of the Guidance is to reveal our barriers against it. As it descends, it pushes against and challenges the parts of our mind and psyche that deny it, that don't believe in it, that doubt it. And these are the first places that we need to expose and understand. You need to find out for yourself whether you believe in the existence or the nonexistence, the possibility or the impossibility, of such a presence, of this specific, precise, articulate, dependable and objective guidance or guiding principle. You need to explore your beliefs and your positions, and your intellectual, emotional, and historical biases. If we say there is no such thing as guidance, for whatever reason—because we were deceived or disappointed before by erroneous guidance; because we've never experienced inner guidance; because we never felt that anyone helped and guided us; or because we are cynical about such things—it will block us from opening to the Guidance.

It is true that guidance is a grace, a benediction, a blessing from beyond, from the source that is unseen; however, blessings do not arise if we are not open to them. Blessing does not try to bore into us like a power drill. It is very delicate in its operation. It doesn't come to us when we are defended, doubtful, resisting, and disbelieving in guidance. It arises only when we relax, open up, and don't take positions against it. This has to do with the very nature of how our consciousness functions. Guidance is not something sitting over there saying, "Pay attention to me—I'm here to guide you." It has to do with our own inner Being opening up and revealing some of its possibility. Only when we open up through whatever means—necessity, calamity, or true sincerity—does the blessing arise and guide us.

Even if you believe in such a guidance, but you believe that the guidance must arise as a person with a long beard, as an angelic being, or as a diamond spaceship, that could block it as well. Both negative beliefs and positive beliefs become barriers if they are inaccurate. So openness means that you are spacious and allowing about the possibility that guidance exists, that it can come in unfamiliar forms, and that you are interested in finding out what is true. So I am not saying to replace negative belief with positive belief. Openness is the absence of belief.

FAITH IN GUIDANCE

As our understanding unfolds, the Diamond Guidance takes us from knowledge to mystery. The Guidance reveals to us the truth and richness of our Being, but the more it reveals these things, the more we are in touch with its mystery. This is a paradoxical, strange, and mysterious situation. Over time, the Guidance reveals to us more and more about our true nature, reality, and about what and who we are. However, the more knowledge and understanding we gain through this revelation, the more we approach the depth, the essence, of our Being, which is mystery. So the increasing and deepening insight and knowledge do not lead us to a satisfying conclusion about who and what we are. We don't end up with a static picture of ourselves and reality. The more understanding and insight we have, the more our soul becomes transparent to the mystery, and the more we recognize that our Being is mysterious.

So understanding doesn't create or add anything; in fact, it removes what is there to start with. That is why ego tends to experience objective understanding and guidance as some kind of a loss. The ego keeps losing its beliefs, ideas, positions, identifications, and attitudes. But the more we feel this loss that we experience as understanding, the more in touch we are with the essence of our Being, and the more mysterious we recognize it is.

In other words, Being reveals its mystery through revealing its truth. By revealing to us more of what it is and how it functions, it shows us how little we know, and that the more we know, the more we realize how little we know. This shows us that the operation of guidance is to take us from a place where we feel we know to a place where we don't know—a place of mystery. The Guidance takes us from a place where we know how to walk to a place where we don't know how to walk; from a place where we know how to know to a place where we don't know how to know; from a place where we can find our orientation to a completely new place in which we feel disoriented. That's why the Guidance always takes us to the precipice, and why following the Guidance always means jumping off the cliff. It is always taking us to someplace new that we are not familiar with.

The unfamiliar place may be an aspect of our unconscious, a forgotten part of our childhood history, or a certain element of our essence or our soul that we have never experienced. Just as a child doesn't know what growing up will bring the next day, in spiritual development we don't ever know how or where we are going to be in the next moment.

This brings in another consideration, which is that we not only need to be open to the Guidance, we also need to have faith in it. We need to have confidence in its efficacy and capacity; otherwise, it won't guide us. Or if it is already guiding us, we won't *know* that it is guiding us. We have faith in our guidance when we have the trust that it will take us to the places we need to go. Faith is the confidence and trust that the Guidance will send us in the right direction, that it won't deceive us, won't lie to us, and won't put us into situations that we can't handle. If we don't have this kind of faith, our openness to guidance is limited, which will limit the capacity of the Guidance to help us.

There's no rule that says you have to have faith in the Guidance for it to work; this is just the nature of reality. The fact that Guidance will keep taking you deeper into the mystery is the reason why you must have some faith in it, why you must trust where it is taking you. Since you do not know where it is going to take you, there is no other way but to trust it and take its promptings on faith. Opening up to the Diamond Guidance requires a lot of faith, confidence, and trust, because as we said, to move from knowledge to mystery means to continually jump into unknown places. So just as seeing our beliefs, positions, ideas, and biases will open up the space for the Guidance, developing faith and confidence in the Diamond Guidance will open up the peacefulness and the stillness required for it to operate.

When we have preconceptions and presuppositions, and believe that we know what is going to happen or should happen, we assume that our mind can be our guidance, and that is how we block our connection or access to the Diamond Guidance. If we have faith in the Guidance, we can accept its direction; we can follow it and depend on it. This ability to accept, follow, and depend on the Guidance can become a way of life. And it needs to become our way of life if our evolution is going to be truly guided.

DOUBTING THE GUIDANCE

A subtler level of this issue is doubt about guidance. Let's say you are aware of the Guidance, but you doubt whether that's what it is. You doubt its reality, its truth, or its dependability. This doubt blocks the Diamond Guidance from continuing to operate. For example, if you have worked with the Black Essence, you know that its center—what the Sufis call *khafi*, "the hidden"—is in the middle of the forehead, which is exactly where the Diamond Guidance functions. The subjective state of doubt is one of the main barriers against the peace of Black Essence. Doubt of any kind will block this center because doubt is partly an expression of hatred; it is not the same as authentic questioning or curiosity.

All of us have doubt about all kinds of things, depending on our ignorance or our history: how many times we were hurt or deceived, how often we were betrayed, disappointed, or abandoned, and so on. From these experiences comes ambivalence—a combination of hope for what we want and fear that it won't happen. From this ambivalence, doubt arises, and the doubt has a destructive, hateful quality in reaction to our history of pain and betrayal. As a result, the doubt tries to discount the insights or the messages of the Guidance. Openness to the Guidance can easily be destroyed by doubt. Normally, when truth first arises, it is very subtle, very delicate; if we doubt it right away, we kill it before it develops.

However, not to doubt doesn't mean not to question. Questioning means curiosity and openness, while doubt expresses skepticism and fear. Curiosity says, for example, "Well, let me find out. I am open and curious and I'm happy to really inquire into whether guidance exists or not." Doubt says, "I don't know if there is such a thing, and I am suspicious and distrustful."

Some people say that doubt is good because it is a scientific approach. That is not true. The scientific approach is not doubt or skepticism; it is inquiry, it is questioning and challenging. Doubt or skepticism is a negative energy, a distorted expression of our Being, while curiosity and inquiry is a positive energy, an expression of the optimizing force. We don't need skepticism and doubt in science; what we need is questioning, inquiry, and a curiosity that embodies openness.

So inquiry, which is questioning based on a joyous curiosity, is not only good but also necessary for invoking the Guidance. In contrast, doubt or skepticism is a paranoid, aggressive attitude that cuts life off before it has a chance to grow. Doubt is a direct manifestation of the absence of faith in guidance. Yet some people feel that doubt is needed to avoid being duped, taken for granted, or led by the nose into something they will later regret. However, the absence of doubt is neither compliance nor dependence but instead a curiosity and openness. Only these qualities will reveal what is truly needed for our soul's unfolding.

Questioning and inquiry evokes and invokes the Guidance through an inviting attitude: "I don't have a position, I don't need to protect any belief or point of view. I am open to finding out what is true." Doubt, on the other hand, is protective and defensive: "I want to protect myself by doubting the truth, the reality, or the existence of things in my experience that I can't explain." So doubt is clearly a different energy than curiosity. The questioning that arises out of doubt reveals aggressiveness, blame, negativity, harshness, and rejection. That is why, in order to open to the Guidance and to the faith needed for following that Guidance, we must really explore the question of doubt. We need to question doubt, inquire into its presence, and explore how it operates. Because if we don't see our doubt, we will be subtly disconnected from our guidance without even knowing it.

Whether it was due to doubt, lack of faith, contrary beliefs, insufficient or distorted parental guidance, fear of surrender, or attachment to worldly rewards, most of us have lived our life without the benefit of true guidance. This has meant being cut off from our soul's depth. We have lived with a diminished potential for discrimination, knowledge, and understanding of the experiences and qualities in our life that touch us most deeply. We have lived in a world devoid of true meaning, using only our mind to make connections and draw conclusions about how best to proceed. Consciously or not, we have looked outside ourselves for teachers, friends, and guides to support us in navigating our life journey, not realizing that the true source of all these functions exists in our own nature.

THE GUIDANCE AS BELOVED

When you have seen through the doubts that block your faith in the optimizing force of Being, your heart relaxes and opens. As your experience of truth in your life deepens, your heart is nourished. As your knowing of the Diamond Guidance as the revealer of truth grows, your heart awakens to what it most appreciates. The Diamond Guidance is the wisdom that leads you home, to the place where your heart knows its greatest joy. This is the land of truth and true nature.

The Guidance is not simply a path to the truth, it is the manifestation of truth, the knowingness of truth, and a discerning intimacy with the truth. So the attitude in the soul that can most directly invite this blessing of truth to arise is one of heartfelt love. This is not only the heart's openness but its active love and interest in knowing and being intimate with the truth. To love to know the truth means to love the operation of the Diamond Guidance. And to feel the love of truth for its own sake means at the essential level, "I'm happy to surrender to the Diamond Guidance." That's why this love is an attitude that more than any other calls the Diamond Guidance to arise and operate.

The heart gets what it wishes for much more often than we think. What the heart deeply wishes for, it ends up having in some way. So if we wish for the immediate and intimate knowingness of the truth, that's exactly what will happen. Diamond Guidance will arise and operate by revealing the truth. The love of truth is not the only necessary element, but it is a basic and fundamental one. We will explore other necessary elements in future chapters.

The essential aspect of Love functions as the motivational energy of inquiry. It is the impulse of the heart, it is how the heart is involved in the journey. Another way of saying this is that when you feel that you love to find out the truth, you're invoking the Diamond Guidance, for the Diamond Guidance is the revealer of truth. It is equivalent to Gabriel, the angel of revelation. Gabriel is the messenger of God, or the truth, and Diamond Guidance is an essential manifestation whose function is to reveal the essential truth in our experience. So when you say, "I want to know the truth," it means your heart wants the truth to be revealed. This is an invitation for the revealer to descend and manifest. The heart is inviting the angel of revelation, the revealer of truth; it is opening the door and saying, "I want you to come and I want to surrender to you."

Seeing all of this, we recognize that when we engage the Diamond Guidance, when we are traveling on Spacecruiser *Inquiry*, we are engaged in a love affair. We have a love affair not only with the truth, but also with the revealer of truth, the angel of revelation. We end up loving the revealer because it is giving us exactly what we love.

So the Guidance is an expression of truth; it is not something separate from the truth. It is the facet of essential truth whose specific function is to reveal that truth. And the Diamond Guidance reveals in particular the basic truth of Being. Its job is not exactly to reveal the details of everyday life; it does not function when you go to the grocery store and want to know about the contents of some canned goods. That's not the kind of truth it reveals, although it can do that if that is what is needed to develop your soul. What it does reveal is your true nature and what you need for this nature to unfold. It reveals what is necessary in your life, what attitudes and directions you need to take, and what supports you need in order for Being to reveal its truth. So it will reveal the truth, the barriers to the truth, and what is needed for the truth to be revealed.

Appreciation for the way that Diamond Guidance connects us with true nature opens up a heart connection with the Guidance itself. It's the same heart relationship that you find between you and your teacher in the Diamond Approach or any other school. The Diamond Guidance is the inner teacher. So you say to the inner teacher, "I am interested. I would love for you to teach me. I will surrender to the teaching. I'll dedicate myself." You would do the same with an external teacher. It's true that your teacher helps you, guides you, and reveals the truth of Being to you. The teacher does these things out of love for the truth of Being. But in the process, you need to love your teacher, be interested, surrender and open yourself up to the Guidance, to the teaching. The same thing happens on the inner level because Diamond Guidance is the true inner teacher, the guide of Being.

The Diamond Guidance is one of Being's greatest gifts to the human soul. When it descends into our consciousness, this living presence gives us access to the magnificent depth and richness of the spiritual life. It guides our journey of inner awakening. It reveals to us the true meaning of our experience. It aligns us with our potential for Clarity, Peace, Joy, and all the essential qualities of Being. And as we integrate this wisdom of the Diamond Guidance, we come to understand our true home in the larger unfolding of all creation.

CHAPTER 15

Guidance and Understanding

UNDERSTANDING UNDERSTANDING

We integrate the Diamond Guidance when we understand understanding. The word "understanding" is normally used in a more limited way than how we use it in the Diamond Approach. Therefore, we need to discuss understanding more extensively than we have done in previous chapters.

The idea that guidance and spiritual realization can be discovered through understanding our experience is a perspective that is quite accessible to our ordinary mind, even though it is not common in traditional teachings. I like this approach because it doesn't require any esoteric or exotic ideas, beliefs, or symbols in order to engage in the inner work. Understanding is something that we can relate to directly. Our everyday life and our ordinary ways of experiencing and thinking are all we need in order to begin working on ourselves. If we simply deepen these, we arrive at true realization of ourselves without getting into strange or mysterious concepts or rituals.

As we have discussed in previous chapters, inquiry invites the Diamond Guidance, and in turn, the Guidance operates by actively guiding the optimizing force to unfold and develop the experience of the soul. This gives our experience the possibility of deepening and expanding, of optimizing instead of merely repeating itself in customary patterns and concerns. The Diamond Guidance guides the soul through the precise understanding of whatever happens to be currently arising in our awareness, whatever is presenting itself in our experience.

The lack of complete and precise understanding of our experience perpetuates it in a cyclic, repetitive pattern. Therefore, when we precisely understand our experience, it naturally opens up to deeper dimensions. Experience stays on the same level when we don't understand it, but the moment we understand it, it moves deeper. This is a natural law of the inner life: that the understanding of a situation necessitates the awareness of elements that are deeper than how the situation first appears to us.

This precise understanding is not static; it is intrinsically dynamic. It involves change and movement, which means that it involves the element of time. This is because understanding is not a matter of understanding a still picture. It is more like understanding a movie. In fact, understanding requires and implies appreciation of change and transformation. If you experience only one thing, for instance, there is no understanding. If you only feel emptiness, for instance, and absolutely nothing else, no understanding is possible. You will only have the awareness of emptiness. But as the awareness of other things arises, and these things become related to the experience of emptiness, understanding can arise.

So understanding is dynamic in nature. And its continuity is nothing but a deepening of experience, which is the revelation of the hidden potentials of our soul. This revelation does not occur in snapshots— though we often remember it and attempt to hold on to it as though it does—but always as a continuous flow of understanding. Our experience in general is a flow that is always changing, but without understanding, it is usually repetitive; rarely does something new arise.

Understanding is not a matter of bringing something into our experience, and it is not a matter of doing something to it. It is a matter of seeing the true nature of what is there. And as we understand our experience, it will deepen and open up further dimensions. That is the nature of our experience: When we understand it, it opens up. And if we don't understand it, it will stay closed down. Over time, it will tend to become thick, defensive, and repetitive.

In order to see how the Diamond Guidance operates, it is useful to understand the connections between opening up, unfoldment, understanding, revelation, and the Guidance itself.

The Diamond Guidance is the vehicle that opens up our experience, and that opening begins our unfoldment, becomes the unfoldment, and is also an important aspect of the unfoldment. We can see this process, then, as having two sides—opening up and unfoldment. And when we see the complementary nature of this process, we call it "self-revelation." Here we mean self-revelation in the sense that the soul reveals herself.

But self-revelation is actually understanding, because understanding is the disclosing of the truth of what is arising. Thus, the whole process of opening up—which begins the unfoldment, continues as part of the unfoldment, and becomes self-revelation—is what we call understanding. In other words, the opening up, the unfoldment, and the self-revelation together are the understanding. So understanding means both the upwelling of new elements and divulging the significance of these elements. When the Diamond Guidance is operating without restrictions, understanding is the arising of new elements *inseparable* from the recognition of their meanings.

When we say that unfoldment is guided, we mean that it is a deepening revelation of our human potential. We call it guided because it is going toward optimization. We are guided from being closed to being open, and always from a present manifestation to a deeper one. This guidance happens through the opening up of understanding. In other words, guidance is the facilitation of our natural unfoldment.

Diamond Guidance functions through the opening up of our experience, activating it so that it becomes more than simply experience; it also becomes understanding. So our experience itself changes to understanding—it changes from repetitive, everyday experience to dynamic, unfolding understanding. So instead of our just having an experience, the significance becomes available to us as part of the experience itself. Experience divulges its meaning—reveals its significance—through the process of understanding. It is then luminous experience.

UNDERSTANDING AND KNOWLEDGE

We need to distinguish understanding from what is called knowledge. Understanding is not the same thing as knowing. It includes and utilizes knowing and knowledge—knowledge is, in fact, an integral part of understanding—but it is more than knowing and knowledge.

For example, as you inquire into your experience, let's say you realize that you are feeling hopeless. This is knowledge, it is not yet understanding, for even though you know what you are feeling, you do not understand it. But understanding your hopelessness includes—in fact, depends on—knowing that you feel hopeless. The understanding, however, goes further because it is the comprehension of the significance of the hopelessness: how it affects you, what it means, where it comes from, how it's related to the rest of your experience, and so on. When understanding finally reveals itself, it can become knowledge. You can store it as a piece of knowledge, as information in your mind. But as it is happening, understanding *uses* knowledge, yet it is much more than knowledge or knowing.

The other distinction we need to make is between understanding and mental comprehension. Most of us have learned that understanding is a mental process. You associate one thing to another, you reason one way or another, and you arrive at a comprehension that you call understanding. The understanding is ultimately an idea or a mental insight. In the Diamond Approach, we include reasoning and mental association in our use of the word "understanding," but the fundamental element of understanding is direct experience, basic knowledge. That is because we cannot have real understanding if we are not in touch with our present experience, if we don't feel our experience fully and intimately.

So when I say that I want to understand what's going on, I don't mean that I intend to think about it and come to a logical conclusion. I mean that I want to first let myself be present in the experience, feel the experience, be fully in touch with the elements of the experience. The more I am in touch with the elements of my experience, the more clearly the experience will reveal its patterns and meanings. This is so because experience is a manifestation within our consciousness, whose ground and nature is knowing luminosity, so being in touch with experience means being affected by that ground of knowing. This revelation of the patterns as an embodied experience is understanding. I can then formulate this experiential discrimination mentally in concepts and words.

So understanding is a revelation of basic knowledge, an unfoldment of basic knowledge. When basic knowledge opens up and becomes more luminous, more direct, and more intimate, we can say that we understand. Another way of expressing it is that understanding is the insightful and experiential discrimination of the unfoldment of experience.

Discriminating the unfoldment involves all of our perceptual capacities. We feel pressure, sense heat, hear sounds, see images, and are aware of feelings, sensations, tensions, and energy. However, understanding is not just the awareness of these phenomena. First there needs to be a precise discrimination of these manifestations. You really must know that pressure is pressure and heat is heat. When you feel anger, you have to know that it's anger, and when you feel love, you need to know that it is love. And this discrimination has to be direct and experiential, not just mental. Understanding begins with recognizing the discrimination, which means that you are in touch with this discrimination independent of thinking about it, even though you might also have thoughts.

Now, the terminology, the words, the labels we use to describe what we are discriminating will depend upon our ordinary knowledge. And as we have seen before, our direct knowingness is not always immediate. This means that our discrimination is usually not pure; it's a mix— the direct knowingness is mixed with ideas and associations. However, over time, our understanding will purify our direct knowing, freeing it from ordinary knowledge.

By discriminating the various elements of experience clearly, you can see their individual significance and the significance of their interrelationships. For instance, you might be feeling heavy in your chest. Discriminating that sensation clearly, you might recognize that you're also shaking, or that you feel a little nauseated in your stomach. Then the recognition can manifest, "Oh, I'm anxious"—and you realize that what you have been feeling is the energy of anxiety. The meaning of these three interconnected experiences—the heaviness, shaking, and nausea—arises as insight, but that insight includes the direct knowingness of these three elements. But the insight brings in a fourth element, which is the direct recognition of the feeling of anxiety. The insight reveals the presence of anxiety. So there is discrimination, knowingness, and also a comprehension or recognition of the meaning and significance of the totality of the experience.

Knowledge can be a knowingness of one element, so it can be a static picture, but understanding is not static, it is always dynamic. As you are feeling the heaviness, the shakiness, and the nausea, they interact and begin to change. The shaking might move from your arms to your chest, and this may decrease the feeling of heaviness. Perhaps the shaking becomes connected with your nausea, and as that happens, you become more directly and specifically aware of the anxiety. The whole picture is always changing. It is a dynamic flow. So understanding is the entire dynamic flow of the comprehension of the knowledge that is discerned in experience, and is also part of that experience. Understanding means that you're fully aware, wholly cognizant; you are in touch with your experience and completely aware of its meaning and significance.

Practice Session: Your Experience of Understanding

In order to better appreciate this meaning of understanding, you might want to take some time to reflect on a particular time when you have recognized understanding such as this arising in your experience. How did you feel when that occurred? What did you notice about how it arose? Did certain elements seem to be significant in the process of coming to that understanding—such as reasoning, direct insight, discrimination, and so on? Was there a sense of immediacy and personal relevance? Did the understanding you gained clarify the meaning of other experiences in your life? Consider the ways that you may have been affected in an ongoing way by this understanding.

When you finish this exploration, bring the question more into present time. Did you feel the process of understanding at work as you did this inquiry? Notice if you can sense the dynamism of the understanding arising and how it moved the inquiry forward.

REVEALING THE PATTERN

Let us assume that this carpet in front of me is your soul, it is who you are. When you look at this Persian rug, you see the fabric itself, the wool. To be completely in touch with the fabric means that you are aware of the wool everywhere it exists, you are in touch with each atom of the fabric. At the same time, you are cognizant of the various patterns in it as you see the various colors. Each one of these colors could represent a quality of experience in the soul. One quality is pressure, another is density, another is weight. You can discriminate all of these when you are completely and intimately in touch with the very fabric of your experience. When the in-touchness with the fabric is sufficiently clear and precise, the pattern of its qualities becomes discriminated. Understanding now is not only the awareness of the various patterns, but also an overall comprehension of the meaning of the patterns, which together form the overall picture.

Usually, the discerning of the meaning and significance automatically opens up the pattern of our experience. As that pattern begins to unfold, it opens up the deeper parts of the soul. This is because the complete meaning of the pattern cannot be discerned in most cases without taking into consideration other elements, deeper elements not manifest in the initial pattern.

Obviously, understanding requires an intimate awareness of experience. It requires intimate contact with your own consciousness—a deep awareness of your thoughts, feelings, sensations, and actions, of all the colors and impressions that arise in your experience. All these must be present in your awareness, not vaguely but in a very clear, crisp way. When our awareness is crisp, we call it diamond-like, for it is very precise, clear discrimination. Red is red, blue is blue, pressure is pressure, and lightness is lightness.

When the pattern is precise and clear, it automatically reveals its meaning: "This red is not only red but feels strong; it makes me feel strong," and "I'm feeling strong in my upper body, but down here in my pelvis, I am feeling weak." That awareness may lead you to understand why you feel strength in one part of your body and weakness in another part and how that affects your experience of yourself.

Reasoning can be part of this process. It is a faculty used by understanding, by the Diamond Guidance. The Guidance uses reasoning in the usual way: You see dichotomies, positions, and similarities, and you can relate what is similar and what is dissimilar; you can synthesize and analyze. But you do these things within the experience, not only in your mind. The mental faculty, the reasoning faculty, is subsumed in the totality of the experience; it is used as one element within it. Reason helps your discrimination by making it even sharper. So reasoning, and the mental operations in general, make use of your previous experience, your ordinary knowledge. When used intelligently, your experience of your life—your conventional wisdom—can be useful in understanding your present experience.

We can summarize by saying that understanding involves three elements: a full in-touchness with the fabric of experience, the precise discrimination of the various patterns of this fabric, and the insightful comprehension of the meaning and significance of these patterns and their interrelationships.

UNDERSTANDING AND UNFOLDMENT

The patterns of experience, as I said, are dynamic and in constant unfoldment. This dynamism and constant unfoldment bring in the question of time. Understanding can be of an unfoldment that spans two minutes or ten years. The time element expands and contracts depending on how expanded your understanding is and how big the pattern you're seeing is. You might be seeing a pattern now that reminds you of a certain manifestation that you experienced last week—or thirty years ago. And this might bring in other elements of your life that will connect with your present experience to help you see a larger pattern. You become aware of the various elements in present experience, you know precisely what each of these is, you're aware of the relationship between the various elements, and you're aware of their relationship to other relevant elements from the past or from other parts of your life. Part of this awareness is mental, in the sense that memory is needed to connect your present experience to other places and situations.

So even though understanding is present-centered and your experience in the moment is the most important element, your past is not excluded. Understanding does not exclude other times and places; everything can be used as components of the information that will help sharpen your discernment in the moment. And the Diamond Guidance is the presence that operates in such a way to make that possible.

The operation of the Diamond Guidance transforms our usual experience into a clear, direct discernment of the meaningfulness of whatever is arising. One way of stating it is that understanding is intimacy with, knowledge of, and insight into the patterns of the space/time fabric of experience. It is as though space/time were a manifold, a fabric that is constantly unfolding, changing in both space and time, and revealing new basic knowledge. But understanding itself is not limited to the patterns within space and time; it can take us further, beyond space and time.

In the beginning of the journey of understanding, our spacecruiser travels within our individual soul; our individual experience is this unfolding fabric. As our experience deepens and expands, this fabric loses its boundaries as the underlying nature of pervasiveness and unity impacts our experience. Then our entire experience—of the whole universe, not just our inner individual experience—becomes an unfolding fabric of manifestation. We are intimately in touch with this unfoldment, understanding it with knowledge, clarity, and insight. The whole universe begins to reveal its nature to us.

Our experience then becomes the experience of realization and the integration of this realization through the continuity of understanding. Realization is not just an insight, it is the continuity of unfoldment of all manifestation, with complete clarity, intimacy, and comprehension. So understanding turns out to be the ongoing life of realization—the continuity of the realized experience, the continuity of the fully aware, fully integrated experience.

Of course, we can put all that we understand into words and write it down, but that is understanding that has become ordinary knowledge. This ordinary knowledge is useful only if it facilitates further experience and understanding. If we just keep our understanding in our mind and think about it, it is not useful anymore. It becomes a piece of ordinary knowledge that can disconnect us from our experience. Holding on to understanding as knowledge is useful only if it opens up our understanding in the present moment. In this way our wisdom and experience from the past can serve to open up our current experience even further.

As our experience continues to open, new elements and new dimensions of experience arise, elements and dimensions that we might not have thought about before or didn't have access to. Then our experience is not repetitive, it is a true unfoldment. Inquiry, with its openness, intimacy, and discrimination, penetrates the fabric of experience and invites that fabric to unfold.

So inquiry invites the Diamond Guidance, and this Guidance is the agency that can directly discern the patterns and their meanings. The Guidance is an operation of intelligence that uses awareness, knowing, clarity, feeling, memory, and reason—uses all these faculties in a way that encourages and prompts experience to clarify itself, and through clarifying itself, to unfold.

During the first journey, in the initial phases of the practice of inquiry, the fabric of experience is our thoughts, feelings, emotions, sensations, actions, and all of our life situations. Later, in the second journey, the fabric becomes more continuously colored by presence itself. By the third journey, there's nothing but the fabric of presence. Then all experience is presence, with the various discriminations in it. So the immediacy and intimacy with experience is complete only in the third journey. During the first journey, we only see isolated parts of the fabric—a pattern here, a pattern there, but with gaps in between. In the second journey, we recognize that there is presence as well. This presence is inherent consciousness that is part of these patterns and moves through them as the most meaningful thread. In the third journey, we recognize that presence pervades all the patterns. In fact, we recognize that the patterns are nothing but patterns in the presence itself. Then the immediacy is complete. Then we are the understanding of our experience at each moment.

PART FOUR

The Essential Aspects in Guidance

CHAPTER 16

Inquiry and the Essential Aspects

WE DISCOVER AN IMPORTANT truth when we begin to experience our essence, or true nature. We find out that Essence manifests in many different qualities—what we have called essential aspects. In other words, not only is Essence the pure and authentic presence of our Being, the ontological beingness of our soul, but this presence manifests itself in and as various experiential qualities that are clearly discernible. So Essence also presents itself as the sweetness of Love, for example, or the warmth of Compassion, or the fire of Strength, or the solidity of Will, or the stillness of Peace—depending on the needs of the particular situation.

In this fourth part of *Spacecruiser Inquiry*, we will study the essential aspects that are central to the practice of inquiry. These aspects, as we will see, form the essential and timeless prototypes for curiosity, discrimination, determination, sensitivity, clarity, truth, and intelligence, among others—the fundamental elements and faculties that make inquiry possible. We will see how they provide the operational supports for inquiry, so that it can invite the guidance of our Being, the Diamond Guidance.

As we go through these aspects one by one in the following chapters, we will come to appreciate how each functions as part of the integrated operation of the Diamond Guidance in the process of understanding. Guidance relies on each one of these aspects in a very specific way, for each provides our process of inquiry and understanding with one or more unique and important elements. These elements operate both as qualities that support the openness of our attitude and as capacities that make our inquiry intelligent and efficient.

The Diamond Approach's understanding of the essential aspects—the various ways that Essence presences itself—is similar to the view of some of the major spiritual teachings, but each teaching has its own way of defining and classifying these qualities, depending on its particular logos, or metaphysical system. The essential aspects are related to the qualities in the various states and stations of Sufism, and to some of the divine names; to the spiritual qualities of the *sefirot* in the Kabbalah; and to the Buddha qualities in Mahayana Buddhism. The view we have developed of these different manifestations of Being, however, is not taken from any of these ancient teachings. It is the result of original discoveries based on a new paradigm that is fundamental to the Diamond Approach.

THE NATURE OF ESSENTIAL ASPECTS

Each of the different ways that Essence appears has recognizable properties and characteristics that differentiate it experientially from the other aspects. Because Essence is not a physical substance, we do not actually perceive its presence with our physical senses, but it can be clearly perceived and recognized through the functioning of subtle inner capacities that correspond to the physical senses. (Chapter 21 explores in more detail the nature of these subtle senses.)

Subtle perception is readily available to some people and not others, but it is an inherent capacity in everyone. With regular practice and careful attention, one's ability to discriminate the perceptual characteristics of inner experience becomes increasingly clear and precise. In time, we can recognize each essential aspect by its texture, color, taste, and so on. Most important, each aspect has a discernible feeling tone—a specific affect or experiential flavor. This becomes more definite and recognizable the more we are able to perceive the other properties such as color, taste, and texture.

Let's take the essential aspect of Love as an example. Love is the experience of the essence of who we are as a pure and authentic presence. It has the feeling tone of liking, of appreciation, which is an enjoyable and pleasurable experiential affect. This pleasurable appreciation becomes more definitely discerned as Love when we recognize the other properties of its presence: when we can taste the exquisite sweetness that is part of the experience of liking or appreciation; when we can sense the softness, smoothness, and lightness of the presence; when we can see the beautiful pink luminosity intrinsic to this feeling. All of these perceptual properties form a unified gestalt that we term the essential aspect of Love. However, the feeling tone is what is more conventionally understood as the experience of Love, and the one that most obviously differentiates it from other qualities. The other properties of taste, color, texture, and so on, are rarely ever known or discerned clearly in everyday experience.

Our understanding of the essential aspects reveals that they are the elements of the authentic experience of being simply and freely ourselves. They are the richness of the free and creative unfoldment of the human potential of our soul. Their presence indicates a measure of freedom in our experience and a degree of openness to the mysteries of our Being.

The essential aspects also form the true and authentic ground for all of our subtle capacities. Sometimes termed the higher faculties, these are the soul's deeper-than-ordinary capacities for perceiving, experiencing, and inner functioning. The presence of each aspect imbues the soul with a certain property of consciousness that opens it up and develops its potential, providing it with a specific subtle capacity or faculty of functioning.

For example, the aspect of Truth, which we will look at fully in chapter 23, possesses a specific affect discernible as truth. It provides the soul with the capacity to directly differentiate truth from falsehood. Without this capacity, inquiry would not be possible as a path of understanding. In other words, the experience and realization of the aspect of Truth activates in the soul a certain faculty that makes it possible for her to recognize truth without having to resort to reasoning or logic. Over time, this becomes the ability to recognize truth directly and with certainty. One is confident that the capacity to discern truth is functioning because one is aware of the presence of the essential aspect of Truth, which is recognized by, among other things, its clearly discernible affective tone. It feels real, dense, warm, and smooth, but above all, has a preciousness that makes it feel very close to our heart, as if it were the depth of the heart itself.

In the following chapters, we will explore eleven different aspects of Essence as they arise in the vehicle of the Diamond Guidance and activate the inquiry process. The first five qualities—or aspects—of Essence are known as the *lataif*. The lataif comprise a foundational group of aspects that operate as explicit manifestations of the Guidance arising in response to basic needs that everyone encounters in the course of inquiry practice. These five qualities are Joy, Strength, Will, Compassion, and Peace. The remainder of this chapter will be a brief overview of the lataif, before we move into a more detailed discussion of each one in chapters 17 through 21.

The other six essential aspects are also operational in inquiry, but usually more implicitly, forming the capacities of its underlying ground. These qualities—Knowing, Truth, Clarity, Focus, Personalness, and Intelligence—refine and clarify our understanding of the nature of inquiry itself. They will be explored in depth in chapters 22 through 27. We have already discussed the contribution of the aspect of Love in chapter 9.

THE LATAIF

What we all wish for ultimately is to simply and authentically be. This wish to be ourselves is the true motivation for inquiry. And this impulse, this motivation, is actually an expression of one of the aspects of Essence—the Yellow latifa. As they are needed, the other lataif arise to support this movement in our soul. So, for example, one needs the strength and capacity to engage in one's spiritual work (the Red latifa), the will to persevere in the face of difficulties, attachments, and conditioning (the White latifa), the perceptual expansion necessary to perceive and understand what one is experiencing (the Black latifa), and the sensitivity to recognize and rest in one's own true nature (the Green latifa). These fundamental capacities of the soul, which are called the five sacred impulses—I wish, I can, I will, I perceive, and I am—are associated with the lataif.

For this reason, the lataif are the most important essential aspects encountered in the development of the soul. This is true especially in the initial stages of spiritual work as the individual consciousness (the soul) opens up to its essential nature. *Lataif* is the plural of the Arabic word *latifa*, which refers to a certain mode of experiencing our consciousness. *Latifa* or *latif* (masculine form of the feminine *latifa*) means literally "subtle, soft, light, delicate, gentle, refined, pure"—all in one unified impression.

We call these aspects of Essence the lataif in accordance with the Sufi tradition, which devotes a specific area of its teaching to them. This does not mean that our view and understanding of the lataif is identical to the Sufi understanding. Our view is similar in some respects because the truth of the inner nature of the soul is objective, and therefore any capable researcher who explores it will reach similar conclusions. However, there are bound to be important differences because the Sufi tradition has its own system and logos, which were developed in ancient times. Our understanding is original and unique to the logos of the Diamond Approach, which has arisen in the current day and age. We will point out only some of the similarities because our familiarity with the Sufi teaching is not extensive.

THE FIVE CENTERS

Most Sufi writers agree that there are five primary lataif, or centers of perception (though some describe six), and there is general agreement about the colors associated with them and their locations in the human body.

The one at the left side of the body is usually called *qalb*, meaning "heart." The color yellow is associated with it. In the Diamond Approach, the state of consciousness here is that of the true delight in which Essence exists in the condition of unadulterated joy.

The latifa on the right side of the body is usually called *ruh*, meaning "spirit" or "soul." The color is red, and the consciousness is of true and real strength. It is like the fire of Essence.

The third latifa is located at the solar plexus and is associated with the colors white or silver. The name of this latifa is *sirr*, which means "secret." The consciousness is that of true will, which is the support for Essence and its life.

The fourth latifa is at the forehead between and just above the eyebrows. It is called *khafi*, meaning "hidden," and the color is a shining black. The consciousness is a state of peace and absolute stillness.

The fifth latifa is at the center of the chest and is called *akhfa*, meaning "more hidden," and the color is emerald green. The consciousness is that of sensitivity, of loving-kindness and compassion.

Our view recognizes that each of the lataif has several levels or dimensions of spiritual perception and experience. This is a significant difference from the Sufi teaching, which associates each of the lataif with a different level of development of the soul. In the Diamond Approach, these different levels of soul development depend on the development of all of the lataif, as one progresses through deepening levels of realization.

In the Diamond Approach, we work deeply with each of these basic qualities of our consciousness in order to activate the inner journey. Clarifying the distinction between these aspects—Joy, Strength, Will, Compassion, and Peace—and their familiar counterparts (or "false" forms) that exist within the conventional reality of the ego helps to cultivate an awareness of our essential presence. Each latifa has one or more personality issues that are universal barriers to the presence of that aspect. This means that working with the quality and its relationship to our experience will also resolve—through understanding—fundamental personality issues not normally understood to be spiritual difficulties.

ACTIVATING THE LATAIF

The Sufis activate the lataif through spiritual exercises, mostly concentration practices, including the visualization of colors, certain forms of chanting called *dhikr* (remembrance of God through the invocation of his names), and concentration on specific locations in the body. All this is done under the guidance of the *shaykh*, or Sufi teacher. The lataif are activated in a certain progression, with some variations, depending on the particular Sufi order or teacher.*

Idries Shah relates the work of some Christian alchemists to the

---

*See Henry Corbin, *The Man of Light in Iranian Sufism* (Boulder: Shambhala Publications, 1978).

activation of the lataif. In discussing the order of activation by both Sufis and alchemists, he writes, "The alchemical exercises therefore aim at activating colors (locations = *lataif*) in the form of crossing oneself. This is an adaptation of the Sufi method which is thus, in order of activation: yellow-red-white-black-green."*

In our work, we do not try to follow any specific order; instead we allow the intrinsic dynamism of Being to activate the lataif in whatever order is needed by the particular individual. We find that the inherent intelligence of Being activates the lataif differently in each person according to his or her specific needs and situation. Our work, therefore, follows the principle of spontaneous and natural opening that is the response of the dynamism of Being to the specific situation of the individual.

Our approach does not emphasize spiritual exercises and concentration techniques, although occasionally we use them as supports for our primary method: the open and open-ended inquiry into the nature of experience. The inquiry process activates the inner dynamism of Being, revealing the inner potential of the soul—including the lataif—as felt or living understanding.

Frequently the lataif are referred to as organs of perception and action or as centers of experience and illumination. This is partly because the lataif are not only different forms of consciousness (or manifestations of Essence, in our terminology), but are also subtle centers where these qualities of consciousness operate. In other words—and this is specially true in the Sufi system—"lataif" refers to both the subtle forms of consciousness and their associated centers at the corresponding physical locations.

In the Diamond Approach, we do not take this notion of centers as primary. We observe that each latifa is more defined by the quality of consciousness than by the physical location. The connection to the locations seems to occur mostly at the initial activation or opening of these qualities of subtle experience. After that, the lataif may arise independent of the physical centers. This means that they may manifest in any part of the body or may even totally transcend the body and its locations. Idries Shah seems to have this in mind when he writes:

---

*Idries Shah, *The Sufis* (New York: Doubleday, 1964), p. 380.

"These Five Subtleties (*Lataif-i-Khamsa*) do not exist literally. They are located in the body because the postures of extending attention to these areas are held to orientate the mind towards higher understanding and illumination."*

Our observations also indicate that, even after their initial activation, the lataif tend to manifest more in their respective centers than in other areas in the body. For example, the Yellow aspect may manifest in any part of the body—even in the head or legs—but it will manifest most often in the left side of the body at the location of the physical heart. Yet as spiritual development matures to its deeper stages, the body loses its significance as a locus of experience. Essential experience begins to transcend the body, in the sense that the presence of Essence is not defined or limited by the boundaries of the body.

HIGHER FACULTIES

Each latifa sensitizes the soul in a specific way to make it capable of functioning in a new mode or possibility. In other words, the activation and the integration of the lataif accesses and unfolds certain deep and subtle spiritual potentials of the soul.

One useful way to view the higher faculties associated with the lataif is through the Five Sacred Impulses, parallel to Gurdjieff's notion of the Three Sacred Impulses. This table highlights only some of the important higher faculties. The Five Sacred Impulses reflect particular capacities available to the soul as a result of the presence of the five lataif. They are:

Color	Affective Tone	Sacred Impulse
yellow	joy	I wish
red	strength	I can
white	confidence	I will
black	peace	I perceive
green	loving-kindness	I am

So, for example, activating the Yellow latifa opens up one of the faculties of the heart, which is to wish, want, or long for what it misses.

---

*Idries Shah, A *Perfumed Scorpion* (London: Octagon Press, 1978), p. 89.

The wish is for what the soul, or its heart, naturally and spontaneously loves. The Yellow latifa is the presence of pure joy and delight, but it also causes the soul to become curious and activates its sacred impulse of true and innocent wanting. This means that the greater and deeper the realization of the Yellow latifa, the deeper the truth one's heart loves and wants to behold.

Activating the Red latifa provides the soul with the strength and capacity to reach and discern what one loves and wishes to unite with. It gives one the energy and fire, the initiative and courage, to go after one's heart's desire.

Activating the White latifa accesses the soul's inner determination and solid steadfastness, which gives her the capacity to persevere and continue, rather than getting discouraged or losing heart.

Activating the Black latifa opens up the subtle perceptual faculties of the soul: those of intuition, seeing, and spiritual understanding.

Activating the Green latifa develops the capacity of the soul to simply be and not do—in other words, to be sensitive to and abide in her essential presence.

In this book, our focus is on exploring how these faculties contribute to the practice of inquiry. This will reflect only one way that the lataif affect the soul and support her spiritual development. Nevertheless, by understanding the role that each aspect plays in facilitating inquiry and our soul's self-revelation, we can appreciate the way that the essential aspects reflect the intelligence and precision of Being's manifestation in our life. To discover this wisdom we once again board our Space-cruiser *Inquiry* to journey with our newfound friend, Diamond Guidance, as we explore its diamond facets.

CHAPTER 17

Yellow

Joy in Discovery

THE ACTION OF TRUE NATURE is self-revelation. Inquiry is our way of doing what true nature does. But we do it from the perspective of the human being—the soul's version of self-revelation rather than that of the Absolute. To move toward enlightenment we have to operate from where we are.

The possibilities of creativity and depth in our soul are unlimited. And the agent of this creativity is the dynamism of our true nature. Inquiry is the ultimate aesthetic creativity; what is being created is life itself. The more our inquiry and the unfoldment of our understanding is allowed, the more we approximate the beauty of God's revelation and the more we appreciate God's face. As we move closer to the original nature of our experience, that experience opens up and reveals the beauty in all things.

Inquiry reveals not only the aesthetic beauty of all things, but also the exquisite meaningfulness and precision of everything. This revelatory process is pure art and pure science at the same time. Each experience unfolds like a flower opening. The openness of our inquiry approximates the vastness of true nature, manifesting as the love of knowing, the love of what is true.

Openness and loving the truth for its own sake are not the only things necessary for inquiry to commence. If one is simply open to experience, inquiry will tend to remain passive and unfocused. And even though love of the truth begins to activate the process of inquiry, a more engaged quality is necessary to invoke inquiry's penetrating and probing capacities. What is needed is an active openness to discovering the truth. Active openness expresses itself in the essential aspects, the pure qualities of Being—and especially in the five aspects of the lataif. In relation to inquiry, each of the lataif becomes an aspect of dynamic openness.

In this chapter, we will explore the specific qualities that engage the dynamism of inquiry through the expression of the Yellow latifa, the aspect of joy. Curiosity, which is a delight in discovering the truth, is one expression of the yellow aspect. Love is the fuel for inquiry, but the spark that ignites it is curiosity. When this quality is present, openness manifests an engaged dynamism, which can then become an active inquiry. Curiosity activates the openness, imbuing it with a vibrant energy and bringing more personal involvement in the experience. It's just like the captain of the Spacecruiser *Inquiry* giving the order "Engage!"—and the spaceship is set in motion in a particular direction or toward an area of exploration.

So openness is the basis of inquiry, but love expressed as curiosity specifically invites the Diamond Guidance. This active edge of openness is needed for the truth to be revealed. Then there is joy, curiosity, a happy excitement to find out. The not-knowing becomes the beginning of adventure. And because you don't know, it is more exciting. Joy is in the whole process, and the excitement of life intensifies. The soul is turned on to exploring the mystery, and it is curiosity that engages the power drive of your spacecruiser.

There is a relaxed and spontaneous quality to curiosity. This active participation in the investigation has a playful lightheartedness that expands the love of truth in a more selfless way. Playfulness indicates a lack of purpose even though there can be a committed investigation. Inquiry is thus a mirror of Being's unfolding, a process that does not follow a predetermined plan—it is spontaneous creativity.

If you forget the attitude of playful adventure, inquiry will tend to focus more on the ego-self and its problems—the part of you that has the heaviness and pain. This means that you're going to be concentrating on the falseness instead of penetrating to the deeper, essential truth. After a while, you'll see only the surface personality and its painful manifestations. Inquiry needs the quality of joyful adventure for it to move to a deeper level. You need to be playful to open up to things that are light and happy, to things that have sweetness and fulfillment, depth and luminosity.

CURIOSITY AND THE LOVE OF TRUTH

As we have noted many times throughout this book, inquiry begins when there is an active, dynamic interest in knowing the truth, experiencing the truth. If we are present and in contact with our experience, then we have the openness to recognize what we do and do not understand within it. So how does curiosity fit in? Curiosity means: "I recognize that there is something here I do not know, and I want to find out what it is." It's not just "I love the truth" but also "I love to discover the truth." "I want to really investigate, to take this experience apart and look at it, to play with it and experiment with it."

Frequently we are aware of something we don't understand in our experience, and yet it doesn't prick our curiosity. For instance, a person might know that she is often angry, but she doesn't know why, and she is not curious to find out. She might say, "Well, the anger just happens, so I have to live with it." It takes the active engagement of being curious to ignite the process of discovering the truth. It is when we are interested in the truth that we want to dig in and see why we get so angry all the time.

Curiosity is a very important element of our soul, and one that is necessary for our inquiry. Curiosity is a particular expression of the soul that we tend to associate with little children. In their early years, children are curious about everything. For example, when a child is a few months old, he puts everything he encounters into his mouth. He does not want to eat it, he wants to *know* it. The child is really curious: "What is this? What does this feel like? What does this taste like?"

As an adult you have that same kind of deep curiosity when you meet someone and fall in love. The moment that happens, you want to know everything about that person: "What have you been doing all these years? How do you spend your weekends? What do you eat for breakfast? What's your favorite movie? Have you ever flown a kite on the beach?" It's like being a little kid again. And that curiosity is very playful, happy, light; it's not a heavy thing.

I think it is obvious that if you are not curious or if your love for the truth is limited, then you will not become sufficiently engaged or expend the energy necessary to find out the truth. But when you're really curious about something in your experience that you do not understand, the love of the truth will translate into an insatiable hunger—the fuel for Spacecruiser *Inquiry*.

Curiosity expresses this passionate love for the truth, so it wants to be totally immersed in the experience. This force wants to penetrate the situation, to open it up, to illuminate it, to come to know it as fully and as completely as possible. It does not want to just witness it from a distance. Now sometimes the unfoldment can become like watching an intense, thrilling mystery at the movies: You're enraptured and can't wait to see what's going to happen. But even then, you're not just passively watching the mystery, because your own involvement and engagement has something to do with what arises. When your soul wants to know what it feels like—in your body, in your emotions, and in your experience—then you are really curious, then you are really beginning to inquire.

A LIGHTHEARTED PLAYFULNESS

The early stages of practicing inquiry are not easy. We come up against all kinds of resistances, defenses, and blockages. In addition, as things open, a great deal of pain, conflict, fear, anger, aggression, painful memories, and difficult states can arise. Identifying with that content or identifying with the desire to make things better can make inquiry feel heavy, dreary, and serious.

After a while, you don't want to do it. Why inquire if you're going to feel something terrible like that? It doesn't seem like an enjoyable kind of adventure; it's more like some form of torture. So people who encounter a great deal of difficulty or pain from their past can come to believe that the nature of inquiry is to be heavy and serious. And others may feel that inquiry is burdensome because they have to do it to get somewhere, that it is something that is good for them. You might feel you have to do it because your spiritual growth depends on it. That's similar to the way you might feel when you struggle to get good grades on your tests so you can get into a good college.

But inquiry is not a test. It's not a matter of passing or failing. It's a matter of finding out. Let's say you find yourself crying a lot. If you don't take a position about what that means about you, then after a while, what you will naturally start to think is: "That's very interesting. I have to open this up and find out where all this crying is coming from." Not because you want to stop it, but just because you're curious. You look at other people and they don't seem to be crying all the time. So you want to know what makes that happen in you. You're not investigating this to get enlightened; you just can't help wanting to know what is really happening.

When you have this attitude, there is no fear of failure, no anxiety about doing it right—because you have no ideas or beliefs about what is right and what is wrong. You don't know what the result of your exploration is going to be. So with a playful attitude, one isn't afraid of making mistakes. Interestingly enough, when we take this kind of lighthearted approach, when we are playful, the entire process not only happens more easily, but things open up more effectively and we begin to see the truth more precisely. Our experience becomes optimized, maximized.

If we understand that inquiry springs out of the lightness and openness of joyful curiosity, we begin to see that the heaviness and seriousness are not characteristic of inquiry itself. They are only characteristic of some of the content that arises in inquiry and from the beliefs we have about it. So the content can be very happy or very painful, but the attitude of the inquiry itself doesn't have to be influenced by the content. The inquiry itself is an expression of openness, lightness, curiosity and love. When it doesn't have that sense of really wanting to know, of feeling so excited that you can't wait to find out, then the inquiry is not coming from that openness. It's coming from more of a fixed position, with a certain aim or a specific goal. But you could inquire into that. Instead of saying, "Uh-oh, things are heavy—let's stop," or "Let's get away from that," you can inquire into that attitude of heaviness: "Where is that coming from?"

Heaviness cannot be inherent to inquiry itself because inquiry begins with curiosity, which is a delight in the investigation—and that is an expression of love. Curiosity brings to the inquiry a playfulness, a happy interest, a spontaneous, free involvement with the situation, in order to find out what is real, what is truthful. Then the exploration as a whole becomes like play. We know that inquiry is happening, and happening fully, when we recognize a playfulness and a joyful quality, a spontaneous and easy quality, even though there may be pain and suffering.

Playfulness is not just having a sense of humor about the difficulty, though that might be part of it. It means that you're interested in the inquiry itself, not in where it's going. If you're mostly interested in where you're going, things will likely get heavy when there is pain. The openness gets closed down, and the unfoldment will inevitably get stuck. But if you're really interested in the inquiry itself—the movement of the investigation—then even if something difficult arises, it becomes interesting: "I didn't know human beings could experience that much pain." Or, "I can't be *that* depressed I wonder how my nervous system can tolerate that much intensity." If you have that attitude toward inquiry, even the heavy content loses its grip and begins to open up.

When I talk about playfulness, I don't mean that what you inquire into is unimportant for your life. When I talk about being lighthearted, I'm not saying that you should take things lightly—they can be dead serious in terms of their importance. But that doesn't mean you have to be depressed about them, it doesn't mean you have to be heavy and glum. Consider something serious such as getting divorced. Do things work better if you feel depressed about it? That's the way we usually think: "Well, something terrible is about to happen—tomorrow I'm going to get divorced. Feeling miserable is what's appropriate." If you feel depressed about it, you're the one who loses. If you feel open and light about it, you actually might find ways to enrich yourself.

I'm not saying to judge yourself when you're depressed or heavy. Just know that inquiry does not have to be depressing or heavy. We need to appreciate that there can be a playfulness even when the heaviness arises, even when something serious and important occurs in our life. This happy, lighthearted, and playful quality makes our approach to experience much more effective, much more powerful. It opens up the experience even when it is difficult, and may even reveal something in it that is light, that is nourishing, that is beautiful.

And if we love the truth, if we want to find out the truth, there will be lightness and happiness, regardless of what the experience is. Even if you are in the midst of pain, for instance, or have been suffering from rejection or abandonment—if you find something about your situation that is true, a lightness emerges with that recognition, that insight. This shows us that there is great wisdom in our Being. It demonstrates that the liberation of our spiritual nature occurs not through the elimination of the suffering, but through the condition of lightness that comes with our attitude toward the experience—our appreciation of the truth!

AN EXPERIMENTAL APPROACH

Playfulness also means an attitude of experimentation. What we're doing is experimental; we don't have to get stuck with any particular method. Let's say you're exploring the fact that at certain times you get too excited, more excited than you can handle. You can inquire into that situation in all kinds of ways. One way is to reflect on the excitement itself and try to see what that brings up. But nobody said there's only one way to do it. You can, for example, notice situations when you get more excited than at other times and see what it is about those situations that gets you so excited. You might read books about excitement, talk to other people who have a similar experience, or even do things to get yourself excited and then watch what happens.

So when we say inquiry is a natural thing, we don't mean that you necessarily wait for things to happen before you can explore them. You can get engaged and become active in your inquiry. You can have an experimental attitude and try various things. You might use movement or visualization, work with your tension patterns, or get some body-work. You might go to a movie to bring up certain feelings in you. Or you might talk to somebody that you know affects you in a specific way and then inquire into that experience.

Nobody said you have to sit in a chair to inquire, nobody said you have to tell someone your experience to inquire. You can kick and hit, and that could be part of your inquiry. You can yell and scream and that could be part of the inquiry. In other words, there are no particular techniques that you have to adhere to in order to truly inquire. What determines whether your inquiry is true or not is the reason why you're using the techniques: Are you using them to get someplace, to move in a particular direction? Or are you using them to find out what's going on?

Using whatever techniques you choose as a way to explore your reality opens up a whole field of experimentation and playfulness, and that playfulness is not limited. If the playfulness is coming out of openness, there is no problem about what method you use, because whatever you do, you are doing to enhance your inquiry.

Playfulness not only brings in a sense of lightness; it also makes things move, makes things fluid, keeps things from getting fixed, which is necessary to avoid getting stuck in rigidities. To play is to experiment with a light heart. And experimentation is nothing but a disciplined form of play. So experimentation—such as doing trial runs or trying one thing after another—is a valid approach to inquiry. If you're experiencing something and you don't know what it is, it's okay to make up a hypothesis or a theory and then check it out to discover if it's the truth. That's the way scientists inquire.

So speculation, imagination, hypothesis, and assumption are all useful and valid for inquiry. However, you need to have an open-minded attitude. You don't take a hypothesis and try to prove that it is true; you take a hypothesis and try to find out *if* it's true. When this experimental, nonattached attitude is present, there is excitement and delight; but this excitement, delight, and joy in discovery now has an objective quality as well that reveals clarity, transparency, and precision.

PLAYFUL CREATIVITY

This is the action, then, of the Yellow latifa in the Diamond Guidance: It's curious, it's inquisitive, it's experimental—all in a playful way. And this playfulness of inquiry reflects the playfulness of the creative dynamism of true nature. We have discussed how the creative dynamism is responsible for the arising of the various forms and patterns in our experience of the whole world, and that this creative dynamism is the action of love. It is also a manifestation of celebration, a manifestation of joy.

That's why in the Indian tradition this manifestation is referred to as play (*lila* in Sanskrit). The Hindu teachings say that God is playing, trying something here, trying something there: "Oh, this sounds like fun—let's make a mountain here. Let's see, now . . . how about creating a supernova there? It feels exciting when I am a supernova. . . . I wonder what would happen if we added planets all around it. . . . That's interesting, I'm getting dizzy. . . . Well, now let's make something that feels a little more subtle—let's create life on that planet over there." That's the attitude of creativity in our Being—playful and purposeless. Being is not manifesting anything because Being wants to get someplace. The Divine Plan is not a closed or final plan; it's a natural, light creativity that is happening all the time.

Everyone says, "God knows." But God doesn't have a memory or make plans the way human beings do. God is spontaneous creativity. So there is no purpose, in a sense; reality's intelligence arises and just manifests itself more and more and more, in a very experimental way. Take the arising of life on Earth: If you study evolution, you will see that it's very experimental. One species arises here, doesn't get very far—and before you know it, it's gone. Another species seems to go much further. So it's all an experiment—which one works better, which one develops more. The human race tends to believe that it's not just an experiment; we think we're the purpose of creation. We might kill ourselves and most other life on Earth because we take ourselves so seriously, believing this is true. But we are just part of the play that is always arising and changing.

This concept of creation as playfulness manifests in the inquiry as a playful attitude, which brings the same quality into the unfoldment. This playfulness brings in joy and delight, curiosity and celebration. This is the way we participate in the divine joy. Of course, we can make up whatever purposes we like. That's part of the playfulness: You make up a purpose for a year or two and believe that it's the purpose of your life. Wonderful! Two years later, you change it to another one—why not? In fact, people do that all the time, don't they? You don't feel bad that for the first twenty-one years of your life, you had a purpose that you don't have now. You don't say, "I wasted my life." No, you say, "Now I have another purpose." Who knows what will happen next year?

The absence of purpose here merely expresses the openness, the open-ended character of our inquiry. When we have a purpose, we subtly orient our inquiry in a certain way; our attention is then oriented and structured toward a certain outcome, according to that purpose. And then we might miss seeing what is going on. Our openness becomes limited by believing we have to adhere to our purpose. So absence of purpose is the essence of playfulness, and the lightness in our inquiry.

Practice Session: The Presence of Curiosity and Playfulness

Now we're going to experiment with these various qualities in the process of doing an inquiry. Take an area of your experience that you do not understand, that is opaque or not completely clear to you. This means that there is something you don't know about, so you want to explore it further. It can be anything personal—an inner experience, an interaction, a block you are feeling with someone or about a particular situation.

After about twenty minutes, go back over your inquiry and look at the presence or absence of curiosity, as well as the changing quality of curiosity. When was curiosity present? When did it seem limited? What were you feeling in each case? If pain or fear arose, how did they affect your curiosity?

Pay particular attention to the quality of lightheartedness. How playful was your inquiry? Did it get heavy at some points? When and how did shifts between lightheartedness and heaviness occur? What made you heavy and forget to be playful? Did you notice whether particular contents tended to make the inquiry more serious?

THE LIGHTNESS OF THE INNER PATH

Spiritual transformation is about finally becoming convinced that the real treasures lie within us—that our consciousness, our soul, contains all the wonderful things that we want to experience. We only need to be open to our Being and invite it to display itself.

This means that our true nature—with all its beauty and all the experiences of it that human beings crave—is not something that we need to create or accomplish. We don't have to work hard at getting these beautiful experiences; they are already there. We just need to be relaxed about it. We need to be loose inside ourselves. Then our true nature will begin to flow out, to bubble up, and we discover that everything we were seeking so hard for outside is all there inside us.

That is a very difficult lesson for human beings to learn because all of society and much of our experience tells us it is the other way around: When you have more money, things get better. When more people love you, you are happier. When the weather is nicer, you can enjoy yourself more. We believe that it is always something external that makes things better.

But the fact that feelings of happiness, joy, confidence, strength, power, peacefulness, fulfillment, clarity, and freedom are potentialities of our soul means that we don't have to worry too much. It is as Meher Baba used to say: "Don't worry, be happy." That was one of his spiritual instructions. If you really don't worry, everything you're after is already there. We already are that true nature. We already have all the treasures within us.

So the more we recognize that we are the source of what we need, the more we are relaxed and light about the inner path. Then it can stop being a path of struggle, a path of effort, where we try to make something happen as if inner work were a matter of accomplishment. If you realize that the source is within you, then you realize you just need to be relaxed, open, and open minded and to let things happen on their own. You don't need to do anything about them. When we can recognize and allow that ease, then the unfoldment of our souls becomes a natural and spontaneous thing. And then inquiry becomes a lighthearted playful participation in the soul's journey.

So as you see, all of the elements we have discussed in this chapter interconnect. Love of the truth—which fuels the inquiry—will manifest itself as an openness, which will spontaneously give rise to a curiosity. The curiosity brings in a lighthearted playfulness, an ease and a flow, a purposeless engagement in life. This playful quality invites a sense of adventure and experimentation in the process of exploring and discovering the nature of reality. And all of these qualities are natural expressions of the Yellow aspect, the heart's joy and delight in participating in the creative dynamism of the soul's unfoldment.

CHAPTER 18

Red

Bold Adventure

THE DIAMOND GUIDANCE IS a true and objective vehicle, or structure, of our true nature that consists of all the qualities, all the essential aspects, including the lataif in pure and perfect form. This means that it always functions one hundred percent perfectly. When we don't experience this perfection, it means our skill in inquiry is still incomplete. As we learn how to inquire, we're discovering how to integrate these qualities and their functioning, so that we can gradually integrate the operation of the Guidance.

By the time we know how to inquire effectively, we are cooperating so smoothly with the Diamond Guidance that it will be difficult to tell who's actually inquiring—is it we ourselves or is it the Diamond Guidance leading our inquiry? When the Guidance itself is leading, our inquiry becomes the most powerful because then it becomes the ongoing revelation of truth.

In the last chapter, we examined the Yellow latifa, which brings the quality of playfulness, curiosity, and delight into the exploration of our experience. But we all know that sometimes it is difficult to delight in the inquiry process because defenses and resistances, painful feelings and emotions, and a lack of understanding can make the journey arduous and trying. Such challenges often make us lose our sense of openness and love of the truth. This situation would be impossible to transform if it weren't for the openness of our true nature, which manifests an infinite potential for responding to what arises. Foremost in this potential is the intelligence that can provide exactly what is needed in any situation. Our Being can manifest in the form of the various essential diamonds whatever quality we need both in our life and in the practice of inquiry.

STRENGTH AND THE RED LATIFA

In the practice of inquiry, the characteristics of the Yellow latifa—curiosity and playfulness—are very delicate. As expressions of a delicate innocence that doesn't have much oomph or capacity to withstand difficulties and barriers, they will buckle under easily without support. Joyfulness needs another capacity to balance that subtle playfulness: an energy, a strength, an expansive power. Not only does inquiry need to be playful and curious, but this curiosity needs to be supported and balanced by a strong energy that gives our soul—and thus our inquiry—the capacity to withstand a great deal of pressure. Inquiry requires an energy and a strength that will keep it from being crushed so easily—a quality of forcefulness, energy, expansiveness, and capacity. A fiery quality.

So when the going gets tough and we start thinking, "I don't know if I can continue this inquiry; it's too difficult," our true nature can manifest what is needed. In this case, it is the quality of our true nature that we call the Red latifa. It gives us the sense that "Yes, I can do it, I've got what it takes," so we don't feel overwhelmed and give up. The Red Essence is the quality that will keep our inquiry from collapsing.

You have probably noticed that even when you're not confronted by blocks or challenges to your inquiry, simply engaging this subtle process of observing your experience and investigating it requires energy. If you're tired, it will be difficult to effectively engage the process; the most you can do is be aware of what you are experiencing. It takes energy to go beyond that basic awareness—to understand the truth that lies hidden within our experience.

Inquiry takes a lot more energy than doing your job because it takes all of you, all of the capacities of your psyche. Even when you're not tired and not avoiding difficult issues, you still need energy to inquire. You need energy in order to be open and interested enough to remain engaged with such a subtle process, to allow such a subtle capacity as our inner guidance to function. That's why it is important to practice inquiry when you feel energetic and robust, when you have vitality. That is also why you need to live in such a way that you have sufficient energy for inquiry, just as would be needed for doing any other inner practice. So if you're really serious about engaging this work, you need to conserve your energy and balance your life so that you can be effective in your inquiry.

The quality of Essence that gives you this energy also gives you a sense of bigness, the capacity to expand, which provides your inquiry with bigger, more robust and healthy muscles for doing investigation. The Red latifa is the presence of fullness that is not separate from the presence of strength. It is as if your whole body were full of robust blood, pervaded with a pulsing, alive, dynamic quality. You feel as if your blood has a lot of hemoglobin in it, a lot of pure oxygen, and you feel vibrant, vital, and capable.

The Red and the Yellow can be considered the two wings of our spaceship. You need both qualities to stay in balance. These two lataif are fundamental for beginning to engage the inquiry process, and as we continue, we will see that additional capacities are needed as well.

DISCRIMINATION AND INQUIRY

At this point, it will be useful to review how the Diamond Guidance reveals the truth of a situation in the process of inquiring. From where we are now on our journey with Spacecruiser *Inquiry*, let's see if we can understand in a fresh way what truth means. This will help us appreciate more of the specific contribution of the Red latifa to inquiry.

If we consider our experience at any moment, the first and most obvious thing we notice is that it is not homogeneous. That is, our experience contains many elements that are different from each other: colors, shapes, sounds, textures, sensations, feelings, and thoughts all combined in the experience but differentiated. If our experience were only of one thing and nothing else, we would have no experience.

So the fact that there is experience means that more than one impression is present. We technically refer to this by saying that the field of experience is always differentiated. In other words, the elements of experience are differentiated from each other. Maybe differences exist in order that we will be able to have perception and experience.

The interesting thing about perception, and about experience in general, is not only that it is differentiated, but that the differences are identifiable. They are conducive to being known. So, for example, when I look around and notice different colors of shirts or different styles of hair, not only do I know that they are different, I also know what those differences are. So I don't only know that this shirt is a different color from that one, but I know that this shirt is green and that shirt is blue.

If I just see differences, there will be no knowledge, only perception. Differentiation is necessary for perception, but my perception will have no meaning until I begin to recognize what these differences are. For instance, sometimes I might have a feeling of love, and at another time a feeling of joy. These are not just different feelings. When I experience them as distinct feelings with specific characteristics, I can understand a lot about my experience. So we are seeing that differences have identifiable qualities, and the human consciousness is capable of recognizing those identifiable qualities.

As we have seen in chapter 3, whenever we have an experience, we are experiencing basic perception—often called mirror-like awareness—which is the capacity to perceive things simply as they are without knowing what they are. And we also are experiencing knowingness, often called discriminating awareness, which is the capacity to tell what the differences mean, to know what things are. These two levels of awareness are always implicit in our experience.

In inquiry, we make them more explicit. First we differentiate the contents of our perception, and then we discriminate what those differences are. For instance, say I'm feeling some kind of emptiness, an open space, and within this space is a delicate atmosphere of warmth. So there's an emptiness and a subtle presence that feels warm. If I can tell that there is an emptiness or spaciousness, but I cannot separate that from the pervading warmth, I will not be able to know, to fully discriminate, the truth of my experience. And if the warmth has in it some kind of sadness or hurt, without discrimination I won't know that there is hurt separate from the sensation of warmth. I will experience all of it as one thing.

Or perhaps I am able to see that there are differences between elements of my experience, but I don't know what those differences are. Once again I have no possibility of discovering the truth of my experience. However, if I know that there is space, and that the space has in it a warmth, and the warmth is wrapped around some kind of hurt, then I'm aware of three discriminated elements and can see each one for what it is.

If I continue to be aware of these three elements that I have discriminated—in other words, to follow this inquiry—I begin to see how they are related. Experiencing the hurt without doing anything to it allows an emptiness to appear; this becomes the space for a warmth to arise, a warmth that feels like kindness. I begin to see that if I don't fight the hurt, kindness arises to heal the hurt. That's an insight. That's an understanding.

In this example, I recognized some kind of truth, but how did I recognize it? By discriminating what was happening through recognizing the already existing discrimination. In other words, our experience always contains differentiation and discrimination. It is always discriminated. And if I recognize the discrimination for what it is, I'm aware not only that I, as the knowing consciousness, am here, but that there is content to experience, and that I know what the specifics of that content are.

As I recognize the specifics of the content, I begin to recognize the relationship between these specifics. As that happens, I begin to understand what I am experiencing, and that understanding reveals the truth. What is the truth? It is nothing but recognizing the discrimination for what it is. In this process, I don't want to put something on top of the arising discrimination, or have an idea about what it is. I just want to see the discrimination that is arising in my experience. I want to know it for what it is. That is what reveals the truth.

Let's say I'm feeling kindness arising in me and I think it's because I am aware that somebody is crying. But then I realize that the kindness is there because I feel hurt. That's an insight. If I say, "I'm feeling kindness because somebody else is hurt," I'm not seeing the truth yet. I am imposing my own idea about what is happening rather than recognizing the discrimination for what it is. So what the Diamond Guidance does is illuminate the situation to show us clearly—without our subjective bias, without our reaction—the actual truth of the discrimination. What is it that is arising on its own?

That's why the Diamond Guidance is objective, precise, and exact. "Precise" in this case means, "No, this is not sadness, this is kindness. And the kindness is in some kind of spaciousness, and the spaciousness feels empty. And furthermore, this emptiness isn't something bad; it's just the nature of the situation that kindness always arises in some kind of spaciousness."

As we recognize the subtle, precise discriminations that the Guidance shows us, we see that we're arriving at truth. But the truth is not a particular conclusion, such as an answer we have been seeking. Recognizing the truth means that we're seeing the discrimination in our experience accurately, that our soul is unfolding exactly as it is. And when that occurs, we say we understand our experience.

Our consciousness also has the capacity to name the specifics of the discrimination. But the discrimination itself precedes the naming. When we give names to the specifics, it becomes easy to remember them; we can write them down and store them as knowledge. But the experience itself comes first, then the differentiation, and then the discrimination, followed by the labeling. Of course, most of the time, these steps happen so quickly that they seem to be occurring at the same time. So we can't tell them apart.

DISCRIMINATION AND THE DIAMOND GUIDANCE

Understanding discrimination in this way shows us more about the function of the Diamond Guidance. The Diamond Guidance is a manifestation or a reflection of the discriminating awareness. Discriminating awareness means the already existing truth of experience, which has its own inherent objective discrimination. For instance, if you look around the room you are in, you may see chairs and lights. Now, we don't create the lights or the chairs with our mind. The fact that they're there is how reality is manifesting. They are already existing discriminations. Our mind then can recognize them and give them names.

So discriminating awareness means that the field of experience always arises with its own discrimination. When that discrimination is arising in our consciousness completely from true nature, we do not experience reactions or layers of self-image getting in the way. We have a pure experience of discrimination. That is what is usually meant by the discriminating awareness. This pure discrimination is the ground that underlies all of our experience.

That purity of discrimination of all of reality everywhere is reflected in our soul as the presence of the Diamond Guidance. The Diamond Guidance is a function, it is the action in our soul of the discriminating awareness. If you liken it to seeing the moon reflected in a bowl of water, discriminating awareness is the moon, the bowl of water is your soul, and the reflection of the moon in the bowl of water is the Diamond Guidance.

So each soul has its own Diamond Guidance, but it is only a reflection of the discriminating awareness of Being itself. And because it is a direct reflection of the discriminating awareness, it has the capacity to reveal all the discrimination within our experience, just as it is. It's capable of revealing the truth of our experience.

DISCRIMINATION AND SEPARATION

But let's look even more closely at what discrimination means. Frequently, we discriminate one thing from another in order to be able to separate them and see how one is different from the other. So in order to separate things, we must be able to discriminate them.

As a child begins to differentiate herself from her mother in infancy, she must learn to discriminate before she can separate. The ability to say, "That is my mother, and this is me," is an expression of the capacity of discrimination. As the child comes to know the difference between herself and her mother, or herself and her bed, she begins to know herself for who she is. She begins to discriminate herself out from the environment that she's in, especially from her mother. The moment we recognize how we are different from our environment and the people in it, we can feel separate. We begin to separate.

Of course, that brings in all the issues that are difficult to deal with—the anxieties and conflicts around the separation. But the human soul will have to separate in order to know itself, which means fundamentally that it will have to develop a discriminated self. It has to know that it is different and how it is different from other things and other people. Otherwise, there is no self-knowledge, no individuation. However, in addition to discrimination, in order to separate we need strength; we need to feel strong enough to be able to stand on our own. If I don't feel strong enough to stand on my own feet, I won't want to feel separate. I will want to remain connected in order to get support and nourishment from that connection.

So there is a very intimate relationship between discrimination and strength. To be able to separate, I need to be strong. But separation is based on discrimination. Hence, if I'm not strong enough, I won't be able to discriminate. I won't be able to—and I won't want to—know how I am different from you. Then there will be no separation.

More often than not, we tend to be mushy and undifferentiated in our experience—relating to it with vagueness and in generalities. We cannot tell one thing from another. When there is no precision, it means there is no clarity, and then it's not possible to know the truth for what it is. This brings us back to the function of the Red latifa. The Strength Essence is useful for inquiry in giving us the strength to begin to discriminate. The more active the Red Essence, the more powerful, precise, and real our capacity for discrimination becomes. The more we discriminate, the more we separate from our reactions and self-images, and the more we know ourselves for who we are, which lets us open up to true nature. Discrimination is the very heart of inquiry, the heart of the revelation of truth.

So now we see the interconnections between inquiry, the Diamond Guidance, and the Red Essence. We understand how the Red latifa functions in the Guidance and thereby supports our inquiry. At this point, you might want to experiment with these relationships for yourself.

Practice Session: Discrimination in Your Immediate Experience

The true practice of inquiry is not only for the purpose of exploring particular issues. We also inquire in order to recognize discrimination as it happens in our experience, moment to moment. Knowing our moment-to-moment experience for what it is—in a way that is clearly discriminated—is our natural condition. Our experience is always transparent, always clear, and it's always unfolding and changing from one thing to another. Ultimately, inquiry becomes that unfoldment itself, which then becomes the flow of understanding.

So in this exercise, rather than choosing a specific issue or focus, inquire into your experience right now. You want to be able to discriminate your experience as it changes from moment to moment. What is your soul dishing out to you? What kind of experience is it manifesting? For about fifteen minutes, continue the inquiry to see how your experience unfolds.

Then reflect on your inquiry to see the role of discrimination in it. This will help you understand more about your capacity for inquiry. When was your discrimination precise, bold, and courageous? When was it fuzzy, weak, or timid? What was going on at those times? What gave you the strength or courage needed to shift out of periods of unclarity and vagueness?

CONFRONTATION AND THE RED LATIFA

Inquiry also means challenging our positions, our usual patterns, our assumptions, our ideas and beliefs and habits. Inquiry is always a challenge to old knowledge. The strength of our inquiry can manifest not just as discrimination but also in questioning as a form of challenge. I don't mean "challenge" in the sense of hostility or an adversarial attitude, as in, "I don't believe you; you are wrong," or "Do whatever you like—you're not going to convert me." It's more like, "Let me find out if this true. I'm not convinced and I really want to be—so show me." We call this kind of challenge confrontation, and it adds another dimension to the process of inquiry. Confrontation will challenge any tendency to bullshit in our own inquiry.

You might notice, for instance, that you are aware of something but you let it slide, meaning that you don't fully acknowledge the meaning and significance of what you know. You do not look yourself squarely in the face. This is a laxity in inquiry that reflects the absence of the Strength Essence. The presence of strength in this situation would appear as a confrontation of the situation that allows you to see the truth as it is. In other words, confronting yourself means that you are firm with yourself, you are firm with your experience, you are firm with your knowledge. It means looking the truth straight in the face, placing it in front of your eyes and saying: "Look at this! What does this mean, and what am I going to do about it?"

Confrontation is also a support for discrimination. When we don't confront our positions, our experience will often remain vague, unclear, and indeterminate, and we won't get the significance of what's happening. Confrontation means that we are committed to seeing things exactly as they are, to calling a spade a spade. So challenge, confrontation, and discrimination go together; they operate as a unified functioning of the Red Essence in inquiry.

We tend to think of confrontation and challenge in terms of standing up to other people, but you can confront yourself, you can challenge yourself and your assumptions. Let's say you have discovered that you're always scared because your father used to beat you up. Perhaps after three years of firmly believing this, you begin to challenge yourself: "Wait a minute—what is this business? I'm scared because my father beat me up? That was forty years ago! Nobody has beaten me up for the last forty years, so why do I keep saying I'm scared because my father beat me up?"

This is a confrontation; it makes you look at your assumptions more closely: "Oh, I see, what is happening is that I still believe I am the person that my father beat up." Perhaps you are able to go even further and recognize that your fear is connected to identifying with a particular self-image: "Oh, I see—the reason I keep feeling scared is because I keep holding on to this victim role, because I want this self-image to give me a sense of identity. How will I be me if I am not scared?"

Confrontation can be seen as the strength to stay open to your experience, which means questioning the attitudes, beliefs, and assumptions of the past. But this challenge of openness does not have to be only in relation to your own experience; you can question anything in your life. This can include whatever you encounter while reading books or the newspaper, watching TV, listening to and observing other people, and so on. If Strength is present, you're not going to take things at face value, because you want to know the truth and you're strong enough to handle the truth exactly as it is.

RED AND THE SUPEREGO

It is relatively easy to see that much of our opaqueness, much of our lack of openness, much of our stuckness, is due to the attacks of the superego—ours and other people's. These are the criticisms, the put-downs, the comparisons, the judgments, the devaluations, the blaming, the shaming, the rejection, and the hatred that the superego levels at you in all kinds of situations. Here the Red latifa can specifically be used in the service of inquiry, by giving us the strength to defend against the superego.

Initially, we need to defend ourselves against these attacks by directly confronting them. This can happen through challenging the superego's authority—by telling it to back off. Such an internal confrontation requires great strength and intelligence. Later, when the Red Essence is more readily available, it becomes possible to disengage from self-judgment simply by clearly discriminating it for what it is and not going along with it. Disengaging from the superego is, in essence, a separation from your parents—the parents you long ago internalized and have lived with in your mind ever since. This disengagement allows you to see more clearly what is there in your experience, because if you're entangled with these attacks, you won't even know what you're experiencing or what has caused the attack in the first place.

Suppose you find yourself stuck and unable to take action and suddenly your superego attacks you: "You're terrible . . . you're no good . . . you can't do anything right." You defend against the attack by telling the superego, "Shut up, get lost—I don't want to hear you anymore." When the disturbing voice is gone, you have the space to look at your experience and see it for what it is. You realize that what you're experiencing is a feeling of "I don't know what to do." You also see that your superego felt you were bad to feel that, so it attacked you in order to stop the feeling.

Having the space to look at "I don't know what to do" without the attacks and judgments, you recognize, "Oh, nobody actually knows what to do—only God knows." That's a divine insight. But your super-ego was judging your feeling as a sign of deficiency, so you did not recognize it as an expression of the truth. The judgments and attacks made it impossible for you to see what was there in your experience: that the discrimination—"I don't know what to do"—was arising from a very deep level of Being where it is clear that action is always the action of the unity of Being, not that of any separate entity. Getting involved with the attack prevented you from seeing that there is more to the feeling than is conventionally recognized.

COURAGE AND INQUIRY

Inquiry is a process of nuzzling into God's bosom, delving into the secrets of existence. Ego encrustations begin to break up when we start to see images as images, structures as structures, patterns as patterns, and projections as projections. All of these are created and held together by our belief that they are reality. The more you see them as they truly are, the less you believe in them and the more they start to break up and dissolve.

This in itself brings up new challenges. We might begin to feel that reality is shifting under our feet. Unexpected things start happening. Inquiry is revealing that our experience comes in forms we did not expect to encounter. This will tend to upset our equilibrium, because even though we have seen holes in our view of reality, we still believe in the overall shape of it. It's as if you were drilling holes in the ice at the North Pole in order to catch fish. Suddenly you realize that the layers of ice are beginning to break up underneath you. This was not part of the plan. You realize you're probably going to fall into the ice water.

Such a situation generally brings anxiety, insecurity, fear, and often terror. You become afraid that things are going to change too much, that the world as you know it is going to disappear. You're going to be overwhelmed, you don't know if you can handle it, you feel deficient. . . . Of course, you have all these feelings because you don't know that you can actually live under water. You think you're only a land animal, but you're really an amphibian that has ended up living nearly all of the time on land. We are accustomed to seeing ourselves as land creatures who go swimming only once in a while. We don't know that we're originally sea creatures, that we can swim in true nature—our fluid true nature—and that this is where we can truly thrive. Because we don't know that, we think we're going to drown, we're going to die if the land dissolves and we end up in the water. We become terrified.

At this juncture of our unfoldment, we need even more strength in order to go forward. Here strength appears in another form that is necessary for our inquiry. When there is fear, the quality that is needed is fearlessness. Fearlessness does not mean the total absence of fear reactions, it means that fear does not scare you away from your inquiry—you still go on. At such times, you need courage to keep looking at the truth even if it terrifies you—to face the fact that you're going to feel insecure as you go forward into the unknown. It takes a daring attitude to cross that threshold.

In other words, for us to continue with inquiry when we are afraid, we need to be courageous, we need to be strong of heart, we need to become lionhearted. But what we need to become lionhearted about is the truth. All kinds of things can happen—disruptions, hardships obstacles, fears, and inadequacies. You might feel helpless for a few days, or a few years. Some people can go crazy on the spiritual path, and some people even kill themselves. These difficulties of the inner journey are well known and have been documented throughout history.

So there are dangers, and it can get scary. But it can also be exhilarating. The spacecruiser is going into territory you've never seen before. You don't know what kind of creatures you will find; you don't know what kind of perceptions will arise or how they will affect your mind. You don't know whether you're going to experience yourself differently, whether your life will change forever. The journey is exciting, it's beautiful, it's creative, but there's always an edge of fear. If inquiry is truly happening, then you're always walking this edge. You are terrified or completely thrilled at each turn in the road. You're leaving the old and familiar and going to the new and unexpected. Whether it is a step in the dark or a jump into the abyss, the unknown awaits.

A BOLD OPENNESS

This is the time when we need tremendous courage, immense strength, and an adventurous attitude. For the true explorer, the bold voyager, risk is always a part of the adventure. So if you are truly interested in the farthest reaches of reality, and the inquiry is a blazing fire within you, then you too will experience this boldness. If your heart is open, this openness will manifest as courageousness. It will become a courageous, bold openness, a daring openness. In fact, you can become so courageous you dare reality: "Show me! Let me see into your mystery!"

We've seen that openness appears as love, as curiosity; with the Red latifa, it appears as courage and daring, an adventurous attitude. Without this quality, you will tend to stay with what you already know or believe about reality. Then openness will have limits and boundaries to it: "Yes, I'm open, but only if what happens confirms what I already know." You might feel this way especially when you've fallen into the ocean and you feel like you're drowning—it can be hard to stay open to see what's true. You think, "I'm going to die, to disappear. I'm terrified!" But if you let go and let yourself disappear, you might find, "Oh, I didn't die, I'm water—amazing!" To surrender in this way when we're terrified requires courage—not just love, and not just trust.

As part of the process of inquiry, it is necessary to work through the difficulties of early life, the emotional pains and privations of childhood, the unconscious of the personality. Many of the traditional teachings don't deal with this level of mind directly; but our understanding strongly points to the importance of this task for spiritual openness to occur. We have to take care of that first. And to do that, of course, we need courage, we need boldness. With this courage we may be able to tolerate all kinds of pains and fears, rejections and abuses. But to go beyond our familiar story, beyond what we think of as reality, requires courage that is based on original openness—an openness that can allow new forms of experience, new forms of perception. Otherwise, reality will not be invited to reveal itself.

Some people are so used to feeling pain, anxiety, and depression that they're comfortable with it. They complain every day about how unsafe life is, but what truly terrifies them is to feel something light and open that doesn't have pain and heaviness. What they lack is the courage to let go of the familiar ground that defines their experience of the world.

Inquiry is in some sense an invitation for our Being to transform our experience, to change our lives. If our invitation is limited, the revelation of our Being will be limited. However, if our invitation is completely open, then Being will be welcomed to reveal the fullness of its possibilities.

Such a daring and courageous attitude, however, does not come from pushing yourself. It's not that you grit your teeth, act tough, and stop feeling anything. It's more that you're courageous enough to feel, you're bold enough to be vulnerable, daring enough to be open. The openness itself has a boldness; it doesn't buckle under when you feel fear or terror. It embodies a fearlessness that has the capacity to be present regardless of the fear. We may tremble, but we keep piloting our ship.

Furthermore, being courageous doesn't mean being foolhardy—jumping into danger without understanding. The courage we're talking about is the courage to recognize the situation for what it is, to be willing to see the truth as it is, regardless of how frightening it may be. This is the courage of discrimination. Another way of saying this is: Taking a risk is not the same thing as putting yourself at risk. The courage we need for inquiry is not a matter of being counterphobic, where you just jump into the situation without acknowledging your fear. That's foolish, not courageous.

The courage of the Red latifa is what we need in all these situations. This willingness to feel our fear and continue our inquiry appears as a natural resilience—nothing strange or unusual, just a natural sense of how we can experience ourselves. This strength that we feel in our hearts infuses the soul with a boldness that allows her to be open to seeing things she has never seen before—even things she considers to be threatening or terrifying.

From this perspective, you can see that self-realization or spiritual maturity is not for the squeamish, and not for the dilettante. You need to be serious about the journey in the sense of being willing to risk your life for it. If you're going to complain or retreat every time something difficult happens to you along the way, then you are interested in something else; you're not a true spiritual inquirer. The path of inquiry is a path of challenge and adventure always leading us into the unknown.

Such is the fullness of the Red Essence that it arises in many flavors to support the openness of our inquiry: strength, energy, expansion, and the capacities to discriminate and confront our experience as we discover what is true. When this fullness of flavors fills our heart, it gives us the courage to welcome whatever the adventure of life brings us.

CHAPTER 19

White

Staying the Course

W HEN WE DISCUSS INQUIRY and how it invites our true nature
to display its inherent possibilities, we're talking about a magical
journey. It's a journey filled with mystery, beauty, exquisiteness, and
significance. Most of us spend our lives within a thin layer of reality,
unaware of the deeper realms of our consciousness. What we call emotional reality—the layer where most people believe human richness
lies—is only onion-skin deep compared to the totality of reality. Beneath this thin layer of emotions and thoughts lie indescribable beauty
and freedom. Many people wander in that onion-skin layer forever,
but in the inquiry process, it's a layer we need to go through and not
get stuck in. To support us in this movement into and through our
emotions, reactions, and beliefs, the next latifa—the White or Will
Essence—plays an important role.

THE NEED FOR PERSISTENCE

Our curiosity, openness, capacity, and courage make us aware at some
point that the journey takes time. Regardless of how effective and deep
any particular inquiry is, that single exploration will not bring us to
enlightenment or the end of the road, because inquiry is about engaging an ongoing process. It's not an experience, it's not a snapshot. It's
not like taking a potion that suddenly opens our eyes. Inquiry is an

organic process of growth and maturation that has its own rhythm, takes its own time, has its own seasons.

During the early stages of the journey, when you're working through the emotional/psychological layer, it can feel tiresome that the process is so slow. You want it to go faster. After a few months or a few years of anxiety, pain, shame, and rage, you might lose heart, get discouraged, even become despondent. And the experiences of light that penetrate every once in a while can make the situation even more frustrating: An hour of blissful experience can be followed by two or three months of misery. So some people might feel, "I don't know if this work is for me. I don't know if I can handle it—it's too much, it's too difficult, and it takes too long." Or they might just get hopeless: "Getting free is never going to happen to me; I'll never succeed. Freedom happens only for certain special people."

In the beginning, especially when we are engaged in the emotional and physical realms—which are filled with attachments, desires, and conflicts from the past, inquiry feels very difficult due to the pain and suffering we experience. This is natural; human beings don't like to feel pain and suffering. They'd rather feel good and happy. However, the fact that we want the process to go more easily, the fact that we become hopeless, despairing, despondent, lazy, or cynical and then feel like giving up—all these indicate a reaction of the ego.

It also indicates that our openness is limited. We already have an aim in mind; we're not interested in the inquiry itself, we're not interested in the truth. Not only do we want to feel good, we want to get someplace. Maybe we want to become enlightened, maybe we want to reach the other shore. These goals are understandable, but the attitude of inquiry is different. Inquiry itself has no need to go faster or slower, or to get anyplace. Inquiry is simply a matter of becoming aware of what's happening now, just recognizing the meaning of the truth that is arising moment to moment.

However, because we're still identified with the falsehood of the ego, our openness is limited. And so are our courage and our curiosity. At this point, Being may manifest another quality, one that is needed for this particular situation—it is the aspect that makes it possible for us to persevere and not give up. This new quality appears in our experience as a sense of determination: an unwavering dedication to continue with the inquiry and stay the course, a determination to keep opening to our experience as it is. Our journey of inquiry needs this quality in order to keep going, to persist over time, to ripen and bear fruit—for the path is long and full of difficulties.

To see what is there in our experience, to recognize the truth fully and precisely, takes time, energy, and a strong commitment to our own process. What we need for this is the essential quality of Will. And, if we have some trust in Being's intelligence, this quality will manifest in our openness. As we will see in this chapter, the White Essence arises as a presence in our soul that can be recognized through many interrelated capacities. The first we will consider is commitment.

COMMITMENT

Essential Will gives us the determination to persist with whatever thread we're following and not let ourselves get distracted. This determination manifests in different ways. One way of experiencing it is as a dedication and commitment to the practice. This is important not just for inquiry but for any practice. In fact, anything you do in life that is a process requires dedication, commitment, and persistence. All our tasks and endeavors will be accomplished more efficiently and smoothly the more we're focused and the more committed we are to that focus.

So what does commitment mean on the journey of inquiry? Commitment means that when you sign on, you intend to continue. This is needed to begin the process, and the farther we travel, the more we recognize that our commitment must deepen and expand for the journey to continue. It needs to get more solid to handle the various difficulties, barriers, and distractions that happen along the way. These distractions, which originate from our thoughts and emotions, from people around us, and from circumstances in our life in the world, can take us off course.

Having a particular destination tends to motivate you; hence it is easier to commit yourself to the process. But if your aim is to pursue the truth without deciding beforehand what that truth should be, then commitment is more difficult. This commitment to inquire manifests as a determination and a persistence in the openness, which support you in inquiring into and discerning the truth as fully and precisely as possible. So this commitment to the truth means that you're not going to quit. You're not going to jump ship when things get tough.

The commitment to the inquiry—the determination not to give up or let yourself be distracted—is also a commitment to the quality of your experience. It is not a commitment to an ideal of being a good person. It's a commitment to experiencing yourself and reality in the here and now regardless of whether you like what's here or not. It's a commitment to maximizing and optimizing the quality of your experience at each moment through being real, authentic, and focused on the truth.

The challenge is for our commitment to be free of any goal orientation. Will is what underlies our determination and commitment. And essential Will, as an expression of Being, has no goal, no direction, no effort, and hence no intention. However, for a long time, our identification is with our ego-self—regardless of the presence of Being and its manifestations. So we will tend to experience our essential Will and inner commitment as an intentionality: the intention to begin inquiring and the intention to stay the course. Intentionality is the basis of the ego-self's commitment, which manifests as a kind of stubbornness and bullheadedness.

So commitment implies intention, but it also reflects what you value. Commitment to the truth means that the inquiry is more important to you than the distractions that can arise. It means that the open endedness of inquiry is more important than any particular aim or result. It means that you prefer the truth to anything else, that you love it more than merely feeling good or relieving yourself of difficulties.

So our commitment arises from the openness to the truth, and it expresses the love of the truth. Without this love, without this valuing of the truth and its revelation, why would we commit ourselves? And yet, even loving the truth and being curious, strong, and courageous do not guarantee that we will have the commitment, the determination, the will to keep us solid and centered in the face of all the distractions of everyday life. The White aspect itself must be available because it expresses the inherent will of our fundamental openness. Then our openness to the truth is a committed openness.

It is interesting that the color of the Will Essence is white, for the kind of dedication and determination we are talking about implies purity. When you follow distractions, needs, and desires, rather than your love of truth, this creates impurity in your soul. Commitment is an expression of the soul's purity because you don't let yourself get identified with the distractions.

DETERMINATION

So the purity in the openness of the inquiring attitude manifests as a commitment. And this commitment translates into a determination and persistence. We don't give up, even when we feel hopeless, even when we feel despairing. These feelings merely become part of the content we inquire into. Why should we stop the inquiry when we feel hopeless? Some people may think, "If I'm feeling scared, I'll inquire, but if I'm feeling hopeless, I won't." Why is that? Why should we give in to the hopelessness more than the fear? They're both emotions.

The presence of the element of Will makes our inquiry unstoppable, makes it impossible to seduce, because the distractions are all seductions. They are promises that our situation will improve if we go along with them. These seductive distractions are called the devil in some religions: the tempter who is always telling you, "Well, if you just fantasize a little bit, you will feel better." Or "If you just think about tomorrow and plan, that's a more efficient use of your time." Or "Get on the phone and talk to a friend—she'll make you feel better about yourself." Your mind is always tempting you away from staying present and open to the truth, promising something better or easier. That's why the purity of your commitment will have a great deal to do with your access to essential Will. And the more Will you have, the less power the "devil" will have over you and the more your inquiry will be able to continue in its own rhythm. That's why Buddha said on his deathbed, "Just persist, just keep working." Doing this indicates that your will is being actualized. In time, the inquiry will go smoothly, effortlessly. You will be zooming through the layers of obscuration. Thus, being grounded in the Will accelerates the inquiry and the unfoldment.

Of course, none of us is one hundred percent pure. Just as we have not completely realized strength, joy, or courage, none of us has our will fully realized. But all of these qualities are available from our Being, so if one of them is missing or insufficient, then another comes up. Guided inquiry has many arms, just like a thousand-armed deity in a Tibetan *thangka;* each arm holds a different capacity.

Acknowledging these capacities, evoking them, encouraging them, supporting them, nourishing them, valuing them—this is our work. But it doesn't mean that our inquiry has to be totally successful all the time. We all have limitations. If you had no limitations, you wouldn't have to learn these things. No one here can do inquiry perfectly. If that were to happen, then there would be no more inquiry—only pure creative dynamism. So we need to be easy on ourselves when we see we're having difficulty. Maybe our strength is a little shaky or our curiosity seems to be hiding. That's when we need to be patient and kind with ourselves and still keep going rather than giving up.

STEADFASTNESS

The kind of determination that is important for inquiry is not like a bulldozer that pushes through regardless of the situation. We call that "iron will," which is a false, reactive substitute for real will. Our ego uses iron or false will to make things happen when it is out of touch with the will of the truth. The determination needed in inquiry, on the other hand, is responsive and has a sense of appropriateness and subtlety. As an expression of the White or Silver diamond of Essence, it is precise and intelligent. It is also flexible, manifesting in accordance with the requirements of the situation. The determination of essential Will can become firm, dense, and solid, or it can be fluid and flexible. Sometimes it's powerful, and at other times it's delicate and light.

There is no need to fight with the content of inquiry by pushing on it or through it. The true function of the Will is to help us become steadfast so that we are not swayed, and not distracted or seduced away from the inquiry. We keep on exploring regardless of what happens. Keeping on doesn't mean that you have to push; sometimes it can be very gentle and delicate. Steadfastness is mostly a matter of simply being there with your experience, being aware of what is going on, remaining interested in the truth, and continuing to explore whatever limits your openness.

This steadfastness is not possible without love of the truth. In fact, true commitment cannot be present without love. Will expresses your love of truth and your openness to it. Will is not the same thing as love, but you won't be interested in manifesting a steadfast will if you don't love the endeavor. Love underlies all the qualities we have been discussing in relation to inquiry. For example, if you don't love the truth, you won't be curious about it. And if you don't love the truth, why would you be courageous in your search for it?

You could say, then, that the openness of our true nature manifests as the love of displaying the truth, and that love then appears in the various qualities—including the curiosity, the courage, and the determination. Thus the love of truth is what underlies true steadfastness. In contrast, the steadfastness of the personality—the kind of stubbornness of the iron will—expresses a position that we are identified with and want to maintain or defend. It is not an expression of appreciation for reality as it is.

The commitment to the truth that appears as determination manifests as a steadfastness in all the principles of inquiry. We are committed to remaining open and finding the truth. And we are committed to this openness through approaching the process without prejudice, without a position, without a preference about the truth that arises. This attitude will protect us from the tendency to manipulate our experience in order to accommodate a prescribed goal. So we are steadfast not only in the sense that we continue investigating, but we also continue to be interested and open in our investigation. Even though our experience might be difficult sometimes and the truth may be slow to reveal itself, we will stay with the inquiry. We might stop and rest, but we will come back to it from another angle, willing to experiment and curious about what we find.

Steadfastness appears externally as patience. The more one embodies the White quality, the more one is patient. But patience doesn't mean that you are just tolerating things. Most people think that being patient means you don't like a situation but you stick around anyway, feeling frustrated. That is not what patience is. Patience means commitment. It means staying the course. It means that you are really interested in continuing to be there, regardless of the feelings that may arise.

When you are truly being patient, you don't feel that you're being patient; you only know that you're doing what you're doing. If you feel that you are being patient, then you are most likely tolerating the situation, just waiting for things to get better. Though the ordinary notion of patience is the willingness to continue waiting one hundred years without complaining, this kind of patience is nevertheless limited because it is dependent upon a certain attitude toward the situation: that the outcome should be some kind of change.

This is the patience of the ego, not essential patience. Real patience implies an openness to the situation and trust in the process. It is not an attitude of waiting—for waiting implies a desire for a particular kind of change to occur. Many people think I am very patient but, in fact, I never feel patient. I just don't abandon the task—it is as simple as that.

Steadfastness doesn't necessarily have to appear as movement in a straight line. It can manifest as meandering, wandering around as you experiment. The point is to efficiently unveil the truth of the situation; it is not to prove that your will is strong and that you can make something happen. We are not trying to prove anything; we are simply working to see the truth. So in inquiry, you do not know where you are going, but you continue until you discover the truth of your situation. In this sense, steadfastness is a determination to stay in the moment.

As we have discussed in previous chapters, the dynamism of our Being has an optimizing force, an evolutionary intelligence that will tend to move our experience closer to the purity of true nature. It will keep doing that, over and over again, regardless of our resistances, regardless of our conflicts and our ignorance, and in spite of the difficulties. The universal will of the optimizing force appears in our experience as our own will—as our commitment and steadfastness in the process. So when we say that the steadfastness expresses the optimizing thrust of Being's dynamism, we mean that even in stuck, dark, or difficult times, the dynamism is still alive in the form of our determination. Being's dynamism is still exerting its will, exerting its force.

True will displays an intelligent responsiveness to the truth of our situation, including our limitations in dealing with what arises in our experience. Because human beings have inherent limitations, the reve-

lation of human potential is an ongoing process. And as such, it requires patience and steadfastness. This steadfastness, however, is an
intelligent expression of the White Essence. How solid, how soft, how
hard, or how flexible this expression is depends on the particular situation. Sometimes you may need to pay intense attention for many hours
in order to explore your experience. That could include talking with
people, reading books, investigating your own history, perspectives,
and patterns of behavior—doing everything you can to inquire into
your current situation. But after all this activity, the process may require that you relax and let your mind settle. This doesn't necessarily
mean disengaging the inquiry; resting or taking a break for a while is
just another part of the process. You have been committed to finding
out whatever you can, and for the moment, you know all that you can
know. Now it's time to be quiet, to watch and see what arises in your
experience. That is frequently when new insights arise.

INNER SUPPORT

We will encounter a seemingly endless number of barriers and difficulties in inquiry; that is why we need steadfastness. But we can't be
steadfast by making a decision in our mind. This steadfastness depends
on having the inner support to stand on our own feet. Ultimately, it is
inner support that makes it possible for us to stay open and to continue
being interested in the truth. Without it, we lack the solidity, the
groundedness, and the internal center that make us steadfast. The Will
manifests as support when you experience an immovability and solidity
in yourself, as if you were a solid mountain that nothing can move.
This inner solidity, this inner rootedness and groundedness, is what
makes it possible for us to engage in inquiry, to commit ourselves to
it, and to persevere.

At the beginning of the journey, your own inner support is limited
or nonexistent, so you need external supports to sustain you. A school,
a group, or a teacher can keep challenging and confronting you, keep
inspiring you so that you continue inquiring. But little by little, as the
inquiry deepens and expands your experience, you will get more in
touch with your own inner resources, your own support. One thing
this means is that it will be necessary for you to become more con-

scious and responsible about arranging the circumstances of your life so they can support your inner journey.

Inner support implies that we need to be in touch with our experience. Inquiry is not a mental exercise, disconnected from ordinary reality. We have to be rooted in our everyday personal experience and in touch with our own thoughts, feelings, body, and behavior. Inquiry does not require us to leave our body or try to reach unusual transcended heights of perception—and we will not feel our inner support by doing so. Instead, we need to become more concrete, more down to earth, by delving into our own everyday experience. It is the embodied soul that is the entry to all the treasures of Being.

When you are inquiring, it is important to keep sensing your body—to stay in direct touch with its movements and sensations. This includes the numbness, the dullness, or the tensions you may feel. To ground your awareness in your bodily experience is important because your essential qualities are going to arise in the same place where you experience your feelings, emotions, and reactions. They are not going to appear above your head, they are going to arise within you. So your body is actually your entry into the mystery.

We say that discriminating awareness is a field that has its own patterns, but where is this field of consciousness? It is not hovering out in space somewhere; it is here throughout your body. And it is through the body that the field can open up and expand infinitely. The body is the doorway to the adventure of Being. So the inquiry has to begin by activating and enlivening the body. The more active and alive the whole body is, the more our inquiry is vital and our unfoldment is alive. Our experience is more robust, energetic, and dynamic. We need to remember that the activation of the lataif requires that their centers or physical locations be energized.

INNER CONFIDENCE

So inner essential support is experienced as groundedness and rootedness, which means being grounded in our own personal experience through our physical body. The more we have our own inner support, the more confidence we have to simply be open. Then we can see that inquiring is all that is needed. Being, which is our true nature, will do the rest. We can just open up and invite our Being, and it will respond and display its riches. It is a cooperation, like a feedback loop in which inquiry invites and Being reveals. The revelation expands the inquiry, which in turn accelerates the revelation.

Inner support gives us a sense of confidence in this cooperation. Why is that? Because the sense of grounding, which is a function of embodying the Will, is an expression of the universal will in the soul. The universal will is the optimizing force of Being's dynamism, the force that actualizes the revelation that our heart desires—the realization of who we truly are. The more we have our own inner solidity, grounding, and support, the more we feel confident in our inquiry, because this confidence is an expression of the universal will, which is the force of the optimizing dynamism. In other words, having our own inner support makes us aware of the functioning of true dynamism and lets us know that this dynamism functions to optimize experience.

However, not feeling connected with our inner confidence and support doesn't mean we cannot inquire. It simply means that inquiry will be more difficult. We might still have our courage or our love, for example, and we can rely on these qualities until we feel connected to our inner support. However, having our inner confidence will support the process to move much more. Inquiry will then be like a well-oiled machine that functions effortlessly and naturally.

The White gives us confidence in the natural capacities that arise in inquiry, as well as in the inquiry itself. For instance, it gives us confidence in the discernment and discrimination that we recognize in our experience. This means that we stop doubting our experiential knowing, we stop denying or discounting our inherent discrimination. And as we increasingly trust our discrimination, we develop, in turn, more confidence and a greater sense of inner support.

ATTUNED UNFOLDING

Because the process of inquiry is intelligent and responsive to the individual's situation, it is one of the least dangerous and problematic spiritual methods. We have already discussed some of the tribulations and dangers of the spiritual journey. Just the fact that you are confronting yourself deeply can present difficulties, pains, and terrors that most people don't feel or are not aware of.

Furthermore, some spiritual methods can inadvertently cause trouble for their practitioners. Concentration and visualization practices, breathing techniques, movements and postures, and other disciplines that attempt to invoke particular experiences and perceptions can catalyze powerful breakthroughs, but they can also cause physical or psychological stress or breakdown. Some people can even become incapacitated, temporarily or permanently.

The process of inquiry, on the other hand, is one of the safest methods of spiritual revelation. What determines your inner movement is your own openness, your own application of your will, and the fact that you are not trying to get anywhere. Since you are just trying to see where you are, inquiry is responsive to your own needs in the moment and is naturally considerate of your own capacities and limitations. Inquiry is a gradual, guided approach that each does at his or her own pace. And because the guidance is attuned to you personally, what will arise and how much your true nature will reveal to you at any particular time will depend on your capacity and your situation. Nobody is pushing you to experience something in particular. And you are not trying to manipulate your own experience to channel it one way or another. These are the safeguards implicit in methods such as inquiry that are not oriented toward a particular goal and that are responsive to minute-to-minute changes in personal experience.

MATURATION AND EFFORTLESSNESS

We have seen the connections between commitment, determination, and steadfastness and the sense of inner support and confidence. These are all expressions of the same latifa: the Will aspect. It is clear that the quality of Will is very different from the quality of Strength. The Strength Essence is a fiery presence of excitement and energy, while the Will is more down to earth, more steady and solid. You feel more settled. Thus it can bring more depth and subtlety to your inquiry. Will indicates perseverance: You find yourself staying with elements in your experience longer, and you are more patient. As a result, you can see more depth, more discrimination, more subtlety, and more profundity in whatever you are exploring.

When our will is fully engaged, our spacecruiser can go very far—all the way to the most distant reaches of the experiential universe. With the Red Essence alone, you might begin with excitement and energy, but you probably won't get very far because your energy will fluctuate and your ship's engine will run unevenly. You'll find yourself stopping and starting many times. The hard work in inquiry begins after you've been on the journey for a while. So the White Essence is what gives you the steadiness and the staying power needed to stay focused and open as you traverse the long distances in plumbing the depths of your experience. It provides you with maturity and a sense of responsibility that supports you in pursuing an issue fully instead of jumping from one thing to another.

It's okay once in a while—even necessary sometimes—to be excited as you jump from one thing to another, fired up by the Red, but if the whole process of inquiry is like that, there will be no real depth, no integration, no maturation. It's just like a pattern of ending a relationship after six months and immediately falling in love with someone else. There's a great deal of excitement every time that happens, but the relationships never become deep or rich. In that case, one could end up thinking that the purpose of relationship is just to enjoy the initial hit of bliss and excitement. Then you would never find out what a mature relationship can be.

Inquiry presents a similar challenge. We need a lot of support to keep on track as we move toward our own maturation and fruition. Whether we get that support internally or externally does not matter during the early stages of the journey. Here in the teaching situations of the School, we have a great deal of support. But eventually you will need to fly solo, which requires having your own inner solidity and support. So as we study the inquiry process, you are learning to become skilled, experienced pilots who can fly for long distances and operate alone when necessary. Even if you have difficulty and make mistakes, you can recover, learn from those mistakes, and keep going with your will to support you.

Practice Session: Your Ability to Stay with Your Experience

Take some time now to inquire into something personal, an issue that concerns you or something that touches you. Use all the capacities, all the commitment and dedication you have to look deeply into your chosen subject. After about twenty minutes, stop and consider what elements were supporting you during the exploration. Did you experience determination and commitment in your inquiry? How open did you feel toward your experience? Were you able to stay attentive to what was arising in the moment, or did you find yourself waiting for something to happen? If you got discouraged or distracted at some point, what came up to help you persevere? Note the presence or absence of inner support and confidence, how it was limited, and when it appeared and disappeared. How much effort did you need to put in to continue? Did the process feel natural or strained?

Questions and Answers

STUDENT: It seems that for me a big motivation and commitment in inquiry comes from the desire to resolve pain, suffering, and internal conflict. Every time I notice that the pain motivates my capacity and willingness to inquire, I beat myself up.

ALMAAS: It's natural and normal that you don't like pain. Everybody wants to relieve themselves of pain. That's not only human, it's an animal tendency. But why would you beat yourself up for that? Would you beat yourself every time you get hungry and you don't have food?

STUDENT: I guess I have a judgment that coming from my essence is better.

ALMAAS: It's true that it is better if your motivation comes from loving the truth, but why does that mean you have to beat yourself up? Do you always have to be the best? I'm willing to be second best. Maybe that's why your superego has something on you—because you think you should always be the best. In inquiry, the desire to increase pleasure and avoid pain does not have to be a problem; we take that into consideration and include it in our field of inquiry. It's not that these motivations are bad, it's just that other motivations are deeper, more expanded.

Nowhere does the Work say that you shouldn't try to make yourself feel better. You can get massages, take hot baths, go to a movie—everybody here does these things. So when you're feeling pain, you want to do something about it. Inquiry includes the attempt to help ourselves feel better. It recognizes the effort and sees how it tends to move our inquiry in a certain direction. If we don't judge ourselves, we may recognize that the attempt to make the pain go away makes us feel better in the short run, but it does nothing to relieve our more fundamental pain.

You need to keep recognizing your aims and objectives, whatever they are, in order to open up your inquiry. If you don't let yourself see them, your inquiry and openness will be limited without your knowing it. Everybody has objectives when they start inquiring, because as long as there is ego-identification, there are desires and preferences. That's normal.

In inquiry, you're not only inquiring into an issue, you're also inquiring into the inquirer. The arrow of attention always points two ways: You're simultaneously looking at the subject matter and at the attitude you have toward it. As you look at your attitude, you will recognize the preferences, judgments, tendencies, goals, and effort you're bringing to the inquiry. Sometimes even when you recognize all these things, they remain for quite a while, because they have very deep roots.

It helps to remember that we are learning an amazing and multifaceted skill in inquiry. Part of learning is making mistakes, getting stuck, being lost. Remember, the spaceship we're learning to fly is one of the most difficult and complex. When you look at the console in front of you, you don't see any buttons. It's just a smooth, transparent surface over glimmering lights that are constantly changing. You want to touch specific lights just at the right moments, in the correct sequence. To do this, you need speed, nimbleness, and perceptivity. Developing these capacities takes time and dedication, but after a while you become like Commander Data in Star Trek: The Next Generation—you can't see your hands moving because they are going so fast.

In inquiry, we are learning how to be natural, how to stop interfering and allow our natural intelligence to function. That is the interesting thing about the inquiry: In some basic way, the practice is to simply cease and desist. Then a lot happens. There is no need to push and pull, huff and puff. Just being natural becomes the full realization of Will. And the deepest understanding of Will is effortlessness, which we realize when we have integrated our inner support completely. Inquiry then becomes spontaneous, and unfoldment is natural.

From the beginning, inquiry needs to embody a measure of this effortlessness; otherwise, it will be goal-oriented and its openness will be limited. Because the openness allows Being to function intelligently through its various qualities, the more openness there is, the less we have to do. This means that even from the earliest stages of inquiry, when we realize moments of openness, effortlessness will be present in our inquiry. When our inquiry is completely effortless, then it is spontaneous, and openness has overcome all its limitations. This is freedom.

CHAPTER 20

Green

Attuned Guidance

EMPATHIC ATTUNEMENT

We use many words—clarity, precision, strength, curiosity, love, compassion, and so on—to try to say something about the Diamond Guidance. But these words are nothing compared to its direct presence, the taste and flavor of actually experiencing them. Words are completely inadequate to describe the Guidance; but they are useful if they activate something in us.

We have seen that inquiry attunes our soul to be receptive to the particular manifestation of our Being that we call the Diamond Guidance. The reverse is also true: The more this presence guides our soul, the more attuned our inquiry is. But the inquiry needs to become sensitive to our immediate experience and our specific situation in order to successfully invite true understanding. The Diamond Guidance provides this complete sensitivity.

The attitude of inquiry has to have an attunement, a sensitivity, for it to reflect the true attunement of the Guidance, which is absolute. The Diamond Guidance is absolutely attuned to our true nature and to the necessary path that our soul needs to travel in order to open up to that true nature. It is also absolutely attuned to where we are at every moment in order that it can take us along the path. Guidance means taking you from the place you are to the place you are going. You cannot guide somebody if you don't take them from where they are. So, for instance, if someone is not in touch with her feelings and you want to guide her to express them clearly, you don't start by teaching her techniques of self-expression. You start by helping her recognize her feelings; then you can help her learn how to express them. This is attunement.

Not only does the Guidance guide your exploration, but its attunement tempers the inquiry process so that it is not a pushing, an effort, or an imposition, and not motivated by shoulds or judgments. This indicates that the Diamond Guidance, with its precision and clarity in the inquiry, expresses the kindness and gentleness necessary for our soul to trust, relax, and open up. Without this attunement, the soul will not be able to do that; she has no reason to. The inquiry must be attuned so that the soul can know that inquiry is not pushing it toward anything or expecting it to go anywhere. Inquiry is a sensitive and attuned action that expresses a genuine interest in the soul's experience in the moment of inquiry and responds to that experience empathically.

Empathy for yourself means that you know and are sensitive to where you are, rather than operating according to an agenda, a goal, or some ideal of what should happen. Using any method to get someplace or do something means that we are not attuned to exactly where we happen to be. This is because a method is a standardized approach to which the individual conforms. A true guidance, an intelligent guidance, a guidance that cares for you absolutely, will first have to see exactly what is going on with you right now and then respond in alignment with that. Otherwise, how will the guide know what your particular needs are?

Our soul opens up most readily when inquiry addresses our experience in the moment. This is the function of the Green latifa in inquiry—the essential Compassion diamond—for it gives us the capacity to be precisely and clearly sensitive to what is actually happening in the soul. So, not only does the inquiry reveal elements of our experience clearly and precisely, but the precision itself is nothing but the exact recognition of where our consciousness happens to be.

Usually, many things are happening in our life at any given time. However, there is a place where our experience is located, where what concerns us most at the moment is differentiated from all the other things that are happening. For instance: "I am experiencing that I am sick, that I am getting married, and that I have to deal with my late taxes, but what I am most in touch with, what I feel is relevant for me at this moment, is that I am feeling a desire to see my father." Your inquiry has to address that feeling, not the fact that there is an upcoming wedding, that you have liver cancer, and you're behind in your paperwork. Where your heart is is what the inquiry must address.

So inquiry must be cognizant of everything in your experience and take all of it into consideration, but it will have to directly address what really matters to you at the moment. Otherwise, you won't feel that the inquiry is addressing you—it is addressing some idea of what should happen or of what's important. This attunement is the function of kindness or compassion in inquiry. It gives our inquiry an attuned sensitivity, an empathic precision. Inquiry then is attuned to the pain of the soul, her suffering and needs, and to her interests and loves. When inquiry addresses exactly where our heart is, the heart responds; if it is seen and cared for, it will open up.

This is one important reason why the Guidance cannot be a pushing, an attempt to manipulate, or an effort to make things happen, for all of these depend on ideals, judgments, opinions, and positions. In these cases, at some point you will wonder if you are the one who is being addressed, because in your heart you will feel that you have to accommodate to somebody else's opinion of what should happen.

KINDNESS AND COMPASSION

Kindness gives inquiry the capacity to listen to our experience and to be receptive to the communications from our soul. This allows the soul to be wide open to revelation and unfoldment. When our inquiry is characterized by kindness toward ourselves, we are not interested in being judgmental. Our interest is in truly understanding who we are, not changing ourselves or making ourselves fit any model or mold. Kindness gives our inquiry a type of intelligence that is responsive to the actual situation, to the precise nuances of our experience. It expresses our Being's openness in a completely selfless way. This selfless openness is basic to the operation of the Diamond Guidance. Therefore, our attitude has to correspond to and reflect this selfless service that the Guidance offers us.

We are exploring here the quality of Compassion or Loving-kindness, which manifests as a sensitivity, an empathy, an attunement that is necessary for inquiry. This attunement of the Green diamond of the Diamond Guidance is so completely selfless that it has an unlimited capacity to see us exactly where we are. This gives a precision to our discriminating capacity. However, there is a difference between how ego sees attunement and how Being does. What usually passes for attunement is to see where a person is and then to give them what they feel they want. What the soul actually needs is an attuned understanding, one that not only sees where she is in the moment but also recognizes where she is in relation to her true nature. The attunement of the Diamond Guidance provides this understanding and then guides the soul to her true nature, for that is what she truly wants.

So, if you see a person hurting and you want to support them, you don't give them a pat on the shoulder or some sweet words of encouragement. No, you do something to help them go deeper. The prevailing understanding of empathic attunement is that you should make somebody feel safe, assure them that there is no danger. But true support is not a matter of making somebody feel safe. It is a matter of precisely seeing and recognizing where the person is so that the person will trust—not because there is no danger but because there is true understanding.

For example, if somebody was repeatedly hurt by her mother, you can be kind and help her feel that it is okay to be hurt, it is okay to be mad at and hate her mother. But that is only part of the story. Emotional attunement recognizes that there is hatred because the soul has been hurt, and hurt naturally produces hatred when one feels powerless to stop what is causing the hurt. But the true attunement of the Green Essence is aware that the real reason she is suffering is that she has lost touch with her true nature. She is not really suffering because her mother hurt her, but because this hurt has disconnected her from what is most precious in her.

We see here that from the perspective of the Diamond Guidance, the impulse to be kind to this person because her mother hurt her is only the beginning of true Compassion. The Compassion of our true nature responds from the knowledge that even though hurt, pain, abuse, and trauma happen in childhood, the most central element in our soul's suffering is that those experiences disconnect us from true nature. If a guide does not have that perspective, then this person is not a true spiritual guide yet. Such a guide may help you deal with the pain and feel better about yourself. But a spiritual guide will start from this pain and disruption—because that is what feels true for you now—and from there take you on the journey to your true nature. This is a very delicate operation and requires the unlimited openness of Being.

Attunement and compassion of this kind obviously requires a vision that reflects a deep understanding of true nature, of what a human being is, what the path consists of, and so on. But the capacity or element we are focusing on here is that of sensitive attunement. This is an expression of objective and essential compassion, the Green diamond of the Diamond Guidance, which has a warmth and an acceptance to it inseparable from the precision and sharpness. It is not a matter of seeing your situation and feeling, "This is terrible; I'm going to change it." It is a matter of seeing your situation and accepting that this is where you are. You take the attitude, "I want to know exactly how it feels to be here."

When you are listening to a friend, you truly help him by being there, so that you step into his shoes and know as precisely as possible what it feels like to have the experience he is describing. It's the same thing when you are inquiring into your own experience: You want to know just what it feels like to be exactly in the place you are in. You really want to understand yourself because you care.

Most of us believe that there is little or no caring attunement available for us; we don't feel that people have the true desire to understand us. So we put up our defenses to protect ourselves. We close ourselves down because other people want something from us or want us to be one way or another. It is hard to be open in such an environment. Similarly it is only when we recognize that our inquiry is motivated by a true desire to see where we are that we can let go of our need for self-protection.

Questions and Answers

STUDENT: I found out that when my inquiry is real, it is automatically attuned and sensitive. At those times, I am more free from my super-ego and its put-downs.

ALMAAS: Very good point. If you are truly interested in finding out where you are, then you won't adopt standards to judge yourself with. In some sense, inquiry puts the superego to sleep. Having the desire to inquire into your experience means that you want to understand yourself, and that is the most compassionate orientation you can have toward yourself. That is why the superego doesn't come in at those times—it is not a compassionate agency. The superego isn't interested in understanding you, it just wants you to shape up. Inquiry means that you really want to know what is going on, without being concerned about outcomes or consequences. So the inquiry itself definitely brings in compassion.

STUDENT: I found it surprising that as inquiry becomes deep and real, I begin to experience a great deal of gratitude.

ALMAAS: This is the interesting thing that happens as we inquire: Our Being not only unfolds, but in this unfoldment it provides what we need. Inquiry is an intelligent, responsive unfoldment. When you realize that what unfolds is exactly what you need, gratitude arises in the heart. As you saw, it is not only the guidance that is attuned; the unfoldment itself becomes attuned. This is what we mean when we call it a guided unfoldment.

STUDENT: I noticed in my inquiry that the Guidance is not always present. Why is that?

ALMAAS: The Guidance comes and goes depending on two things: the objective need of the situation and how open you are to the truth. The more open you are to the truth, the more the Diamond Guidance arises. If you forget about the truth, then the Guidance disappears for a while. Diamond Guidance reveals the truth, so if you are not interested in the truth, why should it stick around? Its mode of operation is not being invited at such times. It is always interested in guiding us, it is always there ready to show itself. But when we don't invite it, we won't see that it is there, and we won't provide the openness it requires for its operation. So we need to turn toward it.

The Guidance is guiding us all the time. Much of the time, we don't want to listen and don't want to recognize it or listen to it. We are busy with all kinds of other things that we think are more important. That is why the more we attune ourselves, the more we are open, and the more we are interested in the truth, the more we will see guidance everywhere.

Guidance appears throughout the whole world. Everything that happens has some kind of guidance in it. We need to remember that the Diamond Guidance is the essential nous, the microcosm of the universal nous. It is nothing but the expression in our souls of the inherent true discriminating knowledge of Being—what I have termed God's mind. So as we open up to its guidance, it guides us to this universal knowledge, and then guidance is everywhere we look.

SUFFERING, SENSITIVITY, AND TRUTH

When we study the quality of attunement and empathy in openness, a great deal of pain and hurt is bound to come up for most of us. This signifies several things. First, that by being attuned to where we are, we recognize more fully and exactly what we are truly experiencing. The arising of pain signifies that there is much suffering in our human experience. When we look with an attuned, precise lens, this suffering is what we see. In fact, one important reason why our experience is ordinarily so limited is that we resist seeing the amount of pain and suffering we have. The soul closes down to avoid feeling the hurt, pain, suffering, and difficulties that are normal in human experience. Another thing this observation indicates is that the pain and suffering in human experience require the presence of Loving-kindness—the sensitivity, gentleness, and healing quality of the Green Essence. It also shows that our inquiry needs to embody not just what feels good and wonderful, but also a true openness that welcomes our pain and suffering.

When our inquiry is open to our pain, our pain will open up and expose itself to the healing agent of Loving-kindness. Furthermore, our pain and suffering will open itself up and reveal the truth that is hidden when we close down the pain. If our inquiry doesn't open up to our pain, it cannot proceed very far, because the route to our own truth is blocked by our positions and defenses that protect us against the pain we have—the pain that is natural for human beings to experience.

Sometimes we can avoid feeling pain by closing down our sensitivity, and sometimes pain is simply unavoidable; we can't help feeling it. But essential Compassion responds to and welcomes all forms of pain— whether mental, physical, emotional, or spiritual, whether exposed or hidden. The moment the Green latifa is present in our inquiry, sensitivity and openness increase and deepen from all sides. Inquiry is more open and sensitive, and the openness becomes more attuned and empathic. This means that the soul is now more open to reveal her suffering and her vulnerability.

When we are not in touch with our true nature, the emotional pain of our everyday life can begin to feel intolerable. But the more we recognize ourselves as our true nature, the less significant our emotional pains become. Regardless of how deep the emotional pain goes, our true nature is infinitely deeper. But without access to the depth of who and what we are, intense pain feels overwhelming. It threatens our sense of who we are, so we close down or clam up. Over time, we block the pain by deadening ourselves, by making ourselves insensitive, thick, and gross. Without the soft, radiant warmth of Loving-kindness, we aren't going to trust enough to open up. Our field of experience needs to have this sensitivity, because we have become insensitive.

So if our inquiry is going to invite openness in our experience, it must be open to the possibility of experiencing the pain, hurt, and suffering. It not only has to be open in the sense of allowing the suffering to surface in consciousness, but the openness has to embody a gentleness, delicacy, sensitivity, softness, and considerateness. Only this will truly invite the soul to open up her pain.

Simply stated, inquiry requires the presence of Loving-kindness. Our clarity and precision need to embody the sensitivity of kindness to respond to exactly where we are. With Compassion, inquiry considers appropriately—in a very gentle, delicate, selfless way—how we are vulnerable and how we are hurting. So our inquiry must be courageous, curious, and steadfast, but also considerate of the pain and sensitive to our vulnerability. In this way, our soul will feel willing and interested to open up and reveal her hidden pains. This presence of precise and attuned kindness also allows our soul to be touched by the healing element, which is the presence of Loving-kindness—the Green Essence.

However, healing particular pains is not inquiry's major endeavor. The main task of inquiry is to help the soul open up and reveal her treasures so she can become an open and transparent window for our Being. In other words, true healing is not just a matter of healing particular pains; it is healing the rift between the soul and her Being. So the objective of essential Compassion, the Green diamond of the Guidance, is to heal this disconnection or alienation between the soul and her true nature. This is what will truly and finally heal the human soul.

Particular pains from your past can define and limit your experience in the present because you are not connected to who you truly are. When you are connected to your true nature, being rejected or hurt by others doesn't do anything to you. You just feel sad for them; you recognize the wound that makes them behave the way they do. It is when you are disconnected from your true nature that *you* get wounded.

So the inquiry must address your particular wounds, but the kindness of the Guidance responds from a larger perspective that knows the nature of true healing. Specific pains are addressed because this is the only way that deeper truth will be revealed. However, the Guidance does not always heal a particular pain right away. It might keep the wound open so you don't forget that a greater connectedness is possible. This prevents you from dealing with your pain and suffering just so you can feel better and then go sailing, get back to your job, or resume your familiar life. So the Guidance might wait until you become committed to the truth before allowing the healing. Otherwise, it would not be functioning in accordance with its true purpose. The Guidance, however, is absolutely compassionate. Keeping the wound open does not mean allowing pain in order to be hurtful; the purpose is always to deepen the soul's capacity for self-attunement, which means drawing her toward her essence.

We need the kindness of Guidance in order to stay with the suffering of the soul; without that, it is too painful to tolerate the difficulties in our experience, and inquiry would be impossible. Frequently, for example, we close our hearts with our anger and rage. In order to open to the pain that is there, we have to go through the rage and anger. To do this, sensitivity is needed to recognize that the anger is our outrage about the pain. So if we inquire into what the outrage is about, it will reveal the hurt. Otherwise, it will stay hidden. Experiencing the hurt will then reveal the underlying truth, and also open our hearts to the essential quality of Compassion, the Green latifa.

The intelligence of Compassion allows a kindness that does not try to get rid of suffering but creates an openness to whatever is happening so the truth will have the opportunity to reveal itself. In this way, inquiry goes counter to the tendencies of the ego. Ego doesn't want to experience pain. It wants to protect itself from pain; Guidance wants to open up the pain. It wants us to feel the pain as fully as possible, for without that willingness to feel whatever is there, we won't be open to ourselves or our experience.

That is why getting in touch with our Compassion requires us to feel our pain and hurt—because our hurt is what invites the Compassion. Compassion comes out as a response to pain. At the same time, we need the Compassion in order to be attuned to our experience so that we can inquire effectively.

Without our pain, our kindness would be limited, which would limit our attunement, which would then limit our inquiry. Human beings get used to believing that emotional pain is bad, but emotional pain is mostly an invitation for Compassion, an invitation for sensitivity. That is how human beings learn to be sensitive—we get cooked, and by getting cooked, we soften. We become delicate and sensitive.

Of course we need to deal with the pain correctly, for experiencing pain does not in itself develop our sensitivity. It can harden us or distort our perceptions if we have no support from our deeper nature. However, with understanding we can see that if we have a great deal of pain, it gives us a greater opportunity to develop our compassion and sensitivity.

To cause people pain is not compassionate. People already have more pain than they can handle. It is only compassionate to cause pain if the person can open to the pain and if they can benefit more from being in pain than not. Who is going to know whether that's the case? Under certain circumstances, when they know for certain, some teachers cause their students pain to provoke a certain shift. But generally there is more than enough pain to go around, and most people are not willing to open up to the pain they already have. So why cause more?

Practice Session: Your Relationship to Difficult Experiences

Choose an issue or element of your experience that you find difficult to stay with or look at. Perhaps it is a conflictual relationship or an experience of someone not paying attention to you. Perhaps it is some feeling that you have judgments about or some sense of yourself you find disappointing. Take fifteen minutes to inquire into this part of your experience. If need be, start by feeling and inquiring into what makes it so difficult to look at this area. If you are able to open to it in a nonjudgmental way, simply be with the feelings and sensations without attempting to get anywhere in "resolving" them. Be aware of the habitual ways you have oriented to this difficult aspect of your experience. Notice what arises in your experience, describing it as simply and directly as possible.

When you are finished inquiring, consider your experience in relationship to this painful subject. How did you find yourself relating to what you were experiencing? How possible was it for you to remain open to what happened? Were you aware of the presence of the Green Essence in your inquiry? When it was present, what happened? Can you identify any particular qualities of compassion that you experienced, such as kindness, attunement, warmth, gentleness, delicate openness? What were you experiencing when the kindness or attunement wasn't there? If it was difficult to contact your own compassionate presence, can you identify what was blocking it?

THE SENSITIVITY OF CONSCIOUSNESS

To summarize, the Diamond Guidance is an expression of the kindness of our Being. When the inquiry is attuned and receptive to the Diamond Guidance—or when its functioning approximates the operation of the Guidance—the Guidance brings in the capacity of Compassion.

This Compassion manifests as an openness to the pain that allows the pain to open up and reveal its truth. It also provides the capacity for precise, empathic attunement, which becomes the most powerful way of allowing experience to unfold.

But where does this empathic attunement that invites the unfolding of the pain and suffering come from? What is it about the Green latifa, the Loving-kindness, that makes the response to pain possible? To understand this, we need to look at the latifa of Compassion from a more transcendent perspective, from the perspective of Being. In other words, how does Compassion appear in the eyes of God, independent of the needs of the human soul?

From this transcendent perspective, the White, or Will, represents the creative force of Being. The Red, or Strength, represents the aesthetic beauty of this creativity as reflected in the richness and color of its inherent discrimination. The Yellow, or Joy, represents the playfulness and celebration of this beautiful creation. The celebration, the beauty, and the creativity exist whether humans need them or not, whether there is suffering or not. So what does the Green represent? What is the quality of Green, independent of our human needs, that provides the specific capacities we have been discussing in this chapter?

We can approach this question by recognizing that with the Green arising in your experience, you become present and open to the situation in a gentle and sensitive way. You directly feel the content of the soul's experience. You do not mentally deduce what's happening—you know it intimately by feeling it through vulnerable and sensitive openness. Green imbues Being's openness with a transparent vulnerability. This vulnerable awareness points to the quality that the Green Essence represents for our Being—a sensitivity of consciousness.

Consciousness requires sensitivity in order to feel, to experience, to be in touch with itself. The Green latifa provides heart sensitivity, which is not just awareness or consciousness. Our consciousness becomes delicate, supple, soft, and minutely considerate of what's happening. It attains a refined, exquisite awareness, which we feel as a sensitivity. It is as if each atom of our soul had become a tendril, a nerve fiber that can sense and feel in a very delicate, subtle, refined way. This sensitivity pervades the whole field of experience, the whole soul, when the Green aspect of Compassion is dominant. It makes it possible for us to recognize the inherent discrimination in our experience through feeling, through intimacy, through contact.

The Yellow is beautiful, bright, and light; the White is pure and pristine; the Red is brilliant, shiny, and magnificent. The Green, too, can be very radiant—an emerald green that is both luminosity and sensitivity at the same time. It is not the kind of sensitivity of a microscope or telescope. It is a sensitivity of the heart, of the soul herself. This sensitivity is the reason for developing Compassion, a reason that is larger and deeper than the desire to heal our pain. Understanding more fully the nature of the Green Essence makes it more available for our soul to use for attunement and inquiry. It is evident that sensitivity is necessary to attune us to exactly what is happening. Attunement, in other words, like empathy, is a particular expression of this sensitivity.

The quality of sensitivity is obviously very important in our inquiry. The sensitivity makes the content of experience fully and truly available. Without this very present and available content, our inquiry will tend to be intellectual, and disconnected, and it won't unfold the soul. The more we have this sensitivity, this softness, the more directly we become aware of experience—by touching it from the inside.

If God creates the world in order to experience it, how is God going to do that without this sensitivity? What some spiritual traditions refer to as witness awareness perceives things at a distance; it is not an involved awareness. But with the emerald green of Loving-kindness, consciousness becomes an awareness that touches and feels, that knows through intimacy. The inherent knowledge of Being now has an extra dimension, a new kind of depth and fullness, that makes the discriminating awareness full of aliveness and tenderness.

The sensitivity of the Green aspect brings in a vulnerability and openness characteristic of life itself. It creates a sense of delicate, virgin aliveness. All of our feelings and sensations appear as if they were leaves that are just being born—very delicate, very soft, but very alive and very fresh. It is not surprising that leaves happen to be green. The soul's heart is awake and sensing with intimacy the unfolding of its own nature.

CHAPTER 21

Black

The Power of Cutting Through

THE SUBTLE ORGANS OF PERCEPTION

Sensitivity is what makes available to inquiry the various experiences, feelings, and states we inquire into. The more sensitive we are, the more the content of our experience becomes palpable, concrete, vivid, exact, and accessible. When we are more in touch with our experience, we are able to more fully and completely know our arising states, which means that our understanding will deepen. It is not merely that a greater sensitivity helps the inquiry by giving it the data we need; the sensitivity is already part of what the inquiry is seeking—the clear, experiential discrimination of what is happening, the truth of our experience.

This sensitivity, as well as consciousness and awareness in general, manifests in the various organs of perception. Our sight, hearing, touch, taste, and smell are an extension of our consciousness that allows us to be sensitive to experience in general. The more these senses are clarified, the more vivid our experience is, both enhancing inquiry and actualizing the understanding that inquiry is facilitating.

However, since we are learning the kind of inquiry that will take us into the depths of our true nature, these organs of perception are not sufficient by themselves, because they are limited capacities. In particular, they are limited by our worldview, our assumptions about reality. We might not know it, but our capacities of seeing, hearing, tasting, smelling, sensing, feeling, and touching, and our kinesthetic sense all operate through subtle veils. These veils are our self-image and our perception of the world—which are based on accumulated encrustations from our history.

So as our inquiry deepens and becomes more powerful, it will require our ability to sense our experience to become subtler, deeper, and more penetrating. Not only do our physical senses need to become more vivid and intense, but we need to bring in subtler senses as well. We need to sense our bodies and our inner sensations more deeply and clearly. We also need to open the heart center so that we can feel our emotions and our feeling states more intimately and vividly. And we need to have greater clarity, spaciousness, and quietness in our mind to be able to perceive thoughts and their processes.

This refinement of our awareness is a natural development in the early stages of the practice of being present and inquiring. As our inquiry deepens, it goes further and begins to invite the Diamond Guidance. Our inquiry then starts to be infused with this presence and guided by it. The Guidance opens up and develops new capacities of perception that are not physical. I refer to these as the subtle capacities of perception—others might consider them intuitive capacities. This, in turn, intensifies our inquiry and gives it more power. Thus, our powers of perception not only intensify, they also multiply.

This development of the subtle capacities occurs specifically through the activation of the Black latifa, at the center of the forehead. The arising of this essential aspect means the opening up of this center, which we experience as the essence of peacefulness—a quiet and still presence, satin-smooth and luminously black. It is the presence of consciousness as stillness. Our mind becomes quieter, and at times completely still and clean. The totality of our consciousness—the whole experiential field of the soul—is stilled. This is the experience of peace descending in our inner world.

The descent of peace brings up a new quality of Essence, with all of its properties and capacities to support our inquiry, but it also activates the subtle centers, the subtle capacities of perception. The primary perceptual center is the Black latifa, at the center of the forehead. It is also the center of the operation of the Diamond Guidance itself. During inquiry, the Guidance tends to operate as a presence at the center of the forehead. That is why you get clear and crisp in your head when you understand something.

When these subtle perceptions are first activated, intuition means that the experience of knowledge is coming through a quiet mind, which indicates that the Black center is open. You become receptive to insights, ideas, and truths, but you don't know exactly where they are coming from. You become more intuitive in the usual meaning of the word—that is, you are open to knowledge in a way that you do not understand or directly perceive. What this means, however, is that although you are receiving knowledge as insights from a true inner source of discrimination—what we call the Diamond Guidance—this source is not yet present in your direct experience. Its center and its channel are open, but you receive messages or insights indirectly.

The direct awareness of the operation of the Diamond Guidance does not occur until the subtle perceptual capacities begin to function. These capacities can be seen as corresponding on a subtle level to the physical senses. They perceive the inner realm, the discriminations in our field of experience that do not manifest physically. For example, with the inner subtle capacity of touch, we can feel our essence as if we were touching it with our nerve ends. We can feel its texture, its density, its viscosity. It is as if you were touching your essential presence with your fingertips. This inner touch is obviously not physical, because you are recognizing the texture of a state of consciousness, not sensing a state in the physical body. We can make this distinction because it is possible to experience both a state of consciousness and a body state simultaneously in the same location, which indicates that they are on different levels of manifestation.

This particular subtle capacity needs to be activated for us to be aware of our soul as a presence, and to be able to discriminate the essential aspects. When we use our physical senses, we are aware only of the effects of Essence but are not directly aware of Essence itself. We cannot physically perceive the presence of our own consciousness. In the presence of Essence, we merely feel clearer and deeper, maybe happier and lighter, but we don't really feel what is causing these effects in us.

In contrast, if the inner touch is open and active, then you begin to experience the actual palpable Essence itself. You will recognize it as presence—a conscious medium, almost an aware substance. Depending on which aspect is manifesting, the inner touch will feel it as water, or gold, or oil, or mercury, and so on.

Any of the subtle capacities provides our experience in general, and inquiry in particular, with a discrimination that wasn't available before, a discrimination that is necessary for our understanding to go beyond the physical and emotional realms. How can our inquiry penetrate the essential realm if we don't have the capacity to perceive that realm and discern its characteristics? With the inner touch, you can discern each aspect and differentiate it from the others. You can also distinguish each whole dimension of Being from the others by using this capacity to discriminate essential sensation.

The inner touch is also necessary for the embodiment of Essence. If you use the other capacities of inner perception but not the inner touch, you won't be embodying Essence. You will be experiencing it more psychically—perhaps as an image, sound, or smell—in a disembodied fashion. This points to the fact that essential presence, and the presence of the soul itself, has a texture. We say that the soul sometimes feels like a flowing plasma. Plasma is physical; it has substance and texture. When the soul is transformed by an essential state, this texture of the presence may get smoother to the point of complete fluidity, so that it feels just like mercury. At another time, it cleanses all of you and feels like a delicate, pure oil, which is the essential anointing of the soul.

The inner touch can become very precise in its discrimination of these textures in the soul. For instance, you can feel the Water Essence—the quality of human vulnerability—as a crystal-clear stream of water washing you from the inside. But you can also feel it on the subtle lataif level as water vapor, on a deeper level in the fuller form of regular water, or on the diamond level, in the solidified form of an ice crystal. You can discriminate all of these experiences just through sensing the different textures with the sense of inner touch.

For this subtle sense to awaken, however, our usual perception of our physical body must first become quite refined. This means increasing the sensitivity not only to our skin but also to whatever is inside our body—the muscles, organs, and so on. When the subtle sensitivity is highly developed, you can travel the entire journey using only the inner touch, because you can discriminate very minutely with it.

Another important subtle sensitivity is the capacity for inner taste. When you experience your inner taste, it is as if your soul had a tongue. It can taste the personality states. So, for example, resistance tastes like bitter rubber. If you experience the state of the false ego—what I call the false pearl—it often tastes like snot. Everyone knows what snot is like—you need a tissue to get rid of it. Ego-personality states exist in our consciousness as waste products that we hold on to. When a person, for instance, feels he is full of shit, with subtle perception he can actually sense the texture, the taste, and the smell of his own state: pure shit. It is not just a metaphor.

But you can also taste the qualities of Essence. You can taste the sweetness of Love; the minty, cool quality of Compassion; the metallic, warm, gold quality of Truth; the licorice quality of the Black Essence. Differentiating the qualities with taste adds another enchantment to the soul—taste intensifies the experience in a different way than texture.

In addition to having a texture and a taste, essential aspects have a smell as well; you can begin to smell the inner state. Some people say that they can smell fear. We do have a capacity to smell emotions. Not only can you smell fear, you can smell love. Love happens to have the smell of roses, or sometimes jasmine. If you smell the Green Essence, it smells like mint. You can smell freshness, you can smell staleness, you can smell rottenness, you can smell depression. You can taste, smell, and touch the quality of restraint, which is much like leather. You can do the same with the state of inertia, which feels like lead, or with the state of deadness in the soul, which feels like wood.

As we see, all of these familiar ego states have textures, tastes, and smells just like external physical objects do. And different people have developed different capacities for sensing these states. Some people use mostly the inner touch. Some people can perceive taste easily but haven't developed their sense of smell much; others develop smell to an unusual degree. But the development of a given subtle capacity has a direct relation to the corresponding physical capacity. For example, people who develop a fine appreciation for different kinds of food and a discrimination of their subtle differences can develop the inner capacity of taste more easily than the other subtle capacities, and more readily than individuals who are not so attuned to their taste buds. The same is true with smell and with touch. But this is not so in every case. Some people who are great connoisseurs of food and wine, for example, never develop the capacity for inner taste.

The subtle capacity of inner seeing is centered in the forehead, and it has many varieties and degrees. When it expresses the level of development of the Diamond Guidance, you realize what I call the diamond eye—objective sight. Just as our physical capacity to see has an extensive range, so does our inner seeing. The range of inner seeing can be so wide that you can see your own inner state or the inner state of somebody else. So for example, you feel the strength of the Red Essence, and you can also see fiery red, or a flame, or liquid fire, or lava. When the Green latifa is present, you can see emerald green or an actual emerald—a shaped, faceted, beautiful emerald of consciousness.

This seeing capacity can operate on different levels, just as the other subtle senses do. You can see not only the presence of essential states but also when emotional states are manifesting. For instance, you can tell if somebody is lying or telling the truth, because you can see the person's images and thoughts. We see our own images, don't we? In the same way, you can see somebody else's images—not just the energy of thoughts but their content as well. That's because thoughts have different images and different colors. And when you have realized the diamond eye in your inquiry and your thinking begins to reflect the true condition of what is arising, you can become aware of thoughts as diamond thoughts. This means that they are objective and have their own presence that can reflect essential qualities.

The capacity of inner vision can also see the unconscious and the past. Our memory of the past is actually a reflection of this inner seeing capacity. You can also see the physical body from inside. You can see the tensions and blockages, you can see the organs and cells, you can see the DNA, and even the molecules and atoms. The Diamond Guidance possesses many lenses, each with its specialized function. You can change the lens to focus on the cells instead of the organs, for instance. You can change to another lens and see the atoms. So you can see all the physical levels and all the essential levels just by shifting focus.

Then there is subtle or inner hearing. Inner states have sounds and vibrations, just as they have shapes and colors. We can hear rushing winds, flowing water, crashing and crackling, and so on. Essential states have their own characteristic sounds, such as the gentle sound of streaming water, the delicate tinkling of jewelry, the ringing of bells, flute sounds, and the hum of bees, to mention just a few. We can hear inner music and uplifting sounds. Our experience becomes magnified, attaining new levels of vividness.

The deepest subtle capacity is the capacity of direct knowing, which is a function of the Diamond Guidance itself. You don't go through a process, you don't even perceive anything—you just *know* with certainty. All of us experience that sometimes, but this capacity can be expanded and developed.

We are beginning to appreciate how far the capacity of inquiry can go. An individual with these capacities can inquire into medicine, philosophy, physics, or human relationships—any field—and have at their disposal a tremendous capacity for investigation. Unless one does the inner work that is needed to clarify these subtle senses, however, they will not be available or trustworthy for any purpose.

This does not mean, though, that we all have to develop every one of them in order to inquire deeply. We are fortunate if even one is developed. To develop all of them is rare; most people will develop one fairly well, and a second one partially. But the more subtle capacities we develop, the better, because they will make our discrimination deeper, more precise, and more complete. And our field of experience will then be more available to our soul and to inquiry.

THE OPENING OF THE BLACK

All of the inner capacities that we have been discussing become active and begin to develop as the Black center opens up. The opening of the Black center brings out the Black latifa, the black subtlety. What does the Black latifa do? It stills our consciousness. It makes it peaceful. The consciousness needs to become still and peaceful, with no mental activity or emotional reaction, for these capacities to first open up and be perceived. This is because they are very subtle at the beginning. You might miss them if you are busy thinking, engrossed in emotions, or reacting.

Therefore, the more accustomed we are to the inner stillness and peacefulness, the more perceptive we become on the subtle dimensions. This can take our inquiry to deeper levels, to a newer kind of knowledge, to a different kind of experience. Our spacecruiser can now travel to other galaxies of experience, where perception is different and unfamiliar.

It is amazing to be able to experience at such subtle levels, to feel a state and see it and taste it, all at the same time. Sometimes you can't tell whether you are seeing, hearing, tasting, or touching—at these subtle depths, it is all one act. Then your whole soul is ablaze. It is as though each atom of the soul were capable of all of the capacities. For although these capacities initially operate through particular centers, just like the lataif do, ultimately they are not limited to certain locations or particular organs. The whole soul becomes an organ of perception, and all the capacities can operate in any part of the body.

I'm sure that many of us are already using one capacity or another, but you might not have conceived of it in this way. For example, you might have been observing and inquiring and suddenly felt that you were hot and red, without noticing that you were actually seeing the color red. Or you might say, "When I feel space arising, it is really clear and open." What do you really mean by "clear and open"? Or you might tell someone, "The space goes on forever." How do you know that? Perhaps you are seeing it. The perception could already be happening without your being aware of it.

These perceptual capacities develop initially to discriminate our inner experience, but in time, as our soul opens up and reveals that the whole world is a manifestation of consciousness, the perception of the whole world appears in terms of the subtle capacities. The world begins to have colors, smells, and textures we didn't see before. For instance, one day you might realize that you are seeing the night at noon; it is daytime, the sun is shining, but you can see the night behind everything. This is called the midnight sun of the subtle realms.

The seeing I am discussing is not necessarily images arising in the mind. It is not what people call visions, because visions are more like fantasies—manifestations in the mental realm. People who are more visual than others sometimes have visions, but this does not mean they are necessarily seeing their inner state. They may be seeing something happening—a presence, a shape, or an event, and this can be a spiritual experience—but that is different from the direct seeing of where you are. The seeing we are discussing means actually perceiving your state. So when the Black arises, you see blackness. You see luminous blackness that shimmers, almost like a black satin curtain that is moving slightly in the wind. This is the pure seeing of the Black Essence, not a vision.

But sometimes the inner states do present themselves in images that have symbolic meaning. For example, some people have difficulty seeing the Green Essence as it is—just a pure emerald green presence—so they see a green valley in their hearts. But we can go beyond the images and just see the pure state. In any case, it is useful to be able to distinguish, for instance, between an image arising in your consciousness and what you are seeing that is actually present in your heart or your belly.

The capacity for inner seeing goes through a process of clarification as it develops. Whether you see visions or experiential states, inner seeing can be contaminated and distorted, just as our regular vision can be. Projections and beliefs can make us see something different from what actually is present in our experience. Or it can cause us to interpret its meaning according to our subjective biases and positions. In fact, all of the inner subtle capacities have to go through the process of clarification so that you don't deceive yourself.

The fact that subtle capacities exist indicates that perception can extend inwardly to subtler dimensions, which is necessary for our inquiry to go beyond the conventional dimension of experience. The inner realm has many kinds of miraculous dimensions, and inquiry is an adventure into these new dimensions and universes. This is part of the excitement of the journey, and it is a valid excitement because it is our life and our possibility.

Practice Session: Inner Perceptual Capacities in Your Inquiry

Now would be a good time to see how the various perceptual capacities function within your own inquiry. For fifteen minutes, inquire into whatever thread you may be aware of in your experience. Then reflect on your inquiry and see which of the capacities you used.

Did the inner touch, the inner taste, or the inner seeing get activated? Did you sometimes hear or smell the states you perceived? It's also useful to note which of your physical senses came into play. What correspondences did you notice between your regular senses and the subtle senses? Which of the senses seemed most dominant? Were there any that didn't show up at all? Consider whether you had more trouble sensing your body or your emotional states.

It is also interesting to notice the relationship between what you discovered in this inquiry and what you may have observed about your perceptual capacities in day-to-day life. Then, as you go about your tasks for the rest of the day, note the times when either your physical or subtle senses seem to be more acute.

SUBTLE UNDERSTANDING

We began the journey of our spacecruiser by exploring inquiry as a dynamic activity of the soul that expresses the characteristics of our true nature. And we have seen how our true nature is a spacious translucence that is constantly displaying the world, including our experience. Inquiry is a specific approach to recognizing the truth of this display. It invites reality to manifest in its fullness, which coincides with its openness. This open translucence has a dynamism, a creativity rooted in total openness, freedom, and spontaneity. This dynamism in its purity is an unhindered, unconditioned, unencumbered, unattached celebratory display of all that is possible to experience.

But as our ego develops, this reality becomes codified and rigidified into the static world that we know and inhabit, the world that includes our familiar and habitual sense of self. This view of reality, which is reflected in the experience of the conventional world, subverts the free dynamism of our Being into manipulative activity based on positions and preferences, and particular aims and goals. It becomes the activity of an entity that is trying to get someplace. This is what we call ego activity, which is a manipulation of our experience based on the conventional view of good and bad, the belief that some things are better than others, and that by rejecting, preferring, judging, and efforting, we can get to someplace that feels better.

We have seen that inquiry is based on remaining open and without positions. It is guided by the true knowingness of what is happening in our experience, and it is not goal-oriented. Its only interest is the revelation of the truth. You could say that inquiry is the aesthetic appreciation of what our Being reveals. So in some sense, as we learn to do it, we reclaim our free dynamism. In fact, inquiry is an expression of that dynamism. It coincides with the true unfoldment of our Being, which we call understanding.

Learning the open attitude of inquiry counteracts our tendency to limit and subvert the free dynamism. With practice, inquiry becomes a mode of inner life that replaces the inner manipulation of ego activity. So instead of trying to do something about a particular state or feeling, for example, we open ourselves to find out and understand it. This changes the whole orientation of our psyche, because ego activity tends to limit true openness. In fact, ego activity blocks the dynamism from its natural freedom and spontaneity because it is based on what we believe is true.

In ego activity, we take for granted the knowledge we have accumulated, without questioning it. We take our learning to be conclusive, while inquiry is based on recognizing what is possible and not taking anything as final. That is because its kernel, which is a question, is openness, an openness that wants to find out. We choose to invite Being to freely display its richness. So as inquiry becomes central in our lives, and synergistic with the operation of the Diamond Guidance, the Guidance infuses our everyday life as well as our inquiry.

With dedicated practice, we can have moments in meditation or inquiry when we move deeply in ourselves, when we go beyond the usual images and emotions and all the content of our personal history. Then it becomes possible to recognize the basis of ego activity itself—that which determines a great deal of our experience. We begin to see directly and explicitly the tendency to take a position and to try to get someplace. We start to see the beliefs and assumptions we have, the subtle attitudes that orient our experience. Even when some of these beliefs are based on real experiences, they block our natural unfoldment because they become solidified as conclusions.

Eventually, inquiry moves to a deeper level, where it becomes very subtle and very delicate, where we can see the original manifestations of the ego and its activities. Instead of just seeing the content, we also understand how the ego works. This means that our spaceship has crossed to a parallel universe, as if it had undergone a phase shift. That is when Spacecruiser *Inquiry* begins to engage the hyperdrive instead of its power drive. By this time, we generally have more peace, quiet, and spaciousness in our inner experience, so it becomes easier to see these subtle discriminations. These initial stirrings of ego are very subtle and underlie all its experiences, identifications, and reactions.

We can indicate a few ways that inquiry might appear at such a subtle level; and these might be most obvious in silent meditation. First, there is no doing anything to anything. Whatever we experience, whatever arises, we don't do anything about it. If you feel hatred, you don't do anything about it. If you feel love, you don't do anything about it. You don't look at experience from any perspective or dimension or position. At this subtle level, we are not operating from any point of view. Everyone usually looks at experience from a particular perspective, whether it is the perspective of the individual, the perspective of the ego, the perspective of the human being, the perspective of the body—or even the perspective of Essence, the Absolute, or freedom itself. But at this deep, still place, there is no perspective; you just purely recognize, experience, and behold whatever arises. The inquiry is not coming from any position. It is completely free.

Perception, intelligence, and understanding operate in a simple and natural way to see through intentional doing or conceptual attitudes and positions. Inquiry spontaneously begins to merely understand the intentional doing, as it arises, or the conceptual attitude we perceive we are taking, or the positions we recognize we are trying to hold on to. It just sees these ego manifestations and understands their significance. There is awareness and knowingness without any conceptually directed interest about any state or condition. Because we hold no position, no state is conceptualized as preferable. No condition is posited as desirable. As a result, awareness is not directed by any of these conceptualizations. There is no intentional movement toward or away from anything; one is just being there—calm, relaxed, with no ideas of what "being there" means.

This is true nondoing, which can happen only when we have no interest in any doing because we are not striving toward any state. From this place, there is freedom from all teachings, freedom from desiring specific states, freedom from ideas and perspectives—even one's own perspective. For it is implicitly understood that any perspective or teaching will be an overlay on whatever is purely arising. Instead, we merely recognize the subtle movement of the psyche toward goals, and that understanding naturally dissolves the movement and liberates our unfabricated and uncontrived naturalness. The pure perception and understanding of what is actually there in our experience dissolves the subtle movement of the psyche. The Diamond Guidance is present and operational as a natural and spontaneous functioning of intelligence and awareness. The result is a discriminating understanding of what is arising, liberating the display of Being from our opinions.

This discriminating understanding appear as the flashes of insight that are inseparable from our intimacy with the qualities of experience. We recognize here the functioning of the Diamond Guidance as spontaneous curiosity, love of the truth, and steadfastness, which together result in the spontaneous unveiling of truth, as both unfoldment and insight. As this continues, the unveiling finally merges into a nondual condition—the natural perfection, which is the lucidity displaying experience. At this point, lucidity and understanding are inseparable, completely unified. There is unity of presence and discriminating awareness, which is a guided, dynamic flow and unfoldment.

In this natural state, whenever a position happens to arise, the practice of inquiry is merely the recognition of that position. The simple apprehension of the subtle movement of taking a position annihilates it. In other words, understanding itself will reveal the barrier and annihilate it. There is no need to do anything, because our nature inherently tends to display things clearly and to spontaneously reveal the truth. We are not making it reveal the truth. Just by seeing our positions and our attempts to get someplace, we cease and desist. We stop identifying with that activity, without trying to stop identifying—because the moment we try to stop identifying, we are active again.

At this level of insight, inquiry becomes subtle, which means that the Diamond Guidance needs to operate in a very subtle way. This requires the Black diamond to come into play. The Black diamond is the presence of the aspect of Peace in inquiry, as a manifestation of the Guidance. This brings in another capacity that has always been present in inquiry and understanding but which now becomes more obvious. The Black latifa gives the Guidance—and our inquiry—the element of power.

THE POWER OF UNDERSTANDING

Power is one of the ways of experiencing the Black Essence. The Black Essence has two sides—the peaceful side and the wrathful side. The peaceful side is the stillness, mystery, and magic—qualities of the night. "Wrathful" is used here in the sense of the Tibetan tradition of being fierce and annihilating in the service of truth. The wrathful side is the quality of power. What is power? In the language of differential calculus, the definition of power is expressed as DE/DT, which means the rate of change of energy in relation to time. So power refers to the rate of output of energy, not just the quantity of energy that is available. The more energy you put out per unit of time, the more power is generated. That is why a more powerful engine can generate large quantities of energy fast enough to create a bigger capacity for movement or functioning.

Power gives all the essential qualities an added force, efficiency, and speed. But what actually is the power of Being? The power of Being is just an active manifestation of peace, a dynamic application of stillness. It is not a pushing, it is not a destructiveness. When peace touches the soul, it simply stills it. All of her activities, agitation, and reactions simply dissolve the moment the presence of stillness touches them. They are annihilated. That is the power of stillness, the Peace aspect of Essence. So the power of our Being is an annihilating force, which annihilates ego attitudes and positions by revealing that they don't truly exist. The power of Peace takes everything back to its original source, which is total stillness.

All of the qualities of Essence color the field of the soul in their own likeness when they touch it. In fact, the soul transforms into the very quality that touches her. So when the Black Essence touches the manifestations of the soul, it brings them back to its own nature, which is peacefulness, and the Peace of true nature is a sense of stillness in which nothing stirs. It is total stillness, which, when precisely understood, turns out to be one hundred percent annihilation. It is an intense sensitivity, but the sensitivity has become so intense that it is absolute, for absolutely nothing stirs.

Question and Answer

STUDENT: I realize I am afraid of feeling powerful because I think it will be destructive. How is power related to destructiveness and hatred?

ALMAAS: Hatred is fake power; it is black, but a dull, thick blackness. Hatred arises when we haven't actualized the true power of the Black Essence. It is due to frustration in the face of difficulties. Hatred arises when you feel powerless, for it is an attempt to eliminate the frustration by annihilating it. You want to annihilate whatever problem you have, whatever is in your way, whether it is an inner or outer frustration. You want to make it disappear. True Black power does that, but through understanding instead of through aggression. Aggression only creates more frustration.

But if you inquire into the hatred itself, it transforms into power. Just as you would inquire into anything else, you want to feel the hatred, be open to it, welcome it, see what it is about. Where did it come from? What is it trying to do? Feel it fully—without resistance, without judgment, and without acting it out. That by itself unfolds it to reveal the truth lying within it, which is true power.

The capacity of true power appears in the Black diamond of the Guidance as sharpness. It is its cutting edge. Whatever you are seeing, the cutting edge discriminates it so precisely that it shows its absolute relationship to our ultimate nature. In doing so, it annihilates it, because our ultimate nature is absolute stillness. So the slightest deviation from our true nature dissolves into Peace. The Black diamond represents the precise and sharp clarity that annihilates whatever falsehood it encounters by the power of its stilling silence. So the precision of the Black diamond gives insight and understanding a tremendous transformative power.

To express it more precisely, when the Black diamond dominates the functioning of the Diamond Guidance, it embodies the power of cutting through. All the diamonds have the quality of cutting through lies and concepts; however, this capacity attains its full power with the Black diamond. Its sharpness is that of annihilation: The edges of the diamond are so sharp that they actually disappear into absence—they actually cease to exist. So when the Black diamond touches something, it makes what it touches not exist. It doesn't actually cut, it simply eliminates what it touches, because the sharp edge of the diamond is so sharp that you cannot say it is an edge anymore.

ANNIHILATION AND THE OPENNESS OF TRUE NATURE

This is the operation of the depth of true nature, which is absolute nonexistence, absolute annihilation—which is the essence of Peace, which is really the essence of openness. Openness arises from this mysterious absence and total lucidity, for nothing is there. Imagine a diamond whose edge is sharpened to the extent of absence, an absence that is beyond matter and space. That kind of diamond cuts through all matter and space by making it disappear. That is why understanding can be so complete. The moment the sharp edge makes contact, whatever is false is just gone. That is why we don't need to do anything for understanding to happen.

Part of this power to cut through comes from the particular understanding of knowledge that the Black diamond provides. The knowledge that is characteristic of identifications and concepts does not exist in any fundamental or ultimate manner. So when we talk about the sharp edge as cutting, this cutting is merely understanding that, "Oh, what I have taken as truth is just a concept, a creation of my mind. I was identifying with something that isn't real." It is not that somebody comes and slashes through something. Annihilation doesn't mean that something that is there ceases to be there. It is more accurate to say that what is there becomes seen in its true nature. Our mental fabrications are exposed as such, and true manifestations of reality are seen in their ultimate nature, neither existing nor not existing. They appear, but never really exist. This means that as things are displayed, they are never solidified. They just keep getting displayed, without ever really existing.

So the insight is the sharp cut, but it has now become insight into ultimate reality, which is beyond existence and nonexistence. In this way, the annihilating quality of the Black brings everything back to reality.

Annihilation is the first of the characteristics of our true nature in its total openness and freedom. In that openness and freedom, there is no solidity, no content. It is so open, so free, so light, that it is empty. Everything disappears into that stillness. That is why stillness and peace are connected with annihilation.

So the Black diamond, when it functions as part of the Diamond Guidance, gives it the capacity to cut through all the way to the Absolute. Then our consciousness is that stillness and silence that is clear, objective, exquisitely precise, and sharp. There is a sense of silent knowledge and mysterious power, a settled sufficiency, and an unspeakable contentment. This diamond reminds us of the Absolute itself, as if the Absolute had condensed and formed itself into a diamond. The blackness is so black that it glimmers and shines. There is a sense of majesty, awe, and mystery. It is an exquisite consciousness of silence, which silences all chatter and stills it into its own beautiful stillness.

With this diamond in the Diamond Guidance, inquiry becomes so sharp, so effective, and so powerful that it begins to expose the first arisings of the ego-consciousness—the background of all attitudes and positions. We become able to perceive the beginning movements of ego—the tendency to go someplace, the impulse to desire, the impulse to reject, the impulse to hope. And just the clear discernment of these impulses annihilates the ego, for by now we are very near the translucence of our true nature.

This operation of the Black Essence is present in our inquiry from the beginning, as the sharpness of insight, as the precision of understanding. It is what has always given understanding its liberating quality. However, when this quality of freedom is central to our inquiry, the Black diamond is in the foreground; we are seeing it as a specific manifestation and functioning of the Diamond Guidance.

At this stage of inquiry, our experience goes through a radical transformation. By dissolving the inner ego-stirrings of the soul that make her leave home, our soul settles and becomes one with her beautiful and exquisite nature. Our inner atmosphere partakes of that lucidity and silence, that satin smoothness, in which the annihilation of the image or the inner activity of the ego-self is experienced as a blissful cessation, a dying in complete ecstasy. Our soul feels rested, finally at home. There is precision, sharpness, and perception, but also complete stillness, as if the stillness itself had a sharpness and a discriminating quality that has evolved faceted edges. You experience yourself as inside, and part of, this very delicate, completely black, faceted diamond. And the whole world appears as the luminous shimmering of those facets.

So as we learn to value not arriving, we arrive, for true arriving is a matter of not leaving, not departing. Usually, we are always leaving ourselves, always departing; and we think we are going someplace. When we try to go someplace, all we end up doing is separating from our true nature. We are always trying to find our true nature by going away from it. So inquiry takes us to the point where we simply recognize how we are leaving—and the ideas and beliefs that make us feel that we should leave. When it truly reveals its fundamental ground, inquiry teaches us not to go anywhere—because there is nowhere to go.

CHAPTER 22

Knowing in Understanding

HAVING DISCUSSED OUR JOURNEY as it moves through the five operational aspects of the lataif, we now travel to other essential realms that are also part of the Diamond Guidance. Our spacecruiser is guided by the luminous presence of the Guidance in the exploration of its own faceted nature. And our understanding of inquiry continues to deepen.

From our discussion thus far, it is obvious that fundamental to both inquiry and understanding is the element of knowing. Knowingness is always implicit in this process of self-revelation. Understanding is more than knowingness, but knowingness is necessary. Without knowingness, there is no experience and hence no understanding. However, by knowingness we mean a particular kind of knowingness: the fundamental knowingness of basic knowledge. More specifically, this necessary element of understanding is the capacity to know.

KNOWING THROUGH INTIMACY

We have seen in chapter 15 that understanding implies a differentiation in experience. Being presents itself, or our experience, in a differentiated form; it does not normally present us with undifferentiated experience. It gives us specifics: anger, sadness, sickness, health, emptiness, fullness, and so on. Knowingness means not only the ability to differentiate these elements, but also the capacity to experientially recognize them for what they are. This kind of knowing is always implicit in experience. In other words, real understanding implies the possibility of knowing through intimacy, instead of only through mental and conceptual operations.

You can know your body through being intimate with it, you can know your feelings through being intimate with them, you can know your inner state by being intimate with it. Intimacy means that no barrier exists between you and whatever you are knowing. It's a direct in-touch-ness, a direct contact. More than that, it is a mixing of your consciousness with whatever it is you're knowing. There are no barriers, no walls, between you and what it is that you are knowing.

This has been traditionally termed knowing through identity, that is, knowing by being what you know. It has also been termed gnosis (*jnana* in Sanskrit; *yeshe* in Tibetan; *ma'rifa* in Arabic). For example, you know anger by being anger, by experiencing it as part of you when your awareness and consciousness pervade the experience of anger. The nature of the soul is such that when a feeling arises, we can experience that feeling from within the feeling itself. We can intimately mix our consciousness with the specifics of our experience and recognize directly what the experience is. This is the ground of knowingness, which is direct knowing, and it is necessary in the process of understanding. Without this kind of knowingness, this gnosis, there is no possibility of real understanding; understanding remains only a mental operation, which is good for mathematics but is not enough for spiritual transformation.

When you experience love, how do you know you're experiencing love? You just know it. But how do you know it? Through intimacy with it, by feeling it in your heart as part of your heart. Everything we know, we know experientially. There is no experience that doesn't include knowingness. As we have seen, when there's no knowingness in experience, there's no experience. It's as simple as that. Even when you experience not-knowing, it's knowingness. You're knowing that you don't know. You're knowing the experience of unknowing.

So whenever there is experience—whether it's mental, emotional, physical, or spiritual experience—knowing is its ground. Both ordinary and basic knowing are necessary for understanding. But the direct, intimate knowing of basic knowledge is necessary for you to develop and unfold. We need to become aware of this kind of knowingness to develop the capacity for understanding.

Practice Session: Your Relationship to Direct Knowing

Because direct knowing is so fundamental to inquiry, exploring your relationship to direct knowing will be helpful in deepening your process. In what way does direct knowing play a part in your life? What is it like for you to have an intimate, immediate awareness of your experience? Are you aware of any beliefs or attitudes about this kind of knowing in contrast to mental or indirect knowing?

Consider something simple such as your experience of your dominant hand. Perform a routine task such as washing the dishes or vacuuming, and as you do so, take note of how directly you are able to perceive that hand and its actions. To what degree is your immediate experience of your hand filtered through your concepts about what hands are and do? or through your attitudes toward past experiences of doing this particular task? or through judgments you might have about how well you are accomplishing the task? What attitudes support you in having a direct knowing about your hand? How does the relative directness or indirectness of your perceptions affect your overall state?

THE BLUE ASPECT

Knowingness—the capacity to know through direct contact with an element of our experience—is related to a particular essential aspect. It is related to the operation of the Blue diamond, which is the Blue Essence in its diamond presence. The Blue Essence is usually called the aspect of pure consciousness, but it is also the aspect of knowingness. Even intellectual knowledge is based on this capacity; without inherent direct and intimate knowingness, ordinary knowledge would not be possible. Direct knowingness is what gives us the data necessary for our mind to think and spin out its knowledge. Without knowingness, we have no data.

Knowingness is more than just perception, for perception alone indicates only the fact of seeing differentiation. To recognize the differentiation—for differentiation to become discrimination—knowingness is required. This knowingness precedes labeling. For example, an infant knows that it is uncomfortable without having the word or even the concept for being uncomfortable. It simply starts squirming. Its body recognizes that something is uncomfortable. Later on, when we develop language, we call it discomfort.

So this capacity for knowing is preverbal, prelabeling. Labeling arises as the next step. In experience, first there is differentiation, that is, awareness that there are various elements and patterns in consciousness. This awareness functions in the same way that a mirror reflects—it reveals the shapes and patterns of our experience but provides no knowledge about what is reflected. The next step is discrimination: recognizing what these elements and patterns are. Knowing implies both their differentiation and discrimination. The third step is labeling, putting a tag on each known element. Thinking assumes all three of these steps in order to proceed.

The knowing necessary for understanding occurs in the second step: the discrimination of experience. Labeling may arise—it can be present or not. If it is, it will serve as a tool for articulating the understanding, unless we use the labels as a substitute for the direct knowing. In that case, we end up with only mental understanding.

This direct knowing is most obvious when we experience Essence and its aspects. When, for instance, the black quality of Peace arises and we absorb ourselves in it, we know it is peace, we know it is stillness. We don't need somebody to tell us that it's peace. Even if we don't give it the name "peace," something in us recognizes that it is a specific quality different from other qualities, and knows how it is different. This inherent capacity in our soul is provided by the Blue aspect. The Blue aspect gives our psyche the capacity to know through immersion, through identity, through intimacy, through contact, through gnosis. This capacity is very elemental and totally basic to all our experience.

This quality of knowing can be impure, obscured, and limited or very pure, full, refined, and clear. When it is refined and clear, we experience it as essential presence. When it's not, when this knowingness is incomplete, we experience it as our normal knowing of thoughts, emotions, and sensations.

THE ESSENCE OF CONSCIOUSNESS

The aspect of Knowing, as we have mentioned, is the same as the aspect of consciousness. Understanding what we mean by that is important for understanding the basis of this direct and basic knowing. The Blue aspect is a quality of presence, a way that the presence of Essence manifests. It is an aspect that expresses and reveals something significant about our true nature. But it is a very basic quality, in the sense that all other qualities depend on it. By understanding what we mean by consciousness, we can also more fully understand what presence is.

Essence is always a presence of a field that is sensitive in itself. It is—it exists—but it is also aware of itself. It is aware of its isness. Each quality of Essence is the self-aware field that is also aware of the particular quality of the aspect. If it is the aspect of Love, then there is the presence of a field of sensitivity that is aware of its isness, but also aware of the quality of Love. The Love and the isness are not separate here; there is simply the presence of Love that is aware of itself as the presence of Love.

With the Blue aspect, there is awareness of isness, of presence, but the quality of the Blue aspect is very subtle, for it is implicit and yet significant in all other aspects. The experience is simply of a presence of consciousness that is aware that it is consciousness. It is just the recognition that there is recognition. More precisely, the presence of the quality of consciousness is simply the presence of consciousness and nothing more. This consciousness is not aware of any object outside of itself. But since it is consciousness, it is consciousness of itself. It is a field conscious of itself, aware of itself.

It is conscious of itself by being itself, not by reflecting on itself. It is like a medium of a subtle gas in which each atom is sensitive to its own existence. So there is a field of self-sensitivity. The quality highlighted in this aspect is simply that of being a conscious presence. This is true of all aspects, except that the other aspects include another quality as well, that of love or will, for instance. In fact, it is subtler than this. In complete identification with this presence, in full realization of it, there is simply consciousness that is conscious that it is conscious.

This is what makes it knowing. To be conscious of being conscious, or to be aware of being aware, means to know that one is conscious. It is actually knowing that there is knowing. It is the presence of knowing without an object. The presence simply knows that it knows. And what it knows is knowing. It is not knowing anything outside of itself; it is pure knowing.

We see that the ability of the presence to be conscious that it is conscious implies that it knows, and knows it knows. To know, and to know this knowing, is the exact experience of the Blue aspect of Essence. And this is what it means when we say that Essence is conscious of itself as presence. Essence is presence that knows itself as presence. If we continue this subtle analysis, we can see that to know in this way is to *be*, because knowing and being are inseparable. The knowing of presence is presence. But this inseparability of knowing and being is the most fundamental epistemological truth regarding Essence.

BEING KNOWING

The aspect of Knowing arises when one knows that one's very beingness is inseparable from knowing: that one is being knowing and hence this presence is completely one with itself. There is no division between subject and object, absolutely no duality in the knowing. So it is basic knowing. But since it is presence, it is not an *activity* of knowing. It is the *presence* of the quality of Knowing.

Because the aspect of basic Knowing implies a complete identity of knowing and being, the experience of it is of deep abiding, total settling in oneself, complete repose in one's presence. Any agitation, any movement away from oneself, will tend to disconnect us from it. It is complete inner rest, what is referred to in Sanskrit as *sahaja-samadhi*. There is no agitation in the field of consciousness. There is total repose in presence, by being the presence so completely that we only know that we know through experiencing ourselves as a *field* of Knowing.

The Blue aspect is usually difficult for most people to access because their minds are so busy and their inner consciousness is so agitated. Things like worry, guilt, and agitated desire all tend to dissipate such repose and lead us away from our Being. What we are left with is a subject-object kind of knowing, mostly of the mental/conceptual type. Yet this basic knowing inherent in the Blue aspect is the foundation for all knowing, for it is the simple and original element of knowing—the element that every other kind of knowing is based on.

We see here the unity of epistemology and ontology, for this aspect is a presence in which the beingness is itself the knowingness. When knowing splits off from being, we end up with ordinary knowledge, a knowledge that is not sufficient to reconnect us with our Being, no matter how useful it is in the practical world.

Such understanding reveals the necessity for stillness, silence, slowness, and solitude in the initial stages of any inner path. Otherwise, it will be difficult for us to settle down and for our mind to abide in its primordial being. And without this abiding, we have no other way to truly know ourselves.

The Blue aspect is the quality of our true nature that is responsible for direct, immediate knowing. This capacity is essential in inquiry to give us contact with the truth of our experience in the moment. Therefore, though we do not necessarily experience the Blue Essence in our personal inquiry, we still retain its contribution as a basic implied capacity. Each moment that we know our experience directly, we are feeling the action of the Blue diamond of the Guidance.

DIRECT KNOWING

The alignment with direct knowing, with inherent discriminating awareness, is one of the few fundamental principles that the Diamond Approach is based on. The Diamond Approach is built to a large degree on the concept of essential aspects—objectively universal qualities of presence. "Universal" means that everybody can recognize them on their own. And it is this capacity for direct recognition that is the function of the Blue Essence, the essence of knowingness.

This is important because our educational institutions and various systems of knowledge do not focus on this quality of knowingness. They focus on that fraction of knowingness that is our mental knowing. The kind of knowingness we are discussing here is not part of modern scientific theory nor even psychological theory. It's a kind of knowingness that becomes obvious only in spiritual experience, for spiritual experience exists only in the immediacy of experience. The more immediate our experience, the more spiritual it is.

So the more we recognize this capacity for direct knowing, the more there arises in us a trust and faith that we can know, that we can experience direct, unmediated knowing. If we don't know about this kind of knowingness, or if we don't have faith in it, we tend not to have faith in understanding. We think, "What will understanding do? It will just teach me somebody else's ideas." If you don't know about this knowingness, you say, "Well, I'll just apply somebody else's ideas about understanding and I'll probably get her or his knowledge." You don't trust that you can have your own independent knowledge. But the moment you recognize that you inherently possess this capacity of knowingness, you will tend to trust understanding more. You will know that you can be certain through your own experience, not just because somebody said so.

Such knowledge is autonomous knowledge, truly our own. We are not using any intermediary. In fact, this is the only way to have autonomous knowledge. We may find such complete autonomy in knowing intolerable. It might frighten us because it makes us feel our aloneness. Immediate knowing in its purity can also be terrifying because we are left without access to our usual ordinary knowledge. The absence of ordinary knowledge erases the foundation of our usual sense of self, for this sense of self is based on mental constructions that use memory traces from the past.

In other words, without ordinary knowledge we have no familiar identity. Using only pure basic knowing, the self cannot maintain itself; it has to be surrendered, melted. Hence, the Blue aspect is an especially selfless aspect. It is in some sense the most undefined and formless of all aspects.

The Blue aspect arises in the center of the head, just as the Green aspect arises in the center of the chest. From this we can also see that just as the Green is the sensitivity that forms the essence of the heart, the Blue is the consciousness that forms the essence of the mind. This is probably the reason why some Sufis consider the Blue to be connected to the Green, as if they form the two sides of one latifa.

Let's look at this phenomenon of direct knowing experientially. If you pay attention to yourself at this moment, you will see that you are not only aware of your body sensations, you also recognize them. You can recognize when you feel pain or pleasure, you can recognize when there's relaxation or tension. And you know whether you like or don't like whatever you are experiencing. So when you pay attention to yourself, what are you experiencing? Knowledge. It's all knowledge—it's all knowing.

The more precise our discrimination, the more it is possible for us to know. The degree to which we can know each discriminated element in our experience depends upon our development of the Blue essential quality. The integration of this essential quality gives us the capacity to immerse ourselves in any particular experience, to absorb our consciousness in it so much that we are intimately in contact with it in all its nuances. We can mix our consciousness with it so much that we know its atoms, the fundamental particles that make up the experience.

And the more we recognize this capacity, the more it becomes specific, the more it develops and integrates, and our experience becomes more pervaded by that kind of knowingness. So when it is said, "Know yourself," that's what is meant—know yourself intimately and directly; because the abstractions that arise out of direct knowing and form ordinary knowledge will not lead you to true self-knowledge.

Direct knowing is inherent in our perception in general; it pervades all of our senses, and it's happening all the time. Without it, we would have no experience. This knowingness is not that mysterious. But we don't recognize direct knowing as the true source of what we call our experience because it's usually mixed with all kinds of other knowing. Rarely do we recognize ourselves as a field of knowledge where the field itself is nothing but a recognition of its patterns. Yet this is our nature, and it is important to understand that this direct knowing is happening all the time. It informs and underlies—it is the foundation for—all of our experience.

The more our capacity for direct knowing becomes precise, specific, and clearly discriminating, the more we are integrating the aspect in its diamond form. Our knowing then becomes more luminous and vivid. But most important, our knowing becomes objective, that is, free of our associations and preferences. Knowing in the Diamond Dimension brings more precision and clarity—and hence certainty—to our knowing. We are more able to discern correctly and know things as they truly are. How else can we recognize truth?

CHAPTER 23

Truth in Understanding

OBJECTIVE TRUTH

Conceptualizing the phenomenon we call understanding as the discernment of patterns in experience and their meaning implies the presence of something to be known, perceived, experienced, and discerned. Specifically, it implies there is content in any given experience that can be discerned, content not produced by our conceptualizing mind. But is there actually something present in experience, and can it be truly recognized for what it is? Or is everything we experience a product of our mind, our subjectivity? Is it perhaps a mixture? And if our mind adds something to an experience, can we truly say that we recognize the pattern of that experience? These questions all point to the issue of objective truth. We need to consider that understanding will not have real significance or true value if there is not something in our experience to be understood, something that is objectively true, independent of our minds and opinions.

Understanding happens when inquiry results in a discernment of the pattern in experience that clarifies the meaning of the situation. Our ability to discern the pattern implies that there is an objectively true pattern in our experience. Similarly, the fact that we can discern the meaning of that pattern implies that there is such a thing as true and objective meaning. This is what is meant when we say that through inquiry we find the truth in our experience. This implies that there is something in our experience that we call truth, and this truth is not necessarily obvious on the surface. Such a perspective assumes that our experience contains truth and that inquiry arrives at this truth by seeing through what obscures it.

Truth, therefore, is not something we produce in our minds but something already there to be discovered. This is actually a controversial assertion. If we listen to philosophers, dialecticians, and epistemologists, we find no general agreement about this point. Not everybody agrees that there is a given in experience called truth. It is easy to see why our assertion is controversial or questionable: How can we know that what we are calling truth is not our own subjective reflection? How can we be sure it is not an opinion, an ideology, or a result of an ideology?

The view of the Diamond Approach is that there is truth in our experience that is independent of the conceptualizing mind of the person investigating. Science accepts that the assertions of a theory concerning the physical world can be proven or disproven, and that the outcome will be accepted universally. We are saying the same thing about human experience: If different people explore, investigate, and experiment—in other words, inquire directly as we have been describing in this book—they will all come to the same truths about experience. This means that our work of inquiry and understanding can become scientific work. We can find out what in human experience is objectively true independent of our attitudes and our psychological, philosophical, or ideological positions. And this discovery will be a matter of common agreement.

This is an important consideration for our work of inquiry and understanding. When you are convinced that you can discern an objective truth through exploring your direct experience, you will be more motivated to put out the effort to find out what that truth is. But if you take the position that everyone sees things differently, and therefore all inner knowing is relative, your motivation will suffer. You're just going to perceive your experience as an isolated happening whose truth is not relevant to anyone else or to any other situation than this one. But if we believe that there is an objective truth—a discernible meaning—in our experience, then we can see more value in exploring our inner reality. Then our inner experience has significance and can function as a support, as a bedrock of reality. The presence of objective truth in our experience can aid us in developing our basic trust, our commitment, our sincerity, and our openness.

We can explore this question from several angles—epistemological, philosophical, or theological. But regardless of our approach, how we answer the question is very important in determining how we orient to our personal experience, how much conviction and certainty we have in our experience, and ultimately how we relate to our actions and life in general.

It also has important implications for spiritual work. If we take the position that everything in our personal experience is relative, then we cannot have a teaching. That is because a spiritual teaching is based on a set of universal truths about human consciousness.

Practice Session: Your Own View Regarding Objective Truth

At this point, you might want to explore your own view or position regarding this question. Do you believe that there is such a thing as objective truth—something apart from learned knowledge or opinion or perspective—that is actually present in a situation? Maybe you have never thought about the question. If not, you have likely taken an implicit position in order to function. On the other hand, maybe you have thought about it a great deal. Either way, it can be very useful to examine your orientation toward objective truth in order to understand more fully the assumptions that underlie your own process of inquiry.

Do you believe that the meaning and significance of experience is all relative? In other words, do you believe that the truth about a situation completely depends on your vantage point? Or are some views more truthful than others? Is there only one correct view, and all others are wrong no matter how logical or sensible they may be? Is there one truth that is impossible to know, making all views simply approximations or guesses? In that case, would the truth be the view that combines the best elements of all the different perspectives? Or perhaps you believe that the truth is some kind of consensus—a general agreement based on what most people find to be true.

What about the truth in your own experience? Is there such a thing as an objective truth that you can directly apprehend? There are so many different possible positions on this question that it will be helpful to find out which one you hold. Can you see how that position affects your motivation and action in life? What are the ways this happens?

RELATIVE TRUTH

Generally speaking, spiritual traditions and teachings take the position that there is such a thing as objective truth. In fact, a spiritual teaching is nothing but a way to reach this objective truth. However, the various spiritual traditions have different ideas about what this objective truth is. The theistic religions believe in the existence of God. The Hindu systems have other ultimate truths: Atman, Brahman, or Shiva. Buddhism talks of *shunyata* (emptiness) or Buddha nature. But they all believe that we can find some ultimate truth in experience.

The Diamond Approach is also based on the recognition that such a thing as objective truth exists independent of the mind of the person experiencing it. However, what we mean by "truth" is not merely the ultimate truth of reality. We use the word to refer to a specific element in any experience: the truth of the experience (or the situation), which can be confirmed by several independent observers. This objective truth, which is independent of one's subjective positions, is not static, nor is it an object. It's not as though you look into your experience and find the truth, and this truth stays the truth forever and ever. In each moment there is truth arising anew in your experience. The next moment, the truth in your experience might be different from the truth you discovered last. So the truth is dynamic, constantly shifting, changing, and transforming. And inquiry is the dynamic process that reveals increasing degrees and depths of that truth.

But truth always refers to something actually present—how things objectively are at the moment—even though that truth will change. At each moment there is one truth, even though it can be viewed from different perspectives, attitudes, or positions. Seeing it from these various positions will definitely color the perception of the truth, without negating the fact that an objective element of truth is present.

Let's take an example: Suppose you feel sad. The presence of sadness is an objective fact. To say "I'm sad" is the truth in the moment. However, we might see and explain this phenomenon in different ways depending on our perspective or position. And that perspective will most likely affect the experience of sadness. But the sadness as an element in experience is still an incontrovertible truth.

This means that if we perceive our state visually, instead of experiencing it emotionally, we might see the sadness as a pattern of lights and colors. Or we might view it as an electromagnetic, electrochemical process. From a different perspective, we might see it as a psychic event or a mental reaction. If we are Buddhists, we might consider it a specific impurity that is arising in the psyche.

Still, the truth is that there is sadness. But the truth is not the words we might use to describe it. We could call it a feeling, an electromagnetic phenomenon, an electrochemical reaction, a pattern of light and color, or a psychic event; these all refer to the same occurrence. But the truth is what all these descriptions are referring to, even though they might reflect different kinds of perception. The experience will also be different if we look at it from a boundless dimension, where reality does not appear in the form of separate, discrete objects and where we will see this phenomenon of sadness arising as an event, as if it were happening in the mind of God. It will feel and look different, yet it is still the same phenomenon. The truth that everybody is observing is the same, though experienced differently.

The phenomenon itself is an incontrovertible truth in the present experience. If all these observers were to discuss what they're perceiving, they might come to see that they are all talking about the same thing—they are just using different languages and have different perspectives and attitudes toward the phenomenon. Yet a specific phenomenon has arisen that is not totally relative to the person experiencing it. The relativity is only in the perceptual details—the lens through which it is viewed—but not in the actual presence of the particular phenomenon. So the fact that there is sadness is an objective truth.

The kind of objective truth that I have just described is not what is usually called ultimate truth in most spiritual traditions. But in our approach, when we talk about finding the truth, we include this kind of truth. I call it relative truth. By relative I don't mean that different people will experience the same phenomenon differently. For example, what I feel as sadness, another person will not feel as hatred; if another person feels what I'm feeling, he or she will feel sad.

It is relative truth because its arising is dependent upon and in response to one's personal history and the present situation. It is the truth we find in the conventional dimension of experience. So, in the previous example, the sadness is an objective phenomenon, but it is dependent on my present experience, in the sense that it arises in response to specific conditions of this time and place. As those conditions change, the truth will change, which makes it relative. Furthermore, another person will likely have another phenomenon or feeling under similar circumstances, because each person's experience is dependent on personal predispositions and history.

It is easy to see this when we look at percepts such as sadness, anger, or love. These simple percepts always arise embedded in specific circumstances, and they are easy to agree upon as being objective truth. The same is true of actions, reactions, and behaviors; it's easy to see what an angry reaction or a loving response is, for example. Now let's take a more complex relative phenomenon: an insight.

Let's say you find out that you're not only sad, but you feel sad because you have missed yourself. How can we tell whether this is the truth or not? Can we say this is objective truth or is it just your opinion, perspective, or spiritual ideology? This statement can be an objective truth in the sense that it is the unique meaning of the pattern of your experience at the moment. That is, if you see the interrelationship between various elements of your experience—in this case, the relationship between your sadness and other significant parts of your experience—you will arrive at only one particular meaning, which is that you're sad because you miss yourself. You will not be able to say that you're sad because you're hungry or because somebody didn't love you—these possibilities will have been definitely eliminated. If you could claim such things, then you cannot have insight, which means there can be no possibility of seeing into the true meaning of an experience.

But the question is more subtle than this. You might recognize that you feel sad because you miss yourself, but you might care or not care about that fact. You might be moved by it or not, you might become curious about it or not. That will depend on your attitude and your perspective. But the realization that "I am sad because I miss myself" can actually happen and be recognized as reflecting exactly what is happening.

You can express this discernment in other ways, using another concept or metaphor, or words that reflect a different perspective. You might express it as "I am not feeling my depth," because you might not have a view that there is a self to miss. Or you might experience it as an alienation from what you truly are. That is different from saying "I am missing myself," but it is the same state, expressed in different words. Or you might experience it as distance from your essence, or as the absence of self-realization. You might experience it as being superficial or unreal.

If you adhere to certain spiritual systems, you won't say, "I feel that I am missing myself," you'll say, "I am recognizing the delusion of believing that I am separate from ultimate reality." That statement is the same as saying "I am missing myself." It's describing the same sensation, the same arising, but looked at from a different worldview. Depending on our view, ideology, or system, we can describe our experience in different ways, but that doesn't mean we are describing different things. It doesn't mean that we are disagreeing. Objective truth simply means that there is something discernibly true arising in the experience.

We see that all these expressions are equivalent attempts to express the same percepts, but from different positions or perspectives. But some perspectives are deeper and more fundamental than others. To say, for instance, "I am being superficial or unreal" is not as deep a perspective as the one that expresses itself as the delusion that you are dualistically separate from your ultimate reality. The latter is more fundamental and in some sense more accurate. However, either way of putting it refers to the same thing. You are merely describing it from a larger, more fundamental perspective. But that doesn't mean the first expression is wrong.

What I am addressing here is not the scientific mind. I'm addressing some of the traditional spiritual systems that take the position that either you see this experience of feeling sad as the delusion of separate reality or else you are in subjectivity—and hence not in touch with objective truth. I'm saying it is true that you are in subjectivity, but I am also saying that there is some truth in that subjectivity. It is the same truth that is expressed by the nondual point of view, but expressed differently—dualistically. Your particular subjectivity will of course be different depending upon where you are coming from. But what you are experiencing is the same.

DEEPENING LEVELS OF TRUTH

Seeing that the same phenomenon can be experienced from different perspectives and that some of these perspectives can be wiser, more inclusive, or more fundamental than others gives us a particular method. It points to a way of ascertaining truth, a reliable method to help us reveal more truth. It is a method not only for investigating and discovering truth, but also for understanding our attitudes or perspectives—in other words, how we view that truth.

We can explore our worldview, and recognizing what that is may change and deepen it. Even the experience itself may expand and reveal more of its truth. The feeling of sadness, for instance, might change as your view transforms. You might now experience the sadness as a ripple in your soul that has a certain vibration. It's the same thing as the sadness, but now you experience it with an additional dimension. This new dimension has emerged because we have explored and understood the assumptions underlying our view of the experience. This has allowed a deeper perspective to emerge. Our original perspective, which was limited by considering ourselves to be a physical body that has emotions, has expanded now to a perspective that says there is a consciousness that has manifestations in it.

In fact, the understanding we are referring to here is a matter of ascertaining the truth as we see it from our present perspective, which then unfolds to reveal deeper aspects of the truth. We investigate both the truth in experience and the investigating consciousness, which allows experience to unfold and to reveal more truth. As I have said before, truth is dynamic, it keeps changing. For instance, as you continue to investigate, you might find, "I am sad because somebody didn't see who I am." As you keep exploring, you realize a bigger truth: "I am sad not just because somebody didn't see who I am, but also because I am not certain that I *know* who I am. And because I am not certain who I am, it makes me sad that somebody didn't see who I am. Because if they see who I am, that will make me certain."

Does that mean that the truth that you were sad because somebody didn't see you was wrong? No, it was truth within its own perspective. Now you have a larger perspective that expands the truth. And this expansion can go on and on. As you explore more, you might recognize, "Now I see that who I am is really more than I thought I was. I was sad because I was not being myself fully, I was really missing myself." The more you know yourself, and the more your view expands, the more truth keeps unfolding, revealing more dimensions, more depths to it. That is how the process of understanding works.

Relative truth means that it is relative to our history—the specific manifestations of relative truth uniquely reflect our personal situation and background experience. When the objective truth is independent of our particular history and situation—that is, when everybody experiences the same truth regardless of personal situation or background—I call it essential truth. That's when we begin to experience Essence and its various aspects. Essential truth will usually arise when we explore a particular relative truth to the point where it becomes freed from our personal history. What will arise then has nothing to do with our childhood, with our history, but reflects the fundamentals of the human soul. The truth in this case is a manifestation of Essence, a quality of essential presence. It could be the presence of Compassion, of Love, or of Joy, Peace, Clarity, Will, Strength, Truth, Intelligence, and so on.

It is objective truth, but it cannot be found in the conventional level of experience, only in the essential level. And when the objective truth, which is now essential, is independent not only of our personal history and background but of all mind and its conceptualizations as well, we call it nonconceptual truth. Nonconceptual truth is independent of the concepts of love, hate, strength, brilliance—of all concepts.

The process of finding the truth continues further: At the final level, objective truth is independent of existence as a whole, independent of all manifestation. It is then what we call absolute truth. That means it is independent of what manifests—of the universe itself. This revelation of absolute truth, which is hard for the mind to conceive of, is the recognition of a truth that is beyond Being or non-Being.

So to summarize: I have divided objective truth into four kinds, of increasing depth and subtlety: the relative, the essential, the nonconceptual, and the absolute. You can differentiate the kinds of truth in other ways, but that's one useful way of doing it. And we can say that truth changes according to your situation and perspective. Every perspective has truth, regardless how limited. And this means that it is possible to use a gradual method of investigation that will reveal more truth, deeper truth, more fundamental truth, as the investigation continues.

As we have seen, inquiry invites the optimizing dynamism of Being and its guidance, which is its discriminating intelligence. The optimizing force will transform experience from one level to another, and the intelligence will discern the quantic movement of truth through these four levels. So if we follow the truth, the optimizing force will move understanding to deeper dimensions of truth. It will generally go from the relative to the essential, then to the fundamental or nonconceptual, and finally to the absolute.

THE ESSENTIAL ASPECT OF TRUTH

We are exploring the place of truth in inquiry and understanding as an element in the Diamond Guidance. Knowing that there is such a thing as objective truth is fundamental to our process of inquiry and understanding. It is also important to look at the role of the major essential aspects in inquiry, understanding, and guidance. We have seen that the capacity for direct knowing is related to the Blue aspect, the aspect of consciousness and knowing. In terms of the four levels of truth, essential truth means experiencing oneself or consciousness on the level of Essence in any of its aspects or manifestations. Exploring particular constellations of conventional experiences, which is the same as understanding specific issues, leads to the arising of Essence as one quality or another.

All essential qualities are truth, in the sense that they are objectively present in this dimension. However, we also find a particular essential aspect that is the aspect of Truth itself. Inquiry into this essential presence shows us that it is this aspect that makes it possible for us to discern truth.

The specific capacities of our psyche are usually reflections of certain essential qualities that our soul possesses. So we can be bright and clever only because there is an aspect in our soul that is the pure presence of intelligence. And the more this aspect is integrated in our psyche—our soul—the more our understanding and our actions are intelligent. We can also know things in general because pure knowing exists on the essential level, as the Blue aspect.

The same is the case with truth. We are able to discern truth—we can know what is true and what is not true in our experience—because inherent in our soul is a quality that is just Truth. Not a particular truth, but the presence of consciousness that is experienced as the presence of Truth. In other words, we can discern truth in experience in general because one pure element of our soul is Truth as such. We can recognize truth because pure Truth is a facet of our nature. The presence of Truth in the soul makes it possible for us to recognize it in everyday experience—whether in a particular situation or in recurring patterns—and on any level of experience.

So depending on how completely we have integrated this particular essential aspect—how transparent we are to it, how much we have realized it, how close it is to our conscious experience—our capacity for discerning truth will be more or less developed. When we experience our consciousness *as* truth, it attains a solid-gold quality. This is because Truth is the Gold aspect. And when our presence feels like solid gold, we are experiencing the presence of Truth. Similarly, when we experience our consciousness as a delicate Blue presence, it has become the presence of knowingness.

So Truth is a golden presence, a solid, definite, shiny metallic gold. It has an aliveness, a consciousness, an awareness in it, because it is an element of consciousness. The presence of Truth feels real, dense, compact, warm, and quite smooth. It has a sense of preciousness that makes it feel very close to our heart, as if it were the depth of the heart itself.

Because there is such a thing as a Truth aspect, it is possible to investigate in depth and in detail what truth is, in terms of dimensions, levels, situations, whatever. Truth becomes something that can be explored specifically and precisely. And understanding will deepen only if we move to deeper and deeper dimensions of truth.

VALUING THE LIFE OF TRUTH

We move to deeper dimensions of truth only if understanding expands and deepens. And, for the truth to go deeper, for understanding to reveal the greater dimensions of truth, the truth we discover needs to be integrated into the rest of our life. We need to start living the truth that we find. We can't just discover it, experience it, understand it, and then go on living our life as if our discovery were an isolated experience. If we do that, truth won't keep revealing itself.

In other words, if we do not include—if we do not integrate into our actions and choices—the truth that we have found through our understanding, the process of deepening revelation will stop. Why? It's very obvious. If we take action and make choices without taking into consideration the truth that we have discovered, then we are holding on to and fixating on the obscurations that were blocking that truth. It means we believe in this ignorance more than the truth, which amounts to the same as not recognizing the truth as the truth. Then we are living a life of lies when we already know the truth.

And how is the truth going to reveal more of itself when we are disowning the truth we have discovered? How is that truth going to expand to deeper and deeper dimensions? It isn't. Our consciousness is going to go back to the surface, to the place it was before we discovered that truth. So, if we want to cooperate with the process of revelation of truth, we need to live the truth that we know.

Every time we discover truth, we need to put it into action. We have to change our life according to that truth. We have to change our behavior so that it takes that truth into consideration. Otherwise, we will be acting from a place that disregards what we have discovered. We can't be couch-potato explorers. Our spacecruiser journey requires all-out commitment and dedication, and total devotion to the truth that ultimately reflects our true nature and the nature of reality.

For instance, you discover that you are really not the unlikable person that you thought you were. You find that you are really pure love. How are you going to live your life now? How are you going to interact? Are you going to go through life as pure love or as that old unlovable person? If you continue to act as that unlovable person, it's as though your discovery never happened. And that pure love is not going to move to a deeper dimension. In fact, it's going to get blocked again. However, if you don't forget, and you begin to do your best to integrate that insight of being pure love into your life, it will help the process of exploration to go deeper, to reveal more truth. This might mean using the implications of the insight to question the beliefs that support your old identity. Such an inquiry will challenge the inertia of your old identification as unlikable.

So what does it mean to live your life as if you were pure love? That is something you will have to find out yourself, because there are no definite rules to follow. Of course, the moment you inquire into this question, you will come upon various barriers—either about love itself or about the roots of the identification with being unlovable. You may find out that you are not behaving according to the truth you know because your actions are being determined by something unconscious. Understanding these new elements might not make it possible for you to behave as pure love right now, but at least it will take you in the right direction. So you can continue working in the direction that will help you integrate that quality more in your life. In this way, insight becomes wisdom, which is insight in action.

Truth is an element in all our experience; it pervades all parts of our life, in all situations. It is much bigger than just saying the truth. It is a matter of living the truth and ultimately being the truth. Telling the truth is often a part of living the truth, but sometimes it runs counter to living a life of truth. The truth is much bigger than just a true statement. So living a life of truth is a lot more than just being honest or speaking truthfully. To be truthful means to be truthful to yourself, to what you know, and to who and what you are.

To live the life of truth means first to value the truth, and to value knowing the truth. It also means to value the truth such that you make it the center of your life, which means learning to be genuine, authentic, and sincere. At its heart, living the truth is a matter of integrity and respect—for oneself, for others, and for truth itself.

The more our life respects and reflects the truth that we know, the more it will take us to ever deeper dimensions of truth, of true nature.

There is an interaction, an interrelationship, and an inseparability between understanding the truth and living life. We cannot separate the two. We cannot be ivory-tower philosophers and expect to discover truth. It doesn't work that way, because inquiry is a journey of truth-finding that constantly reveals the oneness of Being and life. Our spiritual philosophy must become an action philosophy. We have to let our souls become a manifestation of each truth we discover.

THE CITADEL OF TRUTH

The orientation toward living the truth that we know connects us with another Diamond Dimension, called the Citadel. Like the Diamond Guidance, this manifestation of Being possesses specialized functions that can be used in personal development and life in general. As an integrated expression of our true nature, the Citadel functions as a unit—a Diamond Vehicle—where all the aspects of Essence appear as a structure that functions in a unified manner. While the Diamond Guidance guides the soul's inner unfoldment toward true nature, the Citadel is a vehicle of understanding and guidance for living a life in the world that is aligned with the truth. Its presence provides a specific support for how to live our life, how to relate to our situation, and how to conduct our affairs according to the wisdom of our true nature. This ultimately means creating or arranging our environment to help us live the way we know truth to be.

As the Citadel is realized, it provides the soul with all the essential aspects as specific supports for living a life of truth. We call it the Citadel because it can manifest as an enormous, solid presence—like a mighty fortress—that supports and protects the truth as it manifests in our life. The various defensive ego functions that have helped us operate without the ground of our true nature are replaced by this immense and powerful support of Being itself. The more we learn to bring our awareness of truth into the functioning of our life, the more we gain access to the essential grounding, guidance, and protection of the Citadel.

To activate this new dimension, the process of exploration needs to extend into all areas of our life. We begin to explore our work, our relationships, and our behavior in terms of whether they reflect truth or not. This process brings in an integrity, a self-respect, and a valuing of the truth—all of which invite the arising of the Citadel dimension.

Our focus in this book is on the Diamond Guidance and the practice of inquiry, so we mention the Citadel only to indicate the extraordinary richness of Being's wisdom and the interconnection between its many facets. The Citadel is one of the realms that Spacecruiser *Inquiry* will take us to—a whole star system of diamond knowledge in itself.*

We are seeing that the entire journey of inquiry is a process of revealing truth that cannot be separated from the integration of that truth in our lives. If we truly commit ourselves to contacting the dynamism of Being, it will not only bring insight and realization, it will also bring change and transformation in our life as well as in our soul.

---

*See *The Pearl Beyond Price* (Berkeley: Diamond Books, 1988; Boston: Shambhala Publications, 2000), chap. 31.

CHAPTER 24

Diamond Clarity

THE NATURE OF OBJECTIVITY

One of the cornerstones of quantum theory is the Heisenberg uncertainty principle, which implies that the fact of observation changes what is observed. We cannot objectively know what we observe, we cannot see it as it is, because the attempt to know it will change it. So whenever we observe, whenever we experiment, we can't help but interfere. Quantum mechanics draws conclusions about reality through probability, for certainty is not possible.

Since objective knowledge is so difficult to reach in the physical realm, quantum theory is the best tool we have. However, inner experience tells us that there is such a thing as the objective understanding of experience—even to the point of total objectivity—although it is not easy to get to. This does not mean transcending the uncertainty principle of Heisenberg—not exactly. But it is something analogous to that, in an arena not envisioned by Heisenberg. The best way to understand personal experience objectively is through inquiring not only into the object of inquiry, but also into the inquiring subject at the same time. The physicist does not include his own impact on results when observing an experiment. He merely tries to interfere as little as possible and works on improving his instruments. However, when we inquire into our personal experience, we do not try to avoid interfering, we simply include our interference as part of what we observe.

Our exploration is not only into the nature of our experience or state, but also into the totality of who we are, including the nature of the part of us that observes or explores. All of this must become an object of study and inquiry. This means that to be objective about a situation, we, as the inquirer, will need to become objective—free from subjective influence. For when we inquire into what prevents our understanding from being objective, we find that it is the fact that we bring our subjectivity to our experience.

The truth arises as the truth, but we do not see it as it is because of our own unclarity, our own positions, prejudices, identifications, limitations, preferences, and goals—the totality of which we call subjectivity. However, if we really love the truth for its own sake, we will want to see it as it is, we will want to behold the objective truth. This will translate into the wish and passion to discern all our subjective positions that are preventing objective perception. So, for instance, I do not just realize, "I'm feeling angry," but I also observe and discern how I feel in response to seeing my anger. Do I have a judgment about it? Do I believe that it's okay to be angry or not okay to be angry? What are my opinions and prejudices about anger? I explore everything I bring into the experience of anger. In other words, we always need to be aware of our subjective reaction to our experience in order to see how we interfere with it.

Objectivity about an experience or situation includes recognizing and understanding our attitudes and reactions to it. We need to inquire into our inquiring consciousness until it is impartial, balanced, unprejudiced, disinterested, motiveless, goalless, fresh, and totally open to finding out whatever is there. Only when our consciousness approaches experience this way can it apprehend objectively.

Being objective about an experience means that I'm open to it; I am not trying to make it go one way or another. And this is not because I think that's the way I ought to approach it, but because I have no vested interest in things going in any particular way. I'm not trying to get something; I am merely curious, I love to find out what is so— that's all. Accompanying this open and open-ended inquiring attitude is an impartiality, a balance, a fresh attitude and orientation, an objective, inquiring mind. If I approach experience with an aim or a plan, this is bound to interfere with whatever I'm exploring. I won't know it objectively, for what I come to know will always be mixed with and distorted by my own subjectivity. When we can be objective about our experience—or at least be aware of our subjectivity in the process of our inquiry—then it is possible for us to see things the way they truly are. Hence, learning to inquire includes learning to be objective.

The heart is not initially objective, but when it loves the truth in a motiveless way, it is willing to experience things objectively. Real love is objective in this sense: It doesn't have beliefs and preferences; it doesn't perceive through structures and lenses; it doesn't have ideas of how things should be.

This view is the opposite of the conventional idea of objectivity. We have learned that an objective scientist is one who wears gloves; he's an emotionally uninvolved individual with an antiseptic exterior, more like a machine than a man. In trying not to interfere with the experiment, he becomes inhuman, heartless. That's why we usually think that heart and objectivity don't go together. But it's not that objectivity doesn't go with heart, it's that our usual understanding of objectivity doesn't go with heart. Our usual understanding of objectivity is not real objectivity, it's a schizoid isolation. It is the result of trying to arrive at objectivity through schizoid withdrawal. Because we don't know how to deal with our subjectivity, we shut it off. That has been the accepted way of science, and some people have been advocating this approach even for psychology and spirituality.

Rather than trying to be as careful and antiseptic as possible— putting on gloves and operating through glass doors—we can be more objective by appreciating that subjectivity cannot be taken out of the equation. Real objectivity doesn't mean that there is no heart. In fact, objectivity goes along with the heart, with love. Because we love the truth, we can be objective, for the truth we love is objective truth. And you can't arrive at objective truth while you're being subjective.

Because our heart is so unfamiliar with objective truth and so filled with emotional reaction and preference, it is not easy to be objective or even understand what objectivity is. Consequently, the people we ordinarily think of as objective are the mental types, especially schizoid types who live in their minds and are out of touch with their feelings. However, these types are far from objective, for they bring to their experience ideas, beliefs, and concepts powered by unconscious emotions. These people are very subjective; they just are not aware of it.

So to summarize, we can say that subjectivity means that our approach is dominated or influenced by our personality's positions, feelings, reactions, preferences, and judgments. Objectivity means the absence of all such inner coercive agencies and the presence of an openness that embodies love, sensitivity, and all the essential qualities that constitute the Diamond Guidance.

OBJECTIVITY IN INQUIRY

We have seen that in inquiry, we have to explore both the object of exploration and the explorer simultaneously. This way, we bring objectivity to our inquiry, and this objectivity increases and expands as we understand our experience at deeper and deeper levels. What does this mean?

Let's say an individual finds that it is the objective truth that he is angry at you because you remind him of his mother. However, in the process of exploring the situation and himself, he may discover another level of subjectivity: the position that he is a self who has a mother. This level of subjectivity was not relevant for his inquiry at the beginning, but as he continues exploring, he comes upon the truth that he has an issue with separation. So now we have two levels of subjectivity and two corresponding levels of objectivity. As his objectivity develops, the objective truth he finds is more like: "It's not just that I'm angry at you because you remind me of my mother. What's happening in a deeper sense is that I believe that there is a you and a me, and that there's a separation between us related to my feeling angry. And now I see that I learned to separate from my mother by feeling angry."

When he explores the separation, he may experience and appreciate the Red Essence, the presence of a personal strength necessary for one to be truly separate and autonomous, to be one's own person. Then, if he inquires even more deeply the next time he gets angry at you, he recognizes that his prior understanding of separation was not completely objective. He understands now that separation does not mean separateness, does not mean that there is you and there is he, as two islands. He recognizes that separation simply means difference, that the two of you are simply two waves of the same ocean instead of being one undifferentiated ocean or two self-islands. He sees it is true that there are two waves but that he is not separate in the sense of being isolated. Thus he realizes another level of objectivity.

Absolute objectivity doesn't happen except at the level of the Absolute. At the very moment we reach that level, we transcend the uncertainty principle. This is because we see that the recognizer and what is recognized are one, not two. There is no observer and no observed, no explorer and no explored—only one objective existence. The whole basis of the uncertainty principal—the duality between the observer and the observed—has disappeared. Only on this level of nonduality can objectivity be complete. So understanding continues to deepen as we move through degrees of objectivity. More precisely, for understanding to deepen, we must become more objective, more exact, more precise. We then see things more as they are. We arrive again at the insight about truth stated in chapter 23, "Truth in Understanding": that truth is a moving point.

Another way of saying this is that there is an objective truth within every context. The context in which one takes oneself and others to be persons has its own objectivity. So, using our example, to say that a person is angry at you because he is angry at his mother can be seen as objective truth within this worldview. It has a validity of truth. However, if you challenge some of the parameters of this worldview, then the objective truth changes.

A deeper level of objectivity simply means that we've removed some of the parameters of that world, such as the reality of there being separate persons. Then we realize that it is not that he's angry at you because you remind him of your mother, and therefore he doesn't see you as you are. It's more that the awareness of the universe (expressed in the consciousness of his soul at the present moment) does not perceive the particular energy that the universe is manifesting as you. In other words, the inherent discrimination that is characteristic of pure awareness can be interpreted according to whatever level of conceptualization you are functioning at. If you conceptualize separate people, you will recognize a certain discrimination of objective truth; if you conceptualize something else, you will recognize a different discrimination. Each of these is a world of its own, an entire worldview with its own measure of truth and objectivity. If this were not so, there would be no basis for knowing and action in the conventional world.

Through this discussion, we are introducing another element necessary for inquiry besides love of truth. Love of the truth actually points to this element: the need for objectivity. In inquiry, perception and understanding become objective at some point, which means that they become the perception and understanding of the facts of the matter—what actually is. Then we are perceiving what is truly arising in the situation, and our understanding is the discernment of the truth of what is arising or unfolding. Then neither our understanding nor our perception is colored by our subjectivity.

We usually think that being objective means being cold and heartless, but when we understand true objectivity, we see that it is the most compassionate and loving attitude. When you are truly objective toward somebody else, it means that you allow them to reveal their truth as it is instead of interfering with it by wanting it to be one way or another. True objectivity is the most compassionate, loving attitude because it is totally open to the truth. This truth is not only the savior, it is also the beloved.

CLARITY

How do we arrive at the objectivity needed for understanding what is true? This objectivity is not something we attain once and for all, after which it continues to be present fully without interruption. That is not how it works. Objectivity deepens and unfolds just as the truth does. In addition, to have an objective understanding of a situation or experience requires more than just objectivity on our part.

Objectivity is only one element needed for objective understanding, as we will see by considering the process of inquiry. First we are aware of an experience, perception, or situation. Understanding begins when we realize that we do not understand something about it. Since we love to see the truth, this absence or incompleteness of our knowingness of the objective truth of the situation begins the process of inquiry and understanding.

At this point, our lack or incompleteness of understanding usually reflects our lack of objectivity. So our love of finding the truth begins the process of becoming more and more objective in our attitude. Acquiring an increasing objectivity regarding the situation is a matter of clarifying our experience, in terms of both our attitudes and the object of inquiry. This clarifying is a process of cutting through obscurations—the clouds of prejudice, opinions, reactions, defenses, and so on.

So we experience the lack or incompleteness of understanding as not being clear about the situation. The movement toward clarification is the process of inquiry. We may ask questions, explore, or study certain things. We may observe more and correlate our observations. All of this is guided by the movement toward clarifying the situation. In other words, understanding commences as the opaqueness in the experience—the various levels of obscurations and unclarities—is dispelled through inquiry.

What does inquiry do? It reveals the truth. The truth is already in the experience; we are just not seeing it. In the process of the truth emerging and our discriminating it, experience becomes clearer. Or we can say that we become clearer about our experience. So, as in the example discussed earlier, when that person recognizes that the reason he is angry at me is that I remind him of his mother, whom he is angry at, he becomes clearer about his relationship to me. The process of arriving at the new discrimination is one of clarification. Before that, he feels unclear; there is a dullness, a thickness, a vagueness. There is an unknowingness, an unconsciousness. Now he is clear; the situation is transparent and his experience is more lucid.

In other words, understanding is a matter of clarity shining through the various manifestations, clarifying and dispelling obscurations and illuminating the truth. What is happening as we are clarifying is a rise in clarity. What is this rise in clarity? The whole field of experience, the whole soul, begins to become clearer. We become aware of the resistances and blockages, the wrong beliefs and fixed positions that cause such obscuration, dullness, and unclarity. And as we see them, we become clear about what they are and what they are about. As we become clear about them, we understand them and they are dispelled. Obscurations dissipate like clouds as clarity shines through. We discover more and more of the truth, and experience is illuminated. The truth begins to stand out and become manifest. This is the process we go through when we inquire.

By understanding the experience through seeing its truth, we arrive at an objectivity about it. Arriving at this objectivity happens through clarifying our attitude about the experience as we clarify what the experience is. This process of recognizing the truth coincides with the soul herself, the consciousness, becoming clearer and more transparent, more luminous. We might not experience this directly as luminosity but as a greater intensity or as more specificity in what the experience is. Our awareness is now more intense, purer, clearer, and more lucid.

Questions and Answers

STUDENT: It seems to me that there is also an emotional component when you have that clarity, a sense of satisfaction or completeness.

ALMAAS: Yes, of course. Various things happen that I am not mentioning here. Along with the knowingness, which we discussed, there is the love and the curiosity and the joy of the exploration. And there is the satisfaction of recognizing the truth as well as the appreciation of the quality of truth itself. All this occurs, but I am saying that the whole process can be seen as one of increasing clarity.

STUDENT: As the soul lightens, is there a physical sensation or cluster of sensations that are felt along with the soul's?

ALMAAS: That's what I mean when I say that the soul becomes clearer. The soul herself begins to feel the quality of clarity and transparency. Of course, that will affect your physical experience. You will feel lighter, clearer, cleaner, and more lucid. There is more space and less obscuration, less thickness, less opaqueness, less vagueness, less unconsciousness, less sleepiness. There is an increasing quality of being awake and alert, a brightness and clarity. Clarity is actually nothing but the luminosity of our consciousness, the transparency of awareness.

So as we get clearer in the process of understanding, our consciousness is revealing its inherent luminosity, its underlying nature. To put it differently, as we engage in clarifying our experience through inquiry, we invite and bring to bear the transparent luminosity of our essential nature. This clarifies the details of our experience by making them transparent. This means that we recognize them as they are, but also that they literally become transparent; it is not just a figure of speech. When we fully understand physical reality, for instance, it becomes transparent, literally.

STUDENT: Would you need to have some distance from the experience in order to see that happen? That sounds like objectivity to me.

ALMAAS: Yes. Some people call it distance. I think it is better to call it disidentification. Distance means that you are not intimate with the experience. In inquiry, you are intimate but not identifying with the experience. Objectivity won't happen if you are identifying with the situation. Some people distance themselves in order to be objective, but as I said, that easily becomes schizoid distancing. And it lacks the contact, the intimacy with experience that provides you with the data you need for understanding. Then you can only theorize. We are not discussing theory or logical thinking. Inquiry means being in contact with the experience and becoming clear about it, which means that the experience itself becomes clear.

The clarity and the objectivity are two manifestations of the same thing. To be totally objective means to be totally clear, and to be clear is to be objective. You cannot be clear if you are not objective, and you cannot be objective if you are not clear.

In other words, obscuration is like an opaqueness in our consciousness. This opaqueness is dispelled or clarified by our consciousness becoming transparent. What is this opaqueness? It is just the resistances, the defenses, the positions and beliefs, the identifications, and the various other things that comprise our ignorance of what the situation truly is.

STUDENT: As the process continues and we come upon more transparency and objectivity, we seem to encounter opaqueness in some other part of our personality. Are we encountering something deeper and more heavily defended than before, or does it just feel that way because we've become more sensitized?

ALMAAS: Could be either or both. Becoming clearer definitely does not mean that you never encounter opaqueness. Opaqueness can arise at any point and cause you to be less clear, yet the process of inquiry still continues. Sometimes we come upon an area that we have never dealt with, for instance. Its apparent opaqueness or density might relate to the state of Clarity we have been in recently. We might have been feeling clear and light, and in contrast, this unexplored area feels much more opaque.

The transparent luminosity, which is the most basic property of our true nature, reveals both the relative truth of the situation and, as it goes deeper, the essential truth. Becoming clearer about our experience usually brings up the essential qualities underlying it. Generally, we first see the relative truth, then we see essential truth. Ultimately, this increasing clarity reveals the absolute transparency that is our ultimate true nature. In fact, the clarity we experience from the beginning is nothing but the Clarity of our true and absolute nature that is shining through all the way to the relative level. It is what helps us be clear about the relative level.

CLARITY AND THE DIAMOND GUIDANCE

So as we become clearer, inquiry goes deeper. Clarification brings understanding of our relative truth—the issues and situations of our life. Then it brings understanding of our essential truth—all the essential qualities and pure aspects that arise as a result of this understanding. And at a still deeper level, the increasing clarity reveals our absolute true nature, which is the ground of luminosity. This ground is both a transparency and a luminosity. And clarity is nothing but transparent luminosity.

The clarity we are discussing is a specific element in the process of understanding. This clarity is indistinguishable from objectivity. And objectivity and clarity are the qualities of the Clear diamond of the Diamond Guidance. Both qualities are important and specific to the Guidance, and the Clear diamond brings them into the operation of the Guidance. Or you can say that the operation of the Diamond Guidance is an objective operation of clarity in the process of inquiring into the truth. In its operation, in its guidance, it clarifies our situation. It penetrates or cuts through our positions, beliefs, and ignorance. Cutting through means understanding or getting clear. We are able to discriminate in a very definite and precise way. And if there is any process that is central to inquiry, it is the process of clarification.

I am relating this clarity to our true nature because our true nature, with all of its essential aspects, is the presence of luminosity. What is Essence? Condensed light. The very nature of all aspects is this sense of luminosity, this sense of clarity, the sense of lack of obscuration. Yet, even though all the essential aspects are free of obscuration, each has a particular quality besides its inherent common luminosity. The Clear diamond is free of obscuration, just as all the other aspects are, but its essential, dominant quality is clarity—a sense of freshness, translucence, and lucidity.

In the experience of the aspect of Truth, there is a definiteness, a concreteness, a realness, and a warmth, while in the experience of the Clarity aspect there is transparency and coolness. Yet they are both present in the process of understanding. Truth is more of a heart quality, while Clarity is more of a head quality, but they are both manifestations of Essence. Truth brings Clarity, Clarity reveals Truth. And when the mind and the heart operate together in harmony, we call that understanding.

As we become clear, we become more objective. When we are totally clear, we are totally objective. Totally clear also means that we are totally transparent. If we are totally transparent, then there is no ego identity, no positions, for any identification with the ego is an obscuration, a dullness. So clarity brings objectivity. In fact, clarity and objectivity are two ways of looking at the same quality. Objectivity means that there is no subjective bias, while clarity means there is no obscuration. Subjectivity and obscuration are related concepts, but they are not exactly the same.

This clarity is central for both inquiry and understanding because they both involve the process of gradual clarification. In some sense, what is happening is that our truth is clarifying the soul's manifestations little by little as it approaches the surface, which is our conscious experience. Its light penetrates our consciousness more and more until we recognize the source of the light.

Inquiry is the invitation for our Being to reveal its truth, and this revelation is the understanding. Inquiry invites understanding by engaging the Diamond Guidance, whose operation is a process of clarifying. It is nothing but the intelligent operation of the Clarity of our nature, the intelligent functioning of the luminosity of our true nature. In the process of inquiry, we become more and more objective as well as more present, more real, more authentic, and more loving and compassionate, for our true nature is all of these qualities.

Clarity, which is luminous transparency, is the heart of objectivity, the essence of objectivity. It is also the essence and the core of the Diamond Guidance. The clear, transparent presence is the fabric of the Guidance, the very substance of it. The guidance is fundamentally a clarity that assumes various colors. It is a transparency that luminates with various qualities, while its central nature is revelation and guidance.

Being, in its absoluteness, is mystery beyond any description. It manifests its potential richness by differentiating itself into dimensions and qualities. The qualities of Being are its inherent implicit perfections, now manifesting as essential aspects. These aspects also appear in Diamond Dimensions, where each dimension is a particular synthesis of all of the aspects that operates as one vehicle with specific functions. Diamond Guidance is one of these Diamond Dimensions, whose function is guidance through discriminating, knowing, and understanding. We have been exploring the role or contribution of each of the aspects as we learn how Being functions as guidance. The overall dimension of the Diamond Guidance is that of a functioning vehicle, which operates as guidance or understanding. But each one of the perfections of Being—the essential aspects—has its own contribution to the Guidance.

PRECISION

In this chapter, we have been exploring and integrating the function of the Clarity aspect of Essence, the Clear diamond. We have seen how this aspect of Essence contributes the perspective of objectivity, and how we arrive at objectivity by becoming clear about our attitude, which clarifies whatever we are inquiring into.

We have seen that the clearer we are about where we're coming from and what's going on, the more we see the objective truth. This gives rise to the question: How do we become clear? Or, what is the process of clarification? To understand this, we need to explore the contribution of the Clear diamond in a more specific way.

The Clear diamond contributes the capacities of objectivity and clarity, but its most specific and characteristic property is the sharpness of its facets, which contributes the faculty of precision. More accurately, the objectivity and clarity of the diamond are inseparable from its precision and sharpness, which imbue perception and experience with precise discrimination and knowledge. In other words, the process of clarification in the operation of Diamond Guidance occurs through our basic knowledge becoming exact, specific, precise, and sharp. Inquiry moves our experience not only toward objectivity and clarity, but also toward precise, specific, and sharp discriminations. When we have become specific and precise about a matter, we have arrived at objective understanding.

We eliminate unclarity and obscuration by becoming precise. Precision means a specific, exact, sharp delineation. This sharp delineation needs to be not only in the thinking mind, but primarily in direct experience. We know when we feel heat or anger, for instance. We don't merely feel some kind of energy, or a vague hot emotion. Exploring vague feelings is the beginning of understanding, but the understanding is still not complete, not objective, because it is not precise yet. For example, we might feel sort of feisty, or maybe we're feeling angry, but we're not exactly sure yet. Inquiry asks for more precision: "Am I feeling angry or feisty?" When we recognize that we feel more feisty than angry, we become more precise. Some dullness and unclarity is dissipated by the questioning.

Inquiry continues in its quest for more precision: "What does it feel like to be feisty?"

"Sort of feel energetic, sort of alive."

"What do you mean by 'energetic and alive'?"

"The feeling of the presence of alive energy."

"What do you mean, 'the presence of alive energy'?"

"There is this presence, a sense of being, that makes me feel alive, energetic, and strong. I can feel I'm hot too. I thought I was angry, but I am simply experiencing a presence of strength."

You realize finally that you are experiencing the Red Essence, the

Strength aspect. Now it's clear that there is a heat to it, a strength to it, an energy to it, an aliveness, and it is a palpable presence of fullness.

So how did we go from some vague sense of energy we thought was anger to experiencing the Red Essence? Simply by becoming exact about the nature of the experience. We say now that we have become clear about what the experience is, and that happened by working toward more precision in understanding it. If we had stayed with our original sense of what was happening, understanding would not have developed, and a possible unfoldment would have been aborted through lack of recognition. Being satisfied with a general concept of experience, we don't get precise understanding. So the process of inquiry is guided by the movement of greater precision, and precision means that we want to be more exact about what the experience is. And we want to be exact because we love to behold the truth just as it is, completely.

When we don't investigate our experience, we merely stay with the generalities of conventional language. Then not only are we imprecise in our articulation, we are not even knowing our experience fully. And when we don't know what our experience is and experience it fully, we don't understand it. So the process of inquiry is a matter of investigating and penetrating any unclarity in our minds and experience. To embody the Guidance means to learn to appreciate the clarity, the precision, the understanding, the direct knowingness of our experience in its fullness. That is ultimately what realization is. A person who is realized is one whose experience is always fully clear. That person has full awareness, feeling experience intimately with precise and sharp delineation of its basic knowingness.

So inquiry is a process of clarifying any dullness or muffled edge in our experience. We do this by seeing and experiencing things in a more precise and specific way. Clarity of particulars, of details and patterns, means precision. When the discrimination is precise and exact, the clarity of the patterns and the meaning in these patterns become understanding. In fact, this precision and exactness of experience is itself the recognition of objective truth. In other words, understanding is the intimate discrimination of experience, and discrimination is nothing but clarity and precision. So understanding is nothing but clear, exact, and precise direct knowing of the dynamics of the situation.

The drive toward precision and clarity is the action of the Clear diamond. Experience becomes perfectly clear when the Clear diamond manifests and cuts through the clouds of obscuration with the sword of precision. The sharp edges of the diamond function by cutting through the dullness and vagueness of our obscured experience. The diamond has very sharp facets. When these facets touch our experience, they make us see it in a very clear, precise, sharp way. So the sharp edge of the diamond scepter is the clear, precise and specific perception or understanding. This precision can go quite deep, with increasing subtlety. In some sense, the subtlety itself becomes a matter of greater precision. The more precise our experience, the more it becomes subtle. Perception becomes finer, more subtle, more delicate. Hence we see that inquiry proceeds by our being curious and questioning, and the questioning is guided by becoming more precise. This increases the clarity, the objectivity, the sharpness, the subtlety, the refinement, until we arrive home, at the Absolute, the farthest reaches of reality.

That's why one of the descriptions of absolute truth is that it's the razor edge that cuts at each point of space. It's hard to imagine something that is sharp at every single infinitesimal point, where precision becomes a searing sharpness. Imagine the refinement when that sharpness is present at each and every point—such a refinement is absolute. Then there is nothing to be found. It is complete, one hundred percent transparency. If there is even an atom left, it means that point hasn't been cut. It means that we haven't been absolutely precise in our exploration.

Practice Session: Your Capacity for Clarity and Precision in Inquiry

You might want to explore now your own capacity for clarity and precision in the process of inquiry. Consider the fact that when we don't meddle with our experience—if we are objective and not reacting and thus obscuring our experience—it is naturally sharp, clear, and precise. From this perspective, we can see that the lack of clarity and precision in our experience is a result of some way that we interfere with or obscure that experience.

Your exploration, then, is to consider two questions: What are some ways you interfere with the natural clarity, sharpness, and precision of your own experience? That's the first question. The second is: What's right about not being precise in your experience of yourself? In other words, what are the reasons you give yourself for not being precise in your experience of yourself? Here you want to explore your underlying unconscious motivations for staying imprecise and unclear.

After you have made some observations in relation to these two questions, begin a specific inquiry. As you proceed, notice whether the way you are engaged in your inquiry has in any way altered your usual degree of sharpness, clarity, or precision. What, if anything, arises that seems to dull or obscure your experience?

THE TRANSPARENCY OF TRUE NATURE

The primary insight in the logos of the Diamond Approach is that our true nature is the truth. Second, that true nature is self-revealing; it automatically, spontaneously, and naturally has a tendency to reveal its truth. And it reveals this truth in all situations, at all times, in all ways, in everything we experience.

Since our nature is self-revealing truth, then if we are not seeing or being our true nature, it is because we are stuck in what we think we know. We believe that we understand when we don't. We believe that we see the truth when we are not seeing the truth. This not seeing the truth and believing we see it is the unconscious unclarity, the unconscious obscuration, the omnipresent dullness of the ego-personality. The ego-self constantly recites to itself: "Truth is whatever I happen to be thinking." Inquiry is a way of actively challenging this smug comfort of believing that what we experience and know is the truth. In doing so, it opens up a space for Being to naturally reveal its truth.

We can try to see the truth by doing a yogic practice, such as a concentration technique, because sharp concentration can penetrate to the truth. But that method is not based on the understanding that the truth is revealing itself in whatever is happening in our experience. We don't need to do anything special in order to reach the ultimate truth; it's not necessary to practice any particular technique that removes us from or transcends our daily life. We just need to recognize the truth in our ongoing experience. Inquiry is the path of discerning the truth already present in any perception or experience.

Inquiry doesn't necessarily mean that you're always thinking about things or formulating questions in your mind. You are simply aware and curious; you love to know and feel reality fully and clearly. You are happy to know reality as deeply and precisely as possible. If experience is not clear, you are simply curious about it. Openness to experience becomes dynamic, challenging experience to reveal its truth. Once in a while, this curiosity might formulate itself into a specific question. You recognize that you don't understand something, and out of love, you wish to understand it. So questions come up on their own when necessary. The ongoing practice is therefore more an awareness of your experience, a recognition of when you are transparent and when you are opaque. Your interest is in understanding, and clarity will itself bring the Diamond Guidance, which will reveal the truth of the experience.

CLARITY AND INQUIRY

We can practice the inquiry of Diamond Guidance within any field of study; it does not have to be restricted to our personal experience. The Guidance can aid our inquiries in physics, chemistry, biology, sociology, and other disciplines, by sharpening and enhancing our capacity to uncover truth. Its function is to reveal the truth, and the truth can appear as a social truth, political truth, or scientific truth just as much as a personal truth.

This capacity is the true inquiring and exploring faculty of the soul, potential in all but developed by few. However, I do see this as a definite potential for the scientific mind. The great researchers and scientific explorers have developed and applied this capacity, but usually only partially, because they have not clarified their own inner experience as well. I think it would be quite interesting and exciting to see how the full and conscious application of the Diamond Guidance might affect research in other disciplines.

The truth reveals itself in all our personal situations, in the world, in everything. Every perception, every experience, has truth in it. So if we simply and sincerely inquire into experience, we will clarify our life, and we will clarify the world for ourselves. But we won't clarify only what our inner nature is, we will clarify everything, for the whole world is the revelation of this truth. When we discern the world as it is, we recognize that's it's really nothing but Being itself manifesting in various forms.

But we ordinarily don't see the world as it is; we see it through what we believe we know. We believe that we know what we are, we know what other people are, we know what we are doing; we think we know what we want, what we don't want, what we're going to do. All these convictions solidify and freeze the world into a certain form, a certain perception that we take to be the truth. But as we see through this obscuration—these beliefs, ideas, and positions—the world becomes transparent in the same way that our inner experience does. Then we recognize that everything is actually the revelation of the truth. And we see that since the nature of this truth is self-revealing, a possible realistic modus operandi is to invoke and quicken this self-revelation. This modus operandi is inquiry, and the self-revelation is understanding.

CHAPTER 25

Focused Inquiry

GETTING THE POINT

We have discussed the fact that in the Diamond Approach, understanding is not a matter of mentally connecting concepts; it's a matter of being clear about what's happening in our experience by being intimately in touch with it. In other words, understanding is the process of true living. It is realized life. Real living is the unfoldment of understanding, and inquiry is the way that unfoldment happens. As we inquire, understanding manifests, develops, expands, and deepens.

Understanding is ultimately a precise, clear, objective awareness of our true nature, for as we understand ourselves, our soul keeps unfolding and manifesting her hidden potentials until we are just our true nature, our real self. Ultimately, understanding coincides with the total realization of our true nature. In other words, understanding is the vehicle for the integration of the soul—which is our normal consciousness—with its source and nature beyond time and space.

In the process of inquiry and understanding, the soul first throws away her old garb—all our accumulated images, patterns, and self-concepts. This is a process of purification, part of the overall process of revelation in which inquiry reveals the hidden potentials in our soul. At some point, the purified soul—the soul that has gone through the process of clarification—becomes transparent awareness. What we call true nature becomes the soul's identity. Self-realization and awareness coincide as a coemergence of soul and identity. Our experience continues as an unfoldment in which the identity stays the same and only the content that presents itself to our awareness changes.

This process of the soul revealing herself more and more through inquiry is also called reading, or reading oneself. There's an interesting story about reading in this sense; it's the tale of the first time the angel of revelation, Gabriel, appeared to Muhammad. For years, before he knew he was a prophet, Muhammad would go to a cave and sit alone in contemplation for hours each night. One night the whole cave lights up and Gabriel shows up. The first thing he says to Muhammad is, "Read." That's the very first thing that Gabriel revealed to the prophet. Muhammad said, "I'm illiterate. I can't read or write." The archangel reiterated, "Read. Read in the name of your Lord, who taught with the pen, who taught mankind what it has not known." This was the beginning of the Islamic revelation, and it points to the importance of reading in relation to the Qur'an, and implies that the revelation of truth is similar to reading a book. The Muslims consider the Qur'an to contain all the secrets of the universe; they believe that it corresponds to the creation as a whole. The creation is the word of God and so is the Qur'an.

The soul reads the truth as truth is revealed. Seeing and experiencing one's unfoldment is like reading reality, reading the truth. Self-revelation is similar to reading what's on your computer screen as it is scrolling: As you read, the print appears and disappears. Reading in this way is the same thing as the unfoldment of understanding. What do you do when you're reading? For the reading to be a real reading, you have to get the meaning of what you read. Isn't that true? Otherwise, the reading isn't accomplishing its purpose. It's the same thing with inquiry: The point is to get the meaning. But in this case, it's not an intellectual meaning that you give to the experience. It's a meaning that's inherent in what is experienced. It's a lived meaning. It's about getting the import of the experience, experiencing directly the significance of what's happening. From this perspective, the unfoldment of life's inherent meaning is a natural part of real living.

Linguistically, the word "meaning" has to do with getting to the inside of things, to the essence of things. To get to the meaning of what is happening can also be described as getting to the heart of the matter. That occurs when we have an insight and the whole experience is integrated and unified in a certain way; all the elements make a tapestry that is meaningful. Understanding isn't present until we get to the meaning, until we get to the heart of the matter, until we get the point of what's going on.

It is interesting to know that the essential aspect of identity, which we sometimes call the Essential Identity, manifests as a point, a pinpoint of light and presence.* This has far-reaching implications that are initially difficult to grasp. At the beginning of our journey, we wonder why the Essential Identity is a point. What does that mean? What does that have to do with our experience, and what does that do *to* our experience? How does the fact that our true identity is a point reflect in our experience and in our perception, inquiry, and understanding?

The Essential Identity means the identity with Essence, the identity with Being. It is the true sense of identity. When we feel the Essential Identity, when we're being it, we feel we are being ourselves truly and authentically. And there's a sense of identity, a singular sense of "I" that is definitely, uniquely self-existing. You're there, present as you, without that "you" being defined by any constructed concept. There is "I," and you know there is "I" because you are here as "I." The point is identity, a direct sense of recognition of one's identity without history or mind. And because the Essential Identity is the prototype of identity, it represents the soul's capacity to be her true nature, her essential nature. It represents being the essential nature on any level.

When we are the Essential Identity, there is effortlessness, lightness, simplicity, and unquestioned preciousness. It is the simplicity of being and recognizing that "Yeah, that's who and what I am. I'm here." This is the Essential I as an aspect on its own, as an experiential category within the essential dimension of Being. But just as in the case of all other essential aspects, it has a specific function in relation to the Diamond Guidance. That function is to help us understand our experience through getting the point of what's going on.

This specific function has a lot to do with the fact that the Essential

---

*See *The Point of Existence*, (Berkeley: Diamond Books, 1996; Boston: Shambhala Publications, 2000) chap. 13.

Identity is both essential identity and, phenomenologically, a point. Its existence as identity and as a point of presence are two facets of the same phenomenon, and this two-faceted nature affects our experience in a particular way.

The more we have realized the Essential Identity, the easier it is for us to get straight to the point, which is the heart of the matter, which is the meaning of what's going on. It's true that all kinds of things are going on at every moment, but our experience is not haphazard or chaotic. No, the totality of experience has a pattern, and the pattern has a meaning. It has a point. It has a meaning that has something to do with who and what we are, with our relationship to our life, to our true nature and our evolution, and to where we are in the stream of life. All of this together makes one unified whole. When we get the insight into what that pattern of meaning is, we feel, "Aha, I got the point." If we have difficulty experiencing our true self, it will be very difficult to get the point. So being able to experience the essential Point makes it easier for us to get to the point of any situation or experience.

GOING DEEPER

So this is one of the basic functions of the Essential Identity when it comes to the Diamond Guidance. It guides the inquiry to the Point by guiding us to see the point of all and any experience. That is easy to understand when we remember that the Point is true identity. What is our identity? It is who and what we are. And what are we but our true nature, which goes deeper and deeper and deeper until it gets to the ultimate identity, which is the Absolute? This means that getting to the point of any situation is the same thing as penetrating deeper. The moment we get to the point of any situation, we go deeper. Why? Because the point of the situation always has to do with the Point, which has to do with identity—and identity is depth, is penetration inward into ourselves. The ultimate identity is pure depth; that is why the Absolute is depth itself.

In inquiry, we notice that if we fully understand what we experience, the inquiry naturally sinks inward, goes deeper, becomes more fundamental. Why does this happen? Have you ever wondered why, when you understand something, your understanding doesn't get more superficial and diffuse but rather more focused and deeper? The reason is that understanding means getting to the point. Getting to the point means orienting ourselves toward the essential Point. And orienting ourselves to the Point means getting closer to our true identity. Because our identity is ultimately depth, when we get to the depth, that's intimacy. The Absolute is both depth and intimacy at the same time.

Another way of saying it is that all manifestations—which include all experiences—are ultimately manifestation out of the Absolute. Everything is the Absolute communicating with us, revealing some of its possibilities and potentialities. And inquiry is a matter of reading and understanding this communication. In its communication, the Absolute is always guiding us to itself, pulling us toward itself. It does this through its emissary, its representative in our personal experience, which is the Point. In the operation of the Diamond Guidance, the Point affects our consciousness by always orienting us to the point of the situation, the meaning of experience, the heart of the matter. In guided inquiry, we are always pulled in deeper and deeper.

The Point, the Essential Identity, is needed in order to comprehend our experience—to reveal it as a unified whole—because the Point is the organizing center of our circle of experience. It is the center of our personal mandala. It is also the direction of ultimate understanding. In other words, the function of the Point, as part of the Diamond Guidance, is to continuously deepen our understanding. How? By pointing it toward our ultimate nature, our final identity.

So the Point has to do not only with getting the point, but also with pointing. The presence of the Point points to the depth, so that our awareness and knowledge can penetrate directly to the depth of our Being. It is interesting that the Essential Identity is a point, given that the term "point" is used in our everyday language in relation to meaning and understanding. In this case, our language has a great deal of wisdom. Consider our use of the expression "getting the point." That's how the Essential Identity, the Point, contributes to the function of Guidance.

When we say that the Point points, this doesn't mean that it does anything. By its mere presence, it points. When love is present, it affects our consciousness in a certain way. It makes us generous, it makes us give and appreciate, it makes us do wonderful things. Similarly, when the Point is present, it affects our consciousness in a certain way: It brings us to the point, and it points to the point by its very nature. It doesn't actually point a finger.

If it weren't for the Point, inner guidance would stay on the same level. The nature of the Point causes inquiry to penetrate, to go deeper, because it represents identity all the way to the Absolute. The Point is really nothing but the reflection of the Absolute in the soul. It guides consciousness and inquiry toward itself as if by magnetism.

We're understanding here an essential element for the process of inquiry and understanding. Inquiry is not just a matter of exploring and going all over the place. Each time we have an experience or a process, there is a point to it, a meaning to it, there is a significance that unifies the whole thing. There is an overall meaning that the Absolute is moving to reveal. The Absolute is always exhorting us: "Read." At any moment, our life is a book that can be read and comprehended.

ONE-POINTEDNESS

The Point provides inquiry with the skill of focusing, of not being distracted, of not going off on tangents. Focused inquiry is the skill of gravitating toward the significance of the situation, of going toward the main point instead of becoming scattered, going off on tangents, and getting excited about one thing or another. It is a particular skill. In some of us, this ability is more developed than in others. Some of us can't help getting scattered; others go right to the point, getting the insight.

But what is the process of finding the point? We have discussed how the Point gives us the capacity to get to the point, to comprehend the heart of the matter and find its meaning. What are the actual ingredients of the focusing skill? Two primary capacities are required: one provided by the Point, the other provided by another aspect, Brilliancy. The essential aspect of Brilliancy provides the capacity to see the totality of a situation, to look with a large perspective, to hold the whole experience. The Point, on the other hand, provides the capacity to hone in, to focus, to zero in. These two interacting capacities need to operate simultaneously so that we can get to the meaning of what's going on.

The Point is a point of presence, and when it is in consciousness, it focuses our attention. The moment the Point manifests, our attention is spontaneously focused in a very powerful way. The Point is a point of singular presence and brilliance, so its presence in our experience naturally focuses our soul. It does this by providing the capacity to focus on all the levels of the soul's functioning—perception, thinking, feeling, and action. Later in this chapter, we'll discuss a couple of ways that this focusing happens in inquiry.

As we inquire, we hold the entire experience and yet we are also able to focus on particulars. This happens by seeing all the relevant data within our experience. That might mean our experience at the moment, or during an entire week, month, or year. At some point, we recognize that there is a particular thread connecting all our experience. The thread is a sequence of points, a series of specific significances. At a certain point, one thing is going on; two minutes after that, something else is going on, and so on. If we see the relationship of these points, we find a meaningful thread. And this thread is continuous, for the points of meaning are not isolated or disconnected. Meaning is a continuing process.

FOCUSING TO FOLLOW THE THREAD

The Point gives us the capacity to find the thread and follow it, as we have discussed in chapter 10, "The Personal Thread." That's what focus means: At some point we're able to see what is going on in our experience and to focus on it and follow it. To follow a thread, we need the capacity to focus on the specific meaning of what is going on. And that will always be an unfolding meaning; it's not just a snapshot. The process of inquiry means that we're looking at what our consciousness is and asking questions. Some things we see, some things we can't see. Some things we know, some things we don't know. Little by little, though, we get a picture that shows us a certain meaning, and then we follow that meaning. We call that following the thread. We don't just leave that meaning and go with something else. If we do that, the thread is lost, and after a while we have to start all over again.

I'll give you an example. Let's say you're reading a newspaper article about a problem with the economy. A few weeks later, you realize that your company is having trouble and you may lose your job because they're laying people off. You notice around the same time that when you're talking with your friends, you feel an anxiety you haven't felt before: You're always wondering what they think of you. If you look into your experience, you also notice that when you are with your husband, you start to wonder, "Does he think I'm pretty enough? Does he think I am good enough for him?" You might also notice once in a while that you're feeling a little bit depressed, you're not interested in doing things in your life.

At the beginning, it appears that all these things you are aware of are disconnected. However, as you explore them, you recognize little by little that they are all connected. In fact, they each begin to stand out in your experience, singling themselves out of the plethora of impressions you have every day, simply because you recognize that there is something you don't understand that piques your curiosity. First you were worried about your husband thinking you're not pretty enough for him to want to continue being with you. Now you wonder: "Why would I think about that? Nothing bad is happening in our marriage. What's going on?" Then you may connect that with worrying about what your friends must be thinking about you—whether they value you as a person and as a friend.

As you question why you are concerned about that, you realize you're worried that you're going to be one of the first people laid off at your job. Even when you acknowledge to yourself that you're one of the best and most valued people there, it doesn't help. You're worried anyway. In asking, "Why am I thinking that?" you realize from deep inside you that you're feeling worthless.

So the entire thread began with your concern about the economy, which later emerged as the issue of whether you have your own value. This began to come out in different areas—in your marriage, your friendships, and your job. From this you understand that the issue is about value: "I'm not sure whether I'm valuable or not." You are now starting to see the thread.

Following the thread means that as life goes on day by day, you continue to follow that particular issue. You don't recognize that you're exploring value and then go off on a tangent the next moment and start inquiring, "Am I strong enough?" or "Am I smart enough?" The thread is the question of value. So if you move on to the question of intelligence or beauty or capacity, any of these might be useful, but none of them will reveal the meaning of what is going on because the point is the question of value.

Dealing with the question of value might bring up a sense of deficiency of value—feeling worthless and insignificant. Or it might bring up the psychodynamics of value: seeing what happened in your childhood that made you feel that you're not worthy, that you're not valuable. That's following the thread. And you won't necessarily get it all at once; this kind of inquiry takes time. If you stay with the thread, the issue of value will develop. You might wake up the next day and sense a big hole in your chest. If you look into the hole, you might realize that it is specifically the feeling of no value, of worthlessness.

Other things might be arising besides the central thread of value. The feeling of worthlessness might bring up anger and rage that people don't value you. If you're not focused, you could go on a tangent about anger and start to think about all the other things you're angry about. It's important to explore the anger, but it's better to stay with the anger that's related to the issue of value, rather than be angry about just anything. That's staying with the thread. It doesn't help if you just get into looking at all your anger at your husband, for example. "Why am I angry? Well, I remember that five years ago, he had an affair. What else am I angry about? Before that, he didn't let me buy the house I really wanted, so we had to compromise and now I don't even have a place for my sewing machine!" You can bring up all this anger at him, but that's missing the point; what really is arising is the question of value.

THE THREAD OF CONSCIOUSNESS

So staying with the thread means maintaining a thread of focus. But it's not a mental focus, it's a focus of the consciousness of the soul itself, where the soul is focused on the point: "What is the meaning of what's going on?" What's happening is that the Point is going through your unfolding experience and revealing what's going on. And that going through, that path of significance in your experience, we call the thread.

This capacity for focus comes from the presence of the Essential Identity—the Point—in our experience, as part of the Diamond Guidance. The way I see it is that the Diamond Guidance is a structure of many different colorful diamond qualities, in the center of which is the Point. The Point goes through the consciousness, and the diamond structure focuses there. It is not that you're following the Point; the Point is going through and revealing what is going on. So your consciousness is focused on what is being revealed. That's actually what's happening, although we don't always see it that way when we're inquiring.

It's like a point of light that lights something up as it goes through it. This lighting up of the various experiences begins to compose a thread. As you follow the thread over time, the picture becomes revealed all the way to the essential aspect of Value. Experience becomes the experience of Value itself. That is the essential point, what the meaning is at the essential level.

We may continue following the thread further if we don't stop at the experience of Value. Value will take us to presence, and presence can continue as the central thread. This means that we are now in the second journey. Continuing to follow the essential thread, which is a luminous thread, will eventually take us to a recognition of the essential luminosity penetrating and underlying everything. This is the third journey.

So what we're seeing here is a contribution of the Point to inquiry, not just in the sense of pointing, or of revealing the important point of the situation, but also in the sense of focus, one-pointedness. When you're exploring, you need to look at the big picture, but you also need to zero in and focus on specific things. In addition, you need to have the capacity to continue that focus as a thread, as a process.

Questions and Answers

STUDENT: Is there usually only one thread to explore?
ALMAAS: There might be several threads. But if you recognize what they are, you will see that they actually make up one unified thread. Each thread is composed of sub-threads, and those are also composed of sub-threads. So you might see several threads, but that doesn't mean

there isn't a central one uniting all of them. There is, and that is the point.

STUDENT: I find that I tend to come up against a big obstacle when I try to shift my external focus to an internal focus.

ALMAAS: That makes sense because the external focus is in the opposite direction of the Point. The Point takes you in deeper. You notice that in our discussion of focus, sometimes I talk about focus as going inward, deeper; and sometimes I talk about focus as following the thread. These are two different kinds of focus. They're both the operation of the Point. Following the thread is a focus in terms of being one-pointed. You need to be one-pointed to stay with the same object of exploration. But this object now is a moving object, so as you stay with it, it becomes a thread.

ZEROING IN

Another kind of focus is one that has to do with zeroing in. Zeroing in is not a matter of staying with the same object, but of making the focus smaller and more precise so you can see the specific details. When you focus the lens of a microscope, you can see the details of what you are looking at more clearly. The focus that results from zeroing in is also very important for inquiry, because if you don't zero in on what's happening, you tend not to see the specifics; you see only in generalities. Zeroing in is needed to take us deeper. As you're zeroing in, you get closer and closer to the object of inquiry, and as that happens, it reveals itself more. That is the movement inward, the going deeper.

So, as we have said, the focus of following the thread has to do with one-pointedness. What does the focus of zeroing in have to do with? How do you zero in? Think in terms of a lens, a zoom lens. What does a zoom lens do? It magnifies. And when it magnifies, what do you see? You see that everything else drops away, and the dropping away is the one-pointedness. But why do you want to use a zoom lens in the first place? In order to see more of the details. It's a matter of becoming more specific. The closer you zoom in, the more you see specifically what is going on.

In our inquiry, we zero in to see more specifics in our experience.

We go from the general to the specific. This is a dynamic, continuing process that corresponds to the capacity of penetration. It happens when we are able to discriminate more of the specifics.

Let's say one day you tell me, "I'm not feeling good." I would ask you, "What do you mean, you're not feeling good? You might say, "Grumpy." That's more specific.

But then I would say, "What do you mean by 'grumpy'? Be more specific."

So you look at it a little bit more. "I think I'm a little bit testy."

"Be more specific."

"I think I feel really mad."

"Good, be more specific."

"I feel mad about something that happened yesterday."

"Good, be more specific."

"I remember now a conversation I had with my friend yesterday on the phone—that's when it started."

"Be more specific."

"He made a comment about me, and it really got me. I'm mad at him for saying it."

You're zeroing in by becoming specific. So now the feeling of the anger and what it's about becomes very delineated in your body. That's the way we get to the point. The process is partly a matter of getting more and more specific.

The same thing happens when we're going deeper in our essential realization. At the beginning, you say, "Well, I'm feeling present."

"Good, what do you mean by feeling present?"

"Well, it feels like I'm here."

"Well, okay, you're here. What does that mean?"

"When I'm here, it feels like something is here."

"And what is this something that's here?"

"It feels like it's me, and this me and the hereness are the same thing."

"That's interesting; be more specific. What do you mean, 'me and hereness are the same thing'?"

"Well, it seems as though me and the fact of existing are the same thing. So me and the fact of existing are inseparable."

"Be specific."

"Oh, I'm existence."

In this example, we looked more deeply into our experience; we went from a place of feeling just present to recognizing true nature in a particular aspect that is pure existence. How did that happen? By being specific.

Practice Session: Being Specific in Your Inquiry

This would be a good time to explore your own relationship to this capacity. When you inquire, do you look at the details? Are you willing to zoom in and see specifically what is going on moment to moment in your experience? What effect does it have on your experience when you focus in this way as opposed to staying more general about what happens? Do you notice resistance or concerns about being this detailed in your inquiry?

After considering these questions, close your eyes and tune in to how you feel at this moment. Speak aloud a brief statement that describes that feeling. Using as a model the dialogue above, begin a sequence of asking yourself out loud what each statement means. As you continue to respond, zoom in on your experience and see how specific you can get. Notice at which points you are tempted to say, "That's good enough." What stops you from becoming more specific?

SPECIFICITY VERSUS PRECISION

Let's not confuse being specific with being precise. They are not the same. Being precise is a function of the Clear Essence, the Clear diamond. Being specific is a function of the Point. The Point is the most specific essential presence there is. When you experience the Point, you are a singularity, as specific as one can be. There is no more specific experience of Essence than the Point—a one-pointed, singular, concentrated sense of identity and presence. It is the most specific way one can experience oneself. That's why we say that it is simplicity itself. It has no parts—it's one thing, very simple, very specific. And because it is the most specific quality, it aids us in being able to be specific about anything. Precision, however, is a matter of exactness, of distinguishing one thing from another.

I'll give you a more detailed example. You look in the distance and see this dark thing on the horizon, a dark mound or shape far away. As you come closer, you are able to become more precise and more specific. For instance, suppose two of you are getting closer to this thing. One of you says, "Looks like an animal." The other says, "Looks like a building." When you get closer, you both realize that it's a building. So the one who said that it was a building was more precise, not more specific. As you get still closer, you see that it's a two-story building. That's being specific. If you can identify it as a two-story Southern-style house, then you're getting even more specific. You're not getting more precise, you're getting more and more specific—seeing more details about the object. The precision functioned to differentiate perception, to determine whether it was an elephant or a house, while the specificity identified distinguishing elements of that particular house. So clarifying the fundamental difference between various forms is not a matter of specificity, it's a matter of precision.

When you get precise, you don't necessarily zero in, you just get clearer, sharper. To get more specific, you need to see more details. So in precision, you're seeing the delineation, the sharper contrast—to know that what you are looking at is this and not that—while specificity means that you're seeing things in greater detail. Both are necessary skills or capacities for understanding our experience. And just like precision, specificity is a capacity that can be more or less developed in us. Some of us don't know how to get specific, while some of us can get specific down to minute details. Some of us can keep changing our lenses so that we have a zooming mechanism available to our inner eye. Some of us don't have a zoom lens, so we compensate with other capacities.

So we have now looked at two kinds of focus: a focus that is one-pointed so that you can follow the thread, and a focus that zeroes in by being specific. And both these qualities—the one-pointedness and the specificity—have to do with the Essential Identity. One-pointedness comes from the fact that the Essential Identity is a point, and specificity is derived from its being the most specific presence possible. It's interesting how the geometrical and the affective sides of the Point are interconnected, and how both affect our consciousness and capacity. Geometrically the Essential Identity is a point, but in terms of feeling, it is the most specific kind of feeling—the feeling of identity.

The Point is the shining star, the point of light that focuses the action of the Diamond Guidance as it unfolds our experience. By its light, we are drawn to the point of our experience, and through its focus we unravel the ever deepening thread of meaning that leads to our true nature. Our Essential Identity is truly the only point of existence.

CHAPTER 26

Personal Inquiry

GUIDANCE FOR THE JOURNEY HOME

The Diamond Guidance balances our attitude in inquiry in a dynamic way, by intensifying each aspect as it is needed to address the particular situation. As the Guidance presences itself, whatever aspect appears balances the picture a little more. It brings another needed facet, another element that increases the capacity for optimal inquiry and unfoldment. That is why the Diamond Guidance is a Diamond Dimension, which means an integrated structure. All of the essential aspects are integrated in one functional capacity that operates to reveal the truth of reality.

Operating with one of the aspects is still flying our spacecruiser, but it is more like flying a shuttlecraft, while with the whole Diamond Guidance it is as if the mother ship is descending. If you remember the movie *Close Encounters of the Third Kind*, you might recall that first the little ships came zooming around, and then the mother ship descended in a symphony of colors and sounds, which was its mode of communicating. This is similar to how the Diamond Guidance functions: it has all the qualities as colored diamonds of conscious presence, and some of them become more brilliant and more intense as they are needed in response to the objective needs of experience.

So discussing the various qualities and aspects independently does not mean that each one is separate and functions on its own. They all function as organs within the same organism—as an integrated whole. They might all function at the same moment, or alternate in various combinations. Guided inquiry has the capacity to use all the aspects in an integrated way to support us in discovering the various dimensions of experience. By revealing the truth, it has the capacity to penetrate all the levels of reality. If we follow it, the Guidance can lead us all the way to the source of all manifestations, the ultimate truth, which is our home.

When we make the journey with the Diamond Guidance, the soul at some point becomes the Guidance itself apprehending the absolute nature of everything. During the third journey, the Diamond Guidance is inseparable from the soul's ongoing presence, shining with its exquisite precision, delicacy, refinement, intimacy, and indescribable beauty and freshness. We are sweetness, delight, warmth, appreciation, and preciousness. We experience ourselves at this stage as all of these qualities in a presence that touches the Absolute—perceiving it and unifying with it.

In other words, when our spacecruiser takes us to the Absolute, our consciousness becomes refined until it dissolves into the Absolute's mysterious vastness. But it dissolves through this colorfully variegated, clear diamondness. This becomes a specific way of apprehending the Absolute, with the Diamond Guidance as the connecting lens for the soul. The next step is the self-realization of the Absolute. We become the Absolute witnessing the world through the Diamond Guidance. The Diamond Guidance becomes the organ of perception of the Absolute—its multifaceted, precise eye. We perceive the world as a manifestation full of beauty and knowledge, but this beauty and knowledge appears with pristineness, delicacy, and an exquisite sharp precision. Everything appears diamond-like; it's not only beautiful, it's itself, precisely and exactly.

PERSONAL INVOLVEMENT

So we will continue our exploration of the diamonds of the Diamond Guidance by looking at another aspect needed to balance our inquiry. This is the essential Pearl, the prototype of integration and the quality that allows each of us to manifest in the fullness of exactly who we are.

Because of the abstract elements we have recently discussed—such as knowingness, truth, clarity, one-pointedness, focus, and so on—you might be tempted to think that inquiry is some kind of disembodied process distant from our actual experience. Some people react to discussions of truth, knowingness, and objectivity by feeling that inquiry must be an abstract or philosophical process. And others believe that to be clear, objective, and focused on the truth, we have to distance ourselves from it to make sure that our own personal experience does not distort the truth.

As we discussed in chapter 24, that's how research is usually approached, especially in the physical sciences. You keep a very clear separation from the experiment so that it doesn't touch you. Therefore, when we discuss investigation, exploration, inquiry, and discovery, some might think that these have to be as antiseptic as scientific research. Discussions of witnessing, detachment, nonreactivity, and disidentification—all of which are important in the process of inquiry—can also lead to such an attitude.

The belief that one needs to be outside of one's experience is due to the dilemma that most individuals feel caught in. They do not know how to be objective and detached without being distant from experience. However, if we distance ourselves from experience, we cannot inquire into, cannot read, our soul. For inquiry to happen and be guided by the guidance of Being, we need to be intimately in contact with our experience. We need to be intimately in touch with our feelings, sensations, thoughts, impulses, reactions, actions, ideas. We need not only to know they are there, but also to feel their texture. We want to have as much input as possible, which means that we need to be totally immersed in the experience in such a way that we fully experience it and feel it. We need to be completely in the middle of it so that we can feel all its nuances.

Suppose I'm exploring a feeling of enthusiasm that I don't understand. Exploring doesn't mean that there's enthusiasm here and I'm observing it from someplace else. If I want to know what this enthusiasm is about, I have to jump right into the middle of it, feel it as fully as possible; I need to let it fully unfold without its taking over. In fact, the very process of exploring keeps experience from taking over completely. If we just take our experience at face value and don't explore it, that's not inquiry—it's only an experience. But inquiry means being in the middle of one's experience and feeling everything within it with all our senses, all our nerve ends. We need to feel the texture, the temperature, the affects, the sensations, the kinesthetics and pressures—all of it. In other words, an important part of the inquiry is a total personal contact, a complete involvement with the experience and with the process itself.

Having an inner contact with the totality of our experience means that we cannot avoid being in contact with the world, with other people, and with our life in its totality. There needs to be this overall in-touch-ness, this overall contact for inquiry to be full and meaningful. So, for example, if we're not aware of our feelings about life, what are we going to investigate? In other words, if we investigate only our thoughts or our actions, we will create a distance in the investigation. Even though this is still inquiry, it's not as powerful, not as effective as when we include our emotions and reactions. The inquiry is powerful only when there is enough input and enough information to allow the investigation to be personal. And this comes only from a direct, full contact with experience.

This full contact with experience indicates a certain attitude—an attitude of being personally interested, of loving the process because it touches us personally. It happens when we are so interested, so excited, so turned on, that we jump into it without holding back at all. If, on the other hand, we want to explore merely to get rid of a problem or accomplish a particular goal, then we are not interested in immersing all our nerve ends in the experience; we're interested just enough to get rid of or solve the problem.

So inquiry requires that we dive into experience but continue to be aware and present while in the middle of it. And it is the Diamond Guidance that gives us this capacity to be present and objective in the middle of everything. We can be feeling emotional or cynical, or have all kinds of physical reactions, but right in the center can be an objectivity, an awareness, a presence, and a curiosity about the situation. The presence of the Diamond Guidance provides all these elements in the inquiry. But for it to arise, there must be a personal involvement, a personal investment, a personal passion. We need to have a personal love for the process, for the exploration, for the truth, for our soul, for reality. Otherwise the Guidance will not show up.

We can't just be distant observers; we can't just look at experience as if it were a movie. Many spiritual experiences of transcendence or oneness are similar to watching a movie; but that's not inquiry yet, that's impersonal witnessing. For there to be personal inquiry, the witnessing must occur in the middle of experience—in contact with it—not outside it. We continue to witness, but we're in the middle of it. Our witnessing is embodied.

Why would the soul strip herself, expose her beauty and her richness, if we're not completely and personally interested in her revealing her full truth, if we are inquiring with a prejudice or an aim in mind? Real inquiry coincides with a passionate involvement with one's process, with one's realization, with one's life. That way it becomes the core that goes through our life. All of our life then feeds into it and is an expression of it.

PERSONAL AUTONOMY

This brings us to the issue of autonomy. In the context of the Diamond Guidance, autonomy means recognizing and developing this sense of personal involvement, this personal passion in inquiry. Autonomy means that we do our work of inquiry not because somebody told us to, not because we read about it in a book, not because we want to be good or enlightened, but because we are personally excited about it. If we have our own excitement about the process, then we're autonomous. If remaining excited about our inquiry depends on a teacher or somebody else turning us on or inspiring us, then we are still dependent on others or on the circumstances.

Many people think that autonomy means, "I have my own ideas, my own perceptions," but that definition is superficial; it is not what essential autonomy really is. Everyone has his or her own ideas and perceptions, but to have one's own passion, one's own involvement, one's own interest, one's own excitement about the truth and the process of investigation—that is autonomy of inquiry. This autonomy is what invites the guidance of Being.

It is okay to be dependent for a while on a school, situation, teaching, or teacher. But our process is not going to get very far if we are not able to self-activate at some point. How much can our teacher work with us? At most, a couple of hours a week. What are we going to do the rest of the week? If we have our own excitement, then we can have a twenty-four-hour process of unfoldment. So we need to rely on our own pure love, excitement, and passionate involvement in discovering the truth. Our process will not deepen or continue to unfold without this love of the truth, this desire to discover the truth in ourselves. At some point, we ourselves must want to find out about reality because it is personally important to us.

And to be truly autonomous means we're not just inquiring because we're interested in getting rid of problems. In that case, autonomy is not real—it's motivated by whether we feel good or bad. True autonomy means that the unfoldment itself turns us on. That's why, when somebody has true autonomy in inquiry, it doesn't matter whether the experience is painful or pleasurable. Either way, it's always interesting. There are always things to learn that can turn us on. And the human consciousness functions the same way whether we experience intense pain or intense pleasure; only the affect and our reactions are different. This does not mean that we need to like the painful experiences as much as the pleasurable ones. We're not concerned about loving our experiences, we're talking about loving the exploration itself—the investigation, the inquiry, the truth.

We see here that autonomy and personalness go together. This indicates the role of the Personal Essence—the aspect of the Pearl—in the functioning of the Diamond Guidance. Personal involvement, autonomy, and contact are all qualities of the Personal Essence.* In other words, the effect of the Pearly diamond of the Diamond Guidance is to create contact with, a personal involvement with, our internal and external experience. And that translates into personal autonomy in inquiry.

The Diamond Guidance guides the soul and its process of maturation and individuation. This process is the same as the movement toward the soul's realization of the Personal Essence, and the Diamond Guidance will arise naturally to assist in this development. But if we

---

*See *The Pearl Beyond Price,* Book One.

don't have an intimately and independently personal attitude about our experience, the Diamond Guidance will not descend into our inquiry to do its job. Only when that personal involvement and passion are present does the Diamond Guidance say, "Oh, there's the call. Here I come. I'm happy to do my job." Otherwise, it doesn't matter what we feel, what we do, what we long for—the Diamond Guidance won't hear it because it's not its call; it's a call for something else.

So it's okay to depend on teachers and their encouragement and inspiration, especially at the beginning and once in a while along the way, because we get discouraged and disheartened frequently on the journey. But little by little, we need to develop our own autonomy. The fire must eventually come from within us as a heartfelt passion to understand ourselves and to understand reality.

This is similar to getting turned on to fishing, for instance. How does that manifest? You want to know everything about it. It's not only a matter of learning about fishing so you can catch a fish and eat it. Because you are passionately interested, you want to learn all about hooks, about lines, about sinkers, about bait. You talk to fishing enthusiasts, read books about it, spend money on fishing gear. It's a love affair. When we truly become engaged in inner inquiry, it's the same kind of love affair.

Practice Session: Your Personal Involvement with Your Own Inquiry

You might want to take a look now at your involvement with your own process. A good way to do this is to explore the following aspects of your inquiry. Begin by looking at the ways you are not personally involved in your own process. Are there aspects of your self-exploration that don't feel personal or heartfelt? Do you look at your issues and longings in a way that is removed, generalizing, or judgmental? Are you always focusing on what is familiar?

The second area to explore is what stops you from getting personally involved in your own process. Is there a concern about coming directly into contact with your experience? Does the turning toward direct contact bring up fear, expectation of pain or judgment, hopelessness, desire? Remember that having emotions doesn't necessarily mean that you are personally involved. You might also want to look at why it might be difficult to bring freshness and openness to each moment in your process.

The third exploration is to see how you *are* personally involved in your own process. When do you feel actively involved in your own inquiry? What is it that touches you and engages you right now?

Spend some time with each of these questions in this order, and they will deepen your awareness of your personal involvement with your own inquiry. Then notice how this understanding is relevant as you inquire into an issue you are confronted with or into whatever you are experiencing at present. Do you feel more personally involved now that you've done some exploration of your particular tendencies in inquiry? How do you feel about that? Can you see what tends to limit intimate contact with your experience?

Question and Answer

STUDENT: I have a question about the relationship between self-discipline and the love of truth. It seems like there's a continuum where self-discipline is the motivation for the process of inquiry, and then at some point, love of the process of getting to the truth takes over.

ALMAAS: My experience is the other way around. It is loving the truth that motivates me to discipline myself. Why else would I want to discipline myself? What would motivate me to do that? Love is the source of true discipline. Let's assume that you're really interested in the subject matter you're inquiring into. Then at some point, you discover that you have certain limitations. Because of those limitations, you need discipline. Discipline is a way of dealing with one's personal limitations; to use it in other situations is to turn it into the superego. That's why kids always develop a superego: Their parents try to discipline them, but children don't see the point. They don't see the discipline as addressing their needs or limitations. So it becomes a superego thing that is unavoidable. But that's okay as a transitory stage.

SELF-ORGANIZATION AND PERSONAL REALIZATION

The Pearl aspect is the essential prototype of integration and organization, specifically of self-integration and self-organization. This capacity, or process, is inherent in life in general, in consciousness in general. Natural science has discovered that self-organization is also inherent in physical matter. It can be seen throughout the natural world. Even on the simplest of biological levels, life is self-organizing and self-activating. We see this in an amoeba as well as in a single cell in the human body, and even in a star or a planet.

This integration and organization exists on all levels within the human being: The body, the mind, and the soul are all self-organizing. Similarly, groups of people such as families, tribes, and neighborhoods are self-organizing. The same is true of cities and countries, as well as of ecosystems and planetary weather patterns. The concept of Gaia refers to the same principle at work in the earth as a whole. The more we look, the more we see that the whole universe is self-organizing, self-activating, and self-acting.

Self-organization also exists at all levels of evolution. On the soul level, it occurs when the Pearl is realized, at which point self-organization becomes specific and clear as the culmination of the soul's development from the earliest stages of primitive formlessness. The fact that the universe as a whole is self-organizing means that it too is moving toward individuation and integration, toward being the universal Pearl. On the universal level, complete self-organization is sometimes referred to as God.

What is perhaps most interesting is that the essential aspect that functions as the prototype for self-organization—the Pearl or Personal Essence—also happens to be the aspect that is the basis for contact, personalness, and involvement. This indicates that these two elements—self-organization and personal contact/engagement—are somehow inherently related, if not coemergent: It is as if one cannot occur without the other also occurring. Perhaps this is why some theistic religions conceive of God as personal.

Since the evolutionary movement of the soul is toward greater organization, self-integration, and wholeness, the capacity provided by the Personal Essence is required for inquiry. Inquiry is an expression of that evolution, since the unfoldment of the soul is a movement toward individuation. As the potentials of the soul unfold, they become organized and integrated into our sense of who we are. Obviously, this process of integration is an important element in the guidance of the unfoldment, the guidance that expresses itself in our inquiry. In this context, it is interesting to see the ways in which a human being is an expression of the universe.

PERSONAL FIELD

The aspect of Personal Essence contributes another important capacity and quality to our inquiry and understanding. I am referring to the capacity of bringing oneself into the inquiry as an object of inquiry, not just bringing oneself into the inquiry as the inquirer. In other words, inquiry—even an inquiry motivated by personal passion—can be about anything. We can have a personal passion to inquire into genetic engineering, for instance, or into fishing. That is a legitimate and useful application of inquiry. But that's not our work. The inner journey is a passionate inquiry into our own soul, our own personal field of experience. It's not enough to be passionately involved in a subject or pursuit that we are interested in learning more about; we have to be passionately involved in our own process. We need to inquire into and study our own state, our own soul; our inquiry has to be about what is relevant to us personally.

This can be a tricky situation. Suppose we're really excited about genetic engineering and want to learn all about it. There is definitely something personal for us here. If genetic engineering is our job, then it is even more personal and relevant. But is such an inquiry part of the inner journey or not? If we're excited about studying genetic engineering and it is personally relevant to us, that creates an opening for a wonderful inquiry. For it to support our inner work, however, the inquiry needs to address our own interest in genetic engineering. That means inquiring into our personal experience of genetic engineering and what it is like for us to be involved with it. We must consider how it is related to our own inner experience, to our own unfoldment, to the evolution of our soul—then it will be personally relevant for us in the way we mean here.

So, as we can see, for Spacecruiser *Inquiry* to take us to the farthest reaches of reality, any inquiries into other subjects need to be funneled into the central inquiry of our own evolution, our own nature. This does not necessarily contradict our interest in genetic engineering—

even fishing might be useful in investigating our own soul. If I explore my own experience fishing, it might lead to my unfoldment. But just learning about fish, hooks, and lines will not necessarily further my personal inquiry. Naturally, our personal experience expresses itself in the various situations of our life, such as our jobs, our relationships, our philosophies, our worldviews, and so on. We can investigate the practical, theoretical, or external aspects of these situations, or we can investigate our personal involvement and relationship with them. What will directly activate the unfoldment is the latter. Exploring any subject or interest without including one's own experience will not lead to personal unfoldment.

Recognizing this confronts our many resistances to engaging in inquiry that is truly personal. If we want to study some field within science or the humanities, it's much easier to steer clear of personal issues. The difficulties we encounter in those explorations usually relate to concepts, information, time, energy, and things like that. Sometimes the difficulty might be personal issues related to conducting such an inquiry, but those are much more limited than what we encounter when we inquire into the totality of the experience of the soul.

This points to the reason why our own inquiry encounters many personal resistances: It is when we want to explore ourselves in an intimate and meaningful way that we are confronted with the whole range of personal resistances—fear, pain, grief, resentment, hatred, hopelessness, deficiency, as well as long-held beliefs, attitudes, and positions—that stand in the way of contacting and realizing who we truly are. These are the barriers that we believe are integral to who we are, and therefore they keep us stuck in familiar and limited experiences of self. But they are integral only to our personality, our historical self. To be truly personal is to be open and available to contacting our immediate experience as it is now and not according to past beliefs. To work through any one of these resistances affects us more personally than reading a thousand books on genetic engineering or fishing, because it will affect our ability to contact our life.

We investigate our hearts, our minds, and our souls in the journey of inquiry in order to understand ourselves and the reality we live in. So we're not just learning inquiry, we are learning personal inquiry, even though some of the principles also apply to inquiry in general.

For inquiry to invite the Diamond Guidance in the way we have been discussing, that inquiry has to be into our own personal experience.

The Pearly diamond in the vehicle of the Diamond Guidance grounds our inquiry in the reality of the life we are living. It is this quality of the Guidance that engages us in such a way that we are continually being touched by our life and by the understanding of its truth. And this sense of personal contact and personal meaning is what brings about the integration of our realization. Being personally engaged in the inquiry and wanting to know the truth from that personal place means that the unfoldment of our soul cannot help but transform who we are and how we live our life.

It is important to recognize that personalness is not only in reference to an external focus of inquiry. Here we are challenging the impersonal stance that often occurs in spiritual teachings, mostly the Eastern traditions. Many of their traditions view the inner journey as a movement toward impersonal transcendence. They do not see that a personal life and a personal passion can be spiritual. For them, to be spiritual means to go beyond personal life. In the Diamond Approach, inquiry is open and open ended. We do not posit such a position; we allow the Guidance to reveal what the truth is.

One thing we find is that ultimate truth is impersonal and transcendent—which means that it exists beyond the realm where the personal is relevant—but it can manifest and express itself in personal ways on various levels, including that of the soul. This possibility points to a different kind of completeness that is still totally real.

CHAPTER 27

Brilliant Inquiry

BRILLIANCE OF BEING

Realization and liberation require many things: dedication and commitment, love and devotion, awareness and sensitivity. But more than anything else, they require understanding. Understanding is the central faculty needed for liberation, especially when we go very deep in our experience and arrive at subtle places. That is because when we reach the subtlety of our true nature—the real depth—what is left is our understanding. Everything else, in some sense, has dropped away by then. All that is left is our subtle capacity for discriminating what is manifesting, what is true, and what is false.

All spiritual traditions have known that understanding is what is required for realization and liberation. This is reflected in the Indian tradition of the various yogas, in the recognition that *prajna* (discriminating insight) and *jnana* (discriminating awareness) are the faculties needed for liberation. It is understood in the Buddhist tradition that discriminating wisdom is the function of spiritual guidance, which is required in the deeper states of realization. The Sufi tradition believes that what liberates the soul is the higher intellect. The Kabbalah holds that the higher mind, *hochmah* and *binah,* is what liberates the soul. The Greeks had the concept of the nous for this same function.

So it has been acknowledged and understood by all spiritual traditions that what finally liberates the soul is to see the false as false and the true as true. This is for one simple reason: Our soul is fundamentally faithful to the truth.

Truth is the fundamental ground of our soul, so the soul is fundamentally faithful to the truth. She always lives and acts out what she believes to be true. Yes, we frequently act out of lies and falsehoods, but this is because the soul believes that they are true. When we act out being a little deficient kid, for instance, it is because the soul believes that she is a little deficient kid. When we act from anger, we really believe that the truth is that we should act out the anger. The difficulty is not that the soul loves or likes falsehood, but that she takes a falsehood as truth and lives it out faithfully. For example, the soul will not let go of identification with the ego because the soul is totally convinced that this is who she is. The soul is convinced that she is the body, that she is this person, and so this is what she is going to live, act out, and defend until death. The soul is, in a word, ignorant.

That is why at some point, the most important thing for the soul is to see what the truth really is: to see who she is and what she is, and to know the truth about the soul and about reality as a whole. Only when the soul recognizes the truth and is certain about it will she change. Before that, she will continue to behave according to what she takes to be the truth.

Of course, this situation can become quite subtle and complex because we might have an experience of true nature, recognize "Oh, that's me," and then wonder, "Well, why don't I live according to that?" The reason is that we are more convinced of other things, some of which might be held in the unconscious. We might still believe that we are more this little kid, for example, or that we are our historical identity.

Many deep convictions about what we believe is true have been crystallized in the soul and have never been challenged. Hence, our occasional insights or experiences about what true reality is do not liberate us. We still have to understand ourselves in relation to that reality in order to be liberated from the falsehoods that we take to be true. And of course, we need to see what truth itself is. This is why the role of understanding has always been recognized as the central and final liberating faculty.

For instance, if a person is identified with a particular self-image, he will not let it go before he recognizes it is just an image. It doesn't matter what anybody tells him about that image; as long as he believes the image is really him, it will not dissolve. He won't let go just because somebody loves him, or because he feels good about himself, or even because he has an experience of his true nature. He lets go only when he understands: "I am identifying with this. But it is not me, it is just an image in my mind."

Many methods do not use understanding or inquiry directly, such as those based on action or devotion, but all methods produce understanding at some point. If they don't, they won't liberate us. If at some point, through devotion and passionate love, we don't recognize and understand that we are part and parcel of the Beloved, how will we be liberated? It doesn't matter how much we love the Beloved; we will be separated as long as we do not clearly discern our inherent unity with what we love.

Understanding is our natural, inherent faculty. We see that this is all we've got when finally left to ourselves. When we forget all methods and techniques, when we just rest and be, only our own recognition of what is true is left. From this place, when we recognize our true nature, we understand who and what we are. And when we are convinced—with certainty and without question—that this truth is really our nature, then we change. So liberation is actually a change of mind. At some point, we change our mind about what reality is in a very fundamental way.

The Diamond Guidance is the faculty in our soul that makes it possible for our inquiry to arrive at understanding. As we have seen, each essential aspect functions in the operation of the Diamond Guidance as a faculty needed for inquiry and understanding. And together, all the elements of the Diamond Guidance make it possible for our inquiry to become precise enough to arrive at objective understanding. In this chapter, we will explore another perfection of our true nature that is necessary for inquiry and understanding. We will explore how intelligence contributes to the journey.

How can we understand intelligence on the essential dimension, as a manifestation of Being? We first go to the Absolute, the essence of our Being. The absolute essence of Being is complete in all ways, perfect in all possibilities; it is completeness and perfection in a total way. It implicitly has in it all the essential aspects, all the perfections. These are the perfections of the Absolute, the explications of all the perfections inherent in our deepest nature, which is our absolute identity. All these perfections, all the essential aspects, are implicit in the Absolute. They are not only implicit and unmanifest but also undifferentiated. So the Absolute is completeness, perfect in all ways in an unmanifest, implicit, and undifferentiated state.

In this context, "undifferentiated" means that the qualities of Being are not separate from each other. At this level of experience, we cannot separate or differentiate them even though they are all there. Not only are they not differentiated, they are not manifest. In other words, we can't experience them in a positive sense; we can only know that they are there because there is no deficiency, no need, in the experience of the Absolute. The Absolute is complete when we experience it as qualityless. It is qualityless because although it implicitly has all the perfect qualities, they are all unmanifest. That is why we call it the Mystery. We know its perfections explicitly only when the Absolute is manifest.

At one of the stages of its manifestation, the Absolute presents itself as explicit perfection. Here, perfection and completeness are explicit, with all the various perfections present—but in this stage, the qualities are still undifferentiated. We cannot separate one from another. We can know and recognize Love in this manifestation, for example, but we cannot differentiate it from Will. And we can't differentiate Will from Clarity, Clarity from Strength, Strength from Fulfillment, or Fulfillment from Joy. All the qualities are explicit and manifest but not differentiated.

We refer to this manifestation as Brilliancy. When we experience Brilliancy, we experience perfection and completeness explicitly because our true nature is manifesting to us in a form characterized by perfection and completeness. By inquiring into Brilliancy, we recognize it as intelligence. It is the presence of pure radiance, pure brilliance. The brilliance, the radiance, is like white light that contains all the colors of the spectrum. Clear light does not manifest the prismatic colors, nor does black light. More precisely, the clarity and the blackness have all the colors in an implicit way, not explicitly. In Brilliancy, they are explicit but not differentiated, not discriminated yet. That's why when we experience manifestation directly out of the Absolute, we always see it as a radiance, as a brilliance, as illumination.

Brilliancy is a perfection in the sense that it is completely undefiled true nature, just like the Absolute. We experience and recognize this perfection directly, in a positive sense, not in an indirect or negative sense. Because it is qualityless, the Absolute is perfect, but without the feeling or concept of perfection being present. In Brilliancy, perfection is a discriminated specific quality of the Absolute. That is why we consider Brilliancy to be one of the aspects of Essence. The presence of Brilliancy is so fine, so delicate, so subtle, that it is like a substance of utmost refinement, utmost delicacy, utmost smoothness and fluidity. It is like a substance made out of brilliance itself.

No color can be called brilliance; brilliance is always a quality of a color. The closest experience there is to brilliant light in nature is when we look at the stars at night or glance at the bright sun. The light from these bodies is actually composed of many colors, but it is so intense that our eyes can't discriminate the colors. With brilliant light, however, though the colors are all explicitly present, we cannot discriminate them because they are not differentiated. Thus, the aspect of Brilliancy doesn't exist in the physical world. Neither does clear light. We never see clear light. We never see black light. Black light, clear light, and brilliant light don't exist in nature. But they are all specific dimensions of our true nature that can manifest on their own without characterizing something else.

When we can recognize Brilliancy as the essence of intelligence, we can begin to understand the fundamental elements of intelligence. We begin to see, for instance, that when we say an action is intelligent, we mean that it is complete and perfect—it is the best way to go about something. We interpret its completeness and perfection as intelligence. An intelligent action is an effective action, whether it be mental, emotional, or physical. Why do we want action to be intelligent? Because then it will be most efficient, most economical, most expedient. It will be the most optimizing. And when Brilliancy is present, what we see is that our faculties begin to function more perfectly and completely—that is, more intelligently.

So intelligence reflects completeness, and Brilliancy is the most complete because it has all the perfections and aspects in it, undifferentiated. When we experience Brilliancy, we feel it as Love, Will, Clarity, Peace, Joy, and Truth all at the same time. Our sense of it is completeness. Whenever there is a hole in our soul, that means an aspect is missing. In Brilliancy, nothing is missing because all the aspects are present; there are no holes. We can actually feel the particular affect of completeness.

And because Brilliancy is complete, it brings about the most perfect action possible. It is the most perfect in the sense that it is the most optimizing, which means that it is the most effective in drawing us nearer to our true nature. The optimal direction for the experience of the soul is the one that leads her as close to her home as possible.

Intelligence is a very difficult concept to analyze because it includes many elements, many facets. We first need to realize that the intelligence of Brilliancy is not just mental intelligence, it is intelligence in any dimension, any action. We can have intelligence in the response to a situation, in the way we live our life, the way we think, the way we inquire, the way we interact, the way we communicate. This intelligence is organic and it underlies the actual experience of our consciousness. Brilliancy is the inherent intelligence of our Being. The more in touch we are with it, the more it penetrates and pervades our life, our perception, our experience, and our actions.

DIAMOND GUIDANCE AND BRILLIANCY

Each of the Diamond Vehicles is a particular combination of all the perfections. They appear in a certain pattern, in a certain juxtaposition that gives each one of them a particular, intelligent function. So the Diamond Guidance is a particular patterned structure of the various perfections. Unlike the undifferentiated perfections of Brilliancy, however, the perfections of the Diamond Guidance all operate in a manifest, explicit, and differentiated way. They are explicitly differentiated, but they function together as one unit that activates understanding.

This means that the Diamond Guidance itself is an expression of brilliance, of intelligence. It is the brilliant light that has been differentiated and then integrated in a specific function—that of understanding. This is one way of recognizing the functioning of intelligence in the Guidance, which has prompted us to sometimes refer to the Diamond

Guidance as the discriminating intelligence of Being. However, we can see that the Guidance functions intelligently in three major ways. We have been discussing the first—namely, that the whole vehicle is a manifestation of intelligent action in the sphere of understanding or discerning the truth.

A second way the Guidance acts with intelligence is by modulating its brilliance depending on the situation. Its various colors—Black, Red, Blue, and so on—can become clearer, more transparent, more intense, more brilliant. More intelligence is operating when they do so, and the Guidance is then using more intelligence and brilliance in its operation. In fact, as the Guidance itself becomes more brilliant, the intense luminosity will begin to feel more prominent than any of the particular colors. In other words, as the Guidance luminates more brilliantly, the aspect of intelligence becomes dominant over other qualities. When it gets very bright, we might not even see a color, just brilliance. Then the whole Diamond Guidance is brilliant, is Brilliancy.

Also, there are degrees of brilliance and color differentiation. The more inquiry needs the total functioning of Brilliancy—the perfection and completeness—the more brilliant the Guidance becomes. By becoming more brilliant, our inquiry attains greater intelligence, to the point of becoming Brilliancy itself.

Any color—in this case, we are referring to any essential aspect—can become more or less brilliant. If it grows brilliant enough, it becomes the pure presence of Brilliancy. The differentiated light goes back to its origin, which is undifferentiated brilliance. In other words, through the operation of Brilliancy in the Guidance, our inquiry can become more brilliant, luminous, illuminating, penetrating, complete, comprehensive, and perfect in its functioning.

INTELLIGENCE IN INQUIRY

We want to emphasize in this chapter the third way that intelligence functions in the Diamond Guidance: as one of the self-existing components of the Guidance. The Diamond Guidance—just like any other Diamond Vehicle—is a combination of every aspect in its objective or diamond form, and one of those aspects is the Brilliancy diamond. In other words, intelligence functions in the Diamond Guidance as the presence of the Brilliancy diamond.

By exploring the Brilliancy diamond, we will know objectively and precisely what intelligence is and how it functions in understanding. As we have discussed, Brilliancy as an aspect is a very clear, very explicit sense of presence. Its substance is so pure, so compacted with true nature, that its presence is palpable. It is exquisitely smooth. We can feel it as a flowing, luminous presence, with a density similar to that of mercury but infinitely smoother and finer. If we see the reflection of sunlight in a mirror, and then imagine liquefying it, we get the effect of brilliance. Brilliancy is so intense that it looks almost like a continuous explosion of light.

When we see this beautiful brilliance, we understand why and how Being is intelligent. It is intelligent not only when it manifests in thought but also as intrinsic and organic brilliance, which is the underlying intelligence in any sphere of action. It provides our faculties of inquiry and understanding with an innate intelligence, so that discriminations are subtle, connections are insightful, analysis is luminously delineated, and articulation is lucid and perfect. Brilliancy is so perfectly immediate, so complete, smooth, fluid, and free, that its functioning brings ease, perfection, lucidity, and clarity to any action, whether the action is communication or thinking, interaction or analysis.

The intelligence of Being does not function in a mechanical way as a computer does—by stringing together perceptions and memories. It is not like artificial intelligence, which is why artificial intelligence will never become real intelligence. There is an innate creativity in the functioning of Brilliancy. Intelligent inquiry possesses an organic, intuitive magic in the way it arrives at insights. As a result, there is always a newness in the experience, and always an efficiency in our way of understanding. The inquiry embodies a lucidity, a fluidity, and a radiance that illuminate experience and make it possible for us to see more directly. Consciousness becomes so luminous that it cannot help but see more intrinsically, more to the core of the matter, always in a very smooth, easy, and lucid way, without effort or method.

The more that Brilliancy is present, the more we see directly without having to travel the route of making a series of connections. We are able to bridge big gaps in our understanding of experience without having to go through exhaustive, methodical analysis and correlation. We can jump between places due to the intensity, the fluidity, and the smoothness that is going through our consciousness. It is as though the Brilliancy itself were flowing through our neocortex and leaping across our synapses.

In addition, not only is our consciousness clear and transparent from the clarity of Essence, but a radiance from within illuminates and highlights the various associations and connections. Connections are more readily obvious because of the intense light shining through them.

ANALYTIC INTELLIGENCE

In its functioning, Diamond Guidance uses two primary faculties, two operations, in an organically combined way: analysis and synthesis. It combines the functioning of the right and left hemispheres of the brain in a unified action of understanding.

In order to understand something, we frequently need first to analyze it. In other words, we need to look at the various parts and components, differentiate the significant elements, and discriminate them in more subtle and minute ways. Thus, the faculty of analysis is related to separation and discrimination, which ultimately is the capacity provided by the Red Essence.

The way this faculty generally manifests in the Diamond Guidance is in its diamondness—its clear, objective nature. The diamondness of the Guidance—the fact that it possesses sharp facets—is what gives it a precise capacity for discrimination and analysis. Regardless of what quality is operating, there is always a diamondness to it—always a diamondness to the Green, to the Red, to the Brilliancy, to the Black. This gives the overall diamond structure the capacity to discriminate precisely and sharply, which then becomes the capacity of analysis.

SYNTHETIC INTELLIGENCE

Synthesis has to do with putting things together: seeing the whole picture and comprehending it as a unified truth. We take the analyzed experience—experience broken down into components—and then see the elements in a new combination. So we begin inquiry with disparate elements of experience: memories and impressions, observations and reactions. Understanding emerges only when an integration occurs—seeing all of the elements together in such a way that the whole forms a particular meaning. This meaning of the whole is what we call a synthesis.

Of course, there must be a prototype, an underlying basis for this ability to synthesize. What is that prototype? Because Brilliancy is the original synthesis of all qualities, it is the prototype and archetype of synthesis on the essential level. And because it is an inherent synthesis, an intrinsic unity, its presence makes it possible for us to see the underlying synthesis in the various elements that we have analyzed. Brilliancy functions as the capacity for synthesis in any dimension, just as the Red Essence functions as the capacity for discrimination in any dimension. The dimension we are discussing here is understanding.

So analysis is related to the Red or Strength Essence; synthesis to Brilliancy. Analysis is based on separating elements in a situation or an experience—that is, discriminating parts and specifics, which brings clarity, precision, and knowledge. However, the presence of Brilliancy as the prototype of synthesis gives the soul the additional capacity to see underlying unities. This capacity appears as synthetic insights that engender understanding of larger and larger segments of reality.

The functioning of the Guidance in inquiry is primarily an interplay of analysis and synthesis. Sometimes analysis dominates, sometimes synthesis dominates. But they can also work together. We break down an object of inquiry into components and recombine certain parts; then we analyze other parts and make other combinations, until at some point an overall final synthesis emerges. We call that an insight or realization, which is the understanding of the entire matter we are inquiring into.

INTELLIGENT GUIDANCE

Now, what is the difference between the synthesis of Brilliancy and the synthesis of Guidance? Brilliancy can lead us to an intelligent insight because when it is present in its fluid form, flowing through our veins and nervous system, we experience an intelligence and a quickness in seeing overall gestalts. Since we can operate with Brilliancy by itself and see underlying unities without the presence of the Diamond Guidance, how does synthesis change when the Guidance is present? The difference is slight but significant, and there is an overlap between the two as well.

Brilliancy makes it possible for us to perceive the already existing, underlying inherent synthesis, the unity that is the basis of insight. This is not a matter of combining things together to arrive at an understanding. The synthesis is already present; we just don't see it. When Brilliancy arises, we begin to see the synthesis that is already there. It appears as the discovery of a unity that already underlies our experience. We discover this unity with the help of the unity of the soul, which is the Brilliancy.

The insight of the Diamond Guidance derives also from a synthesis. However, unlike in Brilliancy, the aspects in the Diamond Guidance are differentiated. Therefore, the synthesis of Guidance happens by correlating the various elements in a situation. The way it works is that the elements are first analyzed, seen separately. For example, in a given situation, there may be anger, sadness, a contraction here, a memory there, this action and that defense. These are all discriminated patternings. The Guidance sees all of these and then correlates them to find the connections between them and between the various groupings. It recognizes their relationships and interactions in a precise and detailed manner. It sees how they connect to each other, how they affect each other, how one leads to another: how sadness leads to the anger, how anger leads to fear, and how the fear is related to the contraction, how the whole thing is related to what one's mother did, how what one's mother did led to marrying this or that person, how marrying that person led to having that specific kind of job, which then explains one's present financial difficulty. That is the process that happens when inquiring with the Guidance.

This is usually an organized, orderly, and clear process, a precise seeing of interrelationships and interactions. This process ultimately reveals the unity that underlies all of them. This is how the Guidance uses synthesis in its overall functioning. Why? Because the Diamond Guidance is composed of the various differentiated aspects, and those aspects are differentiated and ordered in a certain combination. So Guidance functions by seeing the various elements of experience in combination until at some point they make a coherent gestalt. Then insight shines through.

By contrast, Brilliancy arrives at insight in one shot, at a glance, as if intuitively. It doesn't need to go through the various correlations. It is fast and breathtaking. However, it does not see the details of interactions and relationships between the various elements of the situation. We arrive at insight, but most of the time we don't know how we got there. There isn't as much perception, understanding, or knowledge in the process of arriving at the insight, which often makes it difficult to communicate it to others.

However, since the Diamond Guidance has Brilliancy as an aspect, it can use the capacity for direct illumination by simply seeing the gestalt without also seeing how the illumination came about. This direct penetration to the insight is possible and sometimes necessary. But frequently what is needed is the understanding of interactions and relationships that led to the insight. This is specifically the case when one attempts to relate many insights about the same subject matter. In order to reach an overarching insight that synthesizes the knowledge in various insights, we frequently need an understanding of how we arrived at them. A more complete knowledge of the different processes and relationships is crucial for such super-insights, such as those required to develop a body of knowledge.

The nature of this process is evident in the realm of scientific discoveries. Usually, a major brilliant insight is preceded, and is also succeeded, by systematic exploration. Seeing the unity in the multiplicity of the data available, which is the major insight, is the breakthrough. This breakthrough insight is preceded by the synthetic and analytic functions of the Guidance. It is the discriminating intelligence in the process of exploration that brings to light the various elements, facts, interrelationships, and interactions needed for the final conclusion to arise. Thus, the process of synthesis and analysis arrives at many insights by seeing the interrelationships of facts and data. When this process reaches a sufficient threshold of completeness, the ground is ready for the leap of intelligence, for the brilliant synthetic insight that is the function of Brilliancy.

So, for example, when a scientist is exploring, it's not that she is doing nothing and suddenly has a brilliant insight. No, the scientific researcher has to wrack her brains with a plethora of data, trying to see the various correlations and connections. This can go on for years. At some point, she sees enough interrelationships and has completed enough analysis that she arrives at the necessary threshold for the true completeness to manifest. This is the arrival of Brilliancy, which ushers in the brilliant vision.

But even this point is not the end, as we know from the process of scientific discovery. The unifying vision then needs to be explored in a process that clarifies the details and relevant elements. In addition, the knowledge already available in the field needs to be integrated into the breakthrough insight so that the unifying vision can then be articulated in a way that makes it communicable and usable.

In other words, we must do a lot of research before we arrive at the unifying vision. However, a unifying vision by itself is frequently useless. Many people have unifying visions from which nothing emerges because they don't have the knowledge and skill to translate their vision into something communicable, something that can be used and applied. This is the point where the trained scientist needs all his knowledge, training, and skills. Without the ability to articulate and explicate the unifying vision, the breakthrough is useless and most likely will be lost.

Again, these are the functions of the totality of the Diamond Guidance. Intelligence operates in the Guidance in both its overall functioning as the synthetic capacity that interrelates the elements, and in the brilliant unifying visions and overarching insights that appear like lightning. Then the discriminating capacity needs to come in again to analyze and synthesize, to relate all the elements in a way that makes the insight not only communicable but usable.

The Diamond Guidance uses both kinds of synthetic capacities (that of correlation/process orientation and that of intuitive bursts) in its overall operation, and specifically in its Brilliancy diamond. Sometimes what is needed is precise discrimination and precise analysis, in order to see the specifics and how they interrelate. That is when the Guidance becomes more transparent, clear, and delicate. The diamonds become quite sharp. At other times, more luminosity, more brilliance is needed. Then all the diamonds become more intense, more brilliant. The process is organic, with one often dominating the other.

But sometimes the two intensify together. Then there is an intense sharpness with a brilliance to the diamondness. The sharpness is so sharp that it shines brilliantly. The cutting edge is not only discriminating, it is also intelligently discriminating. This is the specific arising of the Diamond Guidance in the form of the Brilliancy diamond.

Recognition of the interrelationships between analysis and synthesis, and of the different levels of synthesis, can help us understand why major scientific discoveries are normally arrived at by scientists who have a great deal of knowledge and who have already explored the field extensively. Major scientific discoveries are rarely made by ordinary people, although it may happen once in a while. We need to develop a great deal of discrimination and understanding before we can approach the underlying unity. And it is only when we approach the underlying unity of the situation being explored that the essential unity, which is the Brilliancy, will arise. Then brilliant light penetrates the various elements of the whole situation, all of them are clarified in great relief, and they are all seen united to one center. That is the unifying insight.

This is actually a description of how inquiry arrives at insight. It always functions like that, not just at times of cataclysmic insight. The process of understanding continues through analysis and synthesis, steadily reaching greater and greater unity. Based on this understanding, we can see that spiritual development is a matter of greater and greater unification, greater and greater synthesis, until finally we arrive at the true synthesis, the true unity, the source of Brilliancy itself—our true nature.

Practice Session: Analysis and Synthesis in Your Inquiry

Understanding how analysis and synthesis manifest in your process of inquiry will help you open to the operation of the Brilliancy diamond. One way to begin is through a written inquiry into a burning question—something in your experience that you have a deep curiosity about and an urge to understand. For fifteen minutes, inquire into your question as fully and completely as you can. Then, explore the writing you have just done: Consider how you have used analysis and how you have used synthesis. Since these are the major processes of inquiry, it's helpful to recognize when and how you use each, and how the two are interrelated, so you can more clearly understand your own approach. In your inquiry, did you mostly use analysis and discrimination? Or did you lean more heavily on synthesis? How balanced was your process in terms of these two capacities?

THE BRILLIANCY DIAMOND

The Brilliancy diamond, as an aspect in the Diamond Guidance, is a wonderful, smooth presence, with luminosity and preciousness inseparable from clarity, sharpness, exactness, and precision. When this diamond is present in our soul, it infuses all of our capacities with the same luminosity and precision. Our inquiry and our understanding attain these qualities of brilliance and precision, as one capacity. What does that mean?

One meaning has to do with synthesis and analysis, the unified perception and the discriminating capacity. Synthesis and discrimination happen simultaneously when the Brilliancy diamond is present. They are both present in the same act. We see the specifics of the situation and their interrelationships at the same time that we see their underlying unity. It is the synthesis of Brilliancy that is directly seeing the underlying unity. Simultaneously with this awareness, we also see precisely how the unity manifests in the various elements, the various percepts and experiences.

Consider the following example: You are beginning to experience the essential aspect of Will, the White presence. You are able to discriminate it as Will. You can stop at that—"Oh, this is Will"—or you can begin to discriminate various characteristics of it, such as the feeling of determination, the sense of confidence, the inner solidity of support, the steadfastness Will gives to the soul, and so on. This is analysis, discrimination. "Oh, I see. When I'm feeling determined in this way, I recognize in it a sense of confidence." Then, as you feel the self-confidence: "I see, this confidence is the same as what makes me steadfast. And I recognize that when I'm steadfast, it is because this Will is a sense of inner support." You begin to discriminate the qualities that are implicit in Will.

So if you have a discriminating capacity, you can analyze, you can see more details, recognize more specifics in the same experience. If your discriminating capacity is not developed, if the sharpness of the

diamond isn't there, it will be difficult for you to see the various qualities that make up the aspect.

In this process, you are not only experiencing analysis, you are experiencing synthesis at the same time—understanding how all the qualities are manifestations of the same aspect. There is confidence, there's
support, there's steadfastness, there's determination, there's an effortlessness and a sense of purity, there's a sense of pristineness and a
sense of definiteness. At the very instant of seeing the discrimination
among these, you recognize that they are all the same thing. They are
just slight differentiations of the same presence.

If we have only the discriminating capacity without the synthetic
one, we might sometimes experience will, sometimes confidence,
sometimes determination, but it would be difficult for us to know that
they all belong to the same quality, to the same aspect. In the absence
of the synthetic capacity, we might even conceptualize them as different aspects that do not share an underlying unity. But if the synthetic
capacity is present, we will see the underlying unity; we will see that
all these properties characterize the same aspect—which is the same
presence, the same Will.

In order to help you see this faculty in a larger context, I can use
the example of my beginning experience of essential presence. When
I first became aware of presence, I felt a sense of fullness, aliveness,
and groundedness. At that time, it was simply presence for me. That
was the most I could differentiate: Essence is presence. That's what I
was aware of, and nobody had told me anything else before that; I had
never read anywhere that presence could appear in different ways. So
Essence, I found out, was presence—a fullness, an aliveness, a thereness, an I-am-ness. After a while, I would feel the experience of the
presence changing. It's true that it was presence, but once in a while
it felt somehow different. One day the presence would feel strong and
firm, while the next day it would perhaps feel soft, sweet, and melty.
That was the beginning of discrimination.

And the recognition of what that difference meant brought the jolt
of insight: "Oh, Essence appears in aspects." That was the brilliant
breakthrough. It was a big surprise for me, quite an eye-opener. This
became a basic tenet of the Diamond Approach: Essence is not just
presence but presence that presents itself in various qualities, various

flavors. I could have stayed with just that, with the insight that presence appears in aspects. The exploration continued, however. At some point, I realized not only that presence has qualities and aspects, but that these arise at certain times and seem to challenge particular ego manifestations and deal with specific issues.

The Red Essence, for instance, seemed related to strength and weakness, and the issue of separation anxiety. So in a context where the psychological field and the essential dimensions are seen as one—synthesized—there is more discrimination. Thus, synthesis and analysis go hand in hand. The result is the body of knowledge we now call the Diamond Approach.

The analysis kept going, and every once in a while there was a major unifying insight. But a major unifying insight by itself is useless unless the exploration continues. When synthesis and analysis work hand in hand, what arises is a great deal of knowledge, for the specifics and the connections become what we call knowledge.

But the presence of the Brilliancy Diamond does more than allow us to discriminate and synthesize simultaneously; it also gives precision to our brilliance and brilliance to our precision. This means that there is sharpness and precision to synthesis. There is an exactness to it. The diamondness gives clarity, precision, and objectivity. What is synthesized are objective facts, objective manifestations.

If it were not for the precision and objectivity, our synthesis might consist of a little bit of prejudice, some reaction, an element of truth, and a touch of an essential experience, all of which are combined into some kind of strange theory. This kind of synthesis that lacks objectivity happens frequently, especially in the spiritual sphere.

We need precision in our objective facts, and we need precision in the relationships between them. Precision, when combined with the synthetic capacity, allows us to synthesize in an objective and clear way. This is the function of the brilliancy diamond. It is then possible for our understanding to operate with sharpness, precision, clarity, and objectivity, in both the sweeping, unifying vision and in the process of detailed explication. The process of exploration and the flights of genius can happen simultaneously as the functioning of the same aspect, the same presence.

The objectivity implicit in an essential aspect when it takes on the diamond form allows us to separate our subjective, personal bias from what is actually present in the experience. Then synthesis is informed by this discrimination. That is one way the diamondness adds to the brilliance. However, when the Brilliancy diamond is functioning, the discriminating capacity itself becomes brilliant as it embodies greater luminosity and clarity, and more lucidity and speed in making the discriminations and seeing the connections between them.

When we develop this capacity to discriminate and synthesize in a single act, it can deepen our realization of presence, even the realization of nondual presence. In nondual realization, all manifestations are manifestations of the same presence. However, there are many stages of realizing nondual presence. At one stage, nondual presence can itself be diamondized, and all manifestations have sharpness, clarity, and precision. Then what we see everywhere is a unified presence that is discriminated and precisely clear.

Many of us experience the state of oneness, at least fleetingly. This experience, though profound, is two-dimensional most of the time, in that seeing another person is rather like seeing one cell of an organism where all cells sort of look the same. All is one. The dominant experience is of a unified field of nonseparateness. However, when the oneness has the precision of the diamond, what manifests is an added dimension. Everything presents itself in much greater relief; every element of the oneness becomes more uniquely itself. It is true that there is a oneness—a nonduality—but the uniqueness appears very precisely, very clearly. In this state, the other person is a particular person with his own quality, and at the same time he is part and parcel of the oneness of everything. With the precision of diamondness, uniqueness is clear; with the brilliance in the diamond, the oneness is undeniable. Both discrimination and synthesis are operative in this diamond oneness. It is all one unified field, but everything is precisely itself, clearly delineated without being separate. This is the perspective of the Brilliancy diamond as it applies to a deeper experience of realization, that of nonduality.

DISCRIMINATING THE UNDERLYING UNITY

We have been discussing synthesis as the most fundamental quality of intelligence in Brilliancy. Insights seem to pop out effortlessly, connections do not require much cogitation, and the processes flow as easily as mercury. When these qualities are all present in one's functioning, we say that one is brilliant. However, there is another quality of intelligence that is significant and necessary for exploration, understanding, and synthesis. This has more to do with the completeness of intelligence than with its brilliance.

To be able to discriminate and correlate, to check things back and forth, and to synthesize, Diamond Guidance needs to hold together in the consciousness the various elements to be explored. In other words, we have all this data—percepts, sensations, feelings, memories, actions, presence, and so on. We want to explore them by analyzing, questioning, synthesizing, seeing connections. In order to do that, we need the capacity to hold all these elements together. If we just look at one or two of the elements in isolation and forget about the others, we can never arrive at understanding. We need a way to be with all these elements in our consciousness simultaneously. To consider only some of them may not bring us to the threshold necessary for synthetic insight.

Not only do we need to hold the various elements we are exploring together, we also need to hold the right elements, not just any elements of experience. Our experience is full of things—millions of bits of data—but we need to hold in our consciousness only the particular elements, the specific data relevant for our inquiry. So we select certain elements—certain feelings, sensations, experiences, memories, actions, and situations and hold only those; the rest remain in the background. We hold them so that we can explore them, discover significant correlations and interrelationships, and find the unity that underlies them.

But how do we know which elements need to be synthesized, and therefore which elements to hold? Since we have not yet synthesized them, we cannot see their underlying unity. So how do we know that these particular ones are the ones that are going to be synthesized? How do we discern what they are among the multitude of percepts and facts available to our experience? We normally do that selection implicitly, but did you ever ask yourself how that happens?

Let's look at a specific example: You are sitting across the table from your friend, having tea, and you are listening to her talking. You notice that you are seething with anger. You want to chop her head off. You are angry and a little bit sad. You wonder, "What am I angry about? She is talking as usual. She is always full of herself—nothing new—so why am I angry at her right now?"

As you contemplate your experience—listening to what she is saying, seeing the situation, and noticing what you are feeling—you start remembering that two nights ago when you were making love with your husband, you got a little bit irritated, a little bit hurt, in the middle of it. It was no big deal, but it affected you such that you couldn't climax after that. You didn't give it much thought at the time because that happens every once in a while. But you now realize something new about it. Somehow, listening to your friend and being mad at her reminds you of your husband. And as you contemplate all these elements together, you remember that a couple of days before that evening with your husband, when you were painting, your child threw a ball for you to catch. You realize that at that moment you almost slapped her. You knew that this was an unusual reaction to your child since you play ball with her every once in a while. So what was the big deal?

You begin to feel that all these elements are somehow connected. As you continue listening to your friend, your mind is now holding the sex scene with your husband and the painting scene with your daughter. As you do that, you start to feel empty inside, and with that emptiness comes a memory of when you were a child at home. It is a memory of your mommy busy cooking and your father reading a newspaper, and you were feeling some hurt, some anger, and also mildly empty. You never thought much about it, but it seems to be related in some way to what happened in the sexual interaction with your husband.

Then, in the midst of all of that, you remember your last session with your teacher and how it ended with feeling gratitude for him. You didn't think much about it at the time, but now you wonder why you were feeling so grateful to him. All these elements seem to be connected, but you don't know why you are remembering them together.

As you keep listening to your friend, you realize that something about her being full of herself is getting to you. Why does that make you mad at her? Then you remember that on the night when you made love, your husband was worried about his job. He was somewhat self-absorbed. And as you see that, you recognize that in your opinion, you are self-absorbed. However, in your childhood when you were feeling empty, you were not self-absorbed, but your parents were—your father reading his newspaper all the time and your mother always cooking and changing diapers.

"How is that related to my feeling grateful to my teacher? Something about my teacher felt positive, and with all these other people something felt painful. What is the connection? What happened in that session with my teacher?" You are drifting between all of these pieces while still listening to your friend. The memories seem to simmer, all held in your consciousness at the same time. Then you remember that in the session, as you were experiencing a clear sense of "I am" in your heart, your teacher said, "That is you." And you hadn't even said anything about your experience.

Right away, the insights explode in your consciousness. "My teacher saw me for exactly what I was in that moment! My friend is not seeing me, she is full of herself, fully absorbed in herself. My daughter did not see how absorbed I was while doing my painting when she threw the ball to me. When I was a kid, nobody in my family knew where I was; all of them were full of themselves, totally absorbed in themselves and their activities. They didn't see what I was feeling, or respond and relate to me according to what I needed. That is what happened to me with my husband. He started touching me right on my genitals; he wasn't attuned to where I was. I wanted him to start with the right nipple." Your hurt of not having received the right attunement opens up. All of these situations are unified by this deep wound.

So what was it that was giving you the capacity to select and hold these specific elements? You didn't recall the other times when you were angry at your husband, or angry at your child, or other hurts. You remembered only those particular situations. You were experiencing an innate capacity that can illuminate specifically those elements that have an underlying unity without your consciously or explicitly knowing the existence of that unity in advance.

If we look deeply into our consciousness, we recognize that the soul holds all the significant elements. But we can also see that there is a light, a brilliance, that underlies our consciousness and that shines through those specific elements that need to be synthesized and under-stood, which illuminates them in our consciousness. That brilliance is the underlying unity, and it reveals the unity in our experience even before we recognize it in our understanding.

It is Brilliancy that gives the Diamond Guidance the capacity to discriminate the right elements, the specific elements that have an underlying unity. Specifically, it is the Brilliancy diamond, because it has both the Brilliancy—which is the unity—and the diamondness, which is the discrimination. So we need both unity and discrimination; together they comprise a unified act of knowing.

The content in the above example was about attunement and being seen. At other times it could be other things—the content always changes. We have considered an emotional issue, but the same capacity is needed for the exploration of any topic. Brilliancy shines through whatever elements are relevant to the particular inquiry and illuminates them in our consciousness. That way it singles them out for our recog-nition. Then the Diamond Guidance can use our previously acquired knowledge, our memories, and its capacities for correlating, reflecting, and analysis. In this way, exploration can reveal the underlying unity that is already beginning to shine through those particular elements in our consciousness.

This synthetic capacity makes it possible for the Diamond Guidance to explore a situation by looking at the interrelationships of the ele-ments—analyzing some, synthesizing others—in a process that reveals their interconnections. The resulting combination leads to insight, the experience of realization that reveals the underlying unity of the situa-tion being explored.

The process of insight is a continuing one. So in the above example, it begins when you realize, "Oh, I've got something going on about attunement. Somebody is not attuned to me." This leads to more questions: "Why am I so sensitive these days about somebody not being attuned to me? What is new about that? Those people have not been attuned to me all along."

You then realize that in the past few sessions with your private teacher, you have been working on narcissism and your sense of who you are, your sense of identity, and your feeling of being seen and supported. No wonder you feel so grateful to your teacher, because your teacher is the one who has been attuned to you, helping you, supporting you to be yourself.

And as you recognize that, you not only experience the Point—the timeless self-recognition of "that is who I am"—as you did in your last session, but you also start to feel the inner support, the solidity that is within you. This again is an understanding: "I can have my own support, and that is what I need. So when there is no attunement, it is no big deal. I recognize that other people don't see who the hell I am since they are so busy with themselves, because obviously they don't know who the hell *they* are. So what's new?"

Now you are not only able to disengage from all of that, but you can also be attuned to the other person and actually see what is going on for them. You can ask your friend, "There must be something bothering you. What are you really trying to say?" And it might become obvious now why your friend is talking and talking without even paying attention to you. As you see, understanding continues and can become the source of effective action. And the other person can be impacted by your understanding.

Because the realization of Brilliancy in our inquiry is usually not complete, the capacity to hold relevant experiences together does not always function perfectly. The more we have realized and integrated the Brilliancy aspect—the aspect of completeness—in the Diamond Guidance, the more we are able to hold and recognize the relevant experiences on various levels, past and present. If you do not have the capacity to tell which experiences are relevant, inquiry takes a longer time. That is one of the reasons why having a teacher helps your inquiry. A teacher can see which experiences are related because of his knowledge and sensitivity to you. Over time, you will need to learn to be able to hold your experiences for yourself and to see the thread that connects them.

This capacity to hold all the relevant material is at the opposite pole from the capacity of the essential Point to focus on one particular element. The Point gives us the ability to zero in on one thing and look at it closely, experience it with concentration, and analyze it. But we also need to have the capacity to pull back and consider all the related elements. We need both capacities—the focus and the general holding of all the relevant experiences. Frequently, inquiry needs to go back and forth between focus and the larger field.

Questions and Answers

STUDENT: I am aware that my personality is desperately defended against inquiry and wants to obscure that process as much as possible. There is a definite hierarchy there in the personality. Number one: The worst thing is to inquire. The second worst thing is to recognize a relevant element, and next on the priority list is holding a lot of things simultaneously. *[The room bursts into laughter.]*

ALMAAS: So your personality doesn't like inquiry.

STUDENT: It doesn't like inquiry at all.

ALMAAS: Personalities generally don't want to be exposed. But you want to explore for yourself whether something in your history has made you feel that it is not okay to find out, to know. There might be something specific there.

STUDENT: It seems to me that when you do your inquiry and you have the feeling that you have all the facts, then you have to be really brave if the synthesis doesn't happen right away. It's hard not to attack yourself. You really have to defend while you are sitting there feeling all this stuff and nothing is happening.

ALMAAS: That's true. So when you see all the elements and the brilliant insight doesn't come shooting through, you need to be brave and you need to be able to defend yourself against the superego, as you mentioned. Both of those indicate the need for the Strength Essence in inquiry. In holding our experience, we need to be able to hold pain, anger, fear, conflicts, and other elements. Maybe each one of those elements requires a particular quality. That's why Brilliancy can hold all of them. It has all the qualities. If we need to hold just one thing, such as fear or hurt, for example, then strength or compassion by itself is enough. But Brilliancy gives us the capacity to hold all the various elements at the same time.

STUDENT: I notice in my process that when the inquiry starts to get close to the place in my soul where I have the greatest contraction and hurt, I just go away. I push it away: "Don't do it. Let's not look here. Let's do anything except look in here."

ALMAAS: You mean that when it gets close to yourself, you want to avoid the inquiry?

STUDENT: Yes, when it gets close to the place where there's the greatest hurt and contraction. So what I am also aware of is that there is a certain way that those places in my soul kind of pull my attention. So there is this tension between the pull to look at what hurts so much and absolutely not wanting to look at it, which pushes me away.

ALMAAS: Yes, I can see that those areas will push away the inquiry because they are filled with tension or hurt. But your situation still has to do with Brilliancy because Brilliancy provides another faculty you are needing—the faculty of balance. Brilliancy has all qualities equally, so when it is present in our consciousness, it has a balancing effect. As a result, we don't prefer one thing over another. There's an equality in the way we look at the various elements of our experience. There might be hurt here, anger there; fear here, love there. Balance means that we look at all of those in an even-handed way instead of just wanting to look at one or the other.

When we experience Brilliancy, we experience ourselves as complete and balanced. There is a sense of inner equilibrium that manifests in external life as balance. We balance the emotions with the intellect, the intellect with the body, the outer with the inner, rest with activity.

STUDENT: Are you using the word "balance" to mean "integration"?

ALMAAS: I mean it in the sense of equality: One thing doesn't have more weight than another. Everything has the same importance. And balance is different from equanimity. Equanimity means an inner state of being nonreactive to anyone or anything, being peaceful—not subject to disturbance. Equanimity doesn't speak to a relationship between elements. Balance, on the other hand, means that there are various elements, and that there is an equilibrium or appropriate relationship between them. That balance then allows our development to move in an optimizing way. That's why, when I notice that people don't have balance in their life, it indicates that they're having difficulty with the aspect of Brilliancy. In fact, one indication of the absence of balance is when somebody is strange or weird.

STUDENT: Isn't that kind of a subjective viewpoint?

ALMAAS: Strangeness or weirdness can be subjective, but in my perception, when people say somebody is strange and weird, frequently what they are referring to is an absence of balance, the exaggeration of certain things while other things are not paid attention to.

STUDENT: I've known for a long time that I've been afraid of you. I've been afraid of the Work, and I've been afraid of inquiry and analysis. Today I am understanding that the reason I am afraid of you, and the reason that I have resistance to the Work, is the same reason that I have a difficult time holding all of the elements together and synthesizing them. It is the feeling that if I do everything inquiry requires, it will mean that I have to give up my mother. If I did that, then I wouldn't know where I am. So it's just easier for me to say, "I don't understand what you're saying most of the time." It's easier for me to say, "The Work is not for me."

I get to the same point over and over again, where I have this resistance to synthesizing facts about my life in order to come to some understanding and go forward. I'm aware of this, and at this point I don't know what to do with it except to say that I have an awareness that I'm having a difficult time.

ALMAAS: Sounds good. That's an interesting insight: If you really see the truth, you'll lose your mother, and when you lose your mother, you'll lose your sense of self, your identity; you won't know where you are. That's actually true. If you see the truth, you *will* lose your mother, and finally you will lose your identity. So your fear is justified. You just need to look at that and see if it is something desirable in the overall perspective of what you want in your life. But as far as whether truth will do that to you—definitely, that is what truth does.

It is interesting what that means. It means that having one's mother and having one's identity must be false. It must be some kind of falsehood; otherwise, why would the truth make it disappear? You say that if you see the truth, it will make you lose your mother. But truth can only destroy falsehood. So something about your relationship with your mother is false, not true. The most obvious falseness about having your mother is that in fact you don't have her.

It's false to believe that you have your mother. In your mind you feel that you're attached to an image of her, so you feel that you have her. The reason why the truth will dissolve that image is because it is not true. It is just some kind of belief, a mental position. But this kind of belief is a powerful thing. What we believe has to do with who and what we think we are, or what makes our life run, so it is very scary to have it challenged.

I am glad you are bringing this up. I'm sure many people experience this kind of fear, directly or indirectly. It's clear that behind some of the questions today there is fear, and sometimes anger. I think what I am presenting is quite challenging to deep parts of us. I think it's great that you're seeing your resistance, and that you recognize that that's your difficulty instead of saying, "Maybe this Work is not for me" or "This guy doesn't make sense. He's not clear today" or "Let me say it; I'll say it right." These are effective ways to protect ourselves when we sense an inner danger. I'm glad you're more objective about it today.

PENETRATING INTELLIGENCE

The last question penetrated closer to the truth, which brings us to the next subject matter. I have described how Brilliancy has an intense luminosity, and also an exquisite smoothness and fluidity. Its presence has a fine, smooth texture. These two—the intense brilliance or luminosity and the exquisite smoothness—give understanding its penetrating capacity. Then we can penetrate deeply, as a surgeon does using a fine laser beam.

When we are inquiring, we are holding the content—the various facets of experience—and then interrelating those elements, seeing relationships, and analyzing and synthesizing. But our consciousness not only holds the whole interrelated field, it also sees through things; it sees through the veils, defenses, and resistances to underlying meanings, to underlying parts of our experience. We notice that our perception not only has a wider vision, but also that it can have a penetrating capacity. The penetrating capacity goes directly to the essence of the matter through brilliant illumination that pierces as it illuminates. Our consciousness is so smooth that it can move through little cracks, into tiny, subtle places. Brilliancy can seep into and penetrate those little subtle cracks and allow our consciousness to see things we wouldn't normally see.

This penetrating capacity is different from focus. The capacity of focus brings our attention to a single point. It allows us to look at just one element, and everything else becomes background. We stay concentrated, one-pointed; we can see more of the detail. That's focus. Penetration is a matter of going in: entering deep like an acupuncture needle, seeping in like fine oil, or cutting through like a surgeon's scalpel. We are not stopped at the surface, at what is presently showing itself; we see past what's conscious into what's hidden or buried. Obviously, this capacity is important for understanding our experience, especially when we are trying to see underlying meaning or underlying unity, because to do that, we have to go through many veils. Usually we do that through seeing relationships, by using analysis and synthesis. At those times, Brilliancy gives us the capacity to see underlying unity in a flash.

Sometimes, however, Brilliancy takes us to an underlying unity through penetrating insight, penetrating perception, or penetrating investigation. Even an expression can be penetrating—you can say something to somebody, you can give somebody feedback that is penetrating, and it cuts through a lot of stuff and gets to the point. Because of its utmost refinement and smoothness, Brilliancy can enter without creating resistance, static, or interference as it penetrates our consciousness. Because it is so brilliant, it can operate like the sharpest possible scalpel, the finest laser beam. Remember, you make a laser beam with very intense and coherent light of a certain wavelength, which gives the beam a penetrating quality. And the more intense the light, the finer the beam. When we use the expressions "a penetrating mind" or "a penetrating look," we are referring to this characteristic that comes specifically from Brilliancy.

Now, add the sharpness and precision of the diamond to this penetrating capacity, and we have a capacity for inquiry that approaches completeness and perfection. Not only do we have the smoothness that makes penetration effective, but that smoothness now has the sharpness and exactness of a diamond edge, which brings precision to the penetration. Not only can you drill deeply, but you can do it precisely, at the right spot, and with just the right amount of force.

This is another expression of the perfection and completeness of this essential aspect.

Brilliancy is the most intense that an essential aspect can be in terms of awareness—the most concentrated, immediate, and comprehensive. So the intensity gives it the penetrating capacity, but the fact of its completeness can give it the larger holding for the various contents that are needed for synthesis. In this way, Brilliancy gives us the complementary capacities of holding the relevant elements to be explored and penetrating the veils to reveal what's hidden. Both are necessary for going deeper.

We use our intelligence all the time but don't normally experience it as naturally arising from the completeness and perfection of who we are, from the Brilliancy of Being. Today we have been discriminating the various familiar qualities of intelligence such as the flash of revelation, the penetration of insight, the vision of the whole, and the radiance of illumination. Recognizing the fact that Brilliancy is the source of these capacities gives us a deeper understanding of their nature and functioning. All together, these qualities give us some sense of the functioning of the Brilliancy diamond of the Diamond Guidance. Perhaps we can now see how essential Brilliancy is for our process of inquiry and the effective unfoldment of our inner realization.

Epilogue

INQUIRY IS NOT SOMETHING special or unusual to do—it is not an esoteric technique or a strange ritual. To practice inquiry as described in this book is to sharpen a skill that human beings already have. We can think of it as a method, as a practice, but it is really the development of a natural capacity that our consciousness inherently possesses. And inquiry doesn't require any special place, time, or posture; you can do it when you're quiet or active, when you're walking, sitting, lying down, or taking a bath. Inquiry is a natural process that our consciousness goes through.

When we are committed to the practice of inquiry, it will eventually become a functioning that happens on its own, with its own momentum. The questions will arise on their own, the inquiry will proceed spontaneously, the unfoldment will continue happening. All aspects of our life can become pervaded with this natural exploration—with the attitude of openness and of welcoming our Being to reveal its richness, its possibilities, and its potential.

Inquiry is a playful, celebrative kind of engagement, yet its consequences can be quite profound and significant. That's what is beautiful about this inquiry, and the unfoldment and understanding that come with it. It is fun, and in the nature of discovery; it is an adventure. At the same time, it makes the rest of our life richer and helps us become more effective and capable. The more we understand ourselves, the freer we are and the more our love, our intelligence, and our capacities are liberated to express the fullness of who we are.

When our unfoldment is spontaneous and has its own momentum—what I call runaway unfoldment—an interesting thing occurs: What happens to us in the world, though it may be beautiful and interesting, begins to pale in relation to the experience of inner unfoldment. The inner dynamic is what you're in touch with; it's what you feel, it's your own experience. So what you do and where you are externally becomes less important than the nature and quality of this inner life. The activities of life become secondary to the atmosphere of presence.

You begin to realize that the inner experience doesn't change that much whether you're in Paris or Boulder, Kathmandu or Berkeley, whether you're eating dinner, seeing a movie, or being the first person to land on Mars. The sense of yourself becomes so profound, so deep, so substantial, so significant, that the whole external situation—the environment and what's happening in it—feels somewhat ephemeral. External changes now feel like little things that may or may not affect the inner unfolding. They may be interesting or exciting, dramatic or challenging, but the interest and the excitement arising from the soul's unfoldment outshine any feelings that external reality alone can generate. The sense of presence and contentment, with its unlimited possibilities, is so much more beautiful, so much more vivid, so much more interesting and exciting than seeing the most exotic places on Earth or succeeding at the most challenging tasks.

What this means is that life events tend not to disappoint you that much, because they are not what truly nourishes your soul. You find you are less often looking forward to specific situations and less often getting disappointed by what takes place. Even when you are eating the most delicious food, how you feel inside is one hundred times more interesting—it is the richest food there is.

Inquiry is the practice that constantly reorients us to what is most true in our ongoing experience and then invites us into the vast mysterious realm of that truth. As we come to know this truth as our own presence—the substance of Being and the nature of everything—we are able to see reality more as it truly is. We know what is most real and most important, and that is what guides our life. Inquiry then gives way to simple, natural living. We realize the source of all manifestation, and knowing that, we cannot help seeing all the various manifestations in relation to that source. It is clear that everything is unfolding, everything is luminous.

The richness that is the world only appears when that world reflects its nature as Being, when it is transparent to its ground, its source, its truth. It is the bright, clear radiance of true nature that gives our life its power to delight us. How much more delighted our soul can be if she can see that radiance directly for what it is! From the deepest perspective of Being, there is no external reality of events, activities, and people; there is no physical world: All of it is a play of light and color and delicacy. This is the dance of delight, the true unfolding of Being, and the adventure of discovery that inquiry makes available to the soul.

INDEX

About the Diamond Approach

The Diamond Approach is taught by Ridhwan teachers, ordained by the Ridhwan Foundation. Ridhwan teachers are also ministers of the Ridhwan Foundation. They are trained by the DHAT Institute, the educational arm of the Ridhwan Foundation, through an extensive seven-year program, which is in addition to their work and participation as students of the Diamond Approach. The ordination process ensures that each person has a good working understanding of the Diamond Approach and a sufficient capacity to teach it before being ordained and authorized to be a Ridhwan teacher.

The Diamond Approach described in this book is taught in group and private settings in the United States, Canada, Europe, and Australia by Ridhwan teachers. For information about the various contexts for pursuing this work, we invite you to visit www.ridhwan.org.

If you would like to explore starting a group in your area, taught by ordained Ridhwan teachers, write:

Ridhwan
P.O. Box 2747
Berkeley, CA 94702-0747

For more information on the books of A. H. Almaas, go to www.ahalmaas.com. DIAMOND APPROACH and RIDHWAN are trademarks or registered trademarks of the Ridhwan Foundation.